De Ruyter

Dutch Admiral

Protagonists of History in International Perspective

De Ruyter

DUTCH ADMIRAL

EDITED BY

Jaap R. Bruijn, Ronald Prud'homme van Reine,

and Rolof van Hövell tot Westerflier

K

KARWANSARAY PUBLISHERS

2011

Published in 2011 by
Karwansaray BV
Weena 750
3014 DA Rotterdam
The Netherlands

www.karwansaraypublishers.com

With assistance from M.A.O.C. Gravin van Bylandt Stichting and J.E. Jurriaanse Stichting.

ISBN 978-94-90258-03-0

Copy-editing by Richard W. Unger
Design and typesetting by Jan van Waarden (RAM VORMGEVING), Asperen, the Netherlands
Lithography and printing by High Trade BV, Zwolle, the Netherlands
Printed in the EU

Contents

Introduction

By Jaap R. Bruijn

The commemoration in 2007 of the fourth centenary of the great Dutch admiral Michiel Adriaenszoon de Ruyter's birth at Flushing on the isle of Walcheren in Zeeland resulted in a flood of new publications on his life and times. The number of new works from Dutch authors was surprisingly high. De Ruyter, however, is an individual of more than just Dutch national historical prominence. He traded in Europe, Africa and the Americas. He commanded the Dutch fleet in battles against England, Sweden and France. He rendered services to Portugal, Denmark and Spain on behalf of the Dutch Republic. He fought against privateers operating from Dunkirk and off the Barbary Coast. Following his death at the Battle of Etna (1676), his French opponents reputedly honoured him by firing a salute of cannon shot as the home bound ship bearing his embalmed remains passed the French fleet.[1]

The publishing house «Karwansaray» purposefully chose to start its new series of monographs with a publication on De Ruyter and one which focuses on his international position. «Karwansaray» concentrates its publications primarily on international perspectives in Europe. This continent is a collective of nations on its way to unity. The growth of a collective historical consciousness in Europe will reinforce the process of further unification. The more it is believed and understood that the countries in Europe have shared the same experiences in the past and are following a joint path, the greater the development of such a collective consciousness. Julius Caesar, Charlemagne, the duke of Alba, Louis xiv, Marlborough, Frederick the Great and Nelson are prominent figures in a history which all Europeans share. Far too often, however, the average Dutch person views Caesar as a Roman, Alba as a Spaniard, Louis xiv as a Frenchman and so on. He or she views De Ruyter as purely a national figure. With the intention of promoting the growth of a collective European historical consciousness, «Karwansaray» will publish books where historians from different countries describe figures of international importance. De Ruyter is a suitable figure for the first work in the series.

The military and personal qualities of De Ruyter were well known throughout Europe. In July, 1675, the French minister Colbert confided to his son Seignelay his worries about the naval situation in the Mediterranean, for he had received notification of De Ruyter going there to support Spanish naval forces against the French. Englishmen considered the Dutch admiral their «good» enemy. The royal courts of France, Denmark and Spain bestowed their highest distinctions upon him. In Morocco De Ruyter built up a reputation for being a discrete and affable person. When trading in that country during the 1640's he favoured calm and judicious conduct over rash and bold actions, using that approach to negotiate good deals and settling differences about commodities and their prices.

Most aspects of his reputation cannot be detached from the essential truth that his contemporaries considered De Ruyter the figurehead of the Dutch state, renowned not only for its naval power but also for its political and economic strength and its wealth during the middle years of the seventeenth century. Was De Ruyter not the right hand of Grand Pensionary Johan de Witt? Was he not the man who played a crucial role in stadtholder – the later king of England – Willem III's survival of joint attacks by France, England and two German bishops against the Republic in 1672-1673?

Soon after his death the story of this man's life was written, published and republished, of course in Dutch but also in English, French and German. The flow of books about this admiral has never ceased but the present book is different from all those previous ones. This is not a true biography nor a collection of biographical essays written by Dutch historians. This book does, indeed, contain a group of essays which represent for a great deal views of non-Dutch historians. They position De Ruyter as a man of international significance in relation to their own countries. The Dutch Republic of the seventeenth century was an anomaly in Europe. Other, Dutch, authors sketch the admiral's life and especially one of his more famous exploits, the journey of 1664-1665. In addition there are chapters on the Dutch maritime world of his days and the flag officers with whom he collaborated. This approach generates interesting views on Dutch history in general and Dutch naval history in particular. The book also opens a new window on De Ruyter in paintings. To introduce the varied essays this sort of bird's eye view of De Ruyter and his times is based on and inspired by what the authors of the different essays have written.

There was hardly a single year in the seventeenth century with no war in Europe. The Dutch Republic was often among the belligerents. Its enemies became its allies and vice versa. Erstwhile enemy Spain became its ally in later years. The Eighty Years' War ended in 1648 and Dutch naval support in Spain's Mediterranean struggle against France was only a logical consequence of the war France imposed upon the Dutch Republic in 1672. In previous years France had been a trusted ally. In 1666, for example, the French navy played an essential role in the Second Anglo-Dutch War. Traditional cooperation and naval support, however, could end all too easily. In 1667 France embarked on expansionistic and aggressive economic policies which resulted in the 'Guerre de Hollande' of 1672 and later the Nine Years' War and the War of the Spanish Succession. One of their consequences was the long standing Anglo-Dutch alliance dating from 1677 marked by the cooperation of the so-called Maritime Powers. Three fiercely fought naval wars had by then settled their mutual relations and their relative position in the economic world. The Dutch Republic felt sufficiently strong to intervene regularly in Nordic affairs, siding either with Denmark or Sweden. The free passage of the Sound was crucial for Dutch shipping and trade. The principal Dutch naval and military actions in defence of the Republic and its economic interests took place from 1652 onwards, the very years De Ruyter was active as a naval officer.

The central role the Dutch Republic occupied in these years was quite remarkable. The Republic did not fit in a Europe in which monarchies and centralizing absolutist powers set the tone. That is why the remarkable federal and decentralized political structure of the Dutch Republic has always been a point of discussion in national and international historiography. The assets of this structure are getting more attention nowadays. The Dutch political, fiscal, financial and administrative systems functioned better than in the more centralized monarchies in Europe. One

of the effects of Dutch institutions was an extremely well-armed state. With a population of about 1.5 to 2.0 million living on a very small territory, the Republic nevertheless had such an influence on European politics that it could play the role of one of the major powers. It was better able to raise and deploy large resources for war than the continental powers France and Spain. The Dutch army was huge. The maximum strength was about 70,000 men in the war of 1672-1678. During the War of the Spanish Succession it was more than 100,000. In relation to the size of its population wartime strength was usually three to four times higher than that of the Spanish and later French enemy. Many soldiers were recruited abroad, but the army itself was a state institution with its officers permanently employed by the state, not by private entrepreneurs. That meant the peacetime strength was high as well.

The Dutch navy enjoyed many professional characteristics considerably earlier than recent works of history suggest. From 1652 onwards the navy replaced frigates with ships-of-the-line which then made up the backbone of the standing fleet. The role of private entrepreneurs and hired armed merchantmen was small. Taking into account the size of the population, no other European state made greater naval efforts than the Republic. Instead of a centralized naval organization, as in the other European countries, there were no less than five admiralties, which were federal institutions with a very strong provincial and even local character. As it turned out, this admiralty system was often more successful than a centralized apparatus. Navies were among the most complex institutions of the seventeenth century. The Dutch structure made local rulers willing to coordinate their efforts and commit resources within centrally determined policies. At the height of Dutch political and military power the presence of a politician of the calibre of Johan de Witt as Grand Pensionary from 1653 to 1672 guaranteed a comparatively smooth running of the naval organization.

One may assume that seventeenth-century Dutch men-of-war were manned on average by better trained, better paid and better fed men than the ships in other navies. Administrators in several countries developed systems for efficient recruitment of crews for their navies. Spain, Sweden, Denmark and France under Colbert created huge registers of qualified seamen. Those registered had to serve for a number of years. They had no other choice. Seamen in the Dutch navy were largely volunteers. There was no compulsory service and the navy had no long term contracts for its common seamen and petty officers. Enrolment was for one season or for one voyage. No one was forced to join the navy, that is except when temporary embargoes on mercantile shipping, whaling and the sea fisheries took away most other opportunities for employment in seafaring. Finding a crew and feeding it were a Dutch naval captain's responsibilities. The introduction of marines in 1665 was an important innovation, England being the model for that change.

The truly international labour market of the Netherlands, at Amsterdam in particular, was an essential asset. Sufficient men and boys were at hand to man the huge numbers of all kinds of vessels. There was a constant influx of migrant labourers. The Dutch maritime preponderance of the seventeenth century is even more impressive in light of the small territory where all commercial and industrial activities took place: the three maritime provinces Zeeland, Holland and Friesland. Almost sixty per cent of the total population of the Republic lived there. Distances were short, communication quick. An artificial network of canals and the many other navigable waters facilitated transport of goods and persons. Well-equipped wharves and storehouses, well-stocked with raw materials and foodstuffs, were part of the infrastructure.

From early on Dutch commercial interests stimulated the development of a European-wide convoy system. The protection and defence of groups of merchantmen from the waters of the Barents Sea to deep into the Mediterranean provided productive employment for many a naval captain. Convoying went on in time of war and peace and kept the navy in fighting trim. When it came to fighting during the initial phase of an engagement the favourite Dutch tactic was taking up a windward position, quickly sailing toward an enemy, immediately grappling and boarding him. A few times admirals did use the line ahead formation. In the Second Anglo-Dutch War their adversary compelled the Dutch to abandon their grappling and boarding tactics for good. Already in 1653 the evolution from the frigate design to large two-deckers with increasing numbers of guns on board, resulted in instructions in England for a better order in the fleet when sailing and fighting. From 1664 onwards the two central functions of a navy – the protection of one's own trade and one's own coast from invasion – could be best fulfilled by an outright battle between ships-of-the-line, thus by fighting and defeating a comparable hostile naval force. The formation of a line ahead on either tack became standard, while trying to maintain the weather gauge.

In August, 1665, Dutch commanders as well were instructed that fighting ought to be done in a single line-of-battle, and close-hauled. There were to be no more than three squadrons, each to be divided into three divisions. De Ruyter took command in the middle of this transformation in tactics. He trained his officers in the effective application and use of the single line ahead formation. De Ruyter had returned to naval command at a very propitious moment. Two months before his predecessor had been killed in the battle of Lowestoft. The provisional commander in chief, Cornelis Tromp, was a daring man but also a man of little reflection. The navy required a leader who commanded respect and loyalty. The overall condition of the fleet was very good. Many ships were brand new, that mainly due to the efforts of the Grand Pensionary.

When he returned in August, 1665, De Ruyter had been absent for fifteen months. His operations against the Algerian corsairs had been followed by his secret mission to West Africa, the Caribbean and Newfoundland. The ongoing economic rivalry and antagonism between England and the Republic had resulted in English peace-time operations against Dutch overseas trading posts and settlements. There was no open war as yet. De Ruyter's task was to recapture the English conquests before the English realized what he had done.

The long expedition may be considered crucial in the light of De Ruyter's later career as supreme naval commander. The expedition was a success, and the ships returned full of booty. All original twelve men-of-war arrived home safely. The loss of life was only marginal. The ships had been commanded by twelve officers of whom nine either were already or were soon to become flag officers. These men had learned to understand and accept their admiral's views on order and discipline as well as on tactics and strategy. Most of them would later be his flag officers again. During the first part of the expedition some bitter disputes had arisen but during the voyage De Ruyter had learned to work with colleagues who were not fully compatible.

Unlike during the First Anglo-Dutch War adequate numbers of permanent flag officers were available in later wars. Though they were not all even-tempered they began to form a team under De Ruyter's leadership. The frequency of wars meant that being a flag officer was now a full-time job. The professional and also the social background of flag officers became more homogeneous. De Ruyter succeeded in transforming these men into such a unified force that the great battles of the Third Anglo-Dutch War became masterpieces of clever manoeuvring and brilliant application of the new tactics of breaking through a hostile line and concentration of forces.

What strikes the imagination of an historian in the early twenty-first century most, is the fact that a common seaman of humble descent managed to become such a well-known person in the world of his day, a world in which social position and preferably noble parentage were so important. De Ruyter gained his greatest renown during the Second and Third Anglo-Dutch Wars and in their many great sea battles. These battles were fought in the North Sea and the Channel, not far away from the Dutch homeland. English and French contemporaries were familiar with his name and reputation as an admiral to be reckoned with. His reputation, however, spread more widely in Europe. Already in 1642 he was third in command of an auxiliary fleet for Portugal, the Portuguese then fighting for their independence from Spain. Much later, in 1675, the royal court at Madrid considered De Ruyter commanding another auxiliary fleet a great asset in the struggle with France. An unexpected corollary of De Ruyter's presence in the Mediterranean was the liberation of 26 Hungarian reformed and Lutheran ministers. At De Ruyter's request, the Spanish viceroy at Naples dismissed these poor enslaved creatures from the galley fleet. This deed of mercy still is annually commemorated in the city of Debrecen in Hungary.

The place of De Ruyter in the history of North Africa is twofold. From 1644 to 1651 he did business in Morocco after the arrival of the merchantman he captained in the ports of the country. He understood Moroccan society better than most Europeans. The reputation he acquired for fair dealing paid off later. As an admiral from 1655 to 1657 he facilitated the conclusion of Dutch-Moroccan treaties. During three naval expeditions to Algiers between 1655 and 1664, however, De Ruyter failed to make a breakthrough in the quarrels about the principle of *free ship, free goods*, a key issue since Dutch traders and shippers did not want their goods and vessels subject to arbitrary search and seizure. Open war was the end result. Dutch relations with Algiers and with Tunis as well were dominated by permanently conflicting commercial interests and the dissimilarity of the Dutch and their economic systems. This book offers a view of the Barbary States and their relations with Europe, which is unconventional in the historiography.

In Nordic waters De Ruyter impressed local rulers as well. In 1656, he and several other Dutch flag officers were invited to attend the Danish royal court. In those years Dutch naval squadrons operated quite frequently in the Baltic and adjacent waters, which were the battlegrounds for Denmark, Sweden and other countries. In 1658 Denmark was almost completely overrun by its Swedish neighbour. De Ruyter was singled out especially to be asked to command one of the auxiliary fleets. The young promising Danish naval officer Niels Juel (1629-1697) supported the idea. In previous years Juel had served with De Ruyter in the Mediterranean. De Ruyter made good his reputation by recapturing the island of Fyn in 1659-1660. A Danish knighthood and an annuity were his rewards.

'Is that an admiral? He is an admiral, a mate, a sailor, and a soldier. Yes, that man, that hero, is all these things at the same time', said an English lieutenant on board De Ruyter's flagship after his own ship had been burned. De Ruyter inspired universal respect in England, the country whose fleet he defeated several times, the victories contributing more than considerably to his fame. His activities in West Africa and the West Indies in 1664-1665 made De Ruyter well known in the London business world and after the Medway raid his fame was well-established along the coast and near the Thames, Medway and East Anglia in particular. The duke of York admired him as a naval officer and seaman. Newspapers and even satirists praised him. It should, however, be kept in mind that speaking and writing so laudably about this Dutchman was an indirect way of criticizing their own policymakers and admirals. The war of 1672, for example, was deeply unpopular in England.

De Ruyter's last and terminal enemy was France. Only from 1672 were the Republic and France at loggerheads with each other. As late as 1666 king Louis XIV had honoured the admiral with the knighthood of Saint Michel. This and his later successes had made him a much respected, but also feared, opponent. The admiral's final journey had a tragic background. In the war of 1672-1673 he had proved his historic value for the Dutch Republic. Its destruction had been averted and De Ruyter could now be moved aside. He had outlived his usefulness. He could be sent on a secondary mission with inadequate forces. The death of an admiral whose name had been so often mentioned in England, was barely reported in the London Gazette and was little commented on. De Ruyter was 69 when he was killed in the Battle of Etna on 22 April, 1676. The great naval hero received a state funeral on March 18, 1677.

In the Netherlands a chapter on De Ruyter was quickly added to a collection of biographies of Dutch naval heroes and explorers, the book being published in 1677. Within a year after his death also an anonymous Englishman produced a fitting biography, though omitting to mention the raid on the Medway of 1667. In the late 1670's, the admiral's son Engel initiated a grand biography of his father. Gerard Brandt, a poet, author, historian and minister, was asked to take up the job. The family put all the admiral's papers at his disposal. The biography was published in 1687, a fitting monument like the magnificent tomb by the sculptor Rombout Verhulst which still covers his body in the Nieuwe Kerk of Amsterdam. A well known modern French encyclopaedia rightly remarks about De Ruyter: *'L'Europe le considéra comme le plus remarquable homme de mer de sa génération'*.[2]

---

[1] H. Granier, *L'Amiral De Ruyter au combat (1607-1676). Le Zélandais qui fit trembler l'Angleterre*, Paris 1992, 138.

[2] F. Bluche, *Dictionnaire du Grand Siècle*, Paris 2005, 1369.

Maps

La Rochelle ·
Vienna ·
Budapest ·
France
Venice ·
Genoa ·
Livorno (Leghorn) ·
Black Sea
Perpignan · Marseille ·
Toulon ·
Ottoman Empire
Portugal
Madrid ·
Castile
Spain
Agosta ·
Constantinople ·
Lisbon ·
Naples ·
Sevilla ·
Granada · Alicante ·
Stromboli
Lipari Islands
Alicudi
Palermo ·
Lepanto · Salamis ·
Cadiz · Málaga ·
Cartagena ·
Sicily · Messina
Strait of Gibraltar
Gibraltar ·
Etna Syracuse
Barbary Coast
Algiers ·
Mediterranean
Marrakech ·
Tunis ·
Malta ·
Atlas
Morocco

ENGLAND
Lowestoft ·
North Sea
Terschelling
Vlie
Leeuwarden · Delfzijl
Southwold ·
Solebay
Texel
Harlingen · Groningen ·
Den Helder ·
Friesland
Kijkduin ·
Enkhuizen ·
Harwich ·
Haarlem ·
Hoorn ·
Leiden ·
Edam ·
DUTCH
Scheveningen ·
Amsterdam ·
London ·
The Hague ·
ter Heide ·
REPUBLIC
Thames
Sheerness ·
Kentish Knock
Brielle ·
Delft ·
Utrecht ·
Chatham ·
Hellevoetsluis ·
Rotterdam ·
Medway
Walcheren
Schiedam ·
Dordrecht ·
Plymouth ·
Portsmouth ·
Downs
North Foreland
Middelburg ·
Zeeland
Dover ·
Schooneveld
Breda ·
Portland
Hastings ·
Flushing ·
Dungeness ·
Ostend ·
Bergen op Zoom ·
Calais ·
Dunkirk ·
Hulst ·
Nieuwpoort ·
Antwerp ·
The Channel
SPANISH
NETHERLANDS
FRANCE

GREENLAND

Faroer
Islands

Bergen
NORWAY

Shetland
Islands

Delfzijl
6 August 1665

Amsterdam

Terraneuve
(Newfoundland)
•St. John's

New Amsterdam
(New York)

5 October 1664

Gibraltar

Cadiz
•Alicante

Malaga
•Algiers

Salé •Barbary Coast
Safi •Fés
Mogador
Santa Cruz (Agadir)
Massa
Marrakech
Iligh
Meknes

Atlas
ALGERIA
MOROCCO

Bermuda

Atlantic

Ocean

Havana
•
Cuba

Bahama Islands

Jamaica

St. Maarten
St. Eustatius
St. Kitts
Guadeloupe
Martinique

Caribbean Sea

Curaçao
St. Vincent
Grenada

Cape
Verde
Islands

Goree

Cape Verde

GAMBIA

Elmina
*around the 10th
of January 1665*

Cormantijn

Barbados
30 April 1665

Witsen
*Gold
Coast*

Trinidad

27 February 1665

GUYANA

B R A S I L

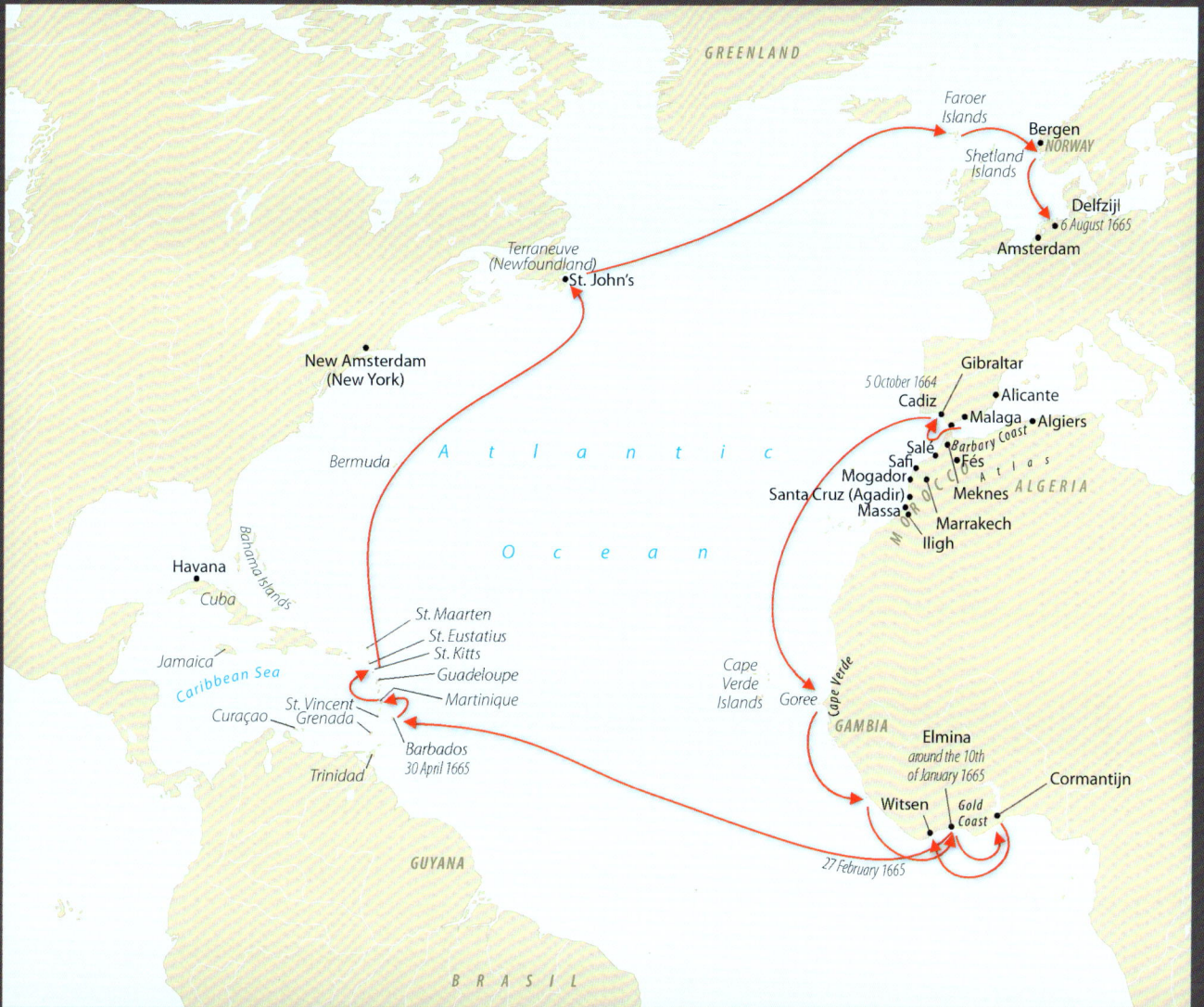

*Michiel de Ruyter's expedition to
West Africa and America, 1664-1665*

Allegory for the restoration of prosperity after the Second Anglo-Dutch War (1665-1667) with great Dutch admirals such as David Vlugh, Aert van Nes, Tjerk Hiddes de Vries, Isaäc Sweers, Adriaen Banckert, Michiel de Ruyter, Engel de Ruyter and Pieter Florisz pulling in the nets filled with fish.

Painting attributed to Willem Eversdijck, 1667-1671, Rijksmuseum, Amsterdam

CHAPTER 1

The Maritime World of the Dutch Republic

Jaap R. Bruijn

The maritime world of the Dutch Republic in the seventeenth century had many faces. Jan Ibess, born on the Wadden island of Terschelling in 1579, was at his death in 1652 a major owner of shares ('parten') in ships at Amsterdam; he had shares in no less than 120 merchant vessels. After a seafaring career (he finished as a master) he married and settled in Amsterdam around 1608. Jan Ibess then became a merchant and ship's husband, while investing his money in ships and acquiring a rope-yard, powder-mill, three storehouses, five ordinary houses and some land in the country-side. In 1652 the value of his shares in ships amounted to 94,000 Dutch guilders; the total estate was valued at 200,000 guilders. His fellow citizen Pieter Allen (1567-1643) from London, left shares in 78 vessels and had become an important merchant in trades to Northern Russia, the Baltic, Bristol and London. The shares in ships of these two successful businessmen ranged from various fourths to eights to even sixty-fourths.[1] Both men illustrate some of the main aspects of the Dutch maritime world of the seventeenth century: inland and foreign migration to the great magnet Amsterdam, the opportunities to profit from an expanding economy and the spread of risks in maritime enterprises. Nobody wanted to be the single owner of a ship.

The maritime world offered other people great uncertainty, and even death. In November of 1664 Jannetje Cornelis at Rotterdam was alarmed by the news that her beloved boy friend's warship had suddenly been sent off to an unexpected destination. A naval force under the command of vice admiral De Ruyter had to sail from the Mediterranean straight to West Africa and the Caribbean. She wrote her boy friend, a common seaman, about her distress and her wish to have him home. This letter never reached him because the vessel carrying this and other correspondence was captured by the English. Luckily, her boy friend returned safely and in September 1665 Jannetje married him. Life was short for Louwerens Louwerensz. By accident he fell overboard and drowned. It happened in early November 1683. He was the cabin boy of captain Johan – he called himself Jean – de Witte, son-in-law of De Ruyter. The boy's sister lived in Amsterdam just around the corner from where the admiral's widow, Anna van Gelder, had her house.[2] These two young men demonstrate the impact the navy could have upon personal lives during the seventeenth century.

■ A glance at the Netherlands

The maritime world was very much a part of the lives of many other inhabitants of the Dutch Republic, not only for Ibess, Allen, Jannetje and Louwerensz. Most of the seven provinces all had borders on the sea: the North Sea or the Zuider Sea or both. Zeeland, Holland and also Friesland, though in a different way, were the real Maritime Provinces. Holland, in particular, was highly urbanized by the standards of early modern times. Most of its cities were port cities. Maritime activities were present in a whole range of harbours along both seas, from Flushing, Zierikzee, Maassluis and Rotterdam to Hoorn and Amsterdam. There were nearly twenty ports in all. There were also several villages along the duned coast of Holland, where fishers harboured their flat-bottomed vessels on the beach.

Most of the people – about forty per cent – lived in the province of Holland, almost 800,000 out of 1,900,000 around 1650. The estimates for Zeeland and Friesland are 100,000 and 160,000 respectively. Less than half of the labour force in the

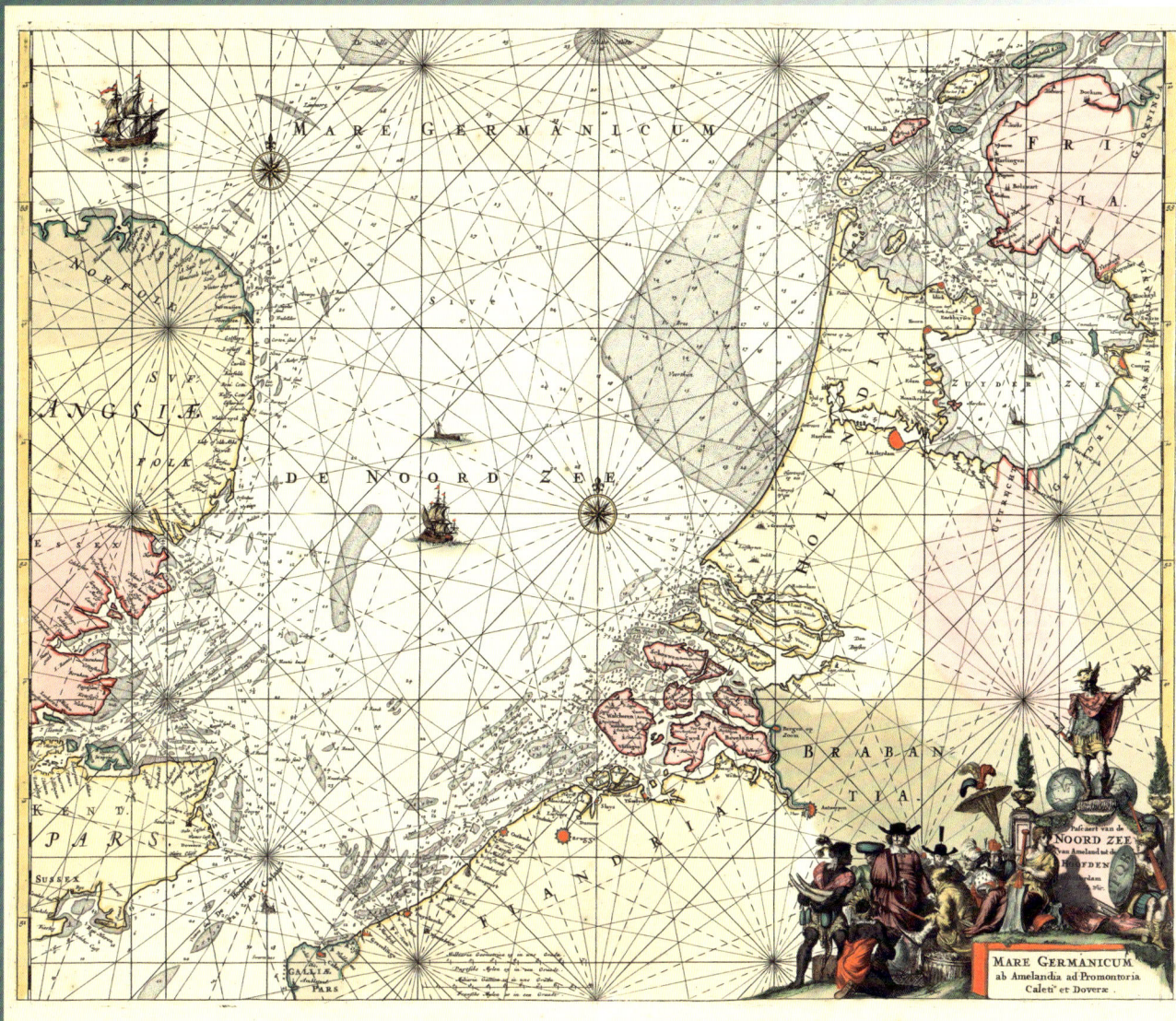

Netherlands as a whole was required for agriculture. The industrial and artisanal sector formed the most important source of employment, in cities in particular. In Holland, the growth in city size was high and pushed the urbanization rate to 60 per cent by around 1675. Industry was not restricted to the cities. It was also certainly present in the countryside. A unique example was the Zaan region, northwest of Amsterdam.

Windmills, so characteristic for the Netherlands, stood in the open countryside as well as on or near the walls of cities and in villages. Improved technology had given them great capacity to pump water for drainage. Regularly improving technology in industrial mills gave them the ability to enhance production. Of great importance had been the introduction of the lumber-sawing windmill in 1594. Along the river Zaan 128 industrial mills were in operation in 1631 for pressing oilseeds, grinding grain, beating hemp, paper making and of course for sawing lumber. Their number increased at an impressive rate. One hundred years later there were 584 windmills. In both cases sawmills made up 40 per cent of the total.[3] Shipbuilding was one of the main industries in the district and closely tied to other industrial activity.

Transportation over water was self-evident in the Netherlands. Thanks to the many outlets to the open sea (the Zuider Sea included) international commercial relations had always existed. Inland transportation by ship was facilitated by routes through Holland via lakes, rivers and channels. The changing flows of river water, tides and other actions of the sea continually influenced the navigability of the waterways. Shoals and sandbanks seldom remained at the same spot. Buoys and other markers were essential for safe navigation. Dredging was unavoidable in many harbours. Tides were not always adequate to keep them accessible to ships. The city of Amsterdam had to dredge enormous quantities of mud annually. Special floating mud mills with their accompanying mud boats did the work, an expensive activity for the city government.[4]

Inland commercial relations were supported by regular transportation service between points: the so-called '*beurtveren*' along waterways. Licensed skippers were committed to depart on regular schedules to destinations. The '*beurtveren*' had developed into a regular and dependable service to almost every city and large village in the Republic. The network of passenger boats ('*trekschuiten*'), pulled by horses, was not dependent upon wind and tide. Their routes reached thirty cities over no less than 658 kilometres of canals which were specially built for the boats between 1631 and 1665. This system offered frequent service, often hourly, and was used by thousands of passengers each year. The network of '*beurtveren*' and '*trekschuiten*' was used for transportation much more than the existing roads. There were only a few paved roads and the unpaved clay roads were hard to use in the winter and the sandy roads were hard to use in the summer.[5]

The habitable area of Holland was enlarged by the drainage of shallow lakes in the northern part, begun around 1560 and completed in 1624. The *Haarlemmermeer*, however, a vast lake between Haarlem and Leiden, grew extensively; it almost tripled in size during the sixteenth and seventeenth century. In Zeeland, the main island, Walcheren, harbouring the cities of Middelburg, Flushing and Veere, suffered from having large pools of mud in wintertime as a result of settling of the clay stratum.

■ A cold age

The seventeenth century was in the midst of the 'Little Ice Age' (c. 1430- c. 1860). Very severe winters occurred more frequently than before. This change in climate had its impact upon all kinds of human activities, in daily life and the maritime world as well. Heavy snowfall often accompanied severe frost. Winters lasted long, far into March. A comparatively mild spell around 1650 was followed by a renewed drop of temperatures. Extreme winter in 1684 was followed by inclement years from 1690. The inland system of transportation often broke down for weeks or longer. The harbours in the port cities were covered with ice, prohibiting any kind of shipping, local or overseas. Food and fuel then became scarce and it was not just impoverished people who suffered.

A few examples may indicate how bad the winters were. The Zuider Sea, the seaway to and from Amsterdam, Hoorn and other ports cities around this large open inland sea, iced over at least once in every four to five years on average. The ice was so thick that horse sledging was widely practised. Ice hampered the operations of the '*trekschuiten*' between Leiden and Haarlem quite regularly. During the period from 1675 to 1700 it happened in four out of five winters. For two or more weeks any transportation was impossible, several times for more than ten weeks in a winter. A number of winters was really extreme. In 1622 the North Sea was not only frozen along the beach, but also far into the sea. Seamen coming home said they had encountered huge ice floes which they had been able to walk over. In March 1650 the funeral of stadtholder Willem II had to be postponed for three days. A period of very low temperatures had ended and a thaw had begun, accompanied by blizzards. The streets in The Hague and in Delft were completely impassable because of the huge masses of snow.[6]

■ Magistrate and Mercurius

The Dutch Republic was a federation of seven sovereign provinces. Sovereignty lay with the States of each province, also called a '*gewest*'. Members of these provincial States were delegates from the cities and the nobility. In the States of Holland and Zeeland, the cities had an overwhelming majority: 18 votes to 1 and 6 votes to 1 respectively. As a consequence power was in essence in the hands of the city councils, the '*vroedschappen*', which appointed their delegations to the States. Taking a decision against the wishes of the most powerful city of Amsterdam was almost unthinkable. Policies of persuasion and consensus building in order to reach mutual agreement were the hallmark of the Dutch ruling system. At all levels – municipal, provincial and national – decisions were taken by boards, by groups of men, and not by one single person. Collective consensus, reached through negotiation, was a characteristic of all aspects of public life.

A number of matters were the responsibility of the States General in The Hague. The delegation of each province in those meetings had an equal vote, Holland the same as Utrecht. Foreign policy, the navy and taxes on imports and exports were in the hands of the States General. The governors of the five admiralties were representatives of each of the seven provinces. The number of governors from the province in which an admiralty was located was equal or greater than the number of those from the other six provinces. Regional influence on an admiralty board was in practice very great. That was true in the admiralties of Zeeland, Holland or Friesland. Members representing Holland in the admiralty of Rotterdam, for instance, came from Rotterdam itself and from cities in the neighbourhood. As a matter of course the boards at Amsterdam and Rotterdam always had a provincial noble man as a member. His influence with his 'commoner' colleagues was often greater than his single vote would suggest. The stadtholder of Holland and Zeeland was admiral-general of the five admiralties and supreme commander of the fleet, though only in theory.

The heart of the ruling system in the Maritime Provinces were the '*vroedschappen*', the city-councils. Their members were the so-called regents. They were the ruling class in each city. All doors were open to them for any desired office at local, provincial and national levels. At the end of the sixteenth and in the early seventeenth century, the ruling class did not yet operate as a closed group of Protestant families. There was still room for newcomers, for those who were successful in the maritime and industrial world. Jacob van Neck (1564-1638) is an example. He had been a shipping agent and merchant in Amsterdam before he became the commander of two large fleets that sailed to the East Indies in 1598 and 1600. In 1608 he acceded to the '*vroedschap*', was four times burgomaster and member of the admiralty boards in Zeeland and Amsterdam. Another example is Joost van Coulster (d. 1649). Born at Schiedam, he moved to Rotterdam, started seafaring and became master of a merchant vessel, developed commercial activities, and also started a brewery. In 1624, he entered the city council of Rotterdam and soon thereafter joined the admiralty board as well. In the following twenty-five years, he would serve both bodies. Six times he was a burgomaster.[7]

Already in Van Coulster's days, though, things began to change. New members for city councils came from amongst the regents, those city councillors, themselves. This process began at Amsterdam. Another important development was the separation between those who ruled and those who were involved in trade, commerce and industry. Initially, nearly all city councillors had been in business. Some had been simultaneously cloth-makers, soap boilers or salt makers. Others were merchants in grain, herring or wines and owned shares in ships. Amsterdam was one of the first cities in which this combination of commercial and political activities began to stop from about 1630. Magistrate and Mercurius were separated. Personal knowledge of and experience with the business world began to disappear amongst the members of the city councils. As city councils were closed to newcomers there were no seats in Amsterdam for successful entrepreneurs like Jan Ibess and Pieter Allen.

A representative example of the trend is what happened at Dordrecht in the family De Witt. It was one of the well established ruling families. Cornelis de Witt (1545-1622) personally managed his timber business while also being active as a town councillor and burgomaster. His son Jacob (1589-1674) continued the family business, but sold it, a couple of years after he had taken his father's seat on the town council. He concentrated increasingly on his official duties, finally at a national level. Grandson Johan de Witt (1625-1672) had the full fledged education of a regent's son (university, grand tour) and was appointed Grand Pensionary of Holland in 1653. Though also a gifted mathematician (he wrote a treatise on life-annuities) and always keenly aware of the commercial interests of Holland, Johan never had any personal link with business.[8]

This split between magistrate and merchant did not take place in each city nor at the same time. The split was neither universal nor absolute. In cities like Hoorn, regents continued to invest their money in shares of ships and in other businesses. Well into the seventeenth century, many a regent was surrounded by relatives involved in all kinds of commercial and industrial activities. In Flushing, for instance, links continued between members of the city council and the world of privateering. By and large, however, the commitment of the ruling class to trade and industry became smaller and smaller. Around 1700, the safe return of a convoy of merchant ships from the Baltic was no longer the concern of all 'vroedschap' members in Zeeland, Holland and Friesland, as it had been early in the century. The city council of Hindeloopen in Friesland was perhaps an exception since some members were still active masters ('schippers'). Spending time away from their houses along the prestigious city canals at their country mansions, though at first only during the summer months, was symptomatic for the change in the regents' attitude. Daily presence at city hall, at the exchange and in the office was no longer required.

The 92 ships built by the shipbuilder
Jacobus Matijssen Osterlinck at Edam.

*Painting by Jan Molenaar, 1688,
Edams Museum, Edam*

■ Maritime industries

Without ships there can be no maritime world. For each sort of seafaring Dutch shipbuilders could offer the desired type of ship. Ships were not ordered abroad. On the contrary, foreigners from the king of France to merchants in Copenhagen and Bergen had ships built in the Netherlands. The Dutch themselves needed massive numbers of new ships, either for expanding activities or for the replacement of worn-out, lost or captured ships. Maintenance and repair were also continuous sources of work in ports.

Usually each city or village situated along navigable water had its own building site of whatever size, just as it had its brewery. Easy access to shipbuilding materials was a great asset. A location near a centre of trade and shipping stimulated ship-building, while also guaranteeing sufficient demand. The Zaan region is the prime example, with its strong links with Amsterdam. Dordrecht and the adjacent area around Rotterdam is another. Each district in the three Maritime Provinces had its shipyards. Some specialized in the construction of fishing, mercantile or inland vessels, others built warships and East Indiamen.

The admiralties and the six chambers of the East India Company (*Verenigde Oostindische Compagnie*, abbr. voc) had their own yards for construction, mainte-nance and repair. These were the largest yards in the country. The naval yard at Amsterdam, opened in 1655, was an impressive 260 metres wide and 54 metres deep.[9] Private yards were much smaller. Around 1610, the city government of Rotterdam gave out lots in a new area. A lot was 6.25 metres by 56 metres. Most shipbuilders bought four neighbouring lots, thus a piece of land 25 metres wide. Authorities were keenly aware of fire hazards. In most cities, the favourite locations of shipyards were located outside the walls. At Rotterdam, in 1704, private shipbuilders were obliged to move to an adjacent area because the government wanted their ground for housing and storing. At Amsterdam, comparable policies had already been applied around 1650.

Exact figures do not exist for the numbers of people employed in shipbuilding. A substantial private yard had one hundred men, not only carpenters, but also sawers, borers and porters. The admiralty and voc yards at Amsterdam each often had a labour force of 500 to more than 1000 men. In 1700, the VOC yard at Middelburg had 300 names on its payroll. A total for the Republic of about 10,000 men employed in shipbuilding would not be too far from the mark.

Neither capacity nor production is known. An annual output of 400 to 500 seagoing vessels seems to be a reliable figure. Losses in war and to privateering forced the building of substantial numbers of replacements. Demand and supply were often completely out of balance. There is a painting that gives the total production for one wharf but the time span when all the ships were built is not given. In 1682 shipbuilder Jacobus Matijsen Osterlinck at Edam had all his 92 ships painted on one piece of canvas. Among them were 8 armed ships and 22 smaller fluyts. An archival source mentions that in February 1694 about 57 merchant vessels were under construction along the Zaan. Their average cargo carrying capacity was 300 tons.[10] That was in the midst of the Nine Years' War.

We know more about production at the Admiralty and Company yards. The majority of warships and East Indiamen were built at these yards, but an unknown number of mostly smaller vessels came from private shipbuilding enterprises. Fully reliable figures of output for those yards are available for the period 1653-1700: 213 ships-of-the-line and 428 East Indiamen.

Ships were expensive assets. A new herring buss cost 3 to 4,000 guilders around 1620. Thirty years later a small fluyt cost 5,000 guilders and a bigger one 12,500. A sea-going lighter ('kaag') cost 500 guilders. Ships carrying armament were always more costly, because carrying and firing guns required heavier construction of decks and beams. In 1632, warships cost the Admiralties 19 to 22,000 guilders. Admiral Jacob van Wassenaer-Obdam's flagship, blown up in the battle of Lowestoft in 1665, had a building price of 60,000 guilders. A big East Indiamen around 1700 cost almost 100,000 guilders.

It was cheaper to have a ship built in the Zaan region than in cities where guilds by stipulating fixed wages and working hours drove up prices. The Zaan region dominated private shipbuilding. One could profit there from several locational and cost advantages. The number of wharves in the area rose from 13 in 1608 to a peak of 60-65 around 1670. Annual production figures stood at 100 to 150 vessels in the peak period. A characteristic feature of the building technique used along the Zaan was the so-called shell-first method, instead of the more common frame-first method, in use around Rotterdam and in Zeeland.

Shipbuilding was dependent upon adequate supplies of sawn timber and other materials. The Zaan region had by far the most sawing mills located, as we have seen. [11] There was plenty of open space, the river was easily navigable and access to Amsterdam was easy. Sawmills operated, of course, in many other places, in the cities in particular, but nowhere else in such concentration. Sailcloth was an indispensable aspect of shipping. Though sailcloth had long been imported in substantial quantities from Brittany in France, its production in the Zaan region and in a number of adjacent villages ousted this import from 1660 on. Hemp was the raw material for sailcloth weaving while for rope making, which was done all over the country, flax was the raw material. The shipyards of the admiralties and the chambers of VOC even had their own ropeyards providing cordage of varied lengths and thicknesses.[12]

*A mail boat comes alongside a fluyt to
deliver a mail bag.*

*Print published by Jacob Quack, 1665,
Gemeente Archief, Rotterdam*

■ The infrastructure for the world of trade and commerce

From the 1590's, Amsterdam grew to be the centre of world trade. The city government vigorously stimulated this development. It took care that the rather simple meeting place for merchants was replaced in 1611 by a new well laid out exchange building which provided all sorts of services. An exchange bank started two years before, accepting deposits of all current currencies and converting them at a fixed rate into bank guilders. Middelburg in 1616 and Rotterdam in 1635 also got their own exchange banks, though with much smaller deposit levels. The Amsterdam Loan Bank, set up in 1614, helped to arrange commercial credit. Bottomry loans financed trading voyages to distant and risky destinations, carrying high rates of interest to be paid on the return of the ship on which the loan was raised. If the ship was lost, nothing had to be repaid.

Another great asset for a proper functioning of the trading world was the publication of weekly printed commodity price lists, initiated in the 1580's. Around 1600 it already listed the quoted prices of more than 200 commodities, of bullion and of currencies. In 1635 the number had risen to 350 goods. The publication of price lists was from 1613 closely regulated by a committee of brokers. The lists soon got spread all over Europe. A grain exchange was formed in 1617. Provisions of these kinds formed the infrastructure for trade, commerce and industry.[13]

Communication was essential as well. News coverage between the cities was arranged by municipal postal services and by reports. The 'trekschuiten' often formed a chain in the transportation of letters. Amsterdam was the nexus for communications to and from Hamburg and further eastwards. Mail traffic with France and England traditionally passed through Antwerp. Amsterdam merchants could also hire a fishing boat from Katwijk to carry letters to Calais where the vessel had to wait for a couple of days in order to collect letters for Amsterdam, as happened, for instance, in May 1637. From c. 1660 merchants felt a need for a direct link with England so packet boats started direct services between Harwich and Holland. Both

Amsterdam and Rotterdam were involved, but from 1668 Amsterdam became the prime participant. Twice a week English packet boats sailed between Harwich and Hellevoetsluis, carrying mail and passengers. Hellevoetsluis, however, was a naval base. The '*Royal Charles*', the great booty of the raid in the Medway in 1667 was moored there. During the Third Anglo-Dutch War (1672-1674) it was thought wise to switch the port-of-call from Hellevoetsluis to nearby Brielle. The packet service itself, apart from this switch, continued as in peace time. Commercial information remained of great interest for belligerents, both in Amsterdam and in London. In August 1673, while the two opposing fleets manoeuvred along the Dutch coast preparing to fight each other, the packet boat was permitted to enter and leave the harbour of Brielle.[14]

■ The mercantile marine

In 1645, an Englishman called Amsterdam the great staple of news. From all corners of the world all kinds of information came together there. Other Dutch port cities often took advantage of this in their own enterprises. Historians have called Amsterdam 'the great staple market'. This is wrong, as Clé Lesger has recently demonstrated. The staple function had to do with (commercial) information. The commodities themselves were not physically present. The numerous storehouses along the city canals and elsewhere suggest otherwise, but they were only used to store foods, goods and raw materials for inland consumption and production and to store finished products for export. The exception were some goods from Asia which were kept in Amsterdam warehouses. Lesger has also demonstrated that a substantial part of the huge merchant fleet was involved in direct ('*doorgaand*') sailings between different parts of Europe, bypassing Amsterdam completely.[15]

The merchant fleet was huge. Fully trustworthy figures for the size were and are not available. In 1634, when estimates were made for fiscal purposes, the fantastic number of 13,650 seagoing ships was mentioned. It was immediately revised and in 1636 reduced to 1750 for Holland only. This number compares rather well with two other data for the fleet operating in European waters: 1433 Dutch ships in 1694 and 1600 in 1699. The 1636 estimate for Holland makes distinctions among the different main destinations, the average number of annual voyages per ship and the average tonnage. Norway, the Baltic and France were the prime destinations for 350, 400 and 450 ships respectively. These vessels were estimated at an average carrying capacity of 200 to 300 tons, while making 2½ to 4 trips in a year. Another 200, bigger, ships sailed to Portugal, Spain and the Mediterranean. The rest mostly sailed to England, Scotland, Northern France and Northern Germany, with capacities of no more than 100 tons.[16] Pieter Allen's shares were in the biggest ships and were more valuable than those of Jan Ibess while shipbuilder Osterlinck at Edam constructed ships of various sizes for various trades.

Merchants had a wide choice of vessel types in which they could have shipped their commodities. Smaller types such as boyers and galliots were appropriate for sailing in shallow waters along the Wadden Isles to Bremen and Hamburg or along the Flemish sands to Dover and Calais. Fluytships were available in many sizes, from 25 to 35 metres in length and with widths of one fourth to one fifth the length. Fluytships were the most common freighters, the larger ones carrying some guns. There were also types with the hull of a fluytship, but with different upperworks. 'Hek-boten' and cat-ships, specialized in the transportation of lumber for example.[17] Frigates were more heavily built. They had flat sterns and often sailed in more dangerous waters. The more numerous guns on board required more crew members. De Ruyter's ship '*Salamander*' in the 1640's was probably a merchant frigate though we lack concrete evidence.

African and West Indian trades used bigger ships than those operating in Europe. The journeys took more time, in particular on a triangular trip to West Africa and to the Caribbean. Adequate armament was compulsory. A crew of forty to fifty men and boys was the rule rather than the exception. An estimate of 1635 mentions 280 vessels involved in the Atlantic trade. It was the period in which the Dutch were very active in Brazil. For 1694 the estimate was much lower at a mere 90 ships.[18]

Dutch vessels sailed all over Europe. In many a port city their masters had to find merchants and cargoes. They had access to good maps for navigation and to descriptions of the main characteristics of each port and what commodities were available where. In the main shipping centres masters could also rely on the presence of relatives of Dutch merchant families and/or representatives of the States General: consuls, residents, agents, etc. who could give practical advice. An important centre of information was Helsingør near Kronborg Castle at the entrance of the Sound, where the famous tolls were collected. Around 1600 there was a lively Dutch colony there. Masters could get information and find orders for the remainders of their voyages. At least from 1637, a Dutch official resided at Helsingør, helping his compatriots passing the Sound. La Rochelle played the same role in Western Europe, later replaced by Nantes and Bordeaux. Naval officers profited as well from this elaborate network of Dutch representatives abroad, of whatever kind they may have been.[19]

Late sixteenth century merchants and ship owners expanded their sailings to Northern Russia via the White Sea and also to the Mediterranean. A sort of Europeanization in commerce started. Wine was brought from France to the Baltic, salt from Portugal to Dutch herring ship owners, and Baltic grain went to Spain and so on. This was not new in 1600. But from this time, Europe formed one commercial entity. Russian fur now went to Leghorn in Italy and Cretan currents or Turkish silk to Amsterdam, Polish wheat to southern Italy. Trade was in bulk as well as precious goods. The Dutch were often the carriers as well. Their merchant fleet was much larger in numbers and capacity than that of any other European state.

■ Whaling

Early in the seventeenth century whaling opened up in far northern waters near Spitsbergen (Svalbard). Initially international competition was fierce. English ships of the Muscovy Company chased Dutch 'intruders' off the whaling grounds. An organizational structure and armed protection were both required. The States General provided both. The Northern Company was founded in 1614 and was given a charter plus a monopoly. A structure was created with regional chambers in port cities in Friesland, Holland and Zeeland. From then on until well into the 1620's, three to five warships annually protected Dutch whaling vessels in Arctic waters. The whale blubber, boiled into oil, and to a lesser degree whalebone turned out to be profitable products. Whaling expanded rapidly in the 1630's and 1640's. In 1633 and

Try-houses for reducing whale oil of the Amsterdam chamber of the Noordse Compagnie at Smerenburg near Spitsbergen

Painting by Cornelis de Man, 1639, Rijksmuseum, Amsterdam

1635 De Ruyter was mate on board the Flushing whaling vessel '*Groene Leeuw*'.

Around 1640 the monopoly of the Northern Company crumbled away, but the company and its chambers were not officially dissolved. They simply disappeared. Whaling became a free enterprise open to any entrepreneur. Great numbers of fortune-hunters saw new opportunities for quick profits. The most curious combinations of people joined forces in chartering merchant ships for whaling voyages. The whales were flensed in the open sea and try houses were built at home, in the countryside or outside city walls because of the unpleasant smell they generated. Climatic changes and falling temperatures soon prohibited further boiling activities at Spitsbergen. Well-organized and well-equipped voyages brought profit and stimulated further whaling while others less resourceful and committed dropped out. Around 1670 the true whaling entrepreneurs had emerged. They began to equip multiple ships in a year and specialized as whaling ship owners. Most of them lived in the northern part of Holland, near Rotterdam and some in Zeeland and Friesland.[20]

Whaling became a flourishing and stable business in the latter part of the seventeenth century. During the 1680's, often more than 240 vessels departed to the high North. Whaling was of course a typical seasonal enterprise. In late March and April, the ships left their ports and returned in August/September. Because of the labour intensive activities during and right after the hunt many hands were always needed on board, on average 40 to 46, many more than on an ordinary merchantman travelling in European waters. Qualified and experienced personnel were required for a successful expedition, just as the whaling vessel had to meet special requirements. Six whaling sloops with their adequate hanging gear formed the basic equipment, while the ship itself had to have a fortified bow for passage through waters full of ice floes. Of the thousands who enlisted annually, there was a core of people who were very loyal to specific ship owners and commanders, people who made careers as whaling specialists. Most of these people lived at the northern limits of Holland and also on the North German Wadden Isles such as Föhr and Amrun. Leaving their homesteads early in the year via a special boat service, these men and boys returned home in September, bringing sundries which were in demand on the isolated islands plus, of course, the rest of their earnings. These earnings could be relatively high but how much they brought home always depended on how many whales they caught.

■ The fisheries and the impact of privateering

There were two kinds of Dutch fisheries in the North Sea: with keel ships and with flat-bottomed vessels. The first category harboured in cities and villages along waters open to the sea. The second category beached along the coast of Holland in villages such as Ter Heijde, Scheveningen, Katwijk and Egmond. 'Buizen' and 'hoekers' were used for catching herring, to be salted and cod with drift-nets and long lines. 'Bomschuiten' and 'pinken' were used mainly to catch flatfishes with trawl-nets and haddock with long lines. Those vessels mostly made short trips. Icelandic waters were favourite grounds for cod while herring was found in the western part of the North Sea near the British Isles.

The heyday of the herring fishery was in the first half of the seventeenth century. A fair estimate is a number of about 600 '*buizen*' involved. By the end of the century the number had halved. Enkhuizen, in particular, lost a great deal of its herring fleet. It is more difficult to give estimates for the other three types of boats mentioned. There must have been several hundred of them. Their crews, fluctuating from 5 to about 12, were mostly recruited in the local neighbourhoods where the vessels were fitted out. In a rather isolated village such as Katwijk, hardly any occupation other than fisherman was possible, unless one dared to leave his village and go to Amsterdam or Rotterdam. The fisheries were related to many ancillary trades and not just to ship construction and repair. Nets had to be made, mended and tanned, which was partially done by women and girls. Coopering was essential for herring. Salt had to be imported and stored. Part of the herring was cured, not salted. There were inspectors of the quality of the fish. Barrels had to be marked with brands. Salesmen bought and sold the fish products, which were transported to markets all over the Dutch Republic and abroad.

The fisheries were vulnerable to violence at sea. The possibility of encountering trouble was rather the rule than the exception. Privateers from Dunkirk and Ostend formed the greatest danger. Fishing boats were not armed and could not put up any sort of defence. The privateers lured around the fishing grounds and often played havoc among concentrations of fishing boats. The presence of one or more warships did not deter them. During the Eighty Years' War (1568-1648) the losses among fishermen from Zeeland and the Meuse estuary are known. They were high and even increased: in Zeeland in 1600-1607 103 fishermen were captured and in the Meuse estuary 116. After the Twelve-Year Truce (1609-1621), Flemish privateers resumed their activities with even more vigour. They had made 109 and 715 victims respectively made by 1647.[21] The three Anglo-Dutch Wars were too brief to have a lasting impact. In the Nine Years' War (1689-1697), however, hostile privateering left deep and lasting marks on the fisheries. The herring fleet was almost halved and the financial resources of many ship owners and investors were exhausted. Enkhuizen was the main victim.

The impact of privateering upon Dutch maritime activities at large can hardly be underestimated. The period 1627-1646 was very risky for Dutch vessels, not only for the sea fisheries but for the mercantile marine as well. In this period, Dunkirk privateers annually captured 150 to 350 merchant and fishing vessels, with peaks in 1629: 320, 1630: 317, 1631: 295 and 1632: 350! English historians claim that their privateers and warships took no less than 1,000 to 1,700 Dutch vessels during the First Anglo-Dutch War (1652-1654), a figure so far not confirmed by Dutch research. Losses during the Second Anglo-Dutch War (522) were largely counterbalanced by Dutch captures of English ships (453). England and France fought the Dutch in the Third Anglo-Dutch War. The balance was now fully in favour of the Dutch: 500 to 648. The relatively short duration of these three conflicts created opportunities for repair and recovery of seafaring activities. The Nine Years' War and the War of the Spanish Succession (1702-1713) turned out to be the heyday of European privateering. The Dutch lost thousands of vessels but captured or retook almost equal numbers. The use of neutral ship's papers and a neutral flag by Dutch ship owners and masters could not always guarantee an undisturbed continuation of seafaring and trade.[22]

Ship owners, investors and seamen in the Dutch Republic were themselves keen on exploiting chances for good profits from their own privateering enterprises. Ship owners at Flushing, for instance, gave De Ruyter the command of one of their privateering vessels in the North Sea in 1637. During the second part of the Eighty Years' War they operated with great success against Spanish and Portuguese shipping in the southern Atlantic and in the waters near the Iberian Peninsula. Privateering then developed into an activity typical of Zeeland. Holland lagged behind in the activity. Privateering reached its zenith during the heyday between 1621 and 1648. It had its own group of investors and ship owners using ships often especially built and fitted out for long and frequently distant journeys, providing work for large numbers of seamen. A whole apparatus of prize-courts and auctions were part of the world of privateering. It belonged to the Dutch maritime world at large but lasted only as long as war lasted. In peacetime privateers had to turn their attention to other activities.

■ The India Companies

The East India Company was by far the greatest entrepreneurial organization in Europe. Founded in 1602, it had a monopoly – now and again extended by the States General – for all dealings east of the Cape of Good Hope and west of Cape Horn. The management board, the Gentlemen Seventeen, coordinated the activities of the six chambers, located at Amsterdam, Middelburg, Rotterdam, Delft, Hoorn and Enkhuizen. Each chamber operated according to its share in the whole: Amsterdam half, Zeeland one quarter and the four others each one sixteenth. For a long time, the VOC was an expanding organization. Its impact upon economic life in chamber cities was great, not the least in the smaller cities and especially after about 1680 when their local economies shrank.

Three times a year a growing number of East Indiamen departed for Asia: in the 1630's about 16 ships, in the 1680's 23 on average and in the 1730's 37. During the first decades a great variety of ships was fitted out, but later the choice was restricted to three different rates of East Indiamen, constructed according to standards formulated by the Gentlemen Seventeen. Some were hired by the navy during the First and Second Anglo-Dutch Wars, though they collected little if any glory in battle. The last time that this happened was in 1665. In the battle of Lowestoft at least three East Indiamen were taken or blown up: 'Maarsseveen', 'Nagelboom' and 'Oranje'.[23] After that disastrous experience the navy only used its own purpose-built warships.

The arrival of the return fleet coming back from Asia was a great event. It took place in the summer with naval vessels escorting the East Indiamen on the last leg of their long journeys from Asia. Their cargoes were very precious. Part of the goods were auctioned in the autumn, others were stored in the Company's storehouses. In that the Dutch Republic and especially Amsterdam were rightly honoured with the reputation of being a staple market.

The Company devoured manpower. The death rate amongst its personnel was extremely high. Only four out of ten men returned home after service of 3, 5 or even 10 years. Most people fell victim to diseases during the voyage, others during their stay in the tropics. The annual demand for personnel increased gradually: from about 3,000 men in 1635 to 4,000 in 1685 and fifty years later even to 7,000. Despite the bereavements around them, many seamen reenlisted and several of them even made 7 to 10 complete journeys to Asia and back. There were always vacancies for the survivors. Some made good careers and became masters of one of the huge East Indiamen. People with a variety of backgrounds found their way into Company service. Labour conditions were among the worst in the seafaring world. In the chamber cities there were groups of families that had various male members employed by the voc generation after generation. Crew members, seamen as well as soldiers, also came from other parts of the Netherlands and from abroad. This last category had left their homes in the hope of finding employment of whatever sort in the Dutch Republic. Via the hosts of their temporary lodgings in port cities or via compatriots who already lived in the Netherlands these people got in touch with the recruitment offices of the voc.[24]

The voc was a very predictable company. Pattern and rhythm as to departure and return of its fleets did not change nor did dates of auctions and moments when decisions about new ship construction were taken. The West India Company (wic) was similar and different. The first wic, founded in 1621, also got a monopoly from the States General, and in that case for trade to the New World. Its structure was comparable with five chambers. In addition to commerce and shipping, however, the wic was a state instrument in the war against Spain and Portugal. Much energy and money was spent in Brazil, but finally in vain. Privateering was a very profitable business until peace treaties with Spain in 1648 and Portugal in 1661 were concluded. The colony of New Netherland along the Hudson River became a fiasco as well. The wic was not equal to English interests and to political strife on the home front. The first wic lost most of its financial resources and was dissolved in 1674.

Freed of debts, a second wic was founded in the same year. Its structure was not changed, but its objectives were more realistic. The new company was to focus on commercial interests in West Africa and protect the vulnerable trans-Atlantic slave trade. Shipping activities were reduced. About 16 vessels, manned by c. 500 men, were annually fitted out. In the 1650's, the chambers had already abandoned their own shipbuilding. The Amsterdam chamber sold the site of its yard in 1670. The second wic bought or hired the ships as needed. Meanwhile private enterprise expanded business in Surinam and Guyana. In West Africa, the company's monopoly, however, was gradually undermined by smugglers from Zeeland and Holland.[25]

■ The navy and its personnel

The Dutch Republic was a small country with no more than 1½ to 2 million inhabitants, in sharp contrast to its enemies and their allies: Spain, England and France. Maritime and overseas activities were the hall mark of the country, and on a scale unsurpassed by any other state. The different branches of seafaring, as we have seen, deployed thousands of men and boys. As to the hard core of its crews each service had its own recruitment pattern. Perhaps some whalers found winter employment on the traditional autumn merchant fleet to the Iberian Peninsula. By and large, however, shifting to a completely different trade was rare.

Some estimates of the total number of seamen employed in each trade have been

A young sailor

Drawing by Moses ter Borch, 1660-1665,
Rijksmuseum, Amsterdam

presented above. Putting these totals together gives an impressive number of seafaring personnel. Historians have been able to collect relevant data which provide insight into the demand for seamen during the 1630's and 1680's/1690's. In the first period the demand fluctuated annually around 45,000, the navy not included. Merchant vessels employed almost half of the amount. Fifty to sixty years later the same figure was around 50,000. The demand by merchant masters remained more or less the same. The VOC (15,000) and the whaling fleet (9,000) had become very prominent consumers in the maritime labour market. The heyday of the WIC had passed.[26] When looking at the labour market at large the army had to be taken into consideration as well. Around 1640 the army had 60,000 men on its payroll, in the war against France of 1675-1678 about 70,000.[27] Probably half of them were Dutchmen.

The pure Dutch maritime labour market would never have been able to supply 40 to 50,000 men each year for merchant shipping, not to mention men for the navy. Moreover, the VOC was responsible for draining this market by demanding for more and more people, many of whom never returned. Still, the maritime labour market did operate rather well, but that was only thanks to the permanent influx of foreigners from countries around the North Sea and the Baltic. These people came to the Dutch Republic in search of work and a better standard of living than they knew at home. Many of them became sedentary migrants, others repatriated afterwards. These foreigners found jobs in all sectors of the Dutch economy, a very large number in the world of shipping. When new on board, foreigners filled the lower ranks. Those who settled at Amsterdam or any other port city often rose to higher ranks in society. Positions of masters or captains were not excluded. Taking the seventeenth century as a whole, one observation is evident: the presence of foreigners on board in all branches of seafaring increased, including the mercantile fleet. A proportion of foreigners of one third on average was quite normal around 1650, creeping upwards to 40 and almost 50 per cent in the following century.

The navy was another organization which placed heavy demands on the maritime labour market, demands which increased over the course of the century from 10,000 in the final stage of the Eighty Years' War to 20,000 men in 1672 and 1673 and up to 25,000 in 1694. There was no compulsory service and the navy had no long term service contracts. Enlistment was only for one season or for one journey on board a ship, the name and that of its captain having been advertised during recruiting. Finding crews was the captains' own responsibility. In time of peace, a rather rare phenomenon in the seventeenth century, a few thousand hands for convoy trips were sufficient and the navy generally could enlist those numbers. But in wartime big problems usually arose in trying to enlist the desired numbers of seamen. Fleets became larger and larger as did the ships. Recruiting officers were deployed outside an admiralty's own district. This step was also a last resort for De Ruyter. During many campaigns the complements on board his ships were not fully manned.

This difficult situation was ameliorated in two ways. Though force and compulsion were not applied, authorities could create circumstances in which many seamen faced the inevitability of enlisting. Early in the year, the States General put embargoes on mercantile shipping, whaling and the sea fisheries. Ships in these trades were forbidden to sail before a certain date much later in the year. The seamen involved were put out of work so most of them were then obliged to look for alternatives and so could not escape going into naval service. They were unable to live without their earnings and the free facilities of food and lodging. Embargoes had the desired effect.

For example in 1672-1674 seamen in the West-Frisian village of Westwoud, 26 in all, enlisted on warships but only for so long as the war lasted.[28] A naval job was always badly paid despite a bit higher monthly wages being offered at the start of a war. Authorities were afraid of excessive wage increases because then the navy would be manned by the ordinary man in the street, as Grand Pensionary Johan de Witt once said.

The other way to deal with the shortage of the seamen for the navy was the introduction of marines. England was the model. For a long time army soldiers had been on board, but seldom to everybody's satisfaction. The sailors held them in contempt. In December 1665, a corps of marines ('*zeesoldaten*') was established in Holland with Zeeland and Friesland following somewhat later. This corps was only for naval service. It had its own officers and was well equipped with swords and flintlocks. Marines took part in the daily routine of shipboard life. In 1666, Holland aimed at a force of 8,000 marines. During the Second and Third Anglo-Dutch Wars, the corps was considered to be a very successful innovation.

Embargoes and marines did help to alleviate manning problems in wartime. At the core of the navy, however, stood still the Dutch seaman who voluntarily opted for naval service together with his colleagues from abroad. A representative of the first category was mentioned above: Jannetje Cornelis' boy friend at Rotterdam in 1664 and in 1683 captain Johan de Witte's cabin boy from Amsterdam. Magnus Andersen from Kristiania (Oslo) represents the second category. He served on board another warship in De Ruyter's squadron in West Africa in 1664. Andersen and his Norwegian wife, Barbara Piters, lived already for several years in the poorest harbour district of Amsterdam. Barbara wrote him that she and their four children had survived the severe pestilence of 1664 (25,000 victims at Amsterdam!). After Andersen's return the couple would have a fifth child.[29]

The most curious phenomenon, however, was the willingness of seamen from the British Isles to fight the English navy and how easily these people were accepted on board Dutch ships. Large numbers of Scots and Englishmen served in the corps of marines in 1672. On board the '*Gelderland*', at Hellevoetsluis in March 1672, there were no fewer than 120 men from Britain. In 1673 8 per cent of the seamen admiral Cornelis Tromp had on board his '*Gouden Leeuw*' had the same geographical background. The most renowned man among the men from the British Isles was the Irish Roman Catholic Thomas Tobiaszoon. In 1673, he was Tromp's flag captain. Before he had entered Dutch naval service, Tobiaszoon had been on board with admiral Edward Spragge. He was responsible for the highlight of the Dutch victory in the Medway in 1667: the capture of the English flagship '*Royal Charles*'. As the captain of the man-of-war '*Bescherming*' Tobiaszoon was the first man out of a nine men party who stepped, unopposed, aboard the '*Charles*'. Its flag and jack were struck down. Tobiaszoon when he was not at sea fighting against England lived very near to De Ruyter in Amsterdam. Young Jean Bart from Dunkirk had also been present in the Medway. He was on board De Ruyter's flagship the '*Zeven Provinciën*'.[30]

The third day of the Four Days' Battle, 1666

Painting by P. van Soest, 1666, Nederlands Scheepvaartmuseum, Amsterdam

CHAPTER 2

Michiel Adriaenszoon de Ruyter

and his Biographer Gerard Brandt

Ronald Prud'homme van Reine

■ His life, his exploits

He distinguished himself in 55 battles, of which 15 were major sea battles, 9 of them fought under his command. His name was Michiel Adriaenszoon de Ruyter[1] and he is the most famous of all Dutch admirals. In the second half of the twentieth century, the interest in this personage was waning only to revive at the beginning of the twenty-first century. His 400th birthday was lavishly commemorated in 2007 with a naval review, books, lectures and exhibitions.

Michiel de Ruyter, the son of the former seaman and beer porter Adriaen Michielszoon, and of Aagje Jansdochter, was born as Michiel Adriaenszoon in Flushing in the Dutch Republic on 24 March, 1607, at precisely eight o'clock in the morning. Michiel was the fourth child in a marriage which produced an impressive eleven children: six daughters and five sons. Most of the children probably died young because later on in Michiel's life there is evidence of only two close relatives, both of whom were sisters.

The stories of young Michiel growing up in Flushing are so legendary that it is not necessary to dwell upon them. His youthful vigour led him to climb the local church tower and to make his mark by getting into fights on the school playground. In the ropeyard belonging to the Lampsins brothers, shipowners in Flushing, he turned the huge wheel. In the nineteenth century, Anton L. de Rop wrote a song about Michiel at work in his blue-checked smock, and the song is still well known in the Netherlands today. Michiel himself, however, apparently said he could only think of one thing at that time – going to sea.

On 3 August, 1618, when he was eleven years old, Michiel Adriaenszoon heeded his calling and departed as a boatswain's apprentice. Before long he rose to the position of seaman. He also served for a time as a gunner and a trooper in the army of Prince Maurits, before going to sea once more in 1623. In the 1630s, he was a helmsman in the service of the Greenland Company, hunting for whales around Jan Mayen Island. Subsequently, having in the meantime acquired the family name De Ruyter, he went on to spend a number of years as a privateer and as the master of a merchant vessel in the service of the Lampsins brothers for whom he had worked in the ropewalk when he was younger. His duties as a merchant ship captain took him on many trips to Morocco and other countries in the Mediterranean, but he also sailed regularly to Brazil and the Caribbean. During a short period as a temporary Rear-Admiral in the service of the Admiralty of Zealand, he sailed in 1641 with a fleet to Portugal where he fought against the Spaniards and gained his first experience as an officer in a battle flotilla. For ten years after that, he worked once more as a merchant captain, but this time he was the proprietor. Again, he went mainly to Morocco, Brazil and the Caribbean where he repeatedly fought with privateers and pirates.

His first two wives both died young and when De Ruyter married for the third time he decided – with the encouragement of his new wife, seaman's widow Anna van Gelder – to bid farewell to his seaman's life. Due to advancing years, he was looking forward to life on shore in his Vlissingen home located between the Lange Nieuwstraat and the Groenewoud. However, just at that time, duty called.

When the First Anglo-Dutch War broke out in 1652, De Ruyter entered the service of the Admiralty of Zealand as vice commander. In various battles with the English at sea – off Plymouth, for example – he proved to be a very skilled commander.

ZEESLAG tusſen de H.ʳ MICHIEL DE RUITER en den H.ʳ GEORG ASCUE by Plymuyden A⁰.1652.

1. De H.ʳ M. de Ruiter.
2. De Vice Ad.ᵉˡ G. Ascue.
3. Een Engelsch ſinkend Schip.
4. Cap.ᵗ J. Bankert de Jonge.

5. Cap.ᵗ Douwe Ankes ſchiet
2. Scheepen van de Engelſche
10. Cap.ᵗ Jacob Sickels.
6 en 7 in de Grond.
8. Cap.ᵗ Andries Fortuyn.

9. Cap.ᵗ Steendert de Haen.
10. Cap.ᵗ Jacob Sickels.
11. Cap.ᵗ Frans Krynsz Mangelaer.
12. De H.ʳ J. van den Broek Vice Comd.ᵗ

13. Cap.ᵗ Klaas Jansz Sanger.
14. Cap.ᵗ Isaak Sweers.
15. Cap.ᵗ Cornelis Kuyper.
16. Cap.ᵗ J. Gideonsz Verburgh.

17. De H.ʳ Sch. by Nacht J. Verhaaf.
18. Cap.ᵗ Pieter Salomonsz.
19. Cap.ᵗ Rombout vander Parre.
20. Cap.ᵗ Laurens Penſter.

21. De Koopvaardy Scheepen.
22. Cap.ᵗ J. Viſcher voerende een Brander.
23. De Vyf andre Branders.
24. Engelſche Oorlog Scheepen.

The Dutch fleet, under the supreme command of Maerten Tromp, was much too weak and therefore no real match for the superior English, so De Ruyter gained valuable experience that was to prove very useful later on. After Maerten Tromp was killed in 1653, De Ruyter was himself offered the position of supreme commander of the battle fleet though he had served for much less time than many of his colleagues. Even then, he was regarded as the obvious choice for leading the navy. Nevertheless, De Ruyter refused the position, realising that if he were to take it on his senior colleagues would never accept him. He did, however, accept promotion to Vice Admiral in the Admiralty of Amsterdam which meant he had to move from Flushing to what was called the Buitenkant, a quayside street now called Prins Hendrikkade on the banks of the IJ River in Amsterdam.

In the years that followed De Ruyter sailed in many convoys to the Mediterranean. These trips were nothing more than a chance to show the Dutch flag and to demonstrate strength to the privateers and pirates that were endangering Dutch merchant vessels in those waters. He proved himself to be skilled in concluding peace treaties with rulers of the Barbary Coast, in other words Morocco, Algeria and Tunisia, at the same time paying for many Dutch slaves in those countries to be set

The battle of Plymouth in 1652, the Dutch fleet commanded by Michiel de Ruyter and the English by Sir George Ayscue

Print by D. Vrijdag, around 1790, Maritiem Museum Prins Hendrik, Rotterdam

free. During a journey to the Baltic Sea in 1659, he supported the Danes in their war with Sweden in order to protect Dutch trading interests. He conquered the island of Funen (Fyn) as well as the city of Nyborg. The Danish king was so grateful he made De Ruyter a peer.

More convoy duties in the Mediterranean Sea followed from 1660 onwards. In 1664, De Ruyter was given a secret assignment by the States General to sail on further, to the west coast of Africa where the English had captured various forts from the Dutch, that all before war was declared. De Ruyter won back a significant number of the forts and then, following new orders, crossed the Atlantic Ocean where he engaged the English and inflicted considerable damage on them in the Caribbean and along the North American coast. Meanwhile, the Second Anglo-Dutch War had commenced with the battle off Lowestoft that turned out to be disastrous for the Dutch fleet. Only when De Ruyter returned with his ships and was appointed Admiral of the Fleet as well as supreme commander did the tide turn. The Four Days' Battle in June, 1666, was the first major victory for the Dutch in the Anglo-Dutch Wars, however, it was a far from decisive one. In August, 1666, the English fought back remorselessly in the St. James's Day Battle in which losses on the Dutch side were only kept to a minimum by the superb way in which De Ruyter led the retreat. Nevertheless, the war ended in Dutch victory. During the legendary raid in the Medway in 1667, the Dutch fleet under De Ruyter conquered and destroyed a large number of important English warships, including the *Royal Charles*, which had been the English flagship. The peace treaty that was subsequently signed in Breda was advantageous to the Dutch.

War was to break out again five years later. In this Third Anglo-Dutch War, England and France launched a joint sea attack while troops from France, Munster and Cologne invaded Dutch territory from the south and east. The Disaster Year of 1672 had begun. It was said at the time that the country was *reddeloos* (beyond salvation), the government *radeloos* (it realised the situation was beyond hope) and the people were *redeloos* (beyond reason). But De Ruyter and his fleet kept going. In the Battle of Solebay in June, 1672, he beat back a combined English and French fleet, thus averting the danger of soldiers being landed from the sea. In June, 1673, there were two engagements with the Anglo-French fleet on the Schooneveld Bank to the west of the island of Walcheren in the province of Zeeland. De Ruyter led his flotilla, known as his 'little pile of ships', supremely. Despite the flotilla's relative weakness, De Ruyter managed to drive off the opponents with brilliant tactical manoeuvres. The apotheosis of the Anglo-Dutch Wars took place in August of that same year during the battle off Kijkduin which the English call the battle of Texel. For the third and final time, the allied enemy fleet attempted to land on the coast of Holland. Once again, De Ruyter stood up to them and forced them to retreat. The danger from the seaward side had been averted and, in February, 1674, a peace treaty was concluded with the English in Westminster.

The end of the Third Anglo-Dutch War meant the end of the golden era for the Dutch fleet and consequently also for Michiel de Ruyter. The war with France was still going on. After a failed attempt to capture the French Caribbean island of Martinique in 1674, De Ruyter was sent off the following year to the Mediterranean with an inferior and badly equipped flotilla. The Spanish king, an ally in the fight against France, had asked for help in fighting for Sicily. Contrary to expectations, the Spanish fleet turned out to be barely capable of supporting the Dutch ships. On 22 April,

1676, De Ruyter was mortally wounded in his leg during an encounter with the French fleet in the battle off Agosta, in sight of Mount Etna. A week later he died from his wounds.

After his death, De Ruyter was honoured with a large marble tomb in the New Church in Amsterdam. During his career, he had received many gifts: a gold cup, a silver water jug, the complete version of Joan Blaeu's large atlas, the 'Atlas Maior', gold medals and splendidly decorated swords of honour. They just kept on coming. People who admired him had paintings, etchings or engravings of him hanging on the wall. A portrait of De Ruyter also hung on the wall in the assembly rooms of each of the five Admiralty Colleges, in Amsterdam, Rotterdam, Hoorn, Middelburg and Harlingen. De Ruyter had become a well-loved and popular hero of the seas. His name was also praised to the skies in prose and poetry. At the end of 1673, for example, the clergyman Gerard Brandt wrote an ode in which he called De Ruyter 'the State's right-hand man'. Twelve years later, Brandt was to write a weighty biography of Michiel de Ruyter, thus immortalising this hero of the seas. Thanks to this description of his life, many details and anecdotes concerning the Admiral have been kept alive.

■ Supreme commander and human being

Michiel de Ruyter was a practical man. Almost his whole life long, he carried out many and varied functions that had to do with all aspects of shipping. As a result, his experience of maritime matters was unparalleled and his knowledge second to none. De Ruyter's contribution to the navy was significant mainly because of his excellent qualities as a supreme commander. He put his men through training in a way previously unknown. Moreover, he could delegate his powers much better than any other commander. He managed to shape his naval officers and crews into a single unit in a way that could be said to be unique. This was quite an achievement in a period in which five different Admiralties, each with its own flag officers, made the decisions. Together with Grand Pensionary Johan de Witt and later to a lesser extent with Prince Willem III, he built up a Dutch navy that was stronger than ever before. He was able to recognize when reform was essential, for example, as when he set up the Marines Corps or when artillery on the warships required improvement.

He was without doubt a charismatic supreme commander. As a rule, he seems to have addressed his crew as a father would his children. Seamen were pleased to have the opportunity to serve on board with De Ruyter. After all, there must have been a good reason for giving De Ruyter the nickname 'Bestevaer' (grandpa), one which could only be granted to a commander who was enormously popular. The finest example of his willingness to help his fellow human beings was the great lengths he went to in order to arrange the release of 26 Hungarian clergymen. They had been put to work as slaves in the galleys of Naples because of their religious convictions and their release is still commemorated every year in both the Netherlands and Hungary.

For De Ruyter himself, the most important things in life were the sea, the Bible and his family. Although he earned a good salary and made absolutely sure his finances were in order, wealth did not interest him. The simple way in which his house was furnished demonstrates that. The collection of precious objects he had assembled in the 'best room' comprised gifts he had received during his career.

He invested much of his money and his children were later to benefit from it. The fact that the moneybags found in his house on his death were destined for parishes in Amsterdam and Vlissingen was a sign of his philanthropy.

De Ruyter had eight children.[2] From his first marriage to Maeyke Velders (1604-1631) there was Heiltje (1631-1632), who died after only a few weeks. From his marriage to Neeltje Engels (1607-1650), there were Adriaen (1637-1655), Cornelia (1639-1720), a girl who died three days after she was born in 1641, Alida (1642-1679) and Engel (1649-1683). His third marriage to Anna van Gelder (1614-1687) brought forth Margaretha (1652-1688) and Anna (1655-1666). Anna van Gelder was the widow of the ship's captain Jan Pauwelsz van Gelder with whom she had a son Jan (1647-1673). De Ruyter raised this boy as his own child.

■ Gerard Brandt writes *Het Leven en bedrijf van den heere Michiel de Ruiter* (The life and deeds of Mr. Michiel de Ruiter)

Very soon after the death of De Ruyter became known, Lambertus van den Bosch, rector of the Latin School in Dordrecht, produced a biography of the Admiral. It was included as the last chapter in Van den Bosch's work entitled *Leeven en daden der doorlugtighste zeehelden en ontdeckers van landen dezer eeuwen* [Life and deeds of illustrious heroes of the seas and discoverers of countries in these centuries].[3] It appeared at the beginning of 1677, even before De Ruyter's body had arrived in Amsterdam. Despite being extremely informative for that time, this biography had all the signs of a job done in haste with many extensively cited letters, diplomatic texts, terms for peace and ship lists. It contained little about the man De Ruyter. Van den Bosch simply did not have enough time to produce something more thorough. Only the statements made by De Ruyter's son-in-law Bernardus Somer, the husband of Margaretha de Ruyter, added something worthwhile to this biography.

On the other hand, other authors were happy to exploit Van den Bosch's book in the first few years after the death of De Ruyter. The Huguenot Barthélémy Piélat, a clergyman living in Amsterdam, used practically the whole book, translated into French, to produce *La vie et les actions mémorables du Sr. Michel de Ruyter*[4] [The life and memorable deeds of Mr. Michiel De Ruyter]. According to the title page, the publication date was 1677, probably chosen to avoid accusations of plagiarism, but in fact it must have appeared in 1681 or thereafter because the author referred to De Ruyter's tomb. An anonymous English biography with the title *The life of Michael Adrian de Ruyter, Admiral of Holland* was published in 1677 in London by Dorman Newman.[5] This author, too, copied a great deal of Van den Bosch's work but did add some interesting passages from English sources. For example, he wrote that De Ruyter had stayed on the Irish coast in the 1640s, however, he wisely failed to mention the raid in the Medway that turned out to be so humiliating for the English fleet.

At the end of the 1670s, Engel de Ruyter, Michiel's only surviving son, went in search of an author who could compile a readable biography from the enormous pile of documents left by his father. He chose the poet, historian and clergyman Gerard Brandt (1626-1685), who lived in Amsterdam.[6] In previous years, Brandt had already written a number of poems about De Ruyter. Moreover, he had helped the family prepare for the funeral ceremony by, for example, composing the text for the letter inviting people to the funeral.[7] This choice may also have had something to do with

HET
LEVEN EN BEDRYF

VAN DEN HEERE

MICHIEL DE RUITER,

Hertog, Ridder, &c. L. Admiraal Generaal van
Hollandt en Weſtvrieſlandt.

BESCHREEVEN

DOOR

GERARD BRANDT.

Met ſchoone koopere plaaten verciert.

INDEFESSUS AGENDO

TE AMSTERDAM,
Voor WOLFGANG, WAASBERGE, BOOM,
VAN SOMEREN en GOETHALS.
MDC LXXXVII.

Brandt's biography of the famous poet and historian P.C. Hooft (1677) and with the
fact that he was working on a biography of another famous poet, Joost van den Vondel which was to appear in 1682. Another factor was that during his lifetime Engel's
father had always shown a great deal of respect for clergymen. Brandt was a Remon-
strant who held extremely tolerant religious views, very comparable to those of
Bestevaer. What is more: just as De Ruyter Brandt had great respect for the De Witt
brothers, being very upset about their brutal deaths. The clergyman even remarked

that Willem III regarded him as the 'enemy'.[8] In his letters Brandt was full of respect for De Ruyter whom he described as 'the incomparable Hero' and 'the Admiral beyond all praise'.[9] Judging by his enthusiastic correspondence with his fellow clergyman in The Hague, Johannes Vollenhove, about the latter's various elegies on De Ruyter, it seems highly likely that he avidly accepted the commission to write the biography.[10]

Brandt began compiling the work in 1681 but initially he had little time for it and so made little progress.[11] He was devoting a lot of effort to writing his *Historie der Reformatie* [History of the Reformation], a multi-volume study of which the first parts had appeared in 1671 and 1674. He was also kept busy for a long time correcting the proofs of his biography of Vondel. What is more, his health left a great deal to be desired and sometimes forced him to suspend his writing activities.[12] It was not until 1684 that he started making progress with the biography of De Ruyter. He worked with unremitting diligence, consulting De Ruyter's original documents, as supplied by Engel, as much as possible. He also consulted various other sources and writings, including the huge historical work by Lieuwe van Aitzema that contained a description of the Anglo-Dutch Wars. Moreover, countless people who had seen or met or knew De Ruyter in some capacity or other were still alive, so it was sometimes even possible to use eyewitness accounts. These enabled Brandt to intersperse his treatise with anecdotes.

Just before he died on 12 October 1685, Brandt managed to complete the manuscript of *Het Leven en bedrijf van den here Michiel de Ruiter* [The life and career of Mr. Michiel De Ruyter]. He had worked on it for fourteen hours a day for more than a hundred days over the previous few months. [13] In the meantime, Vollenhove had regularly been sent parts of the manuscript and proofs so he could provide comments and corrections regarding both language and historical aspects.[14] Brandt asked him, for example, about the term '*zonsopgang*' (*sunrise*), a term he regularly came across in ship's logbooks. He wondered whether it was good Dutch or purely a nautical term.[15] Vollenhove also advised him on the layout of the book. Brandt initially had his doubts about the title that would also be printed at the top of each page of the book. He had first thought of *Het leven van den Heldt Michiel de Ruiter* [The life of the hero Michiel de Ruyter]. He then crossed out the word 'hero' and changed it into 'hero of the seas', but his final version was the modest 'Mr.'[16]

Brandt even went so far as to involve Vollenhove when he needed some extra information. In February, 1685, for example, he wished to verify just a few more facts about Maerten Tromp, including his date of birth. He marked the relevant passages in red, sent his text to Vollenhove and asked him to show a few things to Cornelis Tromp or his sister who lived in The Hague; all this 'out of love for this faithful and brave Hero'. Brandt did, however, warn him that the Tromp family was still not on the best of terms with De Ruyter, saying: 'However, I do wonder whether it would serve us to say that it will appear in 't Leven van De Ruiter. Perhaps, my dear Sir, you should enquire about these things as if it concerned your own curiosity'.[17] Given the amount of information that Brandt required, this request would not have been an easy one to fulfill. Vollenhove also had to act quickly because Brandt wanted to take the chapters to the printers within a few days. It is almost certain that Cornelis Tromp did not want to co-operate and his sister in The Hague had already died in 1680 so Vollenhove was obviously unable to find out everything. As a result, the biography records the year of Maerten Tromp's birth as 1597, but does not mention the precise date.[18] Incidentally, this information later turned out to be incorrect. The year should have been 1598.

Before his death, Brandt corrected half of the proofs for the book.[19] His sons Caspar and Johannes completed the correction work as best they could but of course they did not have their father's knowledge. This meant that errors, which the author would probably have corrected if he had lived to complete the task, remained in the text. The book, a weighty tome comprising 1065 folio pages, was published in Amsterdam in 1687.

Brandt's biography ensured that De Ruyter's fame became widespread over the centuries.[20] Very soon reprints as well as translations into French and German appeared. In the eighteenth and nineteenth centuries, every family which owned a fair-sized library was certain to possess a copy of one of the many reprints or an abbreviated version, and many a boy decided to go to sea when he was older after having read the book.

■ A critical look at *Het Leven en bedrijf*

It is not difficult to be critical of Brandt's work. Totally consistent with the demands of his time, his most important objective when writing this biography was to produce a eulogy. Furthermore, he was following the example of the Roman historians Plutarch and Tacitus, whom he so admired, in compiling a heroic life story that included various dramatic twists and turns and speeches. Another important fact is that he was not a professional historian. Thus he was insufficiently critical when handling information which had been imparted to him by others or which had become generally accepted. Brandt ascribed to his hero words which were impossible to verify. In addition, Brandt was extremely verbose, not entirely impartial, and his untimely death meant that the second half of his work could not be checked for errors.

On the other hand there has always been much admiration for the literary qualities of Brandt's work. In a short period he had to work his way through a mountain of material but managed, nevertheless, to compile a book that is interesting even to the readers of today. Without Brandt's efforts there would certainly be much less known about De Ruyter's life and his name would probably have been more or less forgotten. It has been remarked, and rightly so, that one should ask who exactly has been immortalised, De Ruyter as a result of Brandt's pen or Brandt because he described the life of De Ruyter. Whatever one thinks, the biography was an impressive description of a life, and no biographer since then has been able to ignore this work.

Many regarded Brandt's book as a sort of bible that required absolutely no additions or corrections. Nevertheless, it is possible to conclude from various passages that Brandt moulded De Ruyter's life story to suit himself, especially the early years, for which there were so few sources. Several examples demonstrate that fact.

Brandt invented a pretext for the lack of information concerning De Ruyter's early years.[21] He tried to let it seem as though De Ruyter had destroyed his logbooks or had torn out pages in order to prevent the information being misused later to write a bombastic biography about him. This must be a romanticised version of the matter, something that occurred quite frequently in previous centuries in the life stories of well-known people. The De Ruyter archives are still available today. Only a few logbooks from the 1630s and 1640s are missing, and just a few pages are missing from other logbooks of that period, or some fragments remain. [22] Why should De Ruyter, afraid of a glorified biography, have wanted to suppress precisely these books? His years on merchant ships emphasised more than anything else his simple origins and they give an account of the long period of time in which he climbed the ladder, rung by rung, on his way to great fame. If De Ruyter really did want to delete all evidence of his rise to fame, would it not have been simpler to destroy all the log-books relating to the period before the First Anglo-Dutch War broke out in 1652 after which he became better known? Is it not rather remarkable that some logbooks from this same early period did remain available? All the evidence points to De Ruyter having kept them as carefully as possible, so it would appear that the odd logbook went missing in his earlier years, when he moved house a great many times.

Michiel grew up in relatively humble surroundings. Brandt emphasised this par-ticularly because it allowed him to draw comparisons with examples from the ancient world which he had read about in the works of Tacitus and others. He referred to the Greek statesman Themistocles, the son of an ordinary citizen who had defeated the Persians under Xerxes in the sea battle off Salamis, and to another Greek statesman Demosthenes, the son of a swordmaker, and to King Ptolemy of Egypt, the son of a soldier, and to the King Agathocles of Sicily, the son of a potter. [23] By referring to such predecessors, Brandt was suggesting that De Ruyter did not have to be ashamed of his background. On the contrary, it was to his credit, according to Brandt. After all, De Ruyter had risen to the highest functions entirely by virtue of his own merits.

Brandt mentions two details about De Ruyter's earliest childhood which he used as metaphors for his subject's later life. They should therefore be quoted with a cer-tain amount of caution. Apparently, Michiel indulged so often in fighting or beating up fellow pupils that he was expelled from school. If this really was the case then it is most remarkable that he nevertheless learned to read and write so well, if his later logbooks are anything to go by. Brandt used this story to show that, even at an early age, De Ruyter was already demonstrating a fighting mentality as well as leadership qualities. It was said that in the fights with other boys, he would lead the way as 'cap-tain'. Every time he was the leader, they were victorious, 'so in his childhood tussles, one could already see the portents of his life and deeds to come'. In order to illustrate this great daring which was present even in his childhood years Brandt related how Michiel climbed the church tower in Vlissingen when he was only ten years old. Dur-ing restoration work on the church tower, Michiel was said to have scrambled on to the spire. The inhabitants of the town had looked on with amazement and fear, more so because the workers had in the meantime removed the ladders on which Michiel could easily have climbed down again. Nonetheless, he managed by making use of his shoe heels in a most adroit manner to reach the ground unharmed having broken just a few slates on the way down. Brandt made use of the obvious metaphor, of course: `So high did he climb in his childhood and with such accompanying danger that, as a man, he would survive the climb through the ranks of all the naval services, as well as all the dangers afforded by the sea and by the enemy, and would reach the highest naval offices '. [24]

Brandt regularly talked piously of Divine Providence as, for example, when the seaman De Ruyter was injured during an encounter with the Spaniards. He narrowly avoided being taken prisoner by escaping to shore with two shipmates and after a long journey through France, arrived back home safely. During the time that De Ruyter was a boatswain's apprentice he received, according to Brandt, a head wound inflicted by a pickaxe while he was boarding an enemy warship. Brandt mentioned that some people claimed this was the only time in his life, that is until the fatal shot in 1676, that De Ruyter had been wounded.[25] However, the biographer had to add the story about his injuries in his encounter with the Spaniards when he was a seaman. If one considers the many battles he was involved in, De Ruyter will most certainly have received other injuries, although nothing about them was written down. A hero's life is all too easily associated with the myth of invulnerability.

The book also contains several exciting stories about the adventures De Ruyter had on his journeys over the years. Besieged by the enemy and in appalling weather conditions, he more than once narrowly escaped death. Years later Gerard Brandt noted down these events on a piece of paper that is now stored in the Dutch National Archives in The Hague.[26] Because Brandt had to rely on oral tradition for his information he was not able to put dates to any of the reported events. It is quite conceivable that De Ruyter recounted these tales on long winter nights while seated with his family around the fireplace. He will have told these stories again and again, probably embroidering them to some extent over the years so they no longer entirely corresponded with the truth.

The most famous story is the one of De Ruyter when returning from Ireland, taking a precautionary measure against the numerous privateers from Dunkirk that were active in the English Channel by ordering his ship to be smeared both inside and out with Irish butter. When privateers tried to board his ship, they slipped and slid over one another as if they were on ice so they could easily be beaten off. On another occasion, so the story goes, his warship, manned by just 17 crew, captured a valuable prize which was the booty of Dunkirk privateers whose own ship boasted 20 cannon and 120 crew. They had mistaken De Ruyter's ship for a heavily armed warship because the attack was so audacious.

It is very unusual to be able to verify something that has been recounted orally but there is one story for which this can be done. Brandt did not report a precise date or year for this incident but he related it as part of an overview of the occurrences in the Disaster Year of 1672. The State Papers Foreign, kept in the Public Record Office in London, contain an anonymous account of an attempt on De Ruyter's life. This had been sent from the Dutch Republic to Lord Charles Henry Wotton (Karel Hendrik van den Kerckhoven) in England.[27] His father Johannes Polyander van den Kerckhoven was married to a daughter of Lord Thomas Wotton. Charles Henry had held a court function as the representative of the nobility in the Dutch Province of Zeeland for five years but when the Second Anglo-Dutch War broke out in 1665, he had decided to return to his native country. He inherited the title Lord Wotton through his mother's side. Around 1670, he worked with Johan Kievit on reclaiming the marshes near Newmarket in Cambridgeshire using windmills. Kievit had performed various important functions in the Rotterdam City Council and had also been a member of the *'Gecommiteerde Raden van Holland'* (the executive committee of the States of Holland). Being a fervent Orangist, he fled to England in 1666 because of his involvement in a plot against the regime of Grand Pensionary Johan de Witt; in his absence, he was sentenced to death and his estate confiscated.

One Thursday in November, 1669, according to this anonymous account, a seaman knocked at the door of De Ruyter's house on the Buitenkant quay in Amsterdam. He was holding a piece of cheese and bread in one hand and a sharp knife in the other, apparently to cut the bread. The Admiral's maid opened the door, upon which the young man asked if Michiel de Ruyter was at home. The maid pretended not to understand him because his request to see the gentleman of the house had been made with so little respect. Irritated, the seaman once again asked whether Michiel de Ruyter was at home, this time adding that it was unclear to him why the maid could not understand him, as there was nothing wrong with his Dutch. Meanwhile, De Ruyter himself had emerged from his office and gone to the front of the house to find out what the commotion was all about. He asked the man, 'Comrade, who do you wish to speak to and what do you want?' whereupon the man asked pointedly if he was speaking to Michiel de Ruyter. When De Ruyter confirmed this, the man, who was described as a vagabond, shouted: 'If you say that Tromp is a blackguard, you will perish in hell'. He then lunged forward and made a stabbing movement with his knife but De Ruyter managed to fend him off just in time with a stick that the maid had fortuitously left nearby. Then another member of the family came to his aid and the seaman fled. The man was seen on another occasion but not apprehended. For a while, there was some anxiety that a plot had been hatched and that another attack was possible. De Ruyter apparently was vigilant, fearing a repetition. The perpetrator was, however, never identified.

It is remarkable that Brandt did not put a date to this incident. He did not even mention what year it was. In addition, a number of details in his version of the story do not correspond with those related above.[28] Brandt had the door being opened by a servant who just managed to rescue De Ruyter in time by throwing, in a reflex reaction, a ladder between him and his attacker. De Ruyter had in fact played a much more active role, having helped to bludgeon his assailant and drive him out of the house. According to Brandt, the law had later tried, without success, to trace the villain. Furthermore, Brandt did not mention the man's remarks about Tromp, although he did say a plot was feared. When Brandt wrote his book Tromp was still living so it is plausible that the writer deliberately avoided any reference to De Ruyter's colleague. Tromp, undeniably Orangist, was dismissed in 1666 when the St. James's Day Battle had ended because, according to De Ruyter, he had not followed orders. De Ruyter had called him a blackguard and told him he never wanted to see him aboard his ship, the *Zeven Provinciën*, again. In the years that followed, Tromp was unable to accept his fate and in 1673, after the fall of the Republican regime of Johan de Witt, he returned to the fleet. There was probably a very good reason for sending the anonymous account of the attempted murder to Lord Wotton who, together with Tromp's brother-in-law and confidante Johan Kievit, was busy reclaiming the marshes near Newmarket.

In Brandt's version, the attack on De Ruyter follows on from his account of the events of September 1672, when an angry mob made up mostly of seamen and their wives almost managed to plunder De Ruyter's house in his absence. By doing this, Brandt gives the impression, at the very least, that the murder attempt was made by the seaman in the autumn of 1672 after the Admiral of the Fleet had returned to shore. He wrote that, during the riot in September, the people had shouted angry slogans concerning De Ruyter who, in their eyes, had betrayed and sold off the fleet. It is perfectly possible that this referred to De Ruyter's treatment of Tromp, but here too Brandt omitted such remarks. Tromp's popularity among the people was unprecedented so there was a great deal of indignation about his dismissal. Unfortu-

The house of Michiel de Ruyter,
Prins Hendrikkade 131, Amsterdam.

Photograph by Ton Sipman

Goblet presented to Michiel de Ruyter after the Raid on Chatham.

Gold and enamel, by Nicolaes Loockemans, 1667, Rijksmuseum Amsterdam

nately, the only sources for details about the riot near De Ruyter's house is Brandt's book.[29] The demonstration failed because a relative of De Ruyter's dealt with it firmly. It was never possible to establish with certainty who had incited the riot. There were rumours that it was someone who lived nearby and Tromp lived just a 15 minute walk away on the Keizersgracht. It is almost certain that the whole affair was planned in advance as one of De Ruyter's daughters had heard rumours in Rotterdam a few days earlier to the effect that her parents' house had been or was about to be plundered.

Passages such as these demonstrate to the reader that De Ruyter was not always especially popular among the ordinary people. According to public opinion the Admiral was partly to blame for the defeat in the St. James's Day Battle in 1666. Popular fury had also turned against him after the sudden raid by the English in the Vlie and their plundering of West Terschelling in the autumn of that year.[30] Precisely as in 1672 his house in Amsterdam just escaped plundering and destruction by an angry mob but because Brandt did not include this story it has remained practically unknown. There was no mention either of a decline in popularity after De Ruyter's failed expedition to Martinique in 1674.[31] Brandt mentions the fact that De Ruyter was rather hot-tempered, one of the few flaws in his personality, in just one passage and then without even intending to do so. To demonstrate that De Ruyter never wanted to hear about mutinies and riots Brandt included the following anecdote: the Admiral of the Fleet had once heard a fellow tow-barge passenger insulting the government.[32] De Ruyter flared up angrily, saying that he, as a servant of the country, would not tolerate such language. He commanded the man to be silent. However, the man continued to shout angrily whereupon De Ruyter asked the skipper to put the man ashore. The skipper refused, so De Ruyter stepped in, grabbed hold of the agitator and threw him overboard, but near the bank so that he could reach safety. De Ruyter reported the skipper to authorities and he was soon after suspended for six weeks.

■ Form and style of Brandt's biography of De Ruyter

The title of Brandt's book, *Het leven en bedrijf van den heere Michiel de Ruiter*, indicated that the author had a real biography in mind. The book's dedication to the widow, Anna van Gelder, written by Brandt's sons Caspar and Johannes, called De Ruyter 'the great water hero'.[33] They placed their father's book in the tradition of Plutarch, the great biographer of Greeks and Romans, and the biography *Hendrik de Groote* [Henry the Great] about King Henry IV of France by Pieter Cornelisz. Hooft. It was at that time the best biography ever to have been written in Dutch. The brothers initially seemed to suggest in their introduction that *Het leven en bedrijf* was a classical biography. Later on in their dedication, they retracted. They stated that the book was not only a biography of De Ruyter but that it was also a Dutch maritime history containing a discussion of the naval wars of the seventeenth century. That suggested a much wider scope and in fact the author often digressed from the life of De Ruyter.

At the beginning of his book, Brandt divulged an important source of inspiration: 'I am commencing a work that is rich in material and is full of all manner of change, relating both successes and misfortunes'.[34] This coincided perfectly with the great retelling by P.C. Hooft of the Eighty-Years War, *De Neederlandsche Histooriën* [Dutch Histories]. Hooft began thus: 'I am commencing a work that abounds with changes in fate and contains many an affair'. Incidentally, this formulation harks back to the start of Tacitus' *Historiae* [Histories].

A true seventeenth-century biography consisted of the *exordium* (beginning), the *narratio* (story), the character sketch and the epilogue.[35] The *exordium* contained the rationale for choosing a particular person and for the manner of structuring the text. The *narratio* contained the hero's life story from birth to death, preceded by an account of his ancestry. There were typically few personal details because the hero's public life was the most important aspect, with letters and other documents being incorporated into the text. The character sketch provided facts about the hero's appearance and an extensive discussion of his good points. The epilogue described the funeral, the posthumous honours bestowed on the deceased, and sometimes also said something about what happened to the surviving relatives. The whole work was usually presented as one compact text without any subdivisions.

On countless points, Brandt did not keep to this pattern. The book is exceptionally long and the content is subdivided into eighteen 'books', in other words, chapters. He included a multitude of documents, some filling many pages, such as letters, instructions, resolutions of the States General, treaties and letters of nobility. The story regularly grinds to a halt because of these meticulously cited documents. Almost everything undertaken by the fleet was prefaced by a list of ships, the names of the commanders of the ships, the numbers of crew on board each and the numbers of cannon. To modern readers this urge to be so complete will seem rather contrived. Even so, historians can sometimes derive benefit from the availability of such facts which may be extremely difficult or totally impossible to find elsewhere. However, the interruptions do rather disturb the continuity of the story.

It is therefore remarkable that, in his biographies of Hooft and Vondel as well as in his *Historie der reformatie*, Brandt did manage to incorporate such documents into the text, and often in a compact manner. In his work about the Reformation he even wrote that his aim was 'brevitas' (conciseness) of form and style in his historical works. In *Het leven en bedrijf* he certainly did not achieve this aim as verbosity is the rule rather than the exception. Although digressions and irrelevant observations occurred regularly in seventeenth-century books, that style was not thought to be of merit even then.

A lack of source material meant that Brandt could swiftly deal with the first forty-five years of De Ruyter's life.[36] He allowed the story to develop totally in accordance with the tradition of Plutarch. Classical parallels and divine omens regularly came to the fore. Then, with the discussion of the First Anglo-Dutch War, Brandt struck a richer vein of source material and started to diverge from his classical source of inspiration. He included whole letters and ship lists in his text. His second book begins with a comprehensive explanation of the different views held by the English and the Dutch regarding the use of the sea. From this point onwards, Brandt's approach was more in the tradition of magisterial historical works, such as P.C. Hooft's *Neederlandsche Histooriën*. That allowed him to go more deeply into the backgrounds to various events and to accentuate certain affairs. This is why there is a great deal about the wars between Denmark and Sweden in the 1650s, about the distant countries that De Ruyter visited during his expeditions to Africa and America in 1664-1665, and about the deeper causes of the Anglo-Dutch Wars. If the biography had been written entirely in the tradition of Plutarch, such topics would not have been included.

The tomb of Michiel de Ruyter in the Nieuwe Kerk, Amsterdam

Sculpture by Rombout Verhulst, 1681
Photograph by Ton Sipman

After having described De Ruyter's entire life, Brandt emulated Plutarch with a character sketch of his subject[37], highlighting his virtues, as was the custom.[38] Brandt emphasised once more that De Ruyter's career was entirely due to his own merits and that he apparently stressed his own comparatively simple background to his seamen because he wished them to follow careers at sea. Brandt sketched De Ruyter as a simple, modest man who could do without all the honours and who reported his victories without any arrogance. Piety was De Ruyter's most important trait, according to Brandt, and it was presented as the basis for all that the Admiral did. His whole way of living was defined by his religion. Going to church and listening to the sermon were said to constitute his greatest pleasures, while reading the Bible was a daily pursuit. In fact, his primary reading were theological works. De Ruyter, just as Brandt, firmly believed in and supported peaceful relations among the different churches. He was also favourably disposed towards clergymen in general. This was probably the reason why two of his daughters married clergymen. Brandt stated that De Ruyter was faithful to his country and obedient to the States General, the Dutch government. Brandt presented him as a lover and protector of the country's freedom. Bravery, prudence, much experience and meticulousness helped him through all the wars. He maintained complete order and discipline on board his ships, but at the same time, he could also be kind-hearted. And where possible, he spared his defeated enemies.

This is how Brandt created an image of an admiral who was perfect in all possible ways without any inferior characteristics and who was famous the world over. It is questionable whether the modest De Ruyter would have agreed with this evaluation. After all, he often complained that his function of supreme commander was too burdensome for him. To end his book, Brandt compiled a description, entirely according to Plutarchian tradition, of De Ruyter's physical appearance and emphasised once more his moderation in terms of eating, drinking and amusement on board ship. According to Brandt, the career of De Ruyter demonstrated that when it came to nautical matters experience gained on the job was much more important than theoretical knowledge and a good family background. Brandt ended with an epilogue in which De Ruyter's funeral and tomb are described.

■ Final conclusion on *Leven en bedrijf*

Brandt did well to break loose from the classical form of biography because adhering rigidly to it would certainly have produced an idealised biographical portrait. There were probably various reasons why he moved towards a broader approach. First, there were huge quantities of documents available to him in the De Ruyter archives. Second, Brandt was probably driven by the need to include everything, feeling he would otherwise not be able to present the historical truth. Another factor that may well have played a role here was the fact that the events were so recent, with the result that Brandt could not distance himself enough from his subject and was unable to be sufficiently selective in his use of sources. One should also remember that he was a theologian, a church historian and a poet. He may, therefore, have had little affinity with maritime or more specialised naval history. He knew little about navigation and nautical strategy so it was extremely difficult for him to understand the material. This handicap from a lack of technical knowledge had certainly not been the case with his earlier biographies on Hooft and Vondel.

Brandt's biography of De Ruyter undoubtedly gives an idealised image of this hero of the sea. By strongly emphasising De Ruyter's piety, Brandt presented the admiral very much as a virtuous Christian hero. This may be the reason why there has always been a more than average interest in this biography of De Ruyter within the Dutch Reformed Church. In addition, Brandt presented De Ruyter as a protector of his country's freedom, one who had a great love for the country of his birth and one who, despite his humble origins, climbed to the highest rung of society. Brandt was thus engaging in the sort of hero worship reserved for naval heroes. This had started in the Republic when Admiral Jacob van Heemskerck was killed off Gibraltar in 1607 and honoured with a state funeral and a monumental tomb, paid for by the nation.[39] In their dedication to Anna van Gelder at the front of Brandt's biography, the sons presented their father's work as the literary counterpart of the marble tomb built for De Ruyter. It is easy to see why.

Here and there, Brandt appears to give De Ruyter's piety a tint of his own religious beliefs, as for example in the case of his tolerance of those with other beliefs and his critical attitude toward schism. These were precisely Brandt's points of view, which makes one wonder whether De Ruyter really did think that way. It would seem so, given De Ruyter's efforts in 1676 to secure the Hungarian Lutheran clergymen's release. However, without other sources to prove the point, no clear answer can be given. Brandt made of De Ruyter a man without any unfavourable characteristics and modern readers may not always find this plausible. The contemporary conventions probably made it impossible for him to do anything else. If a virtuous Christian hero had possessed any unfavourable characteristics he or she would not have been the subject of a biography.

Despite all the criticism, however, some admiration for Brandt's biography of De Ruyter is called for. As well as the description of the life and work of Michiel de Ruyter, it provides an impressive overview of the three Anglo-Dutch wars in the third quarter of the seventeenth century. Even today, this book is a unique source for historians interested in this period. The new way in which Brandt wrote this biography was emulated by Emanuel van der Hoeven in his *Leeven en dood der doorluchtige heeren gebroeders Cornelis de Witt en Johan de Witt* [Life and death of the august gentlemen, the brothers Cornelis de Witt and Johan de Witt] published in 1705. Further, Lieven de Beaufort was inspired by Brandt when he wrote *Het leven van Willem I* [The life of William I], which appeared in 1732.

Probably of even more importance is the fact that *Het leven en bedrijf van den heere Michiel de Ruiter* continues to attract new readers. Reprint after reprint has appeared, including one in 2007. One cannot say that about too many other seventeenth century books.

This map, made in 1694, of the Mediterranean gives 38 views of different ports and coastlines.

Print by Romeyn de Hooghe, 1694, National Maritime Museum, Greenwich

CHAPTER 3

Merchants, Diplomats, and Corsairs

*The Dutch in Barbary in De Ruyter's Time**

Karim Bejjit

The greater part of this essay was conceived during my stay at the Netherlands Institute for Advanced Study (NIAS) in 2007. I would like to thank both the director and staff of the Institute for making my stay both fruitful and enjoyable. I also wish to thank Herman Obdeijn for sharing his learned thoughts with me.

■ Constructing Barbary: an ongoing debate

When Captain Michiel de Ruyter dropped anchor in Santa Cruz (Agadir) on the Atlantic coast of Morocco in February, 1644, on board the *Salamander*, he was indeed navigating in well charted waters familiar to a generation of Dutch merchants, corsairs, and diplomats who had undertaken the itinerary to and fro from the United Provinces to the ports of North Africa. This may be less evident today than it was then. The records of these early journeys and sojourns preserved in European archives and libraries have only lately begun to attract academic attention. While a great deal of work has yet to be done, recent academic writing on Barbary based on archival research has thrown new light on these remote encounters which a mixture of intellectual apathy and willed oblivion have for long contrived to keep obscure.

Indeed one of the enduring misconceptions in the vast historical scholarship on North Africa is that until the French colonial occupation of Algiers in 1830, the region had been a closed territory sealed off from Europeans, and fated to a cycle of internal cataclysmic failures. Even more damaging has been the tendency to construct the pre-colonial Maghreb as a grotesque formation in the maritime world of the Mediterranean, unaffected by the currents of change which swept over Europe from the late sixteenth century. It is often reiterated as a kind of truism that North African states engaged in piracy and erected their entire economic systems and modes of life on the harassing of international trade and the holding for ransom of thousands of unfortunate seafaring men during marauding raids on their vessels.[1] The experiences of numerous European slaves who were condemned to a life of toil and deprivation are paraded as ample evidence of the barbarism and fanaticism of the natives of Barbary. If these vistas of cruelty towards Christians were not enough attention is lavished on the constant fratricidal wars among ruling families, brutal coups, insurrections, and massacres to gain an insight into the mindset of these unruly nations.

The fundamental objection to this historiography is that, in total disregard of archival evidence, it offers an exceedingly simple explanation of what is essentially a complicated state of affairs. While dismissive of the intertwined histories of Mediterranean communities and the complex web of economic interests binding them together, a large number of studies on North Africa have placed undue emphasis on the discrepant politico-economic paradigms that divided the communities across the Mediterranean Sea. Whereas historical annals show that the alternating conditions of war and peace were often conducted on the grounds of expediency rather than a rigid code of ethics, a series of unverified and uninformed claims are bandied about asserting the singularity of North Africa as a zone of institutionalised piracy and terror. The paradox is that this Manichean division premised on racial and religious principles is sustained against scores of volumes of contemporary official documents testifying to the universality of such practices as piracy and slavery. Rather than address these controversial issues in their proper contexts and draw on records to sift fact from fiction, a significant number of belated scholars of North Africa were content to rely uniquely on the *published* narratives of ransomed European captives, thus placing one discursive voice at the centre and erasing a multiplicity of other infinitely entwined and complex *recits*.

These methodological predilections have rarely been brought under scrutiny. Even when a learned and unorthodox historian as Sir Godfrey Fisher calls attention

A squadron of Dutch warships off Salé, Morocco.

Painting by Reinier Nooms, between 1662 and 1668, Rijksmuseum, Amsterdam

to the danger of yielding to a complacent and facile interpretation of the Barbary phenomenon, he is often censored as too liberal and romantic. Yet what informs Fisher's study is a remarkable endeavour to demonstrate the untenability of the conventional view of Barbary as the abode of fanatics and outlaws, whose only resource, in the absence of trade, industry, and agriculture, lay in constant ruthless depredation of Christian commerce. Such a picture, however convenient to the tortuous politics of the age or gratifying to the chauvinism of more modern times, finds little support in contemporary records.[2]

The crucial issue for Fisher is an ethical one. The triumphalist quality, which until recently defined European writings on North Africa, has created enormous illusions of the past and contributed little to the unravelling of the complexities which persist in the present. There is a need for new critical readings of the multiple encounters between North Africa and Europe guided by a sustained will to transcend the lure of tumultuous polemics and engage the collective testimonies of hundreds of contemporary witnesses whose plain texts constitute the massive body of archives.

Although it has become obsolete, «Barbary» continues to be a contested term today. A wide range of incongruous meanings and associations have made the word both vague and confusing. The unsettling semantics of the word emanates less from geographical boundaries which have remained fairly stable than a set of epistemological implications with which, over the years, it has become closely affiliated. Indeed, the dense and conflicting layers of meaning accrued to the term «Barbary» in European writings reflect the subversions and mutations in power relations vis-à-vis North African states dating from the early nineteenth century. The added nuances of colonial authority seem to have blurred the lucidity of earlier notions and images of Barbary as preserved in archives.

A recent essay by Kenneth Parker argues that readings of early English accounts of Barbary redefined in the light of posterior discourses of power and domination continue today to gain currency in academic writing.[3] Parker introduces a number of cases in which not only Victorian but also modern accounts of Barbary have failed to perceive the complexity of English relations with North African states, and subscribed to the poorly documented view that piracy was an exclusively North African practice. How does one account, he inquires, for the existence of a significant number of European renegades serving in the Barbary fleets?[4]

The question has also been posed in another study by Peter Lambron Wilson. Wilson notes that the conventional perception of renegades as traitors and apostates has been adjusted by modern historians to explain the durability of piracy in the Mediterranean.[5] Stated simply, the argument has it that piracy would have been suppressed in its infancy if those skilled European renegades had not joined the ranks of the Barbary corsairs. Their experience in naval warfare and sailing of ships in the high seas, aided by their concrete knowledge of geographical locations, determined the course and pace of piracy. Wilson suggests that this theory of renegades not only has little to support it in the archives, it also leaves out the central question of what induced these veteran Christian seamen in the first place to abandon their nations and faiths to serve under the banner of Islam?[6] Like Fisher and Parker, Wilson comes to the conclusion that European historical production on Barbary, so long operating under edifying notions of European power and supremacy over other nations, needs «a massive revising».[7]

Fortunately, this is already taking place. As a number of recent publications indicate, there is a significant innovative interest among scholars in the issues of piracy, slavery and renegades.[8] The real force of this growing scholarship lies in its extensive recourse to archival materials – unpublished reports, journals, accounts, peace treaties as well as a miscellany of official and private correspondence.

This essay owes a great deal of its information to these ground-breaking studies of the Maghreb. Yet it also does a bit of delving into old records, albeit in a mediated way. Much of the documentation on which this essay is based was collected from Dutch sources, translated into French and published along with original texts in six volumes by Henri de Castries between 1906 and 1923. The salient quality of these volumes is their dense, fluid information covering the period between 1578 and 1660. The last two volumes alone span the years in which De Ruyter made frequent visits to the ports of Santa Cruz and Salé.

The plainness and sheer documentary quality of these numerous papers provide an alternative understanding of these early encounters, unencumbered by the kind of problematics which I have described above. More importantly, the virtue of these collected records lies in the dialogic nature of their discourse typified by the series of letters exchanged between official authorities in the Dutch Republic and North Africa. This voluminous correspondence reveals the contested terrain of international mercantile activity fraught with divisions on the rights and conditions of navigation and trade in the Mediterranean basin and beyond.

Dutch relations with North Africa, 1600-1644

In his study of Dutch relations with the regency of Algiers, Gérard Van Krieken offers an elaborate account of the problems which, since the early seventeenth century, caused constant strain and friction between the two countries. The volume of Dutch trade and shipping in the Mediterranean grew progressively from the 1590s. The huge demand for grain in Italian towns following several dry seasons had paved the way for Dutch merchants to take part in the lucrative shipping business from the Baltic to the ports of Leghorn and Genoa.[9] Dutch corsairs were also drawn into the prosperous commerce and traffic of the Mediterranean and made enormous profits out of the prizes they took and disposed of in the North African ports.[10] There was a further dimension to this association of Dutch and North African corsairs. Until the conclusion of a truce in Madrid in 1609, Dutch corsairs gave chase to Spanish vessels which they considered legitimate targets. In this endeavour they had found support in the ports of Algiers, Tunis, Tripoli and, a decade later, Salé which were traditional bastions of resistance against Spanish imperial ambitions. Although Spanish ascendancy in the Mediterranean had weakened considerably after decisive encounters with the Ottoman fleets in Lepanto (1571) and Tunis (1574), and the defeat of its Armada (1588) by the combined fleets of England and the Dutch Republic, Spain continued to hold possessions along the coasts of Morocco and Algiers. In the Low Countries the threat of a Spanish invasion of the rebellious provinces united under the leadership of Prince Maurice of Nassau was warded off only with the signing of the Twelve Year Truce (1609-1621).[11]

A large fleet of Dutch merchantmen in a fierce engagement with some Muslim Corsairs off the Barbary Coast of North Africa.

Painting by Lieve Pietersz Verschuier, around 1670, National Maritime Museum, Greenwich

The landing and ill-treatment of captives at Algiers.

Print by Casper Luyken, 1706, Amsterdams Historisch Museum, Amsterdam

Despite the shared aim of undermining Spanish interests, the governments of Algiers and the Dutch Republic soon were at loggerheads over the right of Dutch ships to carry cargoes and passengers belonging to countries enemy to Algiers. While the States General insisted on the principle of *free ship, free goods*, and defended the sovereignty of Dutch captains over their ships, the Algerian authorities were adamant in refusing any concessions as to their right to confiscate enemy goods transported on board Dutch ships.[12] It was a matter of time that these fundamental differences in defining maritime rights led to the capture of several Dutch ships which opposed inspection. The States General took several diplomatic initiatives to surmount difficulties with Algiers. In 1612, they dispatched Cornelis Haga to Constantinople and he proved able to negotiate some advantageous terms.[13] The concessions he secured, though, could not be imposed on Algiers or even Tunis where an increasing number of Dutch subjects remained in captivity. In 1616, in an attempt to improve relations, the States General appointed Wijnant de Keyser their first consul in Algiers. De Keyser, who was in a good position to judge the genuine difficulty of safeguarding Dutch interests, soon realised that the capitulations granted to Haga in Constantinople were deemed unacceptable by the Algerian government. He concluded a new treaty in which he consented to the stipulation that Dutch ships were to be subjected to search.[14] This new agreement was doomed to remain ineffectual as it was not ratified by the States General and often not complied with by Dutch merchants.

Van Krieken notes that during the eleven years which De Keyser spent as consul in Algiers, relations between the two states deteriorated considerably. A total of 216 Dutch ships were captured by the corsairs of Algiers.[15] As in the case of Salé some three decades later, hostilities came from both sides. In the absence of any hope of receiving satisfaction, acts of retaliation added further complications to already strained relations. Save for a sequence of short-lived and intermittent periods of peace, the two countries waged a bitter and constant war for over a century. Between 1617 and 1621 the States General sent squadrons to the Mediterranean and even joined forces with the Spanish fleet in 1618 to hunt down and intercept the Algerian corsairs.[16] Nevertheless, military solutions proved to be costly and often yielded meagre results. The English, on their part, had dispatched Sir Robert Mansell in 1620 at the head of a large, well manned and armed fleet composed of 18 ships.[17] The size of the fleet, in fact, failed to make an impression on the Algerians who were secured in the belief that the threat was of an ephemeral nature and only intended to exact a few concessions. Their strategy was to delay their enemies by expressions of good intentions, or counter demands for reparation for assaults suffered.[18] In this prolonged state of indeterminacy, the cost of maintaining the fleet and the risks which emanated from the uncertain condition of the sea often left the assailants with few options.[19]

The Dutch, who had temporarily envisaged a joint action with the English against Algiers,[20] and seen the failure of Mansell's mission, had lent an earnest ear to the request made by the government of Algiers for sending an ambassador with plenary powers to conclude a new peace treaty.[21] Cornelis Pijnacker, who was selected for the mission, was instructed prior to his departure in July 1622 to insist on the right of Dutch merchants to refuse inspection or allow the confiscation of goods or passengers under their charge. He was also directed to seek the release from captivity of Dutch subjects without ransom. In return, he would signify to the Algerian authorities the decision made by the States General to prohibit Dutch merchants to trade with Spanish ports after the end of the truce.

Pijnacker's mission came at an auspicious time. Enmity to Spain and pledges of future military collaboration against the Catholic nation formed the basis of a common understanding which translated into the liberation of Dutch captives without ransom.[22] After Algiers, Pijnacker set sail for Tunis where, after protracted negotiations, he obtained the release of 60 captives but had to acquiesce to the demand of the Tunisians to search and appropriate enemy goods on board Dutch ships.[23]

The treaties concluded with the governments of Algiers and Tunis did not prevent the emergence of new difficulties or resolve pending problems related to the immunity of Dutch ships from inspection. In 1625 Pijnacker was once again in Algiers to demand the release of French fishermen captured by the renegade corsair, Murad Rais (Jan Jansz) while flying the Dutch flag.[24] Two consuls, Pieter Maertensz Coy and Lambert Verhaer, sailed with Pijnacker. They were assigned to Algiers and Tunis respectively.[X25] Coy had been consul in Marrakech between 1604 and 1609. Now he was taking over from De Keyser who seemed to have fallen from grace. As well he had incurred enough personal debt that for some months he was prevented from leaving the city.[26] Pijnacker's mission, however, failed to make any progress on the question of inspection of Dutch ships by the corsairs of Algiers and Tunis. The treaties which he carried home were deemed unsatisfactory and were not ratified. The long pursuit for formal peace between the Dutch Republic and the regencies of Algiers and Tunis had finally come to a deadlock. The two Dutch consuls meanwhile continued to serve amid unfavourable circumstances. Their pecuniary difficulties were immense as their pay was often in arrears and altogether inadequate for the tasks entrusted to them. Eventually, Coy died afflicted by hardship in 1629, and Verhaer, unable to endure his precarious situation, had to escape to his homeland.[27]

If Dutch relations with Algiers and Tunis had undergone a steady decline it was due to the structural conflict of their commercial interests and dissimilar foundations of their economic systems. The principle of *free ship, free goods* was the cornerstone of this sustained discord as it entailed systematic restrictions on Dutch shipping. On the other hand, the lifting of this condition meant that corsairs would be deprived of both political power originating from their policing activities in the Mediterranean, and an enormous source of stable revenues, equipment and skilled labour.

Nevertheless, the so-called Barbary States which are often lumped together as one homogeneous entity did not always share the same policies towards the young Dutch Republic. Unlike the case with Algiers, Dutch relations with Morocco reveal a rather different model of economic and political exchange. In the first place, Moroccan ports on the Atlantic coast provided vital services to Dutch ships bound to or from the East and West Indies. Apart from being advantageous stations for rest and provisioning, the ports of Salé, Safi, Mogador (Essaouira), and Santa Cruz were outlets of the country's rich natural products – animal skins, wax, almonds, figs, honey, and oil. In return, there was always a heavy demand for arms, ammunition, nautical items, and cloth.

On the political side, the Dutch Republic had recognized in the Saadi dynasty a potential ally against Spain. Although the heyday of Saadi power (1578-1603) had been eclipsed by almost a decade of bitter and relentless wars among the descendants of Ahmed Al Mansour, widespread anti-Spanish sentiment remained as strong as before. The terms of the peace treaty which the Dutch consul in Marrakech, Pieter Maertensz Coy endeavoured to consummate during these turbulent years aimed at fostering strong commercial and military ties between the two nations and resisting the increasing menace of the bellicose Spanish authorities. Article 12, for instance, stated that if the ships of the two countries were in pursuit of enemy ships or driven by a tempest or misfortune, they should be allowed to take refuge in the ports of the other country.[28] Article 15, in turn, indicates that if the king of Morocco had need of men, ships, artillery and ammunition, the States General should consent to satisfy his request as far as the circumstances allow. These formal vows of friendship were soon followed by concrete actions. While still fighting his rivals, the king of Morocco Moulay Zidan showed a keen interest in building a maritime force to guard the Atlantic coast from Spanish incursions. Already in 1610, Larache had fallen to the Spanish, and Mamora was not entirely shielded from a similar fate.[29] He, therefore, sought and obtained the consent of Dutch authorities to build three warships and recruit their crews among Dutch seamen.[30] He also demanded assistance for the building of forts in Mamora and Mogador.[31]

These cheerful prospects for cooperation were short-lived. Bent on thwarting Zidan's military plans, the Spanish court sent a squadron of seven vessels in 1611 which succeeded in sinking two of the three warships he had newly received from his

Michiel de Ruyter's ship 'De Liefde' off Algiers.

Painting by Reinier Nooms, between 1662 and 1668, Rijksmuseum, Amsterdam

Dutch allies.[32] In August 1614, a large Spanish fleet of 99 ships and galleys departed from Cadiz and occupied Mamora.[33] These Spanish exploits were largely due to the state of anarchy which had overrun the country and split the population into warring communities. Besides his brothers and nephews, Zidan had to face constant dissension and uprisings from powerful *marabouts*. By the end of his reign in 1627 the country had lapsed into further chaos and division. The once strong and unified kingdom he inherited from his father had shrunk into principalities shifting their allegiances from one pretender to another. It was this divided kingdom, much reduced in power, size and resources that he bequeathed to his sons, Abdelmalek (1627-1631) and El Walid (1631-1636). Their short reigns, in turn, saw a great deal of violence and bloodshed which they paid for with their own lives. Both, it is reported in contemporary chronicles and narratives, were assassinated by renegades enraged by their acts of cruelty.[34] Their successor, Mohamed Cheikh (1636-1654) was of a less repressive disposition but he too failed to expand his power beyond Marrakech and Safi, or subdue his opponents who had grown independent and were conducting their own diplomatic relations with European states. Indeed by the time De Ruyter sailed to the port of Santa Cruz, Mohamed Cheikh had ceased to wield any influence in the south and the north where loyalty was shown to local rulers – the Naksis in Tétouan, Sidi Ali Ben Moussa in Sous, and the Dilaites in Fez and Salé.

This prolonged and destructive turmoil had its impact on Dutch intercourse with the Saadi monarchs. From the outset and for strategic reasons, the commitment of the States General to support Zidan had been firm and took several concrete forms. Besides supplying military equipment and provisions,[35] the Dutch also allowed Zidan to use their naval support.[36] When his international affairs required Dutch mediation, diplomatic missions were conducted on his behalf at the European courts.[37] For his service, Zidan had enlisted a family of Jewish traders, the most notable figure of whom was Samuel Pallache who, until his death in 1616, was Zidan's agent in The Hague. Through the offices of these individuals, Zidan was able to maintain a steady correspondence with the States General, send embassies to the United Provinces and obtain satisfactory resolution of problems that occasionally arose between Dutch and Moroccan traders.[38] In 1624 the Dutch ambassador to Morocco, Albert Ruyl noted, with much resentment, the extraordinary influence which the Pallaches enjoyed in the court of Zidan.[39] Nevertheless, by 1627 even these experienced advisors who continued to serve Zidan's successors were powerless in the face of new difficulties which emerged between the two countries. The corsairs of Salé had become a redoubtable force and carried on extensive raids against European shipping. Although Dutch ships were not their prime target, there were several incidents of attack and capture of Dutch ships and seamen.[40] While the States General still maintained relations with the Saadi monarchs, and occasionally sent envoys to Marrakech, they were perforce brought to recognise the necessity of establishing contact with their rebellious subjects in Salé and in Santa Cruz.

In 1638, the defeat of the king's troops by the forces of the Dilaite *marabout*, Sidi Mohamed el Hadj ended the nominal authority the king Mohamed Cheikh had retained over Salé.[41] For the next two decades the affairs of Salé were decided by the Dilaites who were now the ascendant force in Morocco. In the south, the *marabout* Sidi Ali ben Moussa alias Abou Dmia, or Abou Hassoun Semlali had for years established himself as the legitimate ruler and commanded the port city of Santa Cruz.[42] So diminished had the influence of Mohamed Cheikh become that the States General had to make overtures to his enemies who now were in a position to damage Dutch interests. The embassy of Antoine De Liedekerke (September 1640- December 1641), reported in Adrian Matham's journal of his trip to Morocco, illustrates the symbolic importance of Dutch relations with the Saadi dynasty.[43] The visit which the Dutch ambassador made to the court of Mohamed Cheikh was an occasion to exchange presents and renew pledges of amity and mutual respect. Beyond that, the ambassador had to sail to Santa Cruz to negotiate the release of 72 Dutch captives held by Sidi Ali ben Moussa after their ships, *Erasmus* and *De Maecht* had been shipwrecked.[44] Eventually, the ambassador ransomed the 45 crew of the *Erasmus* while the rest of the seamen remained in captivity as the two parties failed to come to terms on an acceptable ransom price.

■ **De Ruyter in North Africa (1644-1664): the making of a career**

It was amid these scenes of civil strife and gradual collapse of the central government in Morocco that De Ruyter made his early visits to Santa Cruz. It appears that these successive upheavals in the political order of Morocco had not diminished the commercial importance of the principal ports of the country or discouraged Dutch merchants from seeking an arrangement with the new masters of Salé and Santa Cruz. Like many of his countrymen, De Ruyter had a fair knowledge of trade opportunities that the ports of Morocco offered for Europeans. His experience as a merchant and a sea captain stood him in good stead. After years of maritime service conducted for his employers, the Lampsins, which involved cruising against the Dunkirk privateers and trading with the Dutch colony in Brazil, De Ruyter had acquired enough reputation to draw the attention of the military establishment in the Dutch Republic. In

An English ship in action with Barbary corsairs.

Painting by Willem van de Velde the Younger, 1676, National Maritime Museum, Greenwich

1641, he was ordered to serve as the Rear-Admiral of the fleet dispatched to support the Portuguese in their war of independence against Spain.[45]

Now in 1644 on board the merchant ship *Salamander*, laden with rich cargoes bound to the coast of Morocco, he was his own master. Of his mercantile experience much is known thanks to the journals he kept during his voyages. The first of these journals covers the period from 21 January to 3 August 1644. His first stop was Salé which he reached after two weeks of sailing. Once ashore, De Ruyter closed a deal with the local governors and merchants to deliver a quantity of tobacco, cotton, gun powder and shellac to the value of 13.000 ducats payable partly in gold and partly in animal skins.[46] Days after, he set sail for Safi which was still under the king's authority. Much to his disappointment, De Ruyter saw two English ships lying in the harbour. Nevertheless, he visited the town in the company of his Jewish guide, Daniel of Lyon to explore the prospects for trade. The following day he invited the local merchants on board the *Salamander* to examine samples of his goods, but no deals were concluded. As his eyes were on Santa Cruz, De Ruyter hastened to reach the famous port before the English traders. The governor of the *Kasbah* in Santa Cruz to whom he paid a visit advised a journey to Iligh, the capital of Sous and the residence of his master Sidi Ali ben Moussa. Aware of the influence which the *marabout* held in this particular region, De Ruyter proceeded to Iligh which he reached after four days. The land journey to this city was particularly exhausting. Though travelling on horseback, he and his companions had to cross long stretches of desolate land amid occasional showers of rain which nearly spoiled their merchandise.[47] In Iligh, De Ruyter was a welcomed visitor and seemed to have little trouble coming to an understanding with the powerful *marabout*.[48] The value of the deals he agreed with the local merchants was so considerable that the next three months were spent in loading goods on the ship and disembarking sold cargo. In exchange for a large quantity of animal skins, wax, gold and amber, De Ruyter traded tobacco, iron, boards, and different brands of cloth. Having careened his ship and settled his accounts, he embarked on his journey back home carrying with him six of the Dutch slaves left unransomed since the visit of the ambassador Antoine de Liedekerke in 1641.

After the success of this journey, De Ruyter embarked on a second trip to Santa Cruz in December, 1645. When he landed, he noted that all kinds of goods were in short supply which moved him to take the land journey again to meet the *marabout*.[49] As in the previous year, his passage to Iligh was not devoid of picturesque incidents. Not far from Santa Cruz, there was a river that he and his company had to cross with a great risk to their lives. When night fell, they were offered lodging by some villagers. Once they reached a town called Massa, they found the place in floods after weeks of continuous rains. Crossing the Massa river proved even more perilous. It was here that he took some rest and discussed business with captain Wally, the *marabout*'s interpreter. In Iligh, Sidi Ali ben Moussa welcomed De Ruyter warmly and approved the deal he had made with Wally. Back in Santa Cruz, De Ruyter delivered the muskets and cloth which Wally had ordered in the name of the *marabout* in exchange for a quantity of wax, gold, amber and ostrich feathers. Towards the end of January, 1646, De Ruyter set sail for Barbados. Of the Dutch slaves held in Iligh, he was carrying six more.

In January, 1647, he was back in Santa Cruz, riding south to Iligh. The trip to the *marabout*'s town had become an essential part of the circuit. There he struck new deals and bought freedom for six more captives, five Dutch and one Spanish.[50] From the start, the sight of these unfortunate subjects had roused his sympathy. Whether their redemption was an act of charity or a simple transaction commissioned by the state or carried on behalf of the captives' families is difficult to determine. What is evident, however, is that the ransom price he had to pay varied from 85 to 107 gold ducats which far exceeded the sum the ambassador Liedekerke had offered to pay in 1641. Unlike many of his contemporaries who had to deal with North African rulers, De Ruyter proved to be a discreet and affable person. In negotiating deals or settling differences he favoured calm and judicious conduct over rash and bold action.

Over the next four years, he kept his course almost unchanged. The goods he embarked in Santa Cruz varied from one visit to another, but his calls at Iligh were renewed proof of his interest in maintaining these profitable commercial relations. It was during these sojourns that De Ruyter became acquainted with the domestic affairs of Morocco. The South of the country had submitted to Sidi Ali ben Moussa who controlled the only port of the region and imposed monopoly over sea traffic. Besides the vast fertile lands of Sous and Massa, the *marabout* had for some time extended his authority farther to the south across the Dra Valley diverting to his own treasury the revenues of the trans-Sahara trade which had once formed the source of Saadi wealth.[51] There was a mystical side to the *marabout*'s power and this was not lost on a shrewd observer like De Ruyter. Sidi Ali ben Moussa was a descendant of the saint Ahmed ben Moussa held in great esteem by the populace for his attributed miraculous gifts and *barakah*.[52] In assuming a holy demeanour, the *marabout* not only appealed to his numerous followers but also claimed the right to be a legitimate potentate.

Sidi Ali ben Moussa, however, was not the only religious figure to have risen to power in Morocco. The steady decline which befell the Saadi dynasty encouraged a number of *zawiyas*, which were both sanctuaries and religious schools, to develop from educational and charitable centres into full-fledged political institutions functioning as autonomous states. Far to the south, the influence of Sidi Ali ben Moussa was soon countered by another family whose descendants – the Alawite monarchs – rule Morocco to the present day. In the north, Sidi Mohamed el Hadj ben Abou Beker, head of the *Zawiya* of Dila became a dominant sovereign. Until 1660, his influence extended from the Middle Atlas to the plains of Gharb and Sais, forcing the principal cities of Tétouan, Fez and Salé to recognize his authority. After years of constant wars, the communities of immigrants expelled from Spain who came to settle on the banks of the Bou Regrag River declared their allegiance to Sidi Mohamed el Hadj. Once again, Salé seemed to grow into a busy centre of mercantile and piratical activities. The raids of Salé corsairs on Dutch shipping were resumed with such vigour that the States General decided to send squadrons in 1649 and 1650.[53] The outcome of these military pressures led to the signing of a peace treaty on 9 February 1651. Partly because he wanted to curb the ambitions of the governors of Salé and partly to establish cordial relations with powerful nations such as England and the Dutch Republic, Sidi Mohamed el Hadj appointed his son, Sidi Abdallah prince over Salé.

Once the master of Salé, Sidi Abdallah wrote to the States General to declare that he approved the 1651 peace treaty and made sea captains and corsairs to abide by its terms. He also indicated that he had received the newly appointed Dutch consul, David de Vries, very positively.[54] Nevertheless, the commitment displayed by Sidi Abdallah to handling the tortuous affairs of Salé soon turned into disappointment. The articles of the treaty may have seemed clear and well-defined in theory, but the intricate world of maritime trade and the conflicting interests of merchants of Salé and the United Provinces gave rise to several disputes. On his part, De Vries complained of violations of the treaty committed by the Salé corsairs. In December 1651, he informed the States General of Sidi Abdallah's decision to levy new taxes on exported goods.[55] In June 1652, he wrote to the States General about a Dutch ship, *De Jonge Wildeman* captured by a corsair of Salé. The crew and cargoes of the ship were sold in Algiers.[56] To complicate things further, a Salétin ship was taken by a Dutch corsair, which caused considerable indignation in Salé. These breaches did not elicit any immediate reaction from the States General whose attention was fully engaged by the war raging with England (1652-54). De Ruyter who had been summoned to serve the Dutch flag was kept informed of the situation in Salé. In June 1654, a month after the signing of the Treaty of Westminster, he wrote to the Admiralty of Amsterdam to recommend that the States General take a strong position against Salé. It was on the basis of his advice, a week later, that the States General sent a letter to the governors of Salé to demand prompt and satisfactory reparation for the losses suffered.[57]

Still, there were further incidents of reciprocal violence. De Vries contested the right of the Salé corsairs to claim Dutch ships abandoned by their crews who happened to be pursued by other North African corsairs. He wanted Sidi Abdallah to forbid the sale of Dutch ships and cargoes captured by Algerian corsairs. The governors of Salé had their own serious grievances too. After convoying the ship *De Tyger* to Salé, two Dutch war vessels under the command of Cornelis Tromp seized a merchant ship of Salé, *De Windthondt*, killing a number of its crew and forcing the rest to flee. The news of the capture of this Salétin ship caused a great tumult. In retaliation the authorities seized *De Tyger* and two other vessels lying at the mouth of the river and held their crews hostage.[58] The Dutch corsairs operating in the Mediterranean were no less implacable avengers. They captured two more ships of Salé and brought them to Cadiz. The crew of one of them, numbering 44, was sold into slavery.[59] The activity of Dutch corsairs was encouraged by the States General to counter the increasing attacks of the corsairs of Algiers. De Ruyter and Cornelis Tromp were also authorized to head to the Mediterranean to convoy Dutch merchant ships bound to Leghorn and hunt down corsair ships. On 6 October, freshly arrived from his convoy mission, De Ruyter received letters from the Dutch detainees in Salé soliciting his intervention. He was moved to write to the Amsterdam Admiralty to signify his intention to sail to Salé to obtain their release.[60]

Once in Salé, De Ruyter wrote to Sidi Abdallah. He was convinced that «a single personal audience would be enough for me to give satisfaction to your Excellency and to make sure that the bonds of friendship between the Netherlands and your Excellency would be tightened again.»[61] It was perhaps his exceeding confidence in being a peacemaker that concealed from him the complicated state of affairs in Salé. The bitterness which the governors of Salé felt towards Dutch authorities was genuine. In response to De Ruyter's protests, Sidi Abdallah's letter contended that the seizure of *De Tyger* was in reprisal for unprovoked action perpetrated by Dutch warships under the command of Cornelis Tromp.[62] De Ruyter who seemed pressed for time to return to Cadiz to convoy the merchant fleet, was compelled to cut his stay short and promised to send a report of these developments to the Admiralty of Amsterdam.

This short visit did not dissipate the fears of the Dutch detainees in Salé or settle the existing disputes. When news of the capture of the two Salétin ships and the sale of Moroccan seamen in Cadiz finally reached the town, tensions went high. The Dutch consul was instantly committed to prison. His house and magazine were sealed off. He was soon joined by a long list of Dutch captains, seamen and domestic servants. The intervention of Sidi Abdallah permitted the incarcerated consul and his countrymen to be released on bail of 18.000 florins.[63] Resolved to address the roots of the problem with the Salétins, the States General decided in June, 1655, to dispatch Admiral De Ruyter once again to Salé to seek the release of Dutch detainees, negotiate acceptable reparations for the claimed losses, and discuss the terms of a new peace treaty. The crisis in the relations between Salé and the Dutch Republic was attributed to the ambiguity of certain articles in the earlier treaty. De Ruyter was instructed to insist on the inviolability of the person and property of the Dutch consul who under no circumstance was to be held responsible for actions committed by Dutch corsairs.[64]

De Ruyter reached Salé on 1 October 1655. The ceremonious exchange of presents and courteous letters over, he set to get the negotiations under way. To gain a speedy settlement of the unresolved issues, he delegated his accountant, Gilbert de Vyanen and consul De Vries to examine the Salétin claims. Sidi Abdallah who approved the proposed procedures also authorized two commissioners to conduct negotiations.[65] Over the next four weeks, the commissioners met almost daily. Their discussions seemed interminable. Initially they debated the legality of the seizure of the ships and contested each party's estimates of the damages sustained. When these difficulties were overcome, there was the question of deciding the size and nature of indemnity. As both parties claimed to be victims and sought to outdo one another in their demands for satisfactory compensation, negotiations seemed to reach an impasse. De Ruyter who received regular reports of these diplomatic encounters was growing

An engagement at sea in boats.

Drawing by Willem van de Velde the Younger, around 1685, National Maritime Museum, Greenwich

weary. Anxious to join his squadron in Cadiz as his instructions stated, he wrote to De Vyanen to press ahead in his talks with the Salétins and, in case no arrangement seemed likely, make the necessary concessions. De Ruyter's lenient attitude enabled the commissioners to draft a formal agreement calling for the release of Dutch captains and seamen held hostage in Salé, and fixing the terms of reciprocal indemnity.

While the protracted process of negotiations finally came to a happy end, there remained the difficult task of reviewing the old treaty, and modifying such terms which were the source of so much conflict and misunderstanding. It fell to consul De Vries to pursue the discussions with Sidi Abdallah's commissioners. De Ruyter, who left Salé on 2 November 1655, spent the next two months cruising against the corsairs of Algiers. By the end of December, however, in view of the enormous cost of these cruises, the States General adopted the recommendation made by the Admiralty of Amsterdam, and ordered the return of the squadron which he commanded.[66] Despite their willingness to conclude a new treaty, the States General did not send instructions to De Vries until May 1656. Among other things, the consul was directed to insist on the immediate release of Dutch seamen captured while serving on board ships enemy to Salé. He was also to demand that if Dutch cargoes or captives were brought to Salé by Algerian corsairs, the consul alone was to be allowed to undertake their purchase. If Salétin corsairs chanced upon an abandoned Dutch vessel, they were to bring it to Salé and hand it over to the consul who in return for their services was to pay a fixed amount of money. Moreover, the consul was to require that Salétin corsairs should carry in addition to commissions from the Salé authorities, a signed letter from the Dutch consul.[67]

The arrival of the English Admiral Robert Blake in Salé in August, 1656, threw the efforts of the Dutch consul in disarray. Given precarious relations with England, Sidi Abdallah chose to give priority to talks with Blake and kept delaying the resumption of negotiations with De Vries. Since he had taken his position, De Vries had grappled with his difficulties and often complained in his correspondence of the conduct of the Salétins who seemed to take little account of his status as consul. By now he had reached the limits of his patience. Sensing that his safety was no longer guaranteed, he wrote to the Admiralty of Amsterdam to declare his desire to resign or leave for another country.[68] It is unlikely that these feelings of concern communicated a real threat to his life or intended to bring his mission in Salé to a halt. At any rate, his discussions with the commissioners were soon resumed with such vigour that it would have surprised even De Ruyter himself. Assuming that the negotiations were reaching a point of crisis, the Admiralty of Amsterdam sent instructions to De Ruyter on 1 December, 1656, to set sail for Salé to inquire about the course of negotiations and make efforts to bring them forward. In case negotiations fell through, he was to warn the consul and merchants, and stand ready for new orders. If acts of aggression were committed by Salé corsairs, he was to inflict maximum damage.[69] By 25 March 1657, this military option was ruled out when De Vries reported to the States General the conclusion of a 12 article treaty which he requested be ratified.[70] In addition to the articles which De Vries was directed to insert in the old treaty, it was agreed that Dutch merchants should be civilly treated and never molested by the populace. They were also to be free to purchase their own provisions at the local prices without the intervention of intermediaries, a change from previous practice.[71]

When he arrived in Salé in mid April 1657, De Ruyter received these new tidings with distinct pleasure. While in Cadiz, he had heard from the consul that significant progress was being made. The signing of the treaty now relieved him from the laborious task of seeing the negotiations through and enabled him to pursue his hunt for corsair ships. In this contented mood, he wrote Sidi Abdallah a cordial letter, notifying him of his departure.[72] This turned out to be his last assignment in Salé. In the following year, the Admiralty of Amsterdam decided to dispatch commodore De Wildt to obtain ratification of the treaty.[73]

Over the years of his maritime experience as a trader, diplomat, and naval officer, De Ruyter proved to be a respected interlocutor. His repeated journeys to the coast of Morocco pointed to the success of his missions and the particular affection bestowed on him by local rulers in Santa Cruz and Salé. Nevertheless, neither his well-earned reputation as an able sea commander nor his courteous manners and rare skills of persuasion seemed to make a significant difference in his dealings with the Algerian authorities. The dilemma which the States General faced in reaching a peaceful settlement with Algiers that guaranteed Dutch traders' rights of free shipping and navigation in the Mediterranean could not be resolved even by an experienced envoy like De Ruyter. During the three expeditions he undertook to Algiers between 1655 and 1664 his diligence and zeal failed to make a breakthrough in the old dispute over the principle of *free ship, free goods.* Eventually, it was open war that prevailed.

After the death of consul Coy in 1629, the States General made no effort to renew diplomatic contact or repatriate the hundreds of Dutch captives reduced to slavery in Algiers.[74] This policy of non-interference was bound to change. The damage wreaked on Dutch shipping by North African corsairs during the first Anglo-Dutch War

(1652-54) was substantial, and called for rigourous retaliation. To this end De Ruyter sailed to Algiers in August 1655. In the hope of surprising the port, he hoisted English flags and sent three of his eight ships to survey the town.[75] Much to his regret, he found the *Kasbah* and forts in a good state of defence.[76] Affecting prudence over adventurous and risky attack, he repaired in haste to the Straits where, in concert with his subordinate commanders, he succeeded in intercepting a few ships belonging to Algiers, including *De Gouden Dadelboom* commanded by the Admiral Suleiman Rais. The ship proved a tough target and attempts to board her were repulsed with heavy casualties among Dutch seamen.[77] In the end, she was sunk near Asila.

The efficiency of these patrols, as a matter of fact, was not measured by the capture or destruction of a few ships. It was the global impact of these punitive expeditions on the volume of corsair activities that was ultimately the measure of success of these naval operations. The enormous cost of maintaining the Dutch squadron furnished further cause for scepticism. It was on the grounds of the soaring expenses that the Admiralty of Amsterdam recommended the return of De Ruyter's squadron in March 1656.[78]

Given the perpetual menace to which Dutch traffic and trade were exposed, De Ruyter was sent back on several occasions to the Mediterranean to convoy merchant fleets and give chase to Portuguese, French and North African corsairs. Whatever the success of these operations it was apparent that these punitive measures did not diminish the power of corsairs or render Dutch merchant ships less vulnerable. By 1661, the number of active corsair ships in Algiers had risen from 18 in 1559 to 30.[79] The number of Dutch ships seized by Algerian corsairs alone in the period was estimated at 35.[80] Despite the zealous efforts to reduce the threat posed by corsairs, privateering was in full swing.

It was in reaction to the escalation of corsair attacks against Dutch ships that the States General resolved to open negotiations again with North African regencies in 1662. The misfortunes of the English expedition against Algiers in 1661 was a clear proof that little effect was to be expected from mere blockade of the ports and interception of corsair vessels. The impregnable towns of Algiers, Tunis and Tripoli were not easily intimidated by the occasional visits of European squadrons. De Ruyter whose long service in the Mediterranean and remarkable knowledge of North African regencies made him the right candidate to head this delicate mission was instructed to search for and capture corsairs with the prospect of exchanging them for Dutch captives. While disposed for peace, the States General insisted on an end to the inspection of Dutch ships and confiscation of their goods.[81]

During the first phase of his expedition, De Ruyter concluded a favourable deal with the Bey of Tunis. He obtained not only the release of 67 Dutch captives in exchange for 93 Tunisian seamen seized some time earlier but also the consent of the Bey to renounce the inspection procedures. In Algiers, however, his endeavours were not entirely rewarded. The negotiations which De Vyanen conducted were rendered difficult by the uncompromising attitude of the Algerian authorities to accept the principle of *free ship, free goods*. For all his pains, De Vyanen could only secure the ransom of some 55 Dutch captives and the signing of a seven-month truce.[82]

There still remained a large number of captives who looked forward to their release. Their fate depended on a satisfactory resolution of differences between the United Provinces and Algiers by their respective negotiators. Andries van der Burgh whom De Ruyter appointed consul was instructed to determine the exact number of prisoners. In November, 1662, days after the truce came to an end, De Ruyter was given to understand that an eventual ransom of the captives seized on Dutch ships to the number of 700 might persuade the Algerian authorities to agree to the Dutch stipulations. Only days before, John Lawson had concluded a treaty with the government of Algiers that secured freedom of shipping and navigation for English merchants. The prospect of large sums of ready money pledged in exchange for the numerous forlorn slaves who crowded the bagnios proved irresistible, and a treaty of peace was accordingly signed. The relatively smooth process of negotiations permitted the ransom of 130 Dutch slaves.[83]

As so often previously, formal declarations of peace were soon made null and void by reciprocal actions of violence. The restrictions which the controversial article on *free ship, free goods* imposed on the corsairs were detrimental to their interests. Several months after De Ruyter left the shores of Algiers, the pledged money had not yet arrived. Though the 15 months set as a deadline had not expired, there was already a growing sense of doubt that the money would be delivered. The number of slaves was decimated by the raging plague which hit the region.[84] Their deaths meant a substantial decrease in the ransom money, and made peace seem less advantageous.

Seeing that they had gained little from the peace signed with the Dutch, the Algerian authorities gave in to the pressures of corsairs to subject Dutch vessels once again to inspection measures. On the Dutch side, Tromp's relentless hunt for corsairs only aggravated the situation.[85] In January, 1664, he captured two Algerian vessels and caused the majority of their crews to be sold. When De Ruyter arrived in Algiers in mid June, he was beset by the mood of belligerency and defiance which prevailed in the town. Consul Van der Burgh had been committed to prison in retaliation for Tromp's actions. To obtain his release, De Ruyter had to set free 25 Algerian captives. Vyanen's death soon after De Ruyter's arrival deprived the Dutch Admiral of a skilled and reliable negotiator.[86] Aware that the chances to wrest a favourable peace deal from Algiers were slim, De Ruyter focused his efforts on ransoming Dutch captives. Back in 1662 he had set out to redeem all the 700 individuals seized from Dutch ships. Of those some 400 were not Dutch subjects. The States General were reluctant to endorse De Ruyter's agreement and in the end raised just enough funds to ransom captives of Dutch origin. The outcome of negotiations was anything but fruitful. In the absence of a comprehensive deal, De Ruyter was permitted to ransom only 55 Dutch captives at an exorbitant price.[87]

With these freed captives De Ruyter set sail for the Spanish coast. From there, a few weeks later, he was to set out on a secret mission to the Guinea Coast.[88] While leaving the shores of Algiers behind, he was unwittingly turning a page in his remarkable personal history. Soon the smouldering tensions between the Dutch and English governments burst into a full scale naval contest. De Ruyter, whose martial skills were never in doubt, fought hard and emerged out of its vortex an acclaimed hero.

Council of war on board De Zeven Provinciën, the flagship of Michiel de Ruyter, on the eve of the Four Days' Battle, 1666.

Pen painting by Willem van de Velde the Elder, about 1666, Rijksmuseum, Amsterdam

CHAPTER 4

The Dutch Republic as a Great Power:

Political Interaction and Armed Forces

Jan Glete

■ State formation and rules of human interaction

The seventeenth century Dutch Republic often figures in comparative studies of European history. It is not because it was a typical seventeenth century state, shaped by an average society. Quite the opposite. The Republic, and the social and economic structures in the seven provinces which constituted it, were exceptional and in some respects unique. There is broad agreement that the commercial, financial and technical achievements in the Republic made it a leader in seventeenth Europe economy. Whether sustained economic growth typical of modern economies began in the sixteenth and seventeenth century Netherlands or later in Great Britain is open for debate, but the economic transformation of the Netherlands was a decisive part of the process which made north-western Europe the centre of European economy.[1]

The political performance of the Republic and the administrative structures of its armed forces have often been objects of interpretations and international comparisons. While interpretations of the Dutch economy vary within the normal spectrum of different methods and theories, interpretations of the Dutch army and navy and the Republic's administration of its armed forces are deeply divided into two diametrically opposed views. The Dutch state has often been described as weak because its constitutional institutions limited the growth of absolutism, because it was federal and decentralised, and because it was bourgeois. Its international power has been described as handicapped by a complicated and slow decision-making process, and its army and navy as small and made up of temporary forces of mercenaries and armed merchantmen. This is seen as a result of that the merchant domination of the Republic. Those men, out of prejudice or parsimony, were opposed to permanent armed forces and also to having bureaucrats, attributes which many social scientists have seen as necessary for strong early modern states. Even in recent comparative syntheses the Dutch Republic appears as weak or semi-anarchic, its armed forces as transitory and resources extracted for war as small. The fact that the Republic had success in war in the seventeenth century has been explained by her wealth, excellent financial system, favourable geographical position and strong allies.[2]

In other studies a completely different picture appears. The Dutch army has by German and Anglo-Saxon sociologists and military historians often been labelled as a model for the early modern permanent European military force. It has even been described as the first professional army and its officer corps as a product of a new middle-class society. The English historian Michael Roberts has been especially influential by making the Dutch army, and implicitly also the Dutch political system, the origin of a «Military Revolution», which decisively changed the relationship between state and society in Europe.[3] The Republic's successful protection and promotion of its economic interests with armed force was important to Immanuel Wallerstein's «world-system» studies and to Jonathan Israel's synthesis of the period of Dutch trade supremacy, although they did not explore the relations between the political system and military and naval organisations.[4] In recent years, important studies have also appeared offering a more positive view of the strength of the Dutch political system and its roots in an urban and politically sophisticated society.[5] Quantitative studies of the size of the armed forces in Europe in relation to the size of the population place the Dutch Republic at a very high level among seventeenth century states.[6]

The Dutch Republic has been difficult to understand because a dominant tradition in European political history and historical sociology for a long time regarded central and local power as inherently antagonistic. In this perspective the growth of central state power was regarded as reflecting a decline of local power while the presence of powerful local societies was taken to indicate that the central state was weak. States were supposed to be stronger the more autonomous their decision-making and administration were in relation to society and interest groups. In this tradition «absolutism» became synonymous with strong centralised state power rather than with failure to create constitutional links which connected state and society. Spain, France and Prussia became archetypes for «strong» states with large armed forces while the Dutch Republic and often also Britain became archetypes for constitutional, parliamentarian and «weak» states with limited armed forces.[7]

For several decades empirical studies of European state formation have generated quite another picture of what actually went on in early modern Europe. Absolutism is no longer regarded as the same as strong, well-organised, bureaucratic and top-down-rule state power. It was simply difficult to make tax-paying subjects obey if they were not allowed to negotiate with the ruler. Even Louis XIV now appears as a manager of traditional elites rather than as the supreme ruler in total control of a centralized state with professional bureaucrats in all decisive positions. The ability of the French state to raise large amounts through taxes in long wars was rather limited and without constitutional control of the government, its credibility as a debtor was low which restricted its capacity to raise loans.[8] Anglo-Saxon historians also began to re-evaluate the strength of the English state. They found that during the seventeenth century it had developed into a fiscal-military state with a strong tax bureaucracy, a large and well-run navy and an army which in times of war had the potential to grow to a major and efficiently administrated force. This was not the least due to increased parliamentary control of policy-making and public confidence in parliamentary power which markedly increased the state's ability to raise loans at reasonable interest rates.[9]

The seventeenth century Dutch Republic was a success story in both economy and politics. The political success was based on an ability to mobilize large resources for war without creating political chaos, civil wars or tax rebellions of the type which periodically struck sixteenth century France, Habsburg Spain and the British Isles. It may be fruitful to explain Dutch political success as a result of the political system and to interpret strong links and networks between state and local power as positive rather than as obstacles to decision-making and resource extraction. It may also be of some interest to try to find out if the Dutch economic and political successes, achieved by the same elite in the same society, may have had common roots. Explanations of Dutch military (but not naval) success have in one sociological tradition been related to the exceptionally creative features of seventeenth century Dutch society.[10] Its dynamic economic performance shows that it had fewer obstacles to innovations and entrepreneurial experiments than any other European society. Several of these innovations required large and complex organisations; the state, the East and West India Companies. They were also related to contractual relationships among a large number of individuals: financiers, merchants trading European-wide and world-wide, consumers depending on the market for food supplies and essential products.

Trust in large, anonymous structures and organisations for protection and economic activities is not inherently natural for human beings. Interaction with other human beings is guided and restricted by *institutions*. The economic historian Douglass C. North has made such institutions the centre-piece of theories of economic change. He claimed that our genetic heritage makes us prefer to co-operate and make exchanges on a personal level with individuals whom we at least occasionally meet eye to eye. The development of impersonal markets, division of labour and centralized mass production of goods and services (the growth of complex organizations) require new rules of human interaction, which may be in conflict with our genetic heritage.[11]

However, our genetic heritage evidently also allows human beings to think strategically and to achieve new combinations. If they prove successful they may favour new rules of human interaction in politics and on economic markets. Concentration of resources and power in the hands of a state or large private companies may be acceptable if the institutions deliver products and services which otherwise would be unobtainable without prohibitive costs. The early modern Dutch Republic, with its high degree of urbanisation and its dense population in a small territory, was a place well-suited for such interaction between innovations and changes in human rules of interaction. That type of interplay may have developed unusually early and rapidly. Urban environments make it easier for many individuals to develop close contacts, and several towns close to each other make it easier to develop regional networks which favour mutual trust and cooperation. The Dutch Republic was the only seventeenth century bourgeois great power, where a non-noble statesman like De Ruyter's contemporary Johan de Witt could become the key policy-maker in the creation of the world's largest navy. It is probable that future studies of Dutch political and economic behaviour in the Golden Age will profit from applying the same theoretical framework to both spheres. Especially trade, shipping and naval power are sectors where interaction between organisation, entrepreneurship and changing rules of human interaction can most likely be studied fruitfully.[12]

■ The Dutch Republic in Europe. Population and armed forces

In terms of population the Dutch Republic was one of several medium-sized powers of early modern Europe. For rough comparisons, Dutch population was around 1.5 million in the early seventeenth century, growing to around 1.8 million by mid-century. The Spanish monarchy (Spain, large parts of Italy, the southern Netherlands, Portugal until 1640 and Franche-Comté until 1678) had around 15 million inhabitants, with a tendency to fall due to territorial losses and economic crises. Seventeenth century France had a stagnating population, but it rose from around 18 to around 20 million due to territorial conquests. The British Isles had a population growing from six to eight million between 1600 and 1700. Sweden, with which the Republic fought two wars, had around 1.3 million inhabitants in the early seventeenth century. The population rose to close to 2.5 million by 1660 due to conquests around the Baltic and to close to 3.0 million by the late seventeenth century. The demography of the several territories ruled by the Austrian Habsburgs in the seventeenth century is uncertain but their population probably varied between 7 and 10 million. Of the five states which had the largest armed forces in Western and Central Europe in the seventeenth century, the Dutch Republic had the smallest population.[13]

In European history, the Spanish monarchy is usually regarded as the strongest military and political power on the continent from the mid-sixteenth to the mid-seventeenth century, except in southeastern Europe where the Ottoman Empire dominated. From the mid-seventeenth century France rose to dominance in Western Europe while Austria began to press back the Ottomans in Eastern Europe. The European power which fought the longest and most fiercely contested wars with the two giants in Western Europe, first Spain and then France, was the Dutch Republic. The Republic was frequently part of alliances but it also fought Spain alone for several years and Louis XIV usually also had allies when he fought the Republic. In the critical years 1672-73 when Michiel De Ruyter reached the height of his career, the Republic had to fight alone the combined military and naval power of France and Britain.

This performance of the small Dutch Republic makes the idea of Spanish and French supremacy on the continent doubtful. Spain was undoubtedly for a long period, at least up to the 1630s, much superior in relation to France, while France from the 1660s achieved a similar supremacy in relation to Spain. Their wide geographical extension made them power players in several parts of Europe; the southern Netherlands, Germany, Italy and the French-Spanish border regions, but their wide commitments restricted their ability to concentrate forces and defeat other powers which created problems. Neither France nor Spain was able to defeat the Dutch Republic and that geographically small power fought in the southern Netherlands, in western Germany, on the North Sea and in the Channel. The Dutch navy frequently also operated in the Mediterranean and the Baltic Sea, where it markedly influenced the outcomes outcome of major wars. The struggle with Spain (1568-1648) ended with the Republic gaining territories in the southern Netherlands and a trading empire in maritime Asia. The wars with Louis XIV's France (1672-78, 1688-97, 1702-13) ended with the Republic in treaty-bound military control of the fortresses in the southern Netherlands. In 1658-59 the armed forces of the Republic saved Denmark from being swallowed by Sweden and in 1688-89 they placed a member of the Nassau family on the English throne. From a small territory and with a population only around one tenth of the two European super-powers the Republic nevertheless influenced European power politics on a scale that made it one of the major power players in Europe during the whole seventeenth century.

Spanish supremacy over France, French supremacy over Spain and the constant Dutch ability to fight both powers cannot be explained by major changes in the quantities of resources available to them. The seventeenth century Dutch Republic did experience economic growth which was markedly better than that in the rest of Europe, but early in the century before the economic growth took hold the Republic was able to fight on even terms with Spain. The explanation for the relative military and naval performance of the three powers is to be found in differences in their political and administrative ability to raise and organise resources for war, not in quantities of available resources. If resources had been decisive, Spanish and French victories over the Dutch would have been easy and quick and the two big powers would have balanced each other throughout the seventeenth century.

In the sixteenth and far into the seventeenth century, most European states had no permanent state-controlled peacetime armies. The traditional armed forces; the feudal levies and the local militia were of limited importance and not administrated by the central states. Major armies were formed during crises and wars with mercenary soldiers organised into companies and regiments by military entrepreneurs. The entrepreneurs owned the regiments or companies as business enterprises. They appointed officers and recruited and paid soldiers. They were usually ready to serve

AMSTERDAM
PRAGA
CONSTANTINOPOLIS
VENETIA
ROMA
Angli
Galli
Belgi
Castiliani
Venetiani
GROENLAND
PARS
OCEANVS SEPTENTRIONALIS
Circulus Arcticus
OCEANVS
DEVCALEDONIVS
HIBERNIA
Noort zee
OCEANVS
OCCIDENTALIS
MARE
ATLANTICVM
BARBARIA
FESSA
MAROCHO
AFRIC
Cautum est Illustr. DD. Ordinum Hollandiæ et Westfrisiæ privilegio ne quis Tabulas istas quatuor Orbis terræ partium citra voluntatem Auctoris imitetur, sub poena in Diplomate expressa.

PARIS LONDON TOLEDO LISBONA

MYRMANSKOY
MORE

EVROPA
recens deſcriptă
à
Guilielmo Blaeuw.

RVSSIA.

ASIÆ

ALBVM
MARE

MOSCOVIA

TARTARIÆ
PARS

PARS

DVCATVS
SEVERIENSIS

Tartaria
Przecopelis

Bulgaria

PONTVS EVXINVS

ASIÆ MINOR

NATOLIA
nunc

CYPRVS

Cyprus

MEDITERRANEVM

Candia ol Creta

MARMARICA
PARS

AEGYPTVS

Germani

Hungari

Bohemi

Poloni

Greci

any state that was willing to pay them, and their ability to organise and lead military units was an asset with a price on the market. Gradually such armies were replaced by state-administrated armies, with officers and soldiers serving the state in peace and war, although not necessarily their native state. By the late seventeenth century most European states had their own armies. Some states hired additional regiments in wartime, although usually from other states, not from private entrepreneurs. Regiments and companies normally had a fixed nominal size for planning and fiscal purposes, but in wartime it was usually difficult to keep the number of soldiers at the nominal level. Ideally for comparison the size of armies ought to be measured by both their nominal strength and the number of effectives, but reliable figures are often not available.[14]

There is a wide difference in what we know about the size of various seventeenth century European armies. The size of the Dutch, Swedish and Danish armies in terms of companies, regiments and soldiers are known almost year by year, although the effective strength of the Dutch army has received little attention from historians. The size of the Spanish army is only fragmentarily known with concentration on certain periods and certain regions, especially the Army of Flanders. In the first half of the seventeenth century, the Spanish army periodically had as many as 150,000 soldiers, of which 60,000 to 90,000 were in the southern Netherlands. In the latter half of the century the Spanish army did during some war years reach a nominal size of 80,000-100,000 men. The latter figures included hired German regiments in the Army of Flanders, frequently hired jointly with the Dutch Republic. Effective strength was lower and the permanent part of the army was considerably smaller. In the 1690s it was 30,000 men and in 1703 an effective force of only 18,000 men is reported.[15] The total effective strength of the army never exceeded one per cent of Spain's population and the peacetime strength appears to have been as low as 0.2 per cent.

The size of the French army is as difficult to estimate as that of Spain, but considerable research has been made on the quantitative aspects of French military power. France had in the early seventeenth century only a small peacetime army, around 10,000 men. During the long war with Spain from 1635 to 1659 a larger army was formed but its normal effective strength was not larger than 70,000 to 80,000 men. It was probably smaller after 1648. The nominal size of this army is little known although figures as high as 200,000 are mentioned. From the 1660s a drastic increase began, first because Louis XIV after 1659 retained the wartime army as a peacetime force of nominally 72,000 men (possibly 50,000 effectives), and later because the wartime army increased. Its maximum nominal strength was 134,000 men in 1667, 280,000 in 1672-78, 450,000 in 1688-97 and 380,000 in 1701-14. The effective strength was lower, and may have varied between 70 to 90 per cent of the nominal strength. Peacetime strength from the 1670s was 140,000 to 160,000 men.[16] In relation to the French population the effective wartime strength of the army rose from 0.25 per cent in the first half of the century to 1.25 per cent in the 1670s and close to 2 per cent in the 1690s. The nominal strength was around 1.5 per cent in the 1670s, 2.25 percent in the 1690s and 2 per cent in the early 1700s. The peacetime strength rose from practically nothing to around 0.75 per cent of the population in the reign of Louis XIV.

The permanent Swedish army in the 1610s and 1620s was increased to a level of around 40,000 men, that is in the nationally recruited army. The infantry was raised by conscription until the 1680s. This strength remained largely unchanged although a growing number of regiments were also permanently maintained in the conquered

German and Baltic provinces. That force rose to around 25,000 men by 1700. The peacetime strength of the army was thus 3 per cent of the population around 1620, declining to around 2.5 per cent of the much larger population in the later half of the century. Its effective wartime strength was larger, especially in the 1630s and 1640s (70,000-140,000), but also in the 1650s (55,000-70,000) and the early 1700s (90,000-110,000). This expansion was achieved because Sweden extracted resources from occupied territories to pay and feed the additional forces. A precondition for that way of financing the army was that a large and combat-ready permanent army had to be able to quickly occupy enough territory to allow for expansion of forces with new regiments recruited by foreign entrepreneurs or Swedish officers acting as entrepreneurs.[17]

The Dutch army expanded rapidly in the 1590s and the early 1600s to a nominal strength of around 60,000 men. It was reduced to around half that size during the Truce of 1609-21. In the 1620s and 1630s it again increased to 70,000-75,000 men. In brief periods it was larger but stabilised at 60,000 men in the 1640s. After the peace settlement of 1648 its size was again halved, but it rose to a maximum level of 90,000 men during the war of 1672-78, 65,000 to 102,000 in 1688-97 and 94,000 to 119,000 in 1701-14. The peacetime strength of the army after 1678 was 40,000-45,000 men. The effective strength of the Dutch army has never been studied in detail but from its operations against the Spanish Army of Flanders and the armies of Louis XIV it is evident that it cannot normally have been seriously below its nominal strength.[18] The nominal strength of the wartime army rose from 3.5 to 4 per cent of the population in the first half of the century to 4.5 to 6.5 per cent in the years 1672-1714. The peacetime army was 2 to 2.5 per cent of the Dutch population.

The difference in resource mobilisation between Spain and France on the one hand and the Dutch Republic on the other was dramatic. The Dutch *peacetime* army was larger, often much larger, relative to population than the maximum *wartime* strength of the two larger powers. The wartime strength of the Dutch army in relation to the population was usually three to four times larger than its Spanish and French adversaries. In the coalitions against Louis XIV, at least up to 1700, the Republic provided the largest army contingent, larger than the Spanish, Austrian and British contributions, in spite of the fact that those states each had four to eight times as many inhabitants. The variations between peacetime and wartime strength was large in the Dutch Republic but such variations in the French army were of about the same magnitude. Viewed from a European perspective it was not the size of the Dutch peacetime army which was low. It was the size of the wartime army which was exceptionally high.

The Dutch army has often been described as a mercenary army, apparently because many soldiers were recruited from outside the Republic, usually from Germany. The army was however administered by the state and its officers were permanently employed by the state, not by private entrepreneurs. This was in contrast to the system used in Germany before and during the Thirty Years' War, where princes had no peacetime armies and relied on private entrepreneurs for recruitment, administration and command of regiments and armies in the field. From the early decades of the Eighty Years' War there were Dutch regiments of Scottish, English and French soldiers recruited and administered by foreign entrepreneurs, but in peacetime these regiments were maintained as parts of the standing Dutch army. While most states reduced or disbanded their armies by paying off entrepreneurs, much of the variation from wartime to peacetime strength in the Dutch army was achieved by reducing the number of soldiers in the individual companies. Mobilisation for war could be achieved quickly as a permanent structure of companies with officers, non-commissioned officers and a nucleus of seasoned soldiers existed. During the great coalition wars against Louis XIV, an increasing part of the Dutch (and the British) army consisted of regiments hired from German princes and the Danish king, but these forces were normally not run by private entrepreneurs in the old style.[19]

The development of Dutch naval power (permanent forces of warships), relative to the main adversaries of the Republic shows the same general picture as for army strength. The Spanish monarchy, including Portugal, had from the 1590s to 1640 a wartime sailing navy with a total displacement, that is weight of ships, of around 40,000-60,000 tonnes, including ships hired on long-term contracts. Disasters in battles against the Dutch and the loss of Portugal in 1639-40 reduced this force, and until 1700 the sailing navy probably varied between 20,000 and 35,000 tonnes. Independent Portugal continued to maintain a sizeable navy of its own, usually between 20,000 and 25,000 tonnes, which indicates that much of the Habsburg naval power from 1580 to 1640 had been Portuguese rather than Spanish. The Spanish Mediterranean galley fleet was gradually reduced from some 40,000 tonnes in 1600 to around 10,000 tonnes in the later half of the seventeenth century.[20]

The French navy was non-existent until the 1620s when the government formed a sailing navy of about 20,000-30,000 tonnes. From 1660 the fleet increased dramatically from 20,000 tonnes to around 140.000 tonnes by the mid-1670s. Another major increase in the early 1690s brought it up to around 200,000 tonnes. France also had a galley fleet, which gradually rose from a minor force to about 12,000-15,000 tonnes. The English navy was relatively stable at 25,000 to 30,000 tonnes from the 1590s to the 1630s when it rose to around 40,000 tonnes. From the late 1640s to 1654 there was a rapid expansion to 90,000 tonnes, an unprecedented change that took the Dutch by surprise in the First Anglo-Dutch War. Stability followed until 1677-80 when the state rapidly increased the navy to 130,000 tonnes and in the 1690s to 200,000 tonnes. Both jumps were responses to Louis XIV's expansion of his navy. After 1700 the British navy overtook the French navy as the largest in the world and retained that position until World War II.[21]

The Dutch navy increased rapidly in the 1590s and early 1600s, although information about its composition and size is scarce. It was reduced after the truce in 1609 but in 1615/16 it was still of around 12,000-15,000 tonnes and when war with Spain started again in 1621 it was increased to 20,000-25,000 tonnes, excluding some ships that were hired in the early years of the war. The war caused further increases to 40,000-45,000 tonnes around 1630, a size that was maintained until the end of the war in 1649 when the government reduced the navy to 30,000 tonnes. The First Anglo-Dutch War of 1652-54 resulted in an increase to 60,000-65,000 tonnes in a few years and the Second Anglo-Dutch War of 1665-67 to in an increase to around 100,000 tonnes by 1670. For a few years in the late 1660s the Dutch navy was the largest in the world, that until overtaken by Louis XIV's expansion program. In the 1670s the Dutch navy declined to around 65,000 tonnes but from the early 1680s it was again increased and reached a level of around 110,000 tonnes from the mid-1690s.[22]

It is harder to compare navies to population levels than it is with armies where soldier/inhabitant ratios are easy to understand. The costs of shipbuilding, outfitting, armament, manning, provisioning and naval infrastructure are, however, all closely related to the total size of the fleet of warships, which can be measured with displacement figures. To get numbers for quantitative comparisons it is convenient to use a tonnes/1,000 inhabitant ratio as a yardstick. Such a comparison shows that the Spanish monarchy from the 1590s to 1640 usually had a navy of 5-6 tonnes of warships per 1,000 inhabitants, while after 1640 the ratio was down to 2-3 tonnes. The French navy had 1-2 tonnes per 1,000 inhabitants from the 1620s to the 1660s after which the figure rose to 7-10 tonnes. England's navy was at 4-6 tonnes per 1,000 inhabitants until the late 1640s, when it rose to 12-15 tonnes until the late 1670s, 16-18 tonnes until the early 1690s and finally to around 25 tonnes per 1,000 inhabitants in 1700. Already in the 1610s the navy of the Dutch Republic was at 8-10 warship tonnes per 1,000 inhabitants, while in the war years 1621-48 the level was around 25 tonnes per 1,000 Dutchmen. The naval expansion from the 1650s increased the ratio to around 35 tonnes in the 1650s, 50-55 tonnes in the 1660s, 40-50 tonnes from the 1670s to the early 1690s and around 60 tonnes per 1,000 inhabitants in the 1690s.

The Dutch navy was from the 1620s into the eighteenth century the largest in the world relative to the population of the country. In the early decades of the seventeenth century three other medium-sized powers, Sweden, Denmark and Venice (with a galley navy), had navy/population ratios of the same magnitude as the Dutch. After that though the Republic's naval efforts were greater than those of any other state in Europe if the size of the population is taken into account. With that measurement, the Dutch deployed five to ten times as much warship tonnage as their adversary during the war with Spain up to 1648, three to four times the tonnage of the English adversary from the mid-1650s to the 1670s and four to six times the tonnage of their French adversary from the 1670s. The only time after 1620 when another country came close to the Dutch level of naval armament was in the early 1650s, when the rapid English expansion for a few years made that navy almost equal to the Dutch in terms of tonnes per thousand of population.

These comparisons with the largest military and naval powers of Europe in the seventeenth century show that the Dutch Republic throughout this century was an extremely well-armed state, both absolutely and relative to population size. Its peacetime army and navy were in relation to the population larger than contemporary peacetime forces in all other states, that is except for the Swedish army, and its wartime efforts of mobilisation reached higher levels than in any other state which relied mainly on domestic resources. The Dutch political, fiscal, financial and administrative systems worked markedly better than similar contemporary systems in raising resources and translating them into military and naval power. The Republic was also very early with creating permanent state-administrated military forces. It was not a pioneer in forming a permanent navy of purpose-built warships, but that was done in the early years of the Republic. Private entrepreneurs and hired armed merchantmen had only a marginal role in its military and naval efforts. They were less important than in other states, which up to the later half of the seventeenth century often had practically no forces under arms in peacetime.

The Republic for a long time had an advantage in international political power struggles because of superior capacity to deploy veteran armed forces on short notice. It was also able to sustain its war efforts for long periods. In the Second Anglo-Dutch War of 1665-67 the English fleet was left unfunded and in port in the third year, vulnerable to an attack led by Michiel de Ruyter. In the war that started in 1672, the Dutch under De Ruyter successfully fought back against the combined Anglo-French

Chart for navigation of the Baltic

Print by Peter Goos, Amsterdam, 1666,
Map Collection, University of Amsterdam

fleet and started offensive operations against France and its allies from 1674, in spite of the fact that the French navy was nominally much larger. In 1693/94 the French naval efforts had to be drastically reduced due to lack of resources, leaving the Anglo-Dutch fleet free to enter the Mediterranean. This inability to fight long wars at sea became typical for France throughout the eighteenth century. Bourbon France never learnt how to mobilise and organise the vast human and natural resources of the kingdom for war against smaller but constitutional powers. The political system was unable to achieve decisive reforms, and the French ability to build excellent warships mattered little when those ships could not be manned and provisioned for service at sea.

The historical and sociological tradition which interprets the Republic as weak has made much of the Dutch navy's low degree of readiness to meet the rapidly expanded English navy in 1652, and the army's failure to meet Louis XIV's greatly expanded army in 1672. Much less has been made of the fact that these events were rare exceptions to the rule, and that the setbacks met immediate responses in drastic increases in naval and military strength. The seventeenth century political system of the Republic was able to change policy immediately if something went wrong. The Republic was normally able to fight any other European power on more or less equal terms for long periods and often able to intervene far from its own territory to help allies and protect her interests. In European history, the Dutch fiscal-financial-military achievements must be regarded as a challenge to explanations which make monarchical rule, non-constitutional political systems and central bureaucracy crucial to the growth of permanent armies and new types of states. No such state in the seventeenth century was able to repeat the Dutch achievement.

■ The Admiralties, resource mobilisation and naval administration

Successful state formation in early modern Europe was often a process where local and central power developed more intense mutual links such as representative institutions, informal networks, patronage connections, career opportunities in state bureaucracies and market relationships. Those links served to coordinate the resource flow between society and the new type of state. The cost of transferring resources from local society to a centre became lower if the transaction was achieved by negotiation over some mutually agreed purpose. Such negotiations might be easier if the centre and the local societies were connected by representative institutions, which also might exercise control of how resources were used. This required that local elites accepted or actively supported the levying of taxes for central purposes, not necessarily on themselves but on subjects and flows of trade under their influence or control. It also required that the central authority respected local power-holders and gave them influence over the administration of resources raised for the state.

From this perspective Dutch naval organisation is an interesting subject which deserves much further research. The Dutch navy was from the late sixteenth century until 1795 administrated by the five Admiralties of the Maas (Rotterdam), Amsterdam, the Noorderkwartier (North Holland), Zeeland and Friesland. The Amsterdam Admiralty was the largest and Friesland the smallest, while the other three were of approximately the same size. Warfare at sea outside Europe was normally not organised by the admiralties but by the East and West India Companies which had their own ships and used them for both trade and warfare. These ships were often larger than the admiralties' ships. The first major Dutch battle fleet seems to have been made up of the same ships that had been used by the Dutch West India Company in Brazilian waters and in the Caribbean during the 1620s and 1630s. Offensive warfare against enemy trade in European waters was largely left to privateering, an activity that became especially important in Zeeland.

The admiralties were formally federal agencies working in the provinces, although local influence over them was strong. They had the right to sell licenses to trade with the enemy and to raise customs from all foreign trade of the Republic, formally to finance convoys. These incomes, *convoyen en licenten*, were the permanent financial base of the navy, and they were raised by the administrative staff of the admiralties. Apart from their domestic area, each admiralty was allotted an inland territory from which to raise funds. In this way they became the only federal fiscal authority covering the whole Republic.[23] From the time of the First Anglo-Dutch War until the early eighteenth century, when the navy was larger than earlier and later, a significant share of naval expenditure was covered by additional funds from taxes raised by the provinces and allocated to the navy by the States General. These funds were also administrated by the admiralties.[24]

In the eighteenth century, three of the five admiralties endured long periods in crisis. The cause was changes in the Dutch economy which concentrated trade in Amsterdam and Rotterdam and provided only these two admiralties with sufficient funds to support viable naval forces. When a large naval rearmament started in the 1780s, and federal funding again was provided, the resources were mismanaged by the admiralties which had during a long period of peace lost contact with naval administration. The amalgamation in a single naval organisation in 1795 was long overdue and it was one of the reforms which became possible when the revolutionary Batavian Republic swept away traditional power structures. The eighteenth century left a memory of the admiralties as a problem and as an obstacle to efficiency, a view that was for long time dominant in Dutch historiography.[25]

In the seventeenth century the Dutch admiralty organisation was however a result of a recent revolutionary upheaval. It was highly viable and its ability to raise and administer resources for naval power was far greater than that of any other naval organisation in Europe. It not only deployed larger fleets in relation to the population than any other European state, it also sent out highly efficient fleets that fought the Spanish, Portuguese, English, Swedish and French navies with considerable success. The interesting problem with the Dutch seventeenth century admiralties is not to find out why the Republic was unable to centralise resources. It is rather to understand why the Admiralty system proved able to raise far larger resources per capita for naval warfare than any contemporary system in Europe. Why was a decentralised system more successful than a centralised naval administration?

The dominating problem in European state formation was not to shape a streamlined centralised organisation to raise and convert resources to armed forces. It was not a problem for a ruler to appoint a number of central office-holders and define their authority; tax-raising, military administration, naval administration. The problems were political and organisational. How should the central state persuade local society to give up resources and how should the state get access to the several competencies which had to be concentrated to achieve organisational capability? Such capability was especially important for navies, which probably were the most complex organisations in early modern Europe. In historical sociology, state formation

is usually regarded as a penetration of local society from above by ambitious rulers who tried to extract resources and centralise them. The Dutch Republic was however a, probably unusual, example of state formation induced by demand from below. The Revolt started in towns and provinces as a reaction to Habsburg policies and the Republic was formed to make rational use of local resources to fight the powerful Spanish Monarchy. In the case of naval organisation, local Dutch elites who were determined to fight Spain did not have to look far to find the necessary skills and material resources to form a navy. They had it at their doorsteps. Michiel De Ruyter, who joined the navy at the age of 45 after a long career in the mercantile marine, is an obvious example.

The five seventeenth century Dutch admiralties were not a decentralisation and duplication of centralised resources and competencies to satisfy myopic local power-holders. The resources and competencies to create naval power existed in abundance in the maritime Dutch provinces. In a European perspective, seventeenth century Holland and Zeeland had a unique concentration of shipbuilders, sail-makers, rope-makers, seamen, men with experience to command ships and merchants with inter-national networks for supplying naval stores, provisions and weapons. The flow of merchandise through Dutch ports was enormous as Europeans of the day to a con-siderable extent did not trade with each other but rather exchanged various products with the Dutch Republic as an intermediary. This trade could be exploited for fiscal purposes, provided that there were incentives for local interests to pay customs duties rather than to cheat the authorities. To organise provincial admiralties was from this perspective a solution to the overriding problem of early modern state formation: to induce local power-holders to coordinate resources with a centrally determined policy. The officials of the admiralties provided links between the policy of the state and local maritime networks, interests, sentiments, resources and know-

how, links which other states with naval ambitions could only envy. Ironically, Spain tried in the 1620s to imitate the Dutch system by creating provincial organisations to bring maritime interests closer to naval administration and make it easier to recruit seamen and competent officers.[26]

Since Dutch society and the Dutch economy were complex, highly developed and dependent on territorial integrity and open lines of communication with the outer world, the armed forces had to be sensitive to demands from below, that is, from the elite groups. In the case of the admiralties this meant that protection and promotion of Dutch maritime trade was of paramount importance. At least until 1639/40 the Republic was fighting a maritime war where, with a quantitatively inferior navy, it had to defend Europe's largest merchant marine against Habsburg naval power. Normally the inferior naval power has to give up maritime trade and try to attack enemy trade. In the Spanish-Dutch confrontation the nominal underdog consistently behaved as if it was the superior naval power. The Dutch blockaded enemy ports in Flanders and developed a European wide convoy-system that even made it possible for the Dutch to trade in the Mediterranean, close to the centre of the Spanish monarchy. How that was achieved and how trade and the use of the navy were coordinated at the local level has been little studied. The very large size of the Dutch navy in relation to the population does however show that Dutch society was willing to give up a significant part of its resources to pay for naval power.

The admiralties had already in the late sixteenth century decided on a policy of building specially designed warships. There is a common myth, often repeated in the literature, that the Dutch navy until the 1650s consisted mainly of hired merchantmen. Actually, the admiralties hired ships only for brief periods and under exceptional circumstances when the navy needed additional strength immediately. The long-term policy was to build and maintain purpose-built warships. This is not surprising as it was economically rational, and Dutch society normally was quick to respond to economic incentives. The admiralties were permanent organisations, which kept a large number of ships at sea, even during the Twelve Year Truce of 1609-21 and after the peace of 1648. An armed merchantman provided less useful naval service for the same cost of outfitting, repair, manning and provisioning since these costs were recurring while the additional cost of building a warship was rapidly paid off after only a few years. A warship could carry more firepower than an armed merchantman in relation to its displacement and its design could be optimised for naval requirements.

The large Dutch seventeenth century fleet of warships has received much less attention than the English, French, Swedish and Danish fleet of the same century. The loss of sources in the fire in the Navy Ministry in 1844 is not a sufficient explanation as the surviving sources about Dutch warships are little used. Compared to other navies, Dutch warships had unusually heavy armament in relation to their displacement even early in the seventeenth century. This feature clearly separated them from even well-armed merchantmen of their age. The admiralties' close contacts with private investors in armed shipping are however visible in that they were early in providing their warships with cast-iron guns rather than the more expensive bronze guns, which dominated in other navies. Already in the 1620s two thirds of the firepower on the admiralties' warships came from iron guns. Cast-iron guns had to some extent been used in the English, Danish and Swedish navies in the late sixteenth and early seventeenth centuries, but these and other navies preferred bronze guns until the 1650s and 1660s, when the prices of cast-iron guns drastically declined. The Dutch navy was apparently more ready to experiment and take risks with new technology if it offered potential savings.[27]

In the war period 1621-48, Dutch naval warfare was dominated by trade protection and fast, small and medium-sized warships were the most useful types for convoy duty and chasing enemy cruising warships. Vessels of around 300 to 600 tonnes displacement dominated the navy, although the total number of even smaller ships for coastal and riverine warfare was large. Larger warships were rare before 1653, but this navy, temporarily strengthened with hired merchantmen, was able to inflict a crushing defeat on the Spanish-Portuguese battle fleet in 1639. That fleet had on average larger ships but they were not much larger, and they may have been more lightly armed in relation to their size than the exceptionally heavily armed Dutch warships. The large shipbuilding program initiated during the First Anglo-Dutch War (1652-54) was dominated by warships of 700-800 tonnes and around 40-50 guns, ships that later were classified as 4th Rates (*4de charter*) in the Dutch navy. They were built for service as ships-of-the-line but were small enough to be useful as heavy cruisers.[28]

During the great expansion of the navy in the 1660s new construction was dominated by ships-of-the-line of three larger sizes; 900-1,000, 1,100-1,200 and 1,400-1,500 tonnes, with around 60, 70 and 80 guns respectively, although dimensions and armament were not fully standardised. Ships of these three size groups became 3rd, 2nd and 1st Rates, and one of the last was De Ruyter's flagship *De Zeven Provinciën*. Construction of smaller warships was rather limited in those years since the number of older cruisers still in service was considerable and naval policy was dominated by battle fleet expansion, aiming at breaking British blockades of the Dutch coast and deploying powerful fleets in the Baltic and the Mediterranean. During the 24 years Michiel De Ruyter served as a flag officer in the Dutch navy its structure, doctrine and capa-

The siege of Nyborg on Funen in 1659 by the fleet under the command of Michiel de Ruyter.

Print by B. Stoopendael, around 1685, Maritiem Museum Prins Hendrik, Rotterdam

bilities changed radically. He himself had a leading role during those years in the practical implementation of increased Dutch naval ambitions.[29]

The Dutch navy De Ruyter led was not only exceptional in its size in relation to the small Dutch population or in its formal relationship with Dutch maritime and mercantile society. It is also likely that on average it was manned by better trained, better paid and better fed men than any other seventeenth century navy. The Dutch had almost certainly the highest level of consumption in Europe and the Dutch Republic formed an attractive labour market for its neighbours. The seamen in the navy were volunteers and they were unlikely to serve unless they were paid market wages and received decent meals at sea. In seventeenth century Sweden it was observed that Dutch seamen were much better provisioned and less likely to fall ill than seamen served meals of Swedish and Baltic standards. In the Dutch army, regular payment of wages was important to enforce discipline and make soldiers willing to work hard. It is likely that the navy followed a similar philosophy and that in this respect it was a leader among European navies. The combination of a financially strong state, a relatively affluent society and the world's largest mercantile marine was the same constellation which supported the British navy in the eighteenth and nineteenth centuries. Strong naval power was in all cases shaped by the society, the state and the organisational capability to use the available widely different resources in the most efficient way.

The Royal James, the flagship of the Earl of Sandwich, is attacked by a fireship at the Battle of Solebay, June 7th, 1672.

Painting by Willem van de Velde the Younger, around 1676, Nederlands Scheepvaartmuseum, Amsterdam

CHAPTER 5

Navies, Strategy, and Tactics
in the Age of De Ruyter

John B. Hattendorf

The quarter century that lay between 1652, when Michiel Adriaenszoon De Ruyter became a temporary flag officer in the Zeeland squadron, and 1676, when De Ruyter died as the most highly respected Dutch flag officer of the seventeenth century, was a span of years that marked a transformation in the character of European navies.[1] This period marked a change in the way navies were managed, in the weapons and ships with which they fought, and in the objectives for which they fought. These characteristics of navies that were established in this period lasted for more than 150 years, through the Napoleonic Wars and even beyond 1815. The characteristics that were established in the last half of the seventeenth century began to take another direction only in the nineteenth century with the Industrial Revolution, the introduction of mechanical propulsion, turreted guns, and metal hulled warships.

In the context of the broadest developments for war at sea in European history, these years marked the transition that brought an end to the primacy of the galley as an instrument of war and an end to the emphasis on the use of ships for raiding operations with mêlée tactics in grappling and boarding an enemy ship with hand weapons in ship-on-ship actions. While northern Europeans had set out to find a means to counter the overwhelming effectiveness of the Mediterranean galley armed with one or two forward-firing, heavy guns, they ended up with quite unexpected results.[2]

Those wide-ranging interconnected results brought the clear early beginnings of permanent national navies, the development of bureaucratic structures to support them, the gradual professionalisation of the naval officer corps, and the employment of large, heavily-gunned, purpose-built warships that became the predominant and the most potent symbols of national power. Moreover, these warships fought in a very specific, single line-ahead tactical formation that involved using purpose-designed warships in a line-of-battle against warships of similar types, using similar tactics, in engagements that had the strategic object of removing the threat of a rival battle fleet in order to allow one's own merchant ships to pass safely to their destinations as part of nationally defined economic and imperial systems.

The century and half between 1500 and 1650 had witnessed some fundamental developments in European history that set the stage for the specific naval changes that took place during the third quarter of the seventeenth century. At the beginning of the sixteenth century there had been two quite different centres of maritime technology in Europe. One was in the Mediterranean and the other in Northern Europe. These two technologies slowly began to merge as merchant entrepreneurs and rulers in western European countries began to cooperate to develop improved guns and ships that provided the technical basis for long-distance oceanic shipping. While this expansion of European dominion and trade was occurring, rulers and their states paid increasing attention to the promotion and protection of their commercial trade at sea. The Spanish and Portuguese voyages of discovery as well as state patronage for the development of nautical science in this era were part of these developments. In northern Europe, Denmark and Sweden foreshadowed future developments elsewhere as they superseded the dominance of the maritime cities of that region as they developed purpose-built, state-owned, and state-managed naval fleets to contest between them the control of foreign shipping inside the enclosed Baltic Sea.[3]

Meanwhile, the strategically located Dutch and English took over control of trade between northern and southern Europe from their positions on opposite sides of the Channel and North Sea. The Dutch were the first to successfully forge this into a European-wide supremacy in trade. When Spain had attempted to stop this development by embargoes on Dutch trade and trade warfare, Dutch business enterprise was able to offset this by successfully competing with Spain's trade monopolies overseas, thereby establishing Dutch supremacy in maritime trade. While the Dutch Republic dominated, England also shared in the subsequent shift in the balance of political and economic power from southern Europe to northern Europe.

The third quarter of the seventeenth century was marked by a number of European wars that reflected these trends and contributed further to the geo-strategic situation of the maritime countries of northern and north-western Europe. Among these wars, France and Spain had fought a war between 1635 and 1659 which had as one aspect of the larger issues, rivalry over control of territory in the Low Countries. From 1656, England supported France in the conflict. In the resulting peace treaty of the Pyrenees, France won control of additional fortifications in Flanders and Artois, while England acquired Jamaica in the West Indies and Dunkirk. Sweden and Denmark fought a war between 1657-1658 and 1658-1660. Sweden and Poland fought a war from 1655 to 1660, which brought Sweden and the Dutch Republic to the brink of war in 1656 due to the Swedish blockade of Danzig.

This period of conflict ended with Sweden gaining control of the eastern shore of the Kattegat through the permanent acquisition of the provinces of Halland and Bohuslän and controlled the eastern shore of the coast of the Scandinavian Peninsula with Skåne and Blekinge. During the final phase of that war, Sweden granted Dutch citizens some parity with her own subjects in customs duties on trade in 1656, but this proved to be of limited importance as the treaty made exceptions for Swedish trade through privileged Swedish companies, thereby continuing to discriminate against foreign trade. While this war was in progress, the Dutch were also engaged in a war with Portugal over the settlements that the Dutch had maintained in Brazil since the 1630s. By 1661, the Dutch had been forced to leave their claims and acknowledge Portuguese sovereignty over all of Brazil. During the War of Devolution in 1667-1668, King Louis xiv of France claimed part of the Spanish Netherlands as his wife's inheritance, she being a daughter of King Philip iv of Spain by an earlier marriage than her half brother, the current king of Spain Carlos ii, and due by the laws of inheritance a division of her father's estate. The subsequent Treaty of Aix-la-Chapelle, made through English, Dutch, and Swedish mediation, allowed France to control twelve additional fortresses in Flanders.[4]

Within this broad framework of conflict, competition, and development, the series of three Dutch Naval Wars in 1652-1654, 1665-1667, and 1672-1674 that took place predominantly in the North Sea and the English Channel and its approaches were the crucial conflicts in which the new naval developments took place. Traditionally interpreted as expressions of economic and trade conflict, historians have more recently debated the additional roles of antagonistic ideology and mutual suspicion as war causes.[5] One can also justifiably add to these causal elements, the extreme religious polemic that English propagandists increasingly employed across this period in characterising the Dutch as an immoral, treacherous and ungrateful people.[6] Although these three wars have often been lumped together because of their location and relatively close occurrence in time, an overemphasis on this can obscure the differing contexts, causes, and results of the separate wars. Nevertheless, when the development of the naval elements are traced across these three wars, an observer can see a distinctive naval development that occurs during this period that differs from other wars in the period and shows De Ruyter's participation and contribution to naval development at the zenith of the Dutch Republic's economic strength.

■ The European context for Dutch and English naval development

By the end of the Thirty Years' War in 1648, the Dutch Republic was widely recognized as Europe's leading maritime state with world-wide commercial interests that stretched from the Arctic to the Levant and from Asia to the Americas. For the maritime situations that had existed up to this point, the Dutch Republic had maintained a naval force that met their immediate needs. The Dutch Navy had played and continued to play a key role in the Republic's development and maintenance of the world's first global maritime *entrepôt* economy by using violence to open areas for trade and by keeping open the sea lanes for the safe passage of Dutch shipping. The largest navy in the world in the 1620s and 1630s was the Spanish-Portuguese navy that the Habsburgs maintained. The naval battles that the Dutch fought against the Habsburgs in the Channel in 1639 were the largest naval encounters in the first half of the seventeenth century in terms of ships and men.[7]

In this context, the outbreak of the First Anglo-Dutch War was an event that was not predicted in advance. Although the outcome of the English Civil War with the overthrow of the English monarchy, the execution of King Charles I, and the establishment of the Commonwealth under Oliver Cromwell showed a volatility that had international implications, England was in a position to adopt an aggressive naval policy as an attractive tool to advance English mercantilist ideas. Yet, neither side was fully prepared for the war that occurred.

The initial advantage lay with the English Navy. Following the common practice of the time, the Dutch Navy had disbanded much of its force with the end of the war in 1648. In 1650, there was no indication of the major naval arms race that would occur within a few years. In general, the balance of naval power initially appeared to be stable across Europe.

Comparison in Total Displacement Tonnage of Major Warships[8]

Year	England	Netherlands	France	Denmark	Sweden
1640	38,000	45,000[9]	29,000	18,000	29,000
1650	49,000	29,000	21,000	23,000	27,000
1655	90,000	64,000	18,000	21,000	28,000

Comparison in Numbers of Warships over 700 tons displacement[10]

Year	England	Netherlands	France	Denmark	Sweden
1650	32	2	14	8	16
1655	57	52	14	9	13

Clearly, however, the notable growth in the English Navy in the years between 1640 and 1650 was an exception, while the number of Dutch warships dropped nearly in half from 120 ships to 62 ships at the same time that the English numbers rose by ten from 43 to 53 ships.[11] While Dutch naval strength had declined in the absence of any obvious external threats, it grew after 1650 in response to threat, while English strength grew as a result of the internal revolutionary situation in England.

■ English naval development

In the spring of 1649, when the English Commonwealth was established, Cromwell's New Model Army had won over Royalist opponents in England. The military men in charge had no particular love for England's naval men, who had generally been more moderate in politics and many of whom had mutinied and defected to the Royalists at Hellevoetsluis in 1648 and come under the command of Prince Rupert of the Rhine. The new English leaders understood that they were isolated and in a dangerous position, particularly while Ireland, Scotland, the islands in Home Waters, and all of England's colonies remained in Royalist hands. They believed that Royalist forces abroad were being financed and supported from other countries and there were reports that Sweden was preparing a naval expedition to support the Royalists in Scotland. In this situation, a strong naval defence was a key element to maintain their power.[12] At the same time, foreign powers had been slow to grant recognition to the new English state. Among them, France issued letters of marque against English merchant shipping. As a result, England banned trade with France and authorized her own privateers to prey on French trade. Much of French trade, however, was carried in Dutch bottoms and this led to English attacks on Dutch trade.

To deal with this array of maritime issues, the leaders of the Commonwealth immediately set out to take control of the ships and seamen close at hand and to begin a major naval construction and acquisition programme. This took place in a series of rapid ship acquisitions for the English Navy that reflected rapidly changing ideas about warship design. A key element in this was the adoption of the frigate design. It involved the adoption of some of the design elements of the ships used by Dunkirk privateers, characterized by being low-built, fast vessels with finer lines that came to have a length-to-breadth ratio of 10 to 3 in contrast to the earlier heavier warships that had a 3-to-1 ratio. Initially a single-decked, narrow, lightly-built, and fast vessel, the frigate design quickly evolved over a few years as new ships were added to the fleet. In 1649, the Parliamentary Commission for the Admiralty ordered five ships, three of them were similar to the first frigates, but two were designed to be flagships and made considerably larger with two decks. The construction of the two large ships was consigned to two brothers: the master builders Peter Pett at Deptford and Christopher Pett at Woolwich. They each built somewhat different vessels that had a major influence on ships that followed. Peter Pett's *Fairfax* included a forecastle on his two-decked ship, while Christopher Pett's *Speaker* became the direct ancestor of the two-decked ship-of-the-line that developed later with both a forecastle and a small poop deck.[13]

At the same time, the numbers of guns on ships were increased. *Speaker* was originally designed to carry 44 guns, but this was changed to 50 guns by the time she was launched in 1650, and increased to 56 by 1653. This increase in guns was paralleled by an increase in the number of men used to man guns and apparently by undocumented changes in the handling and firing of guns. The experience of the naval actions that had occurred during the English Civil War and the privateering and other actions that took place in the defence of trade from 1649 had led to a primary emphasis on speed and a secondary emphasis on a new system of using large guns firing broadsides in single-ship actions.[14] This cumulative experience had a direct influence on English warship design and on ship acquisition during this short span of years. Since the Dutch had long experience in using their ships for defending trade at sea, they had concentrated more consistently than the English in having fast, frigate-style warships. The English Navy had built its ships on the basis of different rates or classes of warships since the mid-sixteenth century. By 1652, the two navies on opposite sides of the North Sea had developed naval forces that showed a distinctive difference. The English had a strong battle fleet and a large number of smaller ships of the 4th and 5th Rates that were useful as cruisers. In contrast, the Dutch had mainly frigate style ships comparable to the English, 4th, 5th, and 6th Rates. The Dutch ships were heavily armed for their size, but the hired merchantmen that the Dutch often employed were not capable of carrying the large numbers of 18- and 20-pound cannon that the English employed.

At the same time that new English ships were being acquired and new approaches to design instituted, the naval establishment ashore had rapidly begun to support innovation and supervise such change with a more integrated approach than used heretofore. Improving upon earlier organisational arrangements, the Commonwealth's Council of State employed three groups that worked together under the Council to direct naval affairs: (1) The Committee for the Affairs of the Admiralty and Navy, or the Admiralty Committee, that dealt with naval policy and strategy; (2) The Commissioners of the Admiralty and the Navy, or the Navy Commissioners, responsible for the shore establishment and pay, and (3) the Commissioners to go to Sea, or the Generals at Sea.[15] This arrangement brought a basis for the coordination of policy, strategy, logistics, operations, and tactics.

By the Spring of 1651, with the conquest of Ireland and Scotland completed and the risk of royalist counter-revolution reduced, the Commonwealth could decrease military expenditure, and, despite the requirement to maintain a constabulary army in Ireland and Scotland, could lower the army's overall strength by 30%. Financially solvent by having sold state property and having been able to obtain the English government's normal excise, customs, and assessment revenues, the Commonwealth was well positioned to pay its arrears and national debt as well as its current costs for the armed forces. This financial situation allowed enough funds to maintain the fleet to protect British commerce in Home Waters as well as in the Mediterranean and the Bay of Biscay. In January 1652, the Commonwealth planned to have 82 ships at sea, manned by 10,024 men.[16] And this continued to grow, so that by the end of the war in 1654, the Commonwealth owned more than 200 ships that required more than 30,000 sailors, and had a shore establishment of several thousands to support them.[17]

These arrays of changes for the English Navy were the innovations that provided the basis for long-term growth into a great power navy during the century that followed, but at the very outset in the First Dutch War they provided advantage over the Dutch Navy when they worked, but were a liability when they did not.

English warships Fairfax, Assurance, Tiger and Elizabeth

Painting attributed to Isaac Sailmaker, around 1680, National Maritime Museum, Greenwich

■ The First Dutch War, 1652-1654

When war finally erupted between the Dutch and the English in the spring of 1652, it had erupted suddenly, following the breakdown of the diplomatic negotiations over England's Navigation Act and the rejection of England's proposal for a union between the English Commonwealth and the Dutch Republic. While this was in progress, the Dutch Republic ordered the mobilisation of a large fleet of 150 ships under Lieutenant-Admiral Maerten Harpertszoon Tromp to protect Dutch shipping between the Strait of Gibraltar and the Sound. At the time, the five Dutch admiralties had seventy-nine warships collectively available to them, most of which were built in the 1640s and the early 1650s. The Dutch Republic had consistently disposed of older ships and concentrated on acquiring new ships, but during periods when the Republic was at peace Dutch warships were typically maintained for protection of their own

The 80-gun Royal Charles, ex-Naseby, built by Peter Pett in 1655, part of the English move to larger ships in that decade.

Drawing by Willem van de Velde the Elder, 1660, National Maritime Museum, Greenwich

neutral trade at a time when nearby countries, such as England, France, Spain, Portugal, were at war. In the early seventeenth century, the Dutch had concentrated their peacetime naval resources by employing purpose built warships and seldom hired merchantmen. The sudden Dutch mobilization in 1652 brought in a variety of ships to the fleet that were essentially armed merchantmen on lease. Seeing the contrast to recent practice, the English saw this mobilization of such a large fleet at sea as a threat. The very fact of naval mobilization created a volatile situation.

The situation in which the conflict arose did not present opportunities for any extensive thinking about strategy, that is to say, using naval force in a comprehensive manner in order to control an enemy force for the purpose of achieving larger political objectives. Battles were largely fought as opposing fleets encountered one another. Yet, the initial tactical preference that English naval commanders had in choosing to use their warships in gunnery duels in a line-of-battle against opposing Dutch warships that were protecting convoys of merchant vessels and the Dutch acceptance of this challenge with a similar type of naval force created a type of operational reasoning that led eventually to a strategic rationale for naval power.

Although the Dutch fleet was numerically superior, the English Navy was in a far superior condition to fight than the Dutch. In 1652, the Dutch preferred their well tried approach in using a limited number of ships, operating from a windward position, to quickly sail down wind to attack enemy ships to immediately grapple and board them for hand to hand combat. When operating in large fleets with a wide variety of ship-types, they had developed an organization of five squadrons that each sailed from the windward position in a line-ahead formation to approach the enemy, then immediately moved to attack individual ships with initial gunfire, then grappled and overwhelmed them with a large boarding party.[18]

When the English General at Sea Robert Blake encountered the Dutch fleet off Dover on 19/29 May 1652 and demanded a salute in recognition of Britain's sovereignty of those seas,[19] gunfire was exchanged and battle ensured in which two Dutch ships were lost in an incident that marked the beginning of open conflict between the two states. This action illustrated little change in the approach from earlier practices. As a chance encounter, there is no indication of pre-planned approaches on either side, either from a strategic or a tactical point of view. The surviving accounts of subsequent engagements – including those in the Channel near Plymouth when De Ruyter had a minor victory over Sir George Ayscue in an action on 16/26 August 1652; the battle of the Kentish Knock in the Thames estuary in which Blake and Vice Admiral Sir William Penn defeated Admiral Witte de With on 28 September/8 October 1652, the battle of Dungeness in which Tromp defeated Blake on 30 November/10 December 1652 – suggest that no new or distinctive tactics were being used. At Dungeness, Tromp's numerical superiority had won the day for the Dutch.

The following year, Blake and his fellow General at Sea Richard Deane were able to attack the Dutch convoy under Tromp's protection off Portland in a three day-battle that had begun on 18/28 February 1652/3. Similarly, the English defeated the Dutch at the Gabbard off the North Foreland on 12-13/22-23 June 1653, and off Terheide south of Scheveningen on 10/20 August 1653, when Tromp was killed in action. The English suffered a serious loss when Commodore Jan van Galen destroyed the four-ship English squadron at Livorno (Leghorn) in the Mediterranean on 13/23 March 1652/3.

The first minor evidence of any change taking place in tactical ideas occurred on 10/20 February 1652/3, just eight days before the battle of Portland, when Vice Admiral Sir William Penn issued instructions to his squadron directing the smaller ships to stand to windward to observe and to protect the major fighting units from an attack by enemy fire ships.[20] The major change came on 29 March/8 April 1653 at Portland, where the English were refitting after the three-day battle off that port. Preparing for the next encounter, the three English Generals at Sea – Robert Blake, Richard Deane, and George Monck – issued two complementary documents, 'Instructions for the better ordering of the Fleet in Fighting'[21] and 'Instructions for the better ordering of the Fleet in Sailing'.[22]

While much of these were a compilation of standard and existing directives, they included some innovations. First, issued together they established a connection between cruising formations and tactical formations in battle that would be developed in the future. Despite their limitations, these documents were issued as documents to be acted up at sea in the context of preparation for battle, giving the English fleet a degree of discipline under the control of its flag officers that it had not previously seen.

Although the evidence from surviving documents is vague, from this point forward the English fleet began to conduct itself differently than it previously had. The next major battle was at the Gabbard on 2-3/12-13 June 1653, in which Deane was killed in action. Despite that loss, both English and Dutch sources report that the English ships were under better control and that their broadside gunnery while in a line was effective in preventing the Dutch for approaching for grappling and boarding. While this is suggestive of new tactical thinking, there is no evidence that it was employed in the final major battle of the war off Terheide.

These experiences of naval warfare between 1652 and 1654 led naval leaders to think differently and to prepare for future wars. For the Dutch, the reverses at sea led

to an immediate commitment to use federal funds to build a larger fleet of purpose-built warships. While the war was still in progress, the States General voted in February 1653 for the construction of thirty purpose-built warships carrying up to 54-guns. As the peace negotiations were in progress by the end of the year, thirty more similar warships were ordered, but it would require the States General to take repeated steps over the coming half century to provide the funding to maintain, man, and provision these ships as active warships.[23]

With this series of decisions, the most powerful Navy in Europe shifted to adopt the new western European standard of a large, permanent, national navy. At the same time, this led to the tacit acceptance of a strategic corollary: the protection of one's own merchant trade and the protection of one's own coast from invasion – two central functions for navies – was best achieved by fighting and defeating a similar type of enemy naval force in an engagement between warships. The presence of an undefeated enemy naval force gave the opposing nation the ability to use the seaways for either peaceful trade or for military purposes. In this, the immediate focus during these wars was on the tactical development by which large battle fleets could fight.

■ The interwar period, 1654-1665

In the dozen years that lay between the First and Second Dutch Wars, both the Dutch and English navies continued to grow and to develop, as did other navies. The displacement figures reflect not only the increase in numbers of major warships, but also the growing increase in the size of warships as the ship-of-the-line developed to carry increasing numbers of guns.

Comparison in Total Displacement Tonnage of Major Warships[24]

Year	England	Netherlands	France	Denmark	Sweden
1660	88,000	62,000	20,000	15,000	23,000
1665	102,000	81,000	36,000	24,000	31,000
1670	84,000	102,000	114,000	30,000	34,000
1675	95,000	89,000	138,000	29,000	33,000
1680	132,000	66,000	135,000	39,000	21,000

Comparison in Numbers of Warships over 700 Tons Displacement[25]

Year	England	Netherlands	France	Denmark	Sweden
1660	57	51	15	9	8
1665	69	70	25	13	16
1670	60	88	75	17	18
1675	68	73	87	19	18
1680	89	62	83	23	11

Across the two decades during which the Second and Third Dutch Wars took place, one can see a major development taking place. On the one hand is the rapid rise of the English and Dutch navies as they faced each other, but also is the sudden appearance of France as major naval power that adopted the newly emerging approaches to naval warfare and the ship-of-the line. While France had not entirely neglected its Navy before the institution of Colbert's reforms in 1661,[26] French naval policy dra-

The 'raadpensionaris' of Holland,
Johan de Witt (1625-1672).

Painting by Jan de Baen, around 1670,
Dordrechts Museum, Dordrecht

matically changed under Louis XIV in the immediate aftermath of the First Dutch
War as France moved to the front ranks of European navies and quickly adopted the
new approaches to warship design, purpose-built warships, and tactics.[27]

By 1660, when King Charles II was restored to the English throne, he acquired a
Navy with a total of 156 ships, of which 75 carried 40 to 64 guns. Moving to even
larger ships, Peter Pett built the 80-gun *Naseby* at Woolwich in 1655, while his
brother, Christopher, built the 70-gun *Richard* at Woolwich in 1658. Two years later,
the 100-gun *Sovereign* was rebuilt at Chatham.[28] As war between the two maritime
countries approached in the early 1660s, the Dutch also began to strengthen the fleet
in a three-year period of warship construction in 1664 that brought in 60 more warships of 80 and more guns.

In the Dutch Republic, the *raadpensionaris* in Holland from 1653, Johan de Witt,
reflected the commercial interests of the Amsterdam merchants and became a major
political force in helping to modernize the Dutch Navy.[29] In both countries, notable
naval administrators were placed to come to the fore. In Holland, the father and son
team of David and Job de Wildt, whose tenures stretched from the 1640s to 1704, and,
in England, the young Samuel Pepys began his notable career as a novice only in 1660.

England's Royal Navy was now under the command of the Lord High Admiral, a young and inexperienced, but strong, leader in the King's brother, the thirty-three year old James, duke of York. Having seen a number of actions ashore, he had an able advisor for naval matters in the experienced Admiral Sir William Penn and his secretary Sir William Coventry.

■ The Second Dutch War, 1665-1667

As war approached in late 1664, the duke of York took direct command of the English fleet at Portsmouth on 9/19 November. Moving quickly on 11/21 November, he set a new tone for employing heavily armed ships by immediately organizing the fleet by dividing it into three squadrons. While the surviving documentation does not provide all the details, this seems to have been the creation of the English terminology that would last well past the age of sail with seniority given to the Red, followed by the White, and then the Blue, and with each squadron flying a flag to denote this: White in the van, Red in the centre, and Blue in the rear. In turn, each squadron had three divisions, each commanded by an admiral in the centre, with a vice-admiral in the van, and a rear admiral in the rear. This made a total of three flag officers for each squadron and a total of nine in the fleet.

Over the next two weeks, the duke of York issued separate sailing and fighting instructions that were based largely on those issued under the Commonwealth, but the fighting instructions contained two important new articles. One required the formation of a line ahead on either a starboard or larboard tack. The other required ships' captains to hold their fire until their guns came within a distance that their gunfire could have effect. Further innovations seem to have taken place between November 1664 and 1 February 1665, the duke of York issued signals that made it clear that ships were expected to take up pre-planned positions in the line of battle. Thus, a naval order of battle was established. In the coming months, several iterations of the orders were made, along with additional instructions.[30]

On the opening of the war, the English and Dutch fleets immediately took up positions from which they could aggressively use their battle fleets to protect and defend their merchant trade. In April, the duke of York moved to intercept Dutch homeward-bound convoys and to try to force a battle by luring the Dutch war fleet out to protect their commerce.

The effect of the improved English tactical dispositions showed in the Battle of Lowestoft on 3/13 June 1665, when the duke of York's fleet defeated the Dutch by using their line-of-battle tactics. In the course of the battle, the English flagship *Royal Charles* and the Dutch flagship *Eendracht* had engaged. During the action, *Eendracht* received a hit in the powder room and exploded killing the Dutch commander, Jacob van Wassenaer, heer van Obdam. This accident in combat led to the Dutch withdrawal from action, and was the fortuitous event that cleared the way for De Ruyter's promotion to replace Wassenaer as lieutenant-admiral of Holland and West Friesland.[31]

The actual conduct of the English ships in actual combat differed somewhat from the ideals that had been laid out on paper in the instructions issued beforehand. The plans did not work out as planned. A number of ships luffed up to windward and were in three, four, and even five ranks, instead of a single line of battle, even causing some casualties in English ships by friendly fire.[32]

The Eendracht and a fleet of Dutch men-of-war.

Painting by Ludolf Backhuysen, about 1670-75, National Gallery, London

Several months after the battle, the earl of Sandwich reflected on their actions and came up with detailed and practical recommendations for improvement in future actions.[33] The Dutch, too, reflected on their defeat in the battle of Lowestoft. But, their official investigation on the defeat stressed the importance of grappling and boarding an enemy ship, while the Admiralty of Zealand encouraged its officers to think innovatively about how to defeat the English tactics and to avoid 'the long and disadvantageous gun-battle with the English and to bring about the early laying aboard at the first opportunity...'.[34] However, the English tactic of staying in a close-ordered line and using heavy broadside gunnery fire precluded the use of the Dutch tactics of a group attack for grappling and boarding.

Despite these official conclusions, new ideas about tactics were brewing in the minds of the Dutch admirals. After lengthy discussions with sea officers during August 1665, Johan de Witt reflected the results of those conversations in the correspondence and directives coming from the States of Holland. Their thoughts centred on several key conclusions, based on recent experience: (1) the long-acknowledged need to maintain discipline in battle with a well-ordered fleet; (2) the fighting should be done in a single line-of-battle, close-hauled, with three squadrons positioned to windward of an enemy; (3) the flag officers needed to be less exposed at the beginning of an action; and (4) a reserve corps was necessary. A new order to the fleet embodying these ideas was issued to the Dutch fleet under Cornelis Tromp on 15

The Four Days' Battle (1666).

Painting by Abraham Storck, around 1670,
National Maritime Museum, Greenwich

August 1665 and had a number of variant alternatives included. One of these had the centre squadron slightly further from the enemy than the other two squadrons.[35] This became the so-called 'snake-shaped line' that remained in the instructions for more than twenty years, but was rarely, if ever, used. Some further changes to the instructions were made on De Ruyter's return, after more than a year away from home waters in Africa and the West Indies, on his appointment as commander-in-chief on 11 August 1665. Yet, for the Dutch admirals, much remained to be resolved and clarified in their tactical ideas.

Meanwhile, the English victualling and shore-based naval support system had broken down. At about the same time, the overall strategic situation changed in January 1666, when both France and Denmark declared war against England. This placed even greater stress on English logistical support in the naval war, as Denmark closed the Sound, and with it access to the Baltic, to English merchant vessels, creating a further major shortage for England of the essential naval supplies from this region for shipbuilding and repair. England, as well as the Dutch Republic, faced a major shortage in seamen to man their warships. On the part of France, Louis XIV had only a peripheral interest in the war and had agreed, with growing embarrassment, to meet a 1662 treaty obligation with the Dutch. In the event, France secretly instructed her admirals to avoid battle, if possible.[36]

In the Dutch Navy, the issues concerning tactics, the numbers of squadrons, and the presence of a reserve squadron continued to remain issues of debate for some time. Finally, after extensive discussions that involved De Ruyter and de Witt as well as representatives of the States-General and representatives of the five admiralties of the Dutch Republic, it was agreed that De Ruyter could have the discretion to command the fleet in battle in an arrangement of three squadrons divided into squadrons under vice-admirals and rear-admirals. Just one week after this decision was made, the Dutch and English fleets met off the Thames estuary in the Four Days' Battle (1/11-4/14 June 1666).[37]

This huge, prolonged action has earned the reputation for being the largest and bloodiest battle in the age of fighting sail. The experience of the battle, although it included boarding, grappling, and the use of fire ships, showed a marked improvement in Dutch tactics and the Dutch navy's ability to use line-of-battle tactics and to do damage with gunfire to the English with their new 70- and 80-gun ships sailing in the newly adopted line-of-battle. Nevertheless, the Dutch victory was not the crushing defeat of the English that many Dutch observers of the time thought that they had achieved.[38]

An equally interesting aspect of the battle was the English estimate of the strategic situation that led the English to divide their fleet. Earlier in the year, Admiral Lord Sandwich had sailed with thirty ships to protect English trade in the Mediterranean. Now, while De Ruyter was approaching with his large force of 84 ships, the English received intelligence – false intelligence, as it turned out – that the French Toulon squadron under the duke of Beaufort was approaching the Channel to join the Dutch. Leaving Albemarle with 54 English ships of the line, Prince Rupert took 20 ships and spent three of the four days of the battle guarding against the possibility of the French landing ashore in Britain or in attacking England's coastal trade. The situation illustrated England's strategic dilemma in not knowing whether to concentrate its battle force to defeat De Ruyter's fleet or to deal with the multiple smaller threats that she faced on other fronts.

After the action, the Four Days' Battle brought time for the English to reflect on tactics while repairing damage. On 16 July 1666, Prince Rupert and the duke of Albemarle, issued their 'Additional Instructions for Fighting', which emphasized the need to 'keep up with the admiral of the fleet and to endeavour the utmost that may be the destruction of the enemy, which is always to be the chiefest care'.[39] Moreover, it instructed that "all the best sailing ships are to make what way they can to engage the enemy, that so the rear of our fleet may the better come up…'.[40]

At the same time, the duke of York first issued one of the most important and influential English instructions of the era in July 1666, intended to ensure that the English fleet maintained the weather gage:

> "In case we have the wind of the enemy, and the enemy stands toward us and we towards them, then the van of our fleet shall keep the wind, and when they are come to a convenient distance of the enemy's rear shall stay until our whole line is come up within the same distance of the enemy's van, and then our whole line is to stand along with them the same tacks on board, still keeping the enemy to leeward, and not suffering them to tack in the van, and in case the enemy tacks in the rear first, and the whole line is to follow, standing all along with the same tacks on board as the enemy does."[41]

The thought expressed here stood for more than a century as the mandatory Article XVII of the eighteenth century Royal Navy's permanent *Sailing and Fighting Instructions*. Additional points in this document expressed the importance of keeping the line and to divide an enemy's fleet by tacking through the enemy's battle line in order to gain the windward position.

Just over a week after these additional instructions appeared, the English under the duke of Albemarle, and the Dutch fleet, under De Ruyter, met again in the Two Days' Battle of St. James's Day on 25-26 July/4-5 August 1666. In this action, the two relatively equal fleets exchanged heavy gunfire, but the English maintained the advantage with a disciplined van and centre. The aftermath of this defeat for the Dutch provided the opportunity to think again about fleet tactics. In this period, De Ruyter pointed out that it was necessary for ships to keep in their assigned station 'otherwise the train of ships would be too extended and the ships would be left unsupported'.[42] In the weeks and months that followed, Johan de Witt played a key role in institutionalising further changes by establishing De Ruyter's signal to form the battle-line into the general signal book, organizing the battle fleet firmly into three squadrons with three divisions each, and even established a standard diagram for the fleet, making sure that these procedures and copies of the orders were distributed for reference among all commanders afloat and shore-based authorities.[43]

By late in 1666, the English were finding serious difficulties in providing the financial resources and the supplies to keep their fleet at sea. Seamen protested and dockyard workers mutinied as peace negotiations began. In early 1667, King Charles II decided not to attempt to put the fleet to sea and opted instead to have only two small squadrons at sea to serve as coastal guard ships. This sudden weakening of England's main naval defence gave the Dutch Navy an opportunity of a completely different kind that had little to do with the tactical discussions for fleet battles. It was at this point that De Ruyter made his raid on the English coast in the Thames estuary and the Medway River, famously capturing the 86-gun ship named for the king, *HMS Royal Charles*, and towing it back as a prize to Holland.[44]

Aside from firmly establishing the line-of-battle tactics in both the Dutch and English navies, the Second Dutch War left both countries exhausted. The experience of the first two wars continued to urge on the increase in the size of warships. In ship design, stability that went toward a firm platform for gunnery had come to outweigh the importance of speed, as did a stiffness that prevented a ship from heeling too far so that its lower gun ports could not be used. The 70-gun third rate ship-of-the-line became a recognized success in the Royal Navy and the three-deck, 100-gun first rates were returning to favour. Across the North Sea, consideration of the shallow waters and sandbanks led the Dutch to avoid building three-deck ships and to prefer beamy ships, but their large 60-, 70-, and 80-gun warships were fully capable of dealing with the English. Additionally, as the French began to place emphasis on their navy in the early 1660s, they initially turned to the Dutch to supply some important warships. These French ships of Dutch design were larger than their English counterparts and more stable two-deckers with their lower tier of guns higher off the water.[45]

■ The Third Dutch War, 1672-1674

From a strategic perspective, the Third Dutch War was significantly different from the others. The origins of the war lay in the personal enthusiasms of the young Louis XIV and not the more careful judgements of his ministers.[46] This involved a volte face from previous French policy in the Second Dutch war with France's decision to invade and to overwhelm the Dutch Republic. It also involved a *volte face* for English policymakers who had previously agreed in 1668 with Sweden and the Dutch Republic to prevent French occupation of the Spanish Netherlands.[47] As France actively sought to embroil England in the war for its own objectives, on the English side King Charles II's motives for entering into the secret Treaty of Dover and in the Third Dutch War in alliance with France against the Dutch Republic lie fundamentally in internal English politics and the king's struggle for maintaining the Crown's controlling power over Parliament.[48]

The immediate outbreak of the war resulted from the English initiative in sending out two squadrons of frigates, one under Sir Edward Spragg and the other under Robert Holmes, to contrive an incident by asserting English 'sovereignty of the sea' and use this as rationale to attack the homeward-bound Dutch convoy from Smyrna. Although the Dutch forces defended themselves effectively and repulsed the English squadrons, nevertheless, the incident became the *casus belli*. On receiving the news of the incident, Charles II declared war on the Dutch Republic on 18/28 March 1672, followed by Louis XIV on 6 April 1672.[49]

From a naval perspective, this situation in policy and strategy created a distinctive aspect of this war that contrasted with the earlier two conflicts. In retrospect, it implied the need for the English Navy to begin to develop means to cope with a coalition naval force and also to complement military operations ashore. While the English initially anticipated a naval war, the French quickly developed plans of their own for aggressive military operations to invade the Republic. French soldiers with troops from England, Cologne, and Münster, moved from the south and the east. Much Dutch territory was occupied, but the English were not directly part of these operations.

The naval actions were similar to the earlier wars, but showed the more mature tactical development that emerged from the experience of the first two Dutch wars.

Moreover, in every one of the four major actions in this war, a French squadron joined with two English squadrons to create the line-of-battle. Anglo-French naval strategy was focused on blockading the Dutch coasts in order to establish a position from which an invasion from the sea could be launched. To counter this, Dutch strategy lay in flooding the polders of Holland to prevent occupation and creating a formidable naval defence to prevent any such landing.

In this war, De Ruyter had the advantage of having the Dutch fleet in an excellent state of readiness with the new warships from the 1664-1666 building programme available. In addition, De Ruyter had trained his commanding officers in procedures for meeting a superior enemy force in battle. In particular, he had finally succeeded in doing away with the earlier ideas about group tactics for grappling and boarding, concentrating on training his fleet in the effective use of the 'single line ahead' formation that the English had pioneered and the Dutch had taken over after the battle of Lowestoft in 1665. In addition, he built further on this approach with innovative tactical thinking on how to counter the Anglo-French use of these tactics, although this was done by word or mouth and in practice rather than in formal written instructions.[50] In contrast, the duke of York, who commanded the combined Anglo-French fleet, issued fighting instructions to the fleet that were fundamentally the same as those issued in 1666.[51]

The first fleet engagement of the war occurred on 28 May/7 June 1672, when De Ruyter with 62 ships attacked the allied fleet of 82 ships as they lay at anchor in Solebay, off Southwold, Suffolk. Although the English and French had expected an attack, they were still at anchor when De Ruyter appeared. The French squadron, under the comte d'Estrées, and the English separated and two separate actions ensued, in which the Dutch prevailed in both. De Ruyter's attack successfully served to force the English and French to postpone their plans to make a landing in Holland and, at the same time, created a major feud between d'Estrées and his second in command, Abraham Duquesne, whom d'Estrées accused of failing to support him. Similarly, the English admirals traded recriminations.[52]

Following this, the focus of events shifted ashore with the lynching of the de Witt brothers in The Hague and the military defence of Holland under the stadhouder Prince William III, which even utilized some guns and men taken from Dutch warships to defend the homeland. In the meantime, De Ruyter planned to make an aggressive attack on England to sink ships and block the channels to Portsmouth and London.[53] Thwarting this plan in May 1673 just as De Ruyter appeared off the Thames, the new commander of the English fleet, Prince Rupert of the Rhine,[54] forced De Ruyter's fleet back into Dutch waters. Forced to take the defensive, De Ruyter took his fleet to the Schooneveld flats off Walcheren Island, where he made brilliant use of his local knowledge of the sand banks in two actions, the first on 28 May/7 June and the second on 4/14 June 1673.

Outnumbered 76 to 52 ships, De Ruyter used the restricted conditions to advantage. Prince Rupert expected to use his numerical superiority to deliver a decisive blow, but De Ruyter came out to windward of the shoals to gain a tactical advantage and was able to manoeuvre to avoid the advance squadron and the fireships that the allies deployed. Instead of retreating as Rupert expected, the Dutch formed a line to defend their position. Rupert had placed the French squadron in the middle of his line to prevent the situation that had occurred at Solebay. In the van, Rupert engaged with Cornelis Tromp's squadron, while De Ruyter's and Adriaen Banckert's

squadrons dealt with Spragge's and d'Estrées'. As the fleets approached a sandbank, De Ruyter tacked and broke through d'Estrées' line isolating the French rear. As the engaged fleets reformed and separated squadrons rejoined on their new course, De Ruyter brilliantly broke through the French again and doubled it. The general action successfully prevented the allied English and French fleet from making any gains. Although neither side lost any ships, the English and French were unable to approach the Dutch ports and were baffled by the sand banks.[55]

A week later on 4/14 June 1673, the opposing fleets met again off Schooneveld with similar results. The lack of communication between Rupert and d'Estrées caused confusion in the allied fleet and the allies withdrew to the Nore at the mouth

Battle off Kijkduin (Battle of the Texel) 1673.

Painting by Willem van de Velde the Younger and his studio, 1687, Nederlands Scheep-vaartmuseum, Amsterdam

of the Thames, concluding that they could not reach the coast by challenging De Ruyter at Schooneveld.[56]

Meanwhile, the allied fleet cruised off the Texel in order to draw De Ruyter out into open water and clear an avenue for landing. The two fleets engaged on 11/21 August in the battle off Kijkduin (battle of the Texel). With the same commanders, the fleets were slightly larger, with the Dutch outnumbered, 86 ships to 60. In the end, the battle divided into separate squadron actions, with the French taking little part. De Ruyter's manoeuvres forced the Allies back to the English coast and broke their blockade of the Dutch coast.[57] The misunderstandings that had arisen in battle between d'Estrées and Rupert became recriminations after the battle and a public dispute that showed the strains within the alliance, helping to contribute to the discontinuation of allied operations and the conclusion that the war had been a failure for France and England.[58]

The Anglo-French fleet had consistently attempted to break through the Dutch naval defences, but failed in all their attempts to do so. De Ruyter's success in this was the greatest naval achievement of the era and the prevention of an enemy landing in Holland and Zeeland was the critical element for Dutch defence. In this, De Ruyter's actions in the Third Dutch war marked the firm implementation of the range of new European naval developments in the period between 1652 and 1676. Offensive and aggressive tactics with heavily gunned, large warships operating in a line of battle for major engagements dominated naval history for the remainder of the age of sail and continued in spirit for centuries.

During the three Anglo-Dutch conflicts, the navies were used primarily in home waters to fight battles with the strategic purpose of attacking and protecting trade or in breaking or enforcing blockades. The focus in the age of De Ruyter was on the development of the ships, gunnery, and tactical approaches to major battles for these purposes. The few cases during these wars in which battles were fought in America, the West Indies, and the Mediterranean were suggestions of future potential when nations in the eighteenth and nineteenth centuries also deployed their naval forces with ambitious imperial and strategic objectives in far distant seas.

The aftermath of the Dutch raid on the Medway, 1667: the flagship Royal Charles being taken to the Netherlands.

Painting by Ludolf Backhuysen, 1667, National Maritime Museum, Greenwich

CHAPTER 6

The Good Enemy

*British Perceptions of Michiel De Ruyter
and the Anglo-Dutch Wars*

J.D. Davies

Michiel Adriaenszoon de Ruyter inflicted on Britain arguably the most humiliating defeat in the whole course of its military and naval history. Yet despite his responsibility for the Medway raid of 1667, he was regarded with almost universal respect in the British Isles[1]. The first biography of De Ruyter in any language was published in England, in the year after his death (although in a piece of breathtaking historical revisionism worthy of Stalin's USSR, this managed to excise all mention of the events at Chatham)[2]. De Ruyter's old adversary James, duke of York, later King James II, praised him fulsomely as the greatest admiral 'that ever to that time was in the world, [and] that never reported untruths or spoke less of his enemy than they deserved'[3]. Edward Barlow, a seaman who was as patriotic and xenophobic as most Englishmen of his time, described De Ruyter as 'a very stout man and a brave commander'; the duke of Ormonde, Lord Lieutenant and effectively viceroy of Ireland, hung De Ruyter's portrait at one of his many homes[4]. Respect, even admiration, for Michiel De Ruyter in the British Isles, transcended class, and it transcended national enmities.

■ A brave and generous opponent

Unlike many of his contemporaries in the Dutch officer corps, De Ruyter spoke English well. He probably acquired the language at an early age; when he was born at Vlissingen in 1607, the town was occupied by an English garrison under the terms of the Treaty of Nonsuch (1585), and it was only returned to the control of the province of Zeeland in 1616. For the first nine years of his life, the young Michiel would have heard English spoken as a matter of course, and at that highly impressionable age, it was surely likely that he picked up at least a smattering of the language (as young Dutch children still do, with invariably impressive results)[5]. He presumably picked up more of the language during his first two extended voyages to sea at the ages of ten and twelve, which took him to an Anglo-Dutch settlement on the Amazon[6]. His command of English undoubtedly contributed to his popularity in the British Isles in later life; after all, it pandered to the perennial linguistic incompetence of the English, and perhaps generated the warmth (and relief) that most Englishmen abroad still feel when they encounter foreigners who speak their language well. Intriguingly, though, English seems not to have been the only language of the British Isles that De Ruyter spoke with at least a measure of fluency. His anonymous English biographer claimed that he had spent seven years living in Dublin as a merchant's factor, and that he became fluent in English there[7]. His early experiences in Ireland were certainly well known in later years. In 1667, Charles II's authorities in Ireland were convinced that a Dutch invasion was imminent, and hasty attempts were made to enhance the defences. One report on the garrison and forts at Derry noted that De Ruyter had been in the town in 1644, that he therefore knew its strengths and weaknesses, and might be tempted to make an attack against it[8]. It has been argued that as well as improving his grasp of English, De Ruyter's time in Ireland gave him at least a smattering of Erse (Irish Gaelic), and he certainly had at least one close Irish friend, Tobias Tobiaszoon, one of those most responsible for capturing the *Royal Charles* at Chatham, and who became both an 'intimate' and neighbour of De Ruyter.[9]

De Ruyter was a subordinate flag officer during the first Anglo-Dutch war (1652-4), but he played a central role in all the major battles of the campaign, and became

Title page of The life of Michael Adrian de Ruyter, the first biography of Michiel de Ruyter, published in England in 1677.

Royal Library of the Netherlands, The Hague

known as a formidable and skilful opponent. After some initial successes, the Dutch fleet took a severe battering in the engagements of the spring and summer of 1653, primarily because their opponents had learned to take advantage of their overwhelming superiority in firepower. On several occasions, De Ruyter had to command fighting retreats (most notably after the Battle of the Kentish Knock / Hoofden in September 1652, when he condemned Witte de With's suicidal attempt to return to the fray). Although he was referring to the Four Days' Battle in the following war, De Ruyter's anonymous English biographer praised the way in which in such situations, the admiral always preferred prudence to a 'vainglorious bravo'.[10] De Ruyter's skill was commented on in sources that otherwise provided a natural anglocentric gloss on events. According to Pepys, De Ruyter's return to the Netherlands in the summer of 1665, avoiding the British fleet that stood in his path, was 'told to the great disadvantage of our fleet and the praise of De Ruyter'.[11] An official account of the Four Days' Battle (1-4 /11-14 June 1666) praised him for his actions in reorganising his shattered squadrons on the third day, when 'with great courage and skill [he] got them together in good order'.[12] The report of the St James' Day Fight, or Two Days Battle, sent to London by the rising minister Sir Thomas Clifford (who was present in the fleet) again praised De Ruyter's skill and bravery:

> *"The Royal Charles was much disabled by De Ruyter in yards masts and sails so that we were forced to give out to repair which held us almost an hour. De Ruyter was all that time engaged, and then we bore in again upon him and after an hour and a half dispute more, he gave way, but the Charles was again so much shattered that we had not a rope to help ourselves... De Ruyter began to make all sail he could and run but with great gallantry would make several tacks to fetch off his maimed ships and once endangered himself very much for his rescue of his second, who at last was so disabled that he could not get off, but then like a very knowing seaman he chopt to an anchor which presently brought us to the leeward of him."* [13]

It was probably De Ruyter's activities in West Africa and the West Indies in 1664-5 that first made him a household name in Britain. His reoccupation of forts previously taken by Robert Holmes at a time when there was no other significant action between Charles II's kingdoms and the Dutch (or any other power) transformed him into a personification of Dutch policy. Despite the distances involved, frequent reports of De Ruyter's doings reached the educated elites of Charles II's kingdoms, and gave his name a uniquely high profile that no other Dutch commander could rival. Moreover, he clearly already possessed a reputation as a courteous and honourable enemy. When he met the British fleet in the Mediterranean in September 1664, De Ruyter saluted fulsomely both Admiral Sir John Lawson and Vice-Admiral Thomas Allin; as well as rendering the expected gun salutes, he passed under Allin's stern and raised a glass to him[14]. In February 1665 Pepys reported that De Ruyter was responsible for an atrocity in Guinea, which allegedly involved throwing hundreds of English men, women and children into the sea. Pepys found it hard to believe that 'he that was so kind to our men at first' should behave in such a way, and was clearly glad that the informant was exposed as a liar two days later[15]. A few months later, attempts by Sir George Downing to blame De Ruyter for atrocities against English settlers at Newfoundland also foundered on their own innate implausibility[16]. De Ruyter was not only a highly unlikely candidate to be a latter-day Attila; his conduct, and that of the forces under him, was considered to be rather more civilised than the norms of the time. Following the attack on the Medway, the conduct of the Dutch forces that De Ruyter's fleet landed on the north coast of Kent was contrasted favourably with that of the Scottish troops who were meant to be defending it. According to Pepys, who visited the area in question soon after the debacle, the Dutch 'killed none of our people nor plundered their houses; but did take some things of easy carriage and left the rest, and not a house burned', whereas the Scots 'plundered and took all away'. Pepys thought it all 'very remarkable to me, and of great honour to the Dutch' – and, by implication, to the discipline instilled by their commander[17].

The coloured counter decoration of the Royal Charles.

Woodcarving, about 1664, Rijksmuseum, Amsterdam

In the summer of 1666, a false rumour of the death of De Ruyter in the St James's Day fight reached London. The Navy Board celebrated en masse, but then news came that the tale was false, 'which quite dashed me [Pepys] again'[18]. A few days later, Sir William Coventry, the secretary to James, duke of York (the Lord High Admiral) was delighted to hear another rumour that the outcome of the same battle had left De Ruyter out of favour in the Netherlands; his friend Pepys described a subsequent report that De Ruyter dared not come ashore 'for fear of the people' as 'a very good hearing'. Both Coventry and Pepys realised instinctively that any disgrace of the best Dutch commander could only be to Britain's advantage[19]. It is also interesting that such rumours were invariably about De Ruyter, not any other Dutch admiral (notably his great rival, Cornelis Tromp), and the reactions of Pepys and Coventry speak volumes for the soaring reputation that De Ruyter already possessed[20]. He was at once bogeyman and behemoth. In 1666 Sir Robert Lynch, an Irish baronet and Mayor of Galway, kept having recurring dreams in which he killed De Ruyter with his fusil. This was sufficient to earn him a place in the fleet, aboard the ship of his colourful countryman Sir Robert Holmes, but Lynch finally obtained conclusive proof that dreams do not always come true[21].

De Ruyter as mythic hero and plain seaman

De Ruyter's anonymous English biographer reported that at some point during 1665
or 1666, he issued a personal challenge to Robert Holmes to meet him in a single ship
duel intended to settle the differences between the two countries. It was said that
Charles II knighted Holmes to make him worthy of the challenge, and gave him
command of a new ship, named *Defiance* for the purpose[22]. Holmes was certainly
knighted at the launch of the third rate vessel *Defiance* (at Castle's yard, Deptford, on
27 March / 6 April 1666), but neither the *London Gazette* nor Samuel Pepys's diary
mention anything of a single ship challenge; *Defiance* was a traditional warship
name, and had been borne both by an Elizabethan galleon and a Royalist privateer;
and Holmes was hardly the sort of man to keep silent on such a matter[23]. The story
might have been an out-and-out canard, or an exaggerated version of his own life
story that Holmes might have aired in his retirement, but its significance lies in the
way in which De Ruyter was portrayed. The medieval notion of national champions
riding out to settle their sponsors' differences on the field of honour may have been

an anachronism long before the 1660s and 1670s, but the association of Michiel de Ruyter with such chivalric conduct reveals much about the way in which he was perceived (and, of course, the English translation of his surname served only to emphasise the knightly connotations)[24].

De Ruyter was portrayed not only as a paragon of chivalry, but as a classical hero. His English biographer recounted the story of his mother saving 'her young Aeneas' from a burning house. The admiral's heroic role in the survival of the Dutch republic during the *guerre de Hollande* was likened to Atlas, carrying the 'tottering and decaying state' of the Netherlands on his shoulders[25]. His personality was idealised to present him as a latter-day Cincinnatus, a comparison made more pertinent by his reluctance to enter naval service as a commodore at the beginning of the first Anglo-Dutch war, and subsequently by his modest refusal of high command in the navy: 'De Ruyter was a person (as most brave men have been) of a middle stature, a strong and well compacted body, not fat, but fleshy, of a graceful and majestic countenance'. Sanguine, temperate and sober, he was 'generally of a frame of temper so even and harmonious, as rendered him sedate and constant, and altogether free from the mistakes and waverings that accompany fickle and light natures'. Much of this panegyric might have been intended as implicit criticism of many of Charles II's naval officers, or even of the king and his courtiers. This certainly seems to be the case in the passage where De Ruyter is said to have advanced by merit, rather than ambition: 'dutiful to his superiors, respectful to his equals, grateful to his benefactors, affable and courteous to his inferiors; and in a word, obliging to all' (in other words, the absolute antithesis of the arrogant, obstreperous Holmes and some of his fellow sea-officers)[26].

Although the eulogist naturally tended to idealise his subject, confirmation of his opinion came from others, for De Ruyter's humility and lack of pretension impressed many of the Britons who met him. Sir William Temple said of him:

> "*I never saw [De Ruyter] in clothes better than the commonest sea-captain, nor with above one man following him, nor in a coach: and in his own house, neither was the size, building, furniture or entertainment at all exceeding the use of every common merchant and tradesman in his town*[27].

Temple, again, was making the point at least in part as an implied criticism of some of those who served Charles II at sea, and were certainly not as modest, but others who lacked the agendas of Temple and the anonymous biographer confirmed his view of the admiral. The Comte de Guiche, a French volunteer who served in the Dutch fleet during the Four Days' Battle, famously found De Ruyter sweeping his cabin with a broom and feeding his chickens; hardly the behaviour in victory that would be expected from any of his British contemporaries. Three young Englishmen visited De Ruyter in February 1672:

> "*He received us courteously and made us taste a glass of Navarre wine... He spoke all English and not ill... he is now 63 years old, yet he looks very fresh coloured and lusty – under his years he looks, and is dressed perfect citizen-like in a plain velvet coat.*"[28]

These would certainly not have been the only accounts of the admiral to reach the British Isles. Large numbers of Britons served in the Dutch fleet during the period, with many of them presumably returning home when their employment ceased. Britons, especially Scots, made up about 8% of the crew of Tromp's flagship *Gouden*

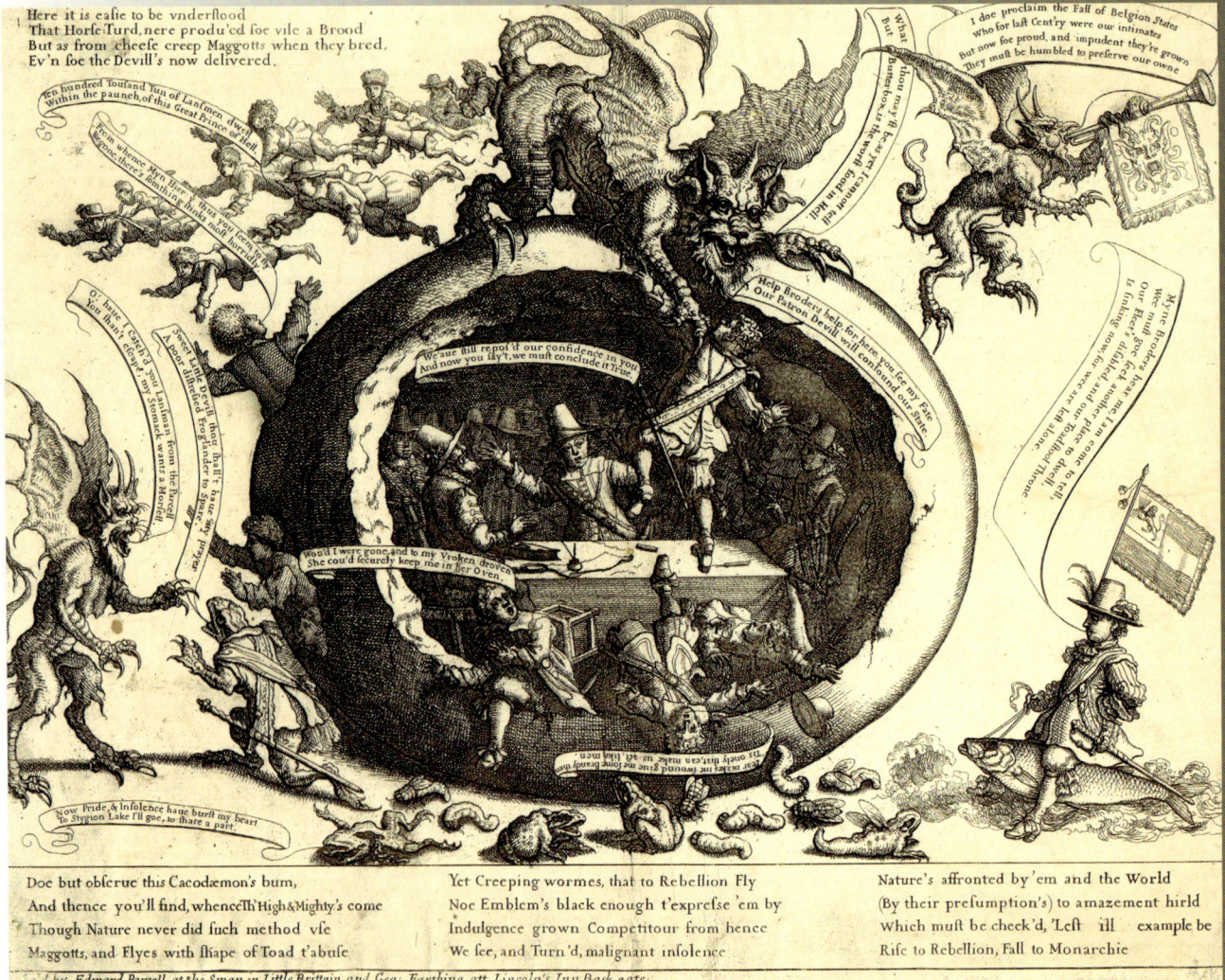

Within the engraving, various text fragments appear:

Here it is easie to be vnderstood
That Horse-Turd, nere produc'd soe vile a Brood
But as from cheese creep Maggotts when they bred,
Ev'n soe the Devill's now delivered.

Ten hundred Touſand Ton of Landmen dwell
Within the paunch, of this Great Prince of hell

From whence then Here, thus you ſee all
Begone, there's Nothing drinks more horrid!

O! have Mercy'd you'd haue Mercy'd you Landmen from the Parcell
Doon't dißeaſed froe Landen to Spare: ſweet prayer

Sweet Land Devil! thear, that't haue Wery Mercy
Sweet Land Devill their, that't haue Very prayer

Now Pride, & Infolence haue burſt my heart
To Stygion Lake I'll goe, to there a part.

We'aue ſtill repof'd our confidence in you
And now you ſay't, we muſt conclude it True.

Would I wert gone, and to my Vroken drovck
She cou'd ſecurely keep me in her Oven

Help Brodery help for here you ſee my Fate
Our Patron Devill will confound our State.

But makes the wound griue me long brandy men
Tis onely that, can make us all liue men

I doe proclaim the Fall of Belgion States
Who for laſt Cent'ry were our intimates
But now ſoe proud, and impudent they're grown
They muſt be humbled to preſerve our owne

What
But Butterbox may fit here the proud Gods in Hall

My the Brothers End
Wee muſt goeral Egled tread
our Elect's fled away and other place
no ſtoe come to dwell
muſt fall, or were are Todded Throne
is finding now her Toddoil alone

Doe but obſerue this Cacodæmon's bum,
And thence you'll find, whenceTh' High&Mighty's come
Though Nature never did ſuch method vſe
Maggotts, and Flyes with ſhape of Toad t'abuſe

Yet Creeping wormes, that to Rebellion Fly
Noe Emblem's black enough t'expreſſe 'em by
Indulgence grown Competitour from hence
We ſee, and Turn'd, malignant infolence

Nature's affronted by 'em and the World
(By their preſumption's) to amazement hirld
Which muſt be check'd, 'Leſt ill example be
Riſe to Rebellion, Fall to Monarchie

Sold by Edward Powell at the Swan in Little Brittain and Geo: Farthing att Lincoln's Inn Back gate.

A satire showing Dutchmen plotting rebellion around a table in a broken egg but as they climb out they are met by devils. The disorder is a sign of Dutch decline and potential for English success.

Untitled print, by Francis Barlow, print-maker, about 1673, published by George Farthing and Edward Powell, London

Leeuw in De Ruyter's fleet in 1673, and the proportion serving on some other ships might have been higher. This meant that reports of De Ruyter's conduct, and both descriptions and opinions of the man himself, could be passed on by those who had witnessed him in action; in the coastal communities of the Thames, Medway and East Anglia, he would not have been simply a name, known only from hostile news-sheets and pamphlets[29].

English satirists of the Restoration usually described the Dutch people as a whole in unflattering and often thoroughly crude terms, but they made an exception for De Ruyter. In Annus Mirabilis, Dryden described him as 'a fam'd commander, bold', while the author of the Third Advice to a Painter referred to him on the eve of the Four Days' Battle of June 1666 as 'inferior unto none for heart'; again, disinterested praise of De Ruyter may have gone hand-in-hand with implied criticism of Charles II's captains and courtiers[30]. However, a certain ambivalence towards the Dutch, even at the height of the wars against them, was not uniquely personal to De Ruyter. For all the scatological propaganda, relations with the Dutch (or at least, with individual Dutchmen) were often remarkably positive, even at the height of the second and third Anglo-Dutch wars. Dublin had a Dutch mayor in 1666, and Limerick had one in both 1666 and 1673[31]. In 1672 and 1673, precisely when the fleet that he was partly responsible for ordering to sea was attempting to destroy De Ruyter's ships in the North Sea, the 'cabal' minister John Maitland, duke of Lauderdale, had Dutch joiners installing sash windows at his southern residence, Ham House, while Dutch floor planks were being installed at his northern seat, Thirlestane Castle[32].

■ De Ruyter in victory and adversity

In the summer of 1667, following its successful attack on the Medway, De Ruyter's fleet made a leisurely and triumphal cruise along the south coast of England. This in itself would have made his name a byword among those who lived near the sea, but the admiral's deportment cemented his reputation as not only a daring and successful opponent, but as a man of mercy, who was worthy of respect. The English coastal defences were either shambolic or non-existent, and even though it was clear that peace was imminent, there was very little to stop De Ruyter causing havoc along the entire coastline, perhaps burning a town or two (as Sir Robert Holmes had done at Terschelling the year before, and as the French would later do at Teignmouth in 1690) or bombarding some ports (as the British did all along the French coast in 1694-5). Instead, he was a model of restraint. His ships attempted to enter Fowey harbour, but only to pursue merchantmen that had taken refuge there, not to raze the town; otherwise, they came ashore to fetch water, caused a brief panic in the Scilly Isles, took some sheep and cattle, and killed precisely one person, an old Cornish woman[33]. As campaigns went, it was hardly 'shock and awe'. At Plymouth, De Ruyter invited the town's governor, John Granville, seventh Earl of Bath, and Sir Jonathan Trelawny of Pelynt, MP for Cornwall, aboard *De Zeven Provinciën* under flag of truce, and there entertained them liberally:

> *"After several compliments and discourses past, they began to drink, first his Majesty's health with 13 guns, then the States-General with 11, and afterwards others with 9, 7 and 5 guns, discharging during their entertainment on board about 80 guns, entertaining Sir Jonathan and his company with great civility and returning them safe to land. That evening, the Lord Lieutenant by Sir Thomas Allin's ketch, sent a present to De Ruyter of some fresh provisions with a fat buck and some fruits, which he received with 7 guns, and dismissed the ketch, with many acknowledgments of the kindness done him."*[34]

The report is taken from *The London Gazette*, the official organ of the state, and disseminating such an account of De Ruyter's courtesy and humanity some three weeks before the Peace of Breda might have been intended as the beginnings of a rapprochement with the Dutch. In any event, it would certainly have helped to cement the admiral's reputation in the British Isles.

De Ruyter's stock rose even higher during the *guerre de Hollande*, or third Anglo-Dutch war. The war was deeply unpopular among large sections of English society: in particular, Charles II's military and naval alliance with a blatantly expansionist, Catholicising France was viewed with deep unease in many quarters, and the spectacle of a combined Anglo-French fleet attempting to sweep the Dutch from the seas was wholly unpalatable to some. In contrast, De Ruyter's brilliant defensive strategy against daunting odds attracted considerable admiration, perhaps in part as a way of

The attack on the Medway in June, 1667.

Painting by Willem Schellinks, about 1667, Nederlands Scheepvaartmuseum, Amsterdam

Sir Frescheville Holles (1641-1672) on the right and Sir Robert Holmes (1622-1692) on the left. They attacked the homeward-bound Dutch Smyrna convoy in the English Channel in 1672.

Painting by Peter Lely, about 1672, National Maritime Museum, Greenwich

implicitly criticising the country's involvement in a widely hated war against what many perceived to be the wrong enemy. Following the first battle of Schooneveld (28 May/7 June 1673) it was reported from London that 'most here give De Ruyter right, magnifying the man's gallantry and conduct with admiration of his, as the greatest feat that ever he performed all circumstances considered, so as if he should be brought over prisoner at [the] next bout, he would be civiller treated'[35]. There were further reports of his gallantry, skill, modesty, and generosity. During the battle of Solebay (28 May/7 June 1672) the lieutenant of the burned flagship *Royal James* was taken aboard De Ruyter's *Zeven Provinciën*, witnessed the Dutch admiral at first hand during the latter stages of the fight, and declaimed to his captors and hosts that same evening: 'Is that an admiral? He is an admiral, a mate, a sailor, and a soldier. Yes, that man, that hero, is all these things at the same time'[36].

Samuel Pepys was certainly among those to be impressed by De Ruyter and his fellow commanders. When, in 1677, he came to note down his preliminary thoughts for his projected history of the Anglo-Dutch wars, one of the great unwritten books of the seventeenth century, he proceeded from the inevitable and entirely conventional assumption that the English were wholly in the right and the Dutch (or at least, De Witt and his so-called 'Loeuvestein faction') were wholly in the wrong. But he wanted express royal permission to moderate his xenophobic agenda in one particular, and one alone: he wanted to be able 'to speak fairly sometimes of the Dutch themselves, and to give due praise upon occasion to some of their most eminent commanders, as De Ruyter, van Tromp, Banckert, the Evertsens and others'[37].

◾ The contrast: De Ruyter and his British contemporaries

The admiration for De Ruyter, who could be viewed safely (but not necessarily accurately) from across the North Sea as a bluff, apolitical seaman fighting solely to save his country from ruin, may have resulted from a conscious or unconscious realisation that the English simply had no commander who even remotely fulfilled those criteria. Almost all of the senior fleet commanders during the second and third Anglo-Dutch wars were tied closely to the court and tainted by association with it and its unpopular policies: in different ways, the Dukes of York and Albemarle, Prince Rupert, the Earl of Sandwich, and Sir William Penn, were all controversial figures with patchy service records, and each of them was deeply unpopular in many quarters. Rupert had the additional disadvantage of being 'foreign', for all his clumsy efforts to prove himself 'more English than the English'. The British also replaced their commanders-in-chief in every campaign, or even in the middle of a campaign (as in 1665): no admiral was entrusted with the supreme command as often on the British side as De Ruyter was on the Dutch, and thus no British admiral had the time to build up such a formidable reputation. The emphasis on De Ruyter's humble background and frugality was another indirect way of attacking the policies of the court. Charles II and his brother James, Lord High Admiral from 1660 to 1673, favoured the appointment of 'gentleman captains', men drawn from aristocratic or gentry families but not necessarily possessing much knowledge or experience of the sea, and certainly not possessing De Ruyter's modest attributes. This policy was politically controversial, and attacks on the competence of the 'gentlemen', so different to the consummate seaman De Ruyter, could also be coded ways of attacking the nature and policy of the Stuart regime[38].

As it was, the closest English equivalent to De Ruyter was probably Sir John Lawson, a Yorkshireman who had risen from skippering east coast colliers to a knighthood and the command of fleets, albeit in peacetime (1659-60) and the Mediterranean (1662-4). However, Lawson was probably too politically naïve and undermined by his republican and religiously unorthodox background to achieve a similar status in Restoration England; in any case, Lawson was killed at the very outset of the second war, long before he could take command of the main fleet in battle and assume the hypothetical mantle of an 'English De Ruyter'[39]. The contemporary English biographer seemed to identify this possible parallel when he compared the conduct of Lawson and De Ruyter at the battle of the Gabbard (June 1653), when the squadrons of the two men went head-to-head, and claimed that they 'fought singly with such courage and emulation as might be expected from two commanders of so much fame and honour'[40]. Sir John Harman also rose from humble origins and was eventually placed in supreme command of an entire fleet – but only in the autumn of

1673, when the campaign (and the war) was effectively over, and then only for a few weeks before his death[41]. Sir Robert Holmes and Sir Edward Spragge both undoubtedly possessed some of De Ruyter's charisma and flair for the bold stroke, but they were both seriously flawed characters (as their detestation of each other proved), too rapacious and factional ever to be serious candidates for fleet command; both were also Irish, and regardless of their achievements, that damned them out of hand in the eyes of many Englishmen[42].

The generals-at-sea Robert Blake and Richard Deane undoubtedly had the stature and ability to have matched De Ruyter, but they were of an earlier time, and both were dead long before De Ruyter assumed the supreme command. De Ruyter's biographer commented on what may have been the only meeting between the Dutch admiral and Blake, the English general-at-sea, which took place in the Straits in 1655: 'they saluted each other, shook hands, and parted on very good terms'[43]. But in the 1660s and 1670s, neither Blake nor Deane were likely to be held up, even posthumously, as rivals for De Ruyter's mantle. After the Restoration, both generals-at-sea were reviled as servants of the hated Commonwealth; the reputation of Deane, who had signed Charles I's death warrant and was thus damned as a regicide, suffered above all, but even Blake's corpse was exhumed from Westminster Abbey and, with Deane's, was thrown into a common grave during a fit of misdirected cavalier wrath. Thus a combination of politics, mortality, and pure luck ensured that during the second and third Anglo-Dutch wars, Michiel de Ruyter simply had no equal in achievements or reputation across the North Sea. This made it easier to cast him as the 'good enemy' in much the same way that stereotypical British portrayals of the enemy during the First and Second World Wars often focused on 'the good German', and found particularly fitting candidates for the role in Manfred von Richthofen and Erwin Rommel.

■ De Ruyter and British politics

In fact, De Ruyter was not quite as apolitical as he seemed. His politics were essentially republican, or more accurately those of the 'state's party' that upheld 'the True Freedom', and this provided a dangerous extra dimension to his professional rivalry with Cornelis Tromp, a staunch Orangist[44]. Charles II's policy from 1660 until 1672 was erratically pro-Orange, if only to the extent that he increasingly envisaged a much reduced rump of the Dutch state under the nominal rule of a suitably amenable Orange puppet, but this does not seem to have particularly affected the way in which Britain's rulers regarded De Ruyter (and Tromp, come to that). After all, De Ruyter was 'almost British', having been born in a cautionary town under English control, and his anonymous contemporary biographer even claimed that his father had been 'a stranger, by some judged a Scottish man', though this may have been a tortuous conflation of the admiral's undisputed Irish connections[45]. Moreover, in the 1660s and 1670s the history of the cautionary towns was no longer just a dim and irrelevant memory[46]. One of the more curious aspects of Charles II's policy of annihilating the United Provinces, which almost came to fruition in the *rampjaar* (year of disaster) of 1672 thanks to the efforts of the French army, was the scheme to bring the cautionary towns, and perhaps the whole province of Zeeland, under direct English rule, with the unmissable opportunity of returning MPs to the House of Commons[47]. It is not inconceivable that Charles II even imagined Michiel De Ruyter as both an admiral of his own fleet and as the duly elected Member of Parliament for the constituency of 'Flushing'.

Regardless of the rather bizarre political fantasies in which the king might have indulged during the years 1670-2, contemporaries were certainly well aware of the various dimensions of the rivalry between Tromp and De Ruyter, and perhaps this was demonstrated most clearly in the convoluted saga of the English honours bestowed on both men. The fact that De Ruyter was seen as a noble opponent, who thus possessed all the traditional English knightly virtues, was carried to its logical conclusion by Charles II's direct offer of a knighthood. This followed a precedent established in 1642, when King Charles I had knighted Maerten Tromp[48]. The honour seems to have been first offered to De Ruyter in 1668, but he turned it down, and it was bestowed instead on his son Engel, who had no opportunity at that point to

accept an honour which transformed him (as far as English clerks were concerned) into 'Sir Angel De Ruyter'[49]. After the conclusion of the third Anglo-Dutch war in 1674, Charles II moved rapidly towards a rapprochement with the United Provinces, though this hardly accorded with his personal inclinations; it was a price he had to pay for better relations with (and thus more money from) Parliament, and the policy advocated by his new chief minister, the earl of Danby. De Ruyter was invited to come to England, but, according to Brandt, his first Dutch biographer, he declined both this and any honours that might accompany it, as he 'did not care for courts and preferred a plain burgher's life'[50].

An identical invitation was issued to Cornelis Tromp, the son of 'Sir Martin Tromp'. He had none of De Ruyter's misgivings, and visited England in January and February 1675[51]. He was well received at court, became particularly friendly with the earl of Ossory (who had commanded a squadron in the most recent war), was feted by the University of Oxford, and even dined with Sir Robert Holmes, the man blamed by some for starting both the second and third Anglo-Dutch wars[52]. However, he did not impress the town youths of Oxford, who found that for all his fame, Tromp was merely 'a drinking greasy Dutchman'[53]. Sir Ralph Verney provided a rather more subjective and political explanation for the cool reception that Tromp received in more exalted quarters:

> "...the King is very kind to him, but the duke [of York] is hardly civil; for the duke
> is of De Ruyter's faction, and you know that he and Trump could never agree.
> De Ruyter is a great admirer of the duke, and hath often professed, if ever he hath
> a convenient kind of leisure, he will make a journey hither purposely to attend his
> Highness".[54]

This is perhaps the only recorded instance of James Stuart being counted a member of a faction that was even vaguely 'republican' in nature.

From the viewpoint of those who had invited him, Tromp's visit had a deeper political agenda to it, and De Ruyter was probably well advised to have declined the invitation. Tromp was cultivated quite blatantly as a prospective intermediary between Charles II and his nephew, William of Orange, and was bombarded with suggestions that William should not blindly follow Dutch national interests alone, the implicit message being that he should follow his uncle's instead. This unsubtle attempt to cultivate Tromp culminated in a gift of £1,000 and the award of a baronetcy, ultimately confirmed on 23 April/3 May, and a measure of the regard in which the admiral was held by the English court was an unusual grant of a special remainder to Tromp's two brothers (baronetcies normally descended to male issue alone)[55]. Even so, Charles II was determined to be seen as even-handed between Tromp and De Ruyter, and thus between the rival factions in the Dutch state. The letters patent confirming that Engel de Ruyter had been knighted in 1668 were conferred at Whitehall on 22 February/4 March 1675, two days after Tromp took his leave of the king, thanks to the useful coincidence that had seen the younger De Ruyter's fleet arrive at Plymouth late in January[56].

■ Conclusion: Britain and the death of De Ruyter

Perhaps surprisingly in the light of the reputation that he had enjoyed, the death of De Ruyter seems to have been little remarked in Britain. The first word of it seems to have been brought by the Hellevoetsluis – Harwich packet boat which arrived on 27 May/6 June 1676, but the event was barely reported in the *London Gazette*, and there is little comment in other contemporary sources[57]. The fact that his last battle had been a defeat, and a defeat at the hands of the French of all people, might have contributed to the neglect; following the controversial events of the third Anglo-Dutch war, many Britons regarded the French navy with unbridled contempt. Nevertheless, within a year De Ruyter's anonymous English biographer had produced a fitting tribute to the man, although like the saga of the honours for Tromp and De Ruyter, this was very much a product of the political circumstances of its times. Showering lavish posthumous praise upon the Netherlands' greatest hero in a work published in 1677 was undoubtedly connected intimately to the marriage in the same year of William III of Orange and the Princess Mary, niece and reversionary heir presumptive to King Charles II; the decision by the anonymous author to omit all mention of the Medway raid ten years earlier can only have been a response to the delicate political sensibilities surrounding the new Anglo-Dutch alliance that the marriage cemented[58]. But regardless of the political agenda that underpinned its publication, the biography provided an exemplary summary of the regard in which the Dutch admiral had been held by his recent opponents:

> *"He was so good a man, so devout and pious a Christian, so stout a soldier, so wise, expert and successful a general; and so faithful, trusty and honest a lover of his country, that he deserves justly to be recommended to posterity, as an ornament of his age, the darling of the seas, and the delight and honour of his country".*[59]

Meanwhile, Michiel Adriaenszoon de Ruyter had returned to Britain one last time. On 14 December 1676, it was reported from Portsmouth that three Dutch warships had anchored at Spithead (where they became icebound), and that the flagship *Eendracht* was carrying the admiral's corpse[60]. Almost exactly 129 years later to the day, the body of another truly great seaman would rest in the same waters before beginning its final journey[61].

The first stage of the battle of the Sound, 1658.

Painting attributed to J.A. Beerstraten, around 1660, Nederlands Scheepvaart-museum, Amsterdam

CHAPTER 7

Danish Perspectives on De Ruyter's Role in the Nordic Conflicts[1]

Niels M. Probst

Michiel de Ruyter's service on the Danish side during the war against Sweden in 1659-60 is well documented but what was perhaps his most important contribution to the Danish navy started much earlier. In 1652 England declared war on the Netherlands starting what was later termed the First Anglo-Dutch war. In 1649 the Netherlands and Denmark signed the Redemption Treaty whereby Dutch shipping was exempted from the Sound Tolls. In conjunction an alliance treaty was signed whereby the Netherlands and Denmark agreed to provide mutual support, specified as 4,000 soldiers, in case either country was attacked by a foreign state. At the outbreak of the war against the English Denmark thus became an ally of the Netherlands. In this war neither England nor the Netherlands had any plans to invade each other's territories so the Dutch emissary in Copenhagen stated that instead of soldiers his country preferred naval support. This was duly given. A sizeable Danish squadron was equipped and put to sea but because the Redemption Treaty had proved just as damaging to Swedish as it had been to English trade, the squadron never went west of Skagerrak. It stayed in Danish waters to curb any Swedish temptation to assault Denmark with most of her navy absent.

By 1652 a 23 years old Danish nobleman by the name of Niels Juel, previously a page to the later king of Denmark, had completed his obligatory educational tour of European universities. He set out to find foreign military service and in that year the natural choice was the Netherlands. According to the long and detailed oration delivered at Niels Juel's funeral, the only source available on his early life, he arrived in Amsterdam during the autumn of 1652 and then participated in four of the naval battles against the English. These must have been the battles of Dungeness in December, 1652, Portland in February, 1653, Gabbard in June, 1653, and finally Scheveningen in August, 1653. During the first two of these battles both fleets seem to have employed traditional frontal tactics, engaging their opponents head on. In the last two the English ranged their fleet in a single line of battle even when they had the opportunity of being to windward. In that formation they could, thanks to their more powerful artillery, prevent the Dutch from coming close enough to attack. Niels Juel's first hand experience of the battles between the relatively small, lightly-built and lightly-armed Dutch ships against the strongly-built and heavily-armed purpose-built English warships no doubt provided him with lessons which would contribute to his later success that earned him the reputation of being the greatest Danish fleet commander.

Niels Juel must have served with some distinction because in 1654 the Danish government awarded him the title of *Junker* with a yearly allowance of 450 *Rigsdalers* and four court dresses. The allowance was equal to that of a senior naval captain. Which ships and under which commanders Niels Juel served during the war is not known but he must at least have met Michiel de Ruyter because it was in his squadron he went to the Mediterranean in the spring of 1654. Although the age difference between the two men was 22 years they had many characteristics in common. Sober-mindedness, utter professionalism and modesty paired with a sense of humour were some of them. The purpose of the Mediterranean expedition was to curb the attacks by Barbary pirates on Dutch shipping. It ended in December, 1654. The following year De Ruyter again went to the Mediterranean with a squadron and Niels Juel also took part in that expedition. The funeral oration reports that he distinguished himself in a heavy fight which led to the capture of a notorious Spanish-born pirate named Oman Diaz. After this action Niels Juel was promoted to

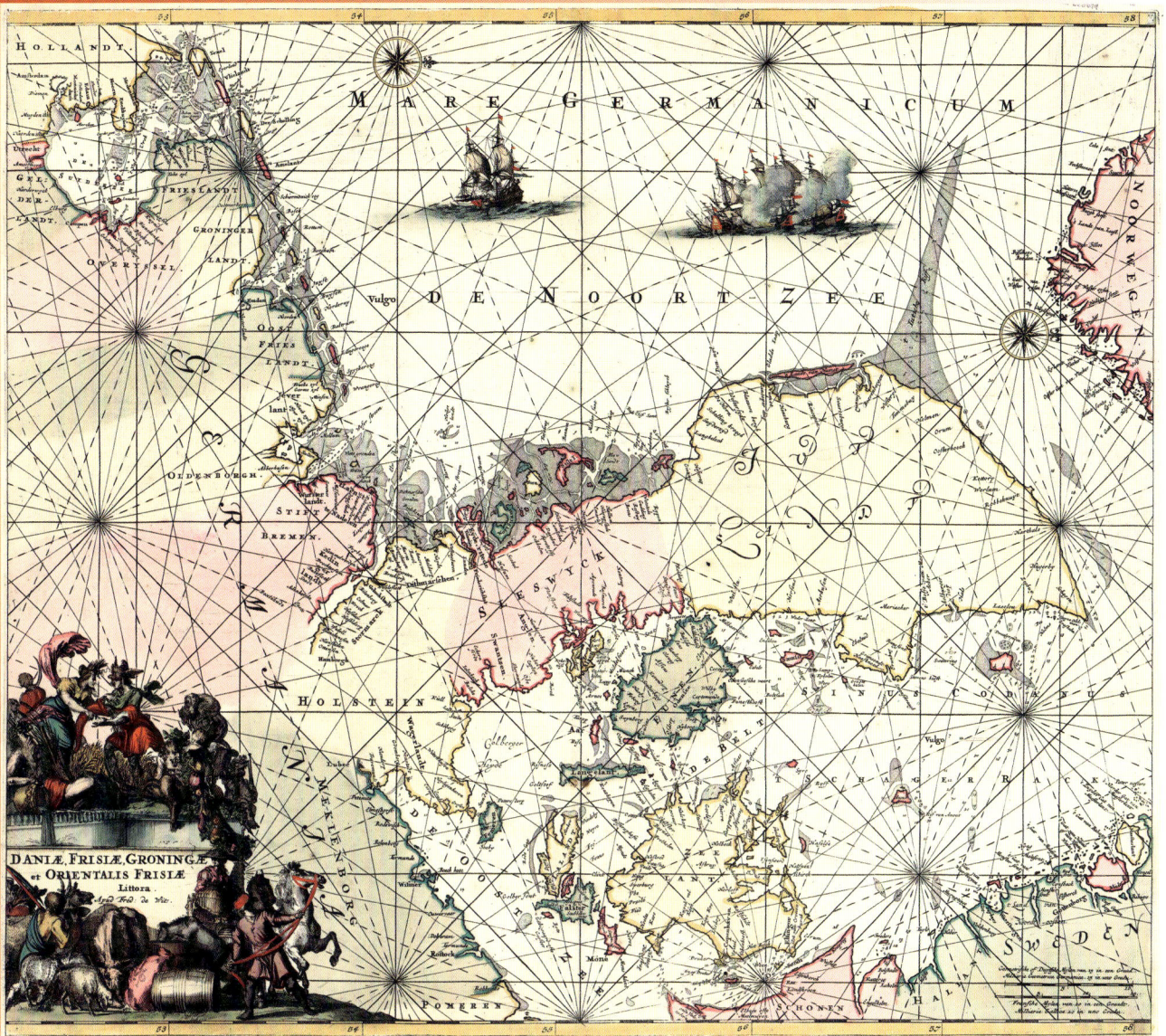

Map of Denmark and surrounding lands and waters.

Print by Frederick de Widt, around 1660, Map Collection, University of Amsterdam

oberkaptain. What exactly that title meant is open to question. It seems hardly likely that a 27 year old foreigner, however proficient, could have been given command of a Dutch warship but perhaps it indicates that he became captain of De Ruyter's flagship. The expedition ended early in May, 1656, and already by the 31st of the month De Ruyter was in command of the strong vanguard of a large Dutch fleet heading for the Baltic, probably with Niels Juel on board.

The purpose of the Gdańsk expedition of 1656 was to break a blockade of the port which the Swedes had established the previous year in connection with the Polish campaign of their king, Carl X Gustav. He had ascended the Swedish throne in 1654 on the recommendation of his cousin, Queen Christina, who had been forced to resign when she converted to Roman Catholicism. Carl X Gustav, a count from the Palatinate in Germany, had spent most of his adult life fighting in the Swedish army during the Thirty Years' War. It was an army he never left for long. Extremely martial, during his entire reign he only spent a few months in Sweden. The trade through Gdańsk was extremely important especially to the Dutch but the blockade was also

against Danish interests. Swedish attempts to dominate the Baltic in general were seen in Copenhagen and The Hague as a major threat. So during the spring of 1656 a general plan was taking shape whereby the concerted action of a combined Dutch-Danish fleet was to force the Swedes to lift the blockade.

De Ruyter's two squadrons totalling 25 ships anchored at the so-called *Lappe-grund* just northwest of Elsinore on June 8. The day after De Ruyter and some companions went by road to Copenhagen. After reporting to the Dutch embassy there,

they were allowed to inspect the naval base and on the following day they visited the
Danish admiral Christoffer Lindenow who treated them courteously. A week later,
on June 17, Niels Juel received his first command in the Danish navy. He was to
embark on the light warship *Sorte Rytter* where he was to supervise its fitting out,
aided by two lieutenants.

On June 27, 1656, the main Dutch fleet under Admiral Jacob van Wassenaer-
Obdam arrived in the Sound. That brought the total Dutch fleet up to an impressive

42 ships. Apart from Michiel de Ruyter, the squadron commanders included well known figures such as Cornelis Tromp, Witte de With and Pieter Florisz. The Swedish ambassador in Copenhagen was both shaken and impressed by seeing "the most illustrious 'sea cocks' here in the middle of the King of Denmark's land and on its seas"[2]. Obdam's preliminary orders dated April 19 instructed him to support Denmark in case it was attacked by "a foreign sea power", and to stay in Danish waters until he received final orders. The latter he received on July 18. The fleet was to proceed to Copenhagen and soon an agreement was reached by the allies to make a united stand against the Swedes off Gdańsk whose city council had pleaded for help both from the Netherlands and Denmark. Here Denmark had the chance, together with a powerful ally, to effectively curb Swedish attempts to dominate the Baltic. To the great disappointment of the Dutch, the Danish King Frederik III (1648-60) decided to send seven or eight warships fully fitted out on a journey to Norway carrying the young prince who was successor to the throne so people there could pay homage to him. Not until those ships had returned at the end of August could a Danish squadron be sent to Gdańsk.

So when the great fleet set sail for Gdańsk on July 23 it included no Danish ships. Nonetheless, the operation proved to be an easy one. From the middle of May the Swedish blockading force off Gdańsk had only numbered three ships and when Obdam arrived on July 27 they seemed to have left. Although the Swedes had managed to equip a fleet of 19 ships in Stockholm, most of them were in such poor condition that they could not serve on the high seas. The Swedish navy was thus confined to protecting the access to Stockholm against a feared Dutch attack. It was not until September 8 that a Danish squadron of ten ships, including Niels Juel's *Sorte Rytter*, under Admiral Christoffer Lindenow set sail for Gdańsk where he arrived on September 11. The effort proved fruitless because on the same day the Dutch had concluded the Treaty of Elbløg with Sweden. Although Denmark was mentioned in this treaty, it primarily benefitted the Netherlands.

Lindenow's orders were to stay off Gdańsk for no more that 14 days. So on September 25 he set course for Copenhagen. Obdam stayed until September 26, when he departed, leaving a squadron of 12 ships under Tromp which stayed on station off Gdańsk for another month. On October 17 De Ruyter had a meeting with King Frederik III who impressed the Admiral as "a very splendid potentate to talk with"[3]. A suggestion made late in September by the State Council (rigsrådet) to furnish the navy with a competent and experienced officer "...where to we now know no one better to suggest than De Ruyter"[4], does not seem to have been acted on.

War broke out between Denmark and Sweden in 1657. The hostilities between 1657 and 1660 actually consisted of two distinct wars which were closely connected although the first one did not involve the Netherlands. The Danish King Frederik III, who had no doubts and rightfully so, that the next target for his belligerent Swedish colleague would be Denmark, decided when reports came back that the Swedish campaign in Poland had run into difficulties, to take the offensive. In the spring of 1657 Denmark prepared for war. The ships of the navy were repaired and equipped, sailors and soldiers were hired, and the army was mobilized. Not all members of the State Council agreed with the decision to go to war. Among those opposed was Admiral Christoffer Lindenow who as a result fell into disgrace with the king. His post as chief of the main naval base at Copenhagen (*Holmens Admiral*) was taken over by the only 29 year old Niels Juel. This very early promotion to admiral indi-

Witte Wittenson

cates that reports on Juel's service under De Ruyter must have been very favourable indeed. For various reasons, mainly political, though he had to wait many years before reaching his deserved position as commander of the entire Danish navy.

It was not until June 15, 1657 that Denmark declared war on Sweden but in late May Niels Juel was already commanding a squadron in the Sound where he took three Swedish prizes. The tasks of the navy in the war were well defined. The Swedish lines of communication on the Baltic were to be severed and when the Swedish main fleet appeared, Danish command of the sea was to be maintained. The navy did well. Under Admiral Henrik Bjelke with Niels Juel as one of the squadron commanders, it harassed Swedish communication along the southern coast of the Baltic, and on September 23-24 it met the Swedish main fleet in battle south of Falsterbo. In spite of Swedish superiority in resources of some 27%, the battle ended in a draw. While the Danish fleet remained at sea after the battle, the Swedes retreated into the Swedish-held harbour of Wismar. The Danish navy bottled up the enemy there until extremely cold and stormy weather forced both fleets to return to their bases early in December.

Unfortunately the army had no such success. Before the war Denmark assembled a large hired army in Holstein. The most logical plan was a massive advance eastward but King Frederik advised an attack on his previous bishoprics of Bremen and Verden. That meant the army was divided. The bishoprics were duly taken but in the meantime Carl Gustav had made his move. Even before he launched the Polish campaign the king of Sweden and his State Council had decided that if Denmark attacked Carl Gustav would drop everything and attack Denmark with his entire army. So when on August 1 he suddenly crossed the border of Holstein with his army of 8,000 seasoned soldiers, the Danish army was unprepared and divided and had to retreat northward into the newly fortified camp at Frederiksodde (present-day Fredericia) on the east coast of Jutland without offering any serious resistance. The Swedish troops rapidly occupied Jutland and late in October Frederiksodde fell. The Danes lost 1,100 men killed and 4,000 captured.

The situation was now almost identical to that during the Thirty Years War in the late 1620's and the Torstenson War of 1643-45 with Jutland wholly occupied by foreign troops. In the earlier cases the navy had been able to effectively stop any advance across the Little and Great Belts but this time those waters froze solid. The winter of 1657-8 was one of the coldest ever during the "Little Ice Age". The thick ice not only prevented any naval operations but also allowed the daring Swedes to cross the Belts. First they attacked the island of Fyn where the defence was quickly overcome. Second they took the island of Lolland and from there they went on to Zealand. Whereas the crossing of Little Belt to Fyn involved a calculable risk the decision to cross the Great Belt to Falster was bordering on the irresponsible. A thaw had set in and only some 5,000 men got across whereas there was a Danish force of some 7,000 soldiers in Copenhagen alone. In case of defeat a Swedish retreat would have been difficult if not impossible. Considering the previous Danish military performance on land Carl Gustav's confidence in his troops is understandable. Indeed, his gamble paid off. The Danish government panicked and on February 28 an armistice was signed. The following negotiations led to the Roskilde Peace Treaty, signed on March 6. The kingdom of Denmark ceded about 1/3 of its territory, including all lands east of the Sound, to Sweden.

During the spring and early summer of 1658 Swedish troops withdrew from Denmark even though the negotiations for the Roskilde Treaty had not yet been

finalised. Disagreements arose mostly about a Swedish requirement that Denmark would provide 10 "well armed warships" if and when a foreign navy tried to enter the Baltic. The Treaty required that the Swedish and Danish navies should unite and "no foreign navy should [be allowed to] force its way through the Sound or the Belts"[5]. This would in reality have given Sweden unlimited domination of the Baltic and so the Danish negotiators refused to sign. Then Carl Gustav changed his mind. Strongly supported by his primary military advisors he decided to attack Denmark again, this time aiming to bring the whole country under Swedish rule. In Kiel a force of 4,000 foot soldiers and 1,200 cavalry set sail in a large number of small craft escorted by a squadron of 11 warships. On August 17 they landed the troops at Korsør on the west coast of Zealand. The warships went to the Sound where they established a blockade of Copenhagen. Carl Gustav led his army towards Copenhagen, which he reached on August 21. Here the suburbs had been set on fire and the king of Sweden realized that this time the Danes were prepared to resist. He nevertheless established a siege and soon most of Denmark, apart from Copenhagen and the castle of Kronborg, was once more occupied by Swedish troops.

In the long run Copenhagen could only hold out if the blockade was broken and that could only be accomplished with help from abroad. The first war had been started by King Frederik III. During that war the 1649 treaty with the Netherlands had therefore not been applicable. This time however, Denmark had been attacked by a foreign power. Moreover, the Dutch did not wish to let Sweden occupy both sides of the Sound. So on August 30, at a meeting called by the States General, the Dutch province states agreed to send a large fleet and an army of 2,200 men to the relief of Copenhagen. On November 2 a fleet under Admiral Obdam anchored at Lappen waiting for a favourable wind to enter the Sound. The fleet consisted of 35 warships, four fireships and 12 merchantmen loaded with provisions and soldiers. Over the next few days the Swedish main fleet assembled south of Kronborg, the castle having fallen by that point into Swedish hands. Under the command of State Admiral Karl Gustav Wrangel the Swedish fleet consisted of 43 warships and six fireships and galiots. So the Swedes had about 12% more warships than the Dutch and their vessels were generally larger and carried 26% more guns. In Copenhagen Denmark had equipped a squadron of seven ships. When the Swedish ships went north to Kronborg this squadron, led by Admiral Henrik Bjelke, went to sea on November 6.

On November 8 the wind at last went to north northwest and Obdam ordered his fleet to set sail. The famous Battle of the Sound could begin. The battle proved to be one of the hardest fought and most bloody ever in Nordic waters. Two of the three Dutch admirals were killed and according to a Swedish source one of them, the veteran Witte de With at one time said that "...here it [the fighting] was somewhat sharper than in any of the [battles of the] English and Spanish wars". Others said that this had not been a regular but a murderous fight[6]. The battle was fought in the northern part of the Sound, between Kronborg and the island of Hven. It lasted for about five hours. In the meantime the Danish squadron, held back by the northerly wind, managed to get as far as Hven, and according to both Carl Gustav and Karl Gustav Wrangel, the sight of these fresh ships caused the Swedes to break off the engagement. Although the Danish ships did not actually enter the fight, their presence was decisive. In fact Obdam's flagship *Eendracht* was at that time so severely damaged that it could hardly have survived any further attacks.

The allied fleet and all the transports reached Copenhagen without further incident. The Swedish fleet went to Landskrona to repair damage. When an allied Dutch-Danish fleet of some 29 ships appeared off Landskrona a few days after the battle most of the Swedish ships were already in the harbour and so the allies set up a blockade. On November 13 Obdam, who suffered from rheumatism, decided to leave the allied fleet, letting Admiral Henrik Bjelke take command, something which probably did not suit the admiralties in the Netherlands. Later a largely unsuccessful attempt was made to block the harbour entrance to Landskrona with old stone-filled hulks and when frost set in on December 10 the fleet was recalled to Copenhagen where it was laid up for the winter.

In fact the situation for Carl Gustav had by now become quite precarious. Command of the sea was lost and in Jutland the Elector of Brandenburg with an army of 30,000 men had forced the Swedes to retreat into Frederiksodde, a fortress they knew was not impregnable. Although both the Danish and Swedish sides made moves towards peace negotiations, the aggressive Swedish king still had plans to attack. If he could take Copenhagen he thought both the Dutch and the Danish fleets would be his, and he would then possess the largest navy in the world. That he might have had trouble with the loyalty of men and commanders does not seem to have entered his mind. So the siege of Copenhagen was maintained and on the night of February 20-21, 1659, the Swedes mounted an all-out attack on the city. It failed, costing heavy casualties not least thanks to the bravery of the Dutch soldiers and sailors. Despite the losses Carl Gustav continued the siege.

At the end of March an allied squadron of some 10-12 ships under Nikolaj Helt left Copenhagen in order to join four ships which had wintered over in Flensborg Fjord. Not long after the main Swedish fleet of 27 ships under Klas Hansson Bjelkenstierna left Landskrona and took up station in the western Baltic between Femern and Langeland, bottling Helt up in Flensborg Fjord. The allied forces in Copenhagen suffered from a lack of sailors and so it was not until May 7 that they succeeded in putting a fleet of 26 ships to sea. Obdam and Henrik Bjelke were in command. Niels Juel, who had not been to sea at all in 1658, served as Bjelke's viceadmiral. Bjelke's orders were to join Helt's squadron, which now consisted of 17 ships, and then seek out and destroy the Swedish fleet. The presence of the Swedish fleet effectively prevented the allied fleet, coming from the East, from joining up with Helt's squadron so the allies were forced to do battle with the ships they had in hand. The Battle of Rødsand was fought on May 10. The wind was east southeast giving the allies an advantage but it was blowing so hard that they could not open their lower gunports whereas the Swedes, lying to leeward, had no such problem. Early in the battle Bjelkenstierna was seriously wounded so the leader of his van, Gustav Wrangel, a brother of State Admiral Karl Gustav Wrangel, had to take command. During a lull Gustav Wrangel succeeded in getting to windward which may have been in accordance with theoretically the best strategy but now it was his turn to be unable to use the lower batteries. On top of that he was no longer able to stop the allies from joining Helt's squadron. The battle ended as darkness fell, the Swedes retiring north through the Great Belt while the allied fleet set course for Flensborg Fjord. Already before the battle King Carl Gustav had given orders that in case the allied force succeeded in joining the ships in Flensborg Fjord the Swedish fleet should retire to the Sound. Gustav Wrangel followed this order and on May 30 his fleet entered the harbour of Landskrona not to reappear in force at sea during the rest of the war.

A squadron of six allied ships was detached from the main fleet and sent to the Little Belt where they were placed at the disposal of the Elector of Brandenburg. He was planning an invasion of Fyn. The rest of the fleet went to the Great Belt where on May 10 an unsuccessful attempt was made to relieve the castle of Nakskov which was holding out against the Swedes. This was however to be the last allied fleet action for the next three months. The reason for the inactivity was an intervention by the two western powers, England and France, who wanted the hostilities to cease. Negotiations between those two and the Netherlands resulted in an agreement signed on May 21. The Concert of The Hague was an agreement among the signatories to try to persuade the two Nordic kings to initiate peace negotiations on the basis of the Roskilde Treaty. The Concert was followed by two extensions, the latter running until late August. In the meantime the Dutch fleet was not allowed to carry out hostile action against the Swedes. The agreements were certainly not to the taste of the Netherlands, but they were enforced by England which had already in April placed a large fleet of 44 ships at the entrance to the Sound. Obdam was not to know the full contents of the Concert of The Hague until June 8 and at the same time he was informed that De Ruyter's fleet had reached the island of Læsø in northern Kattegat.

The Huys te Swieten, the flagship of Michiel de Ruyter during the 1650's, in the company of other Dutch warships.

Painting by Willlem van de Velde the Younger, 1658, Kröller Müller Museum, Otterlo

Obdam was quite shocked by the contents of the Concert which he correctly saw favoured Sweden because the Danish navy was far too weak to mount offensive action on its own.

On June 23 De Ruyter's fleet joined that of Obdam and Bjelke off the island of Romsø in the northern part of the Great Belt. The decision to send De Ruyter's fleet was in part because of the English naval intervention and in part because even before Obdam's departure for Denmark in 1658 it was clear that the 2,200 soldiers he claimed to carry did not meet either the obligations of the 1649 Defence Treaty which had stipulated 4,000 troops or the Ampliation Treaty of June 27, 1657, in which the army contingent was increased to 6,000 "well equipped and well armed footmen"[7] . Frederik III had even complained that instead of the planned 2,200 soldiers Obdam had actually arrived with only some 1,200-1,300 men. In late 1658 plans were made to send a Dutch squadron of four warships and ten armed transports to Denmark with the rest of the troops and Obdam then returning to the Netherlands leaving only 12 Dutch warships to winter in Denmark. The Danish government had specially asked that De Ruyter should be given command of the new force. Cold weather and ice prevented the execution of the plan just as it had thwarted English plans at the time for sending a squadron to northern waters. De Ruyter was ordered to disembark his troops and Obdam was instructed to remain in Copenhagen and assist in the defence of the town. On March 10 renewed Swedish activities before Copenhagen along with rumours that a large English fleet was about to be sent to northern waters caused the

Letter granting Danish noble status to Michiel de Ruyter, 1660.

National Archive, The Hague

Netherlands to decide that a much larger fleet should be sent to Denmark. In the end the fleet was so large that it had to be divided into three squadrons. Johan Evertsen and Jan Cornelisz Meppel were appointed vice-admirals commanding two of the squadrons. Although Johan Evertsen was senior to De Ruyter, the latter was chosen overall fleet commander at the insistence of the States of Holland and the request of the Danish Government[8]. On May 20 De Ruyter set sail from Texel with a fleet of 38 warships, a few fire ships and transports carrying 4,000 soldiers with provisions. Two days later De Ruyter was informed by the Dutch ambassador to Denmark, Govert van Slingelandt about the contents of the Concert of The Hague. The ambassador also brought detailed instructions from the Grand Pensionary Johan de Witt who, contrary to a paragraph in the Concert which forbade uniting De Ruyter's and Obdam's fleets, advised the Dutch admirals to find a way to prevent any Swedish or English attempts to drive a wedge between the two fleets. The two men were, however, to be careful to avoid any direct confrontations with the English.[9]

Shortly after the two Dutch fleets linked up some Swedish ships were observed off the island of Endelave north of Fyn. Obdam and De Ruyter went northwest to intercept them but the English fleet appeared preventing further action. Then two Dutch ships, *Deutecum* and *Jonge Prins*, were sent to escort a third ship carrying two Danish delegates to the Elector of Brandenburg who was then in Jutland. On July 6 Obdam and Bjelke went south through the Great Belt towards Copenhagen which they reached on July 13. De Ruyter followed, arriving on July 16. In those days large English ships were unable to navigate the Great Belt and that only became possible after Nelson had done a thorough survey of the waters in 1801.

While the Concert of The Hague and its extensions paralyzed the allies, King Carl Gustav did not allow them to restrict his activities. During the period when the agreement was in force he sent out three different squadrons from the fleet at Landskrona. The first under Gustav Wrangel had orders to attack the allied ships in the Little Belt. It was his ships that were sighted by the allies off Endelave. On his way westward on June 24 Wrangel encountered the Dutch escorts, probably on their way eastward, and attacked them. *Deutecum* was set on fire and *Jonge Prins* was severely damaged but managed to escape into Horsens Fjord on the east coast of Jutland. Two days later Wrangel reached the entrance to the Little Belt but calm prevented him from entering the Belt where preparations for the invasion of Fyn continued undisturbed. On June 29 the Concert of The Hague was running out so Karl Gustav Wrangel, who was on Fyn, decided to order his brother home. The next day Gustav Wrangel arrived at Landskrona where a furious king Carl Gustav put him under arrest. He was never again given a naval command.

The second squadron under the command of Clas Uggla, later to become known as an accomplished naval commander, left Landskrona on July 7 and set course towards the Baltic. Here he was unfortunate enough to run into the fleets of both Obdam and later that of De Ruyter, which were at that time on their way eastwards to Copenhagen. The English were unable to enter the Baltic, so the allied fleets pursued Uggla, forcing him to retire into the harbour of Ystad on the south coast of Skåne. The third squadron, led by the Englishman Owen Coxe, had more luck. On August 2 he surprised most of the allied Little Belt squadron at Ebeltoft on the east coast of Jutland where it was embarking troops for the planned invasion of Fyn. He destroyed the allied squadron, the ships being either burned or taken, and the Swedes captured 1,000 Imperial and Brandenburg troops. As a result the invasion of Fyn had to be postponed for the time being.

On September 3 the last extension of the Concert of The Hague ran out and when news of Lord Protector Richard Cromwell's resignation reached the English fleet commander he immediately took his fleet home. That put the initiative back into the hands of the allies. De Ruyter soon after the departure established a blockade of Landskrona. In August Obdam and Bjelke had been busy escorting small ships with provisions and troops from northern Germany to Copenhagen but after the English fleet left they went to the Kattegat where they spent September on convoy duty, escorting Dutch shipping. In the beginning of October they joined De Ruyter after which Bjelke stayed with De Ruyter while Obdam went to Copenhagen to prepare for his journey back to the Netherlands with 20 ships. The 48 ships which were to stay in northern waters were deemed sufficient for the forthcoming operations to drive the Swedes from the islands. After Obdam had received the thanks of King Frederik III in the form of various honours, the promise of a sum of 12,000 *Rigsdalers* and a yearly pen-

Niels Juel at age eighteen.

Painting by an unknown artist, around 1647,
Valdemars Slot Museum, Denmark

sion of 1,200 *Rigsdalers*,[10] he set course for home on November 1 leaving De Ruyter as supreme commander of all Dutch armed forces in northern waters.

In the beginning of October De Ruyter left Copenhagen with an invasion fleet of 39 Dutch warships, the solitary Danish warship *Spes* and 76 transports. On board *Spes* was the designated leader of the land forces, Field Marshall Hans Schack and "all the artillery". A few Danish warships were left in Copenhagen to thwart any Swedish attempts at blockade. In Femern Belt Bjelke joined De Ruyter's fleet with two capital ships and together they went to Kiel. There they spent a fortnight provisioning and embarking troops for the invasion of Fyn. Schack was on board Bjelke's flagship and there on November 7 the commanders worked out a detailed plan for the coming invasion. When Bjelke hoisted a yellow and the Dutch admirals a red flag, aft all the ships would follow in line with the transport ships carrying the Danish infantry and their artillery in front but close to Bjelke's and his vice admiral Helt's ships followed by ten large boats from De Ruyters fleet, each armed with a large cannon. The transport ships with the Dutch infantry, supported by 20 similar big boats, would stay close behind the Danish ships followed by De Ruyter's warships. The troops would embark in the boats. When the admirals let pennants fly from the yard arms everyone would make ready and when each admiral fired a big gun the boats would push off and head for the beach. They would be followed in as far as possible by those small ships which carried guns. Later the cavalry would be set ashore[11].

About noon on November 8 the fleet reached Nyborg, which Schack decided to attack. 2,000 men were embarked in boats which took some time. Darkness fell, the weather turned foggy and no one seemed to know the way into the harbour. The Swedes opened fire on the ships, shooting down the main yard on rear admiral Jan Thijszoon's ship and hitting his cabin with a 24 pound shot. Several shots flew over De Ruyter's flagship which took a hit one foot below the waterline. The ships returned the fire but could not see the enemy. The attack had to be aborted but as the wind had come up the freezing men had to stay in the boats until morning. Then the fleet retreated eastward and a war council was held aboard Bjelke's flagship. At this point it was concluded that by now the enemy had probably gathered such strong forces in Nyborg that a renewed attack was not advisable. Instead it was decided to head north towards the small town Kerteminde on the north east coast of Fyn.

Just after noon on November 10, the allied fleet, following the south side of the Bay of Kerteminde, drove a large Swedish force of eight cavalry regiments away from the shore with gun fire. Then the town of Kerteminde was bombarded so heavily that it almost disappeared from view in the rising smoke and dust. This time a man who knew the locality, captain Peder Jensen Kierteminde, had been found. The previous day he had surveyed the entrance to the harbour and now he was in the lead boat, showing the troops the best place to land. As the boats approached the shore the ships had to cease firing, the critical moment in any invasion. Now the enemy, consisting of two dragoon regiments which had taken up positions behind two dikes, could fire freely on the attackers who could only return fire with the small guns in the boats. Fortunately for the attackers there were proportionally few Swedes but at one point the issue was in doubt. The heavily loaded boats could not get as close to the shore as had been anticipated and the spirit of the soldiers began to falter. Fortunately De Ruyter, dressed as an ordinary sailor, was in one of the lead boats. He shouted "Attack men, attack or you will all be killed!" The men now went into the water which was "quite deep and ever so cold". The infantrymen held their muskets high and once ashore they "fiercely attacked the dragoons as magnificent soldiers, step by step, and after a short fight the enemy fled towards the bridge" as De Ruyter wrote in his journal[12]. Before they retreated over the bridge leading southward to open country, the Swedes tried to set the town on fire in two places but the allies, who now occupied the town, quickly extinguished the flames. The invasion had succeeded and the allies established a firm bridgehead.

Shortly afterwards Field Marshall Eberstein crossed the Little Belt with his force of Brandenburger, Polish, Austrian and Danish troops totalling some 5,000 men, mostly cavalry, and 14 guns. He met no resistance, and after the landing he marched towards Odense where he met Schack's army of 6,100 men, 2,500 cavalry and 2,600 infantry and dragoons with 28 field guns. The Swedes had chosen to concentrate all their forces at Fyn in the fortified town of Nyborg. Their army included some 6-7,000 men, mainly German cavalry and some infantry and dragoons, with eight field guns all commanded by Field Marshalls Phillip von Sultzbach and Gustav Otto Stenbock. The Swedish army faced grave difficulties. They were short of provisions and the fortifications of Nyborg were in such a poor state that it was not deemed possible to hold the town for very long. The presence of the allied fleet in the Great Belt prevented bringing in reinforcements or provisions from Zealand. So in spite of the numerical inferiority of their army the two Swedish field marshalls decided to accept battle on open ground where their cavalry could be used to best advantage. On November 24 the two armies met some three kilometres northwest of Nyborg. The allied army was ranged in two lines, Eberstein in the front and Schack in the rear. Both lines were divided into three with the cavalry on the wings and infantry and artillery in the centre. The Swedish army was likewise ranged with a centre of infantry and dragoons along with the artillery under Stenbock and a right and left wing of cavalry. The battle started at eleven o'clock when Eberstein's right wing attacked the Swedish left. A little later Eberstein's left wing attacked the Swedish right. Swedish musket and artillery fire stopped both attacks and then Swedish cavalry drove back the enemy. Both Eberstein's wings were forced to withdraw with heavy casualties, but his centre with the infantry and artillery held its position. The battle had now raged for two and a half hours and had reached a critical phase with the outcome in the balance.

Schack then launched a major attack against the Swedish left wing and centre with his right wing and centre using his Danish and Dutch infantry. The Swedish cavalry broke after a short and bloody fight and retired to Nyborg with the Danish cavalry in hot pursuit. That meant the left flank of the Swedish centre was exposed and Schack's infantry neutralized the Swedish infantry and captured their artillery. The Dutch infantry fought gallantly and Eberstein was full of praise for them. He reported that "it was a joy to see the routine way in which the Dutch infantry used their muskets and pikes"[13]. The remains of the Swedish infantrymen who tried to escape were massacred mercilessly by Eberstein's Polish cavalry. Sultzbach's right wing still held out against Eberstein but then Schack outflanked it and only with great difficulty did Sultzbach succeed in retreating to Nyborg with his cavalry but his infantry and dragoons were either massacred or taken prisoner.[14]

The allies followed the Swedes to the walls of Nyborg and on the following day, November 25, the field marshalls while planning an attack on the town were at the same time encouraging the Swedes to surrender. Then De Ruyter who had been prevented by the weather from supporting the forces on land during the battle sent in six ships to attack a fortress northeast of Nyborg while he himself with some other ships made his way into Nyborg Fjord. On his way there he passed two fortifications, probably Slipshavn and Holmen. They did not fire. On the contrary the garrisons fled when De Ruyter opened fire. He occupied both fortifications, planted the Orange flag and brought back two beautiful 24 pounders, one in his own boat the other in the boat of another ship. Then he went in close to the town which he bombarded heavily for about an hour. A Swedish negotiator then went to De Ruyter offering surrender. He answered that the surrender should be effected within an hour, otherwise he would turn the town into rubble. When the hour had passed

without any sign of surrender the admiral resumed the bombardment. Shortly afterwards some Swedes came running, bringing a letter from Schack thanking De Ruyter for his effort which had hastened the capitulation, which had now been agreed.[15] The battle of Nyborg was is perhaps the bloodiest that has ever been fought in Denmark. About 2,000 of the Swedish troops were killed and the allies lost about 500 men of whom 200 belonged to the Dutch contingent. Some 3,000 enemy troops were taken prisoner as were three Swedish generals and 12 colonels. The two Swedish field marshalls, Stenbock and Sultzbach, managed to escape to Zealand in a small boat.[16]

After the surrender of Nyborg, the town was plundered by the foreign troops. The soldiers, especially the wild Polish cavalry, divided the booty, including the wives and daughters of the inhabitants among themselves. To his regret De Ruyter was unable to do much to prevent these horrors except to forbid the Dutch contingent from participating in the excesses.[17]

Shortly afterwards the islands of Langeland and those south of Fyn were liberated leaving no Swedish troops west of the Great Belt. This ended the sea campaign of 1659 and on December 15 the allied fleets entered the harbour of Copenhagen. Frederik III sent his coach to take De Ruyter to the castle where the admiral spent the night. During the following month there was plenty of contact between De Ruyter and the king. On December 17 De Ruyter was treated to a royal banquet with all the state councils and on December 20 he received a gold chain with a medal with valuable stones, hung around his neck by the Queen herself, and on February 13 he was invited to visit the famous royal cabinet of curiosities where a three-foot long ship model of ivory with masts, sails, anchors and guns in particular drew the attention of the admiral. That model is still in existence, displayed in Rosenborg Castle. In return De Ruyter hosted several banquets aboard his flagship for the king and other dignitaries. Apart from the social activities De Ruyter also looked after his fleet. He even contributed to the defence of Copenhagen which was still under siege. On December 29 he inspected the ramparts and thereafter ordered guns to be supplied, manned by 985 artillerymen and officers with reserves of 400 men to be at the ready in case of emergency.[18]

Niels Juel had resumed his duties as admiral of the naval base Holmen, at the beginning of October. He tried to equip nine Danish warships for spring operations but was hampered by lack of tar, timber, hemp, and, not least of all, money. It seems that only one Danish warship, the relatively new *Lindormen*, was actually able to participate in these operations when the time came. The Dutch fleet on the contrary was quickly made ready. Spring arrived early in 1660 and already on February 27 the blockade of Landskrona was resumed.

By now everything pointed to a rapid conclusion of hostilities. With the departure of Richard Cromwell from the political scene the Swedish king, Carl Gustav, had lost his last potential ally. Late in 1659 he went to Gothenburg where he died on February 23, 1660, only 37 years old. Thereby, as the Swedish government somewhat reluctantly admitted, "an essential prerequisite for the continuation of the war had passed away"[19]. On March 17 negotiations between Sweden and the Netherlands resulted in a ceasefire. Thereafter De Ruyter to his regret as well as that of Frederik III had to raise the blockade of Landskrona and abandon preparations for a planned fireship attack on the closely grouped Swedish fleet in the narrow harbour of that town. The Swedes, quite in the spirit of their deceased king, immediately grasped the opportunity of the raised blockade to send two squadrons to sea, one with the purpose of conquering the Danish held island of Femern, the other to initiate a blockade of Copenhagen. The invasion of Femern faced stiff resistance and the Swedes sustained heavy losses. Thanks to De Ruyter the blockade attempt never became effective. His fleet was lying in the middle of the Sound and he made it clear that he would not under any circumstances tolerate any Swedish attempts to arrest a Danish ship.

The shipyard facilities at Landskrona were insufficient for any major repair work so late in April the Swedes tried to send ten warships that were not up to effective service off to Stockholm loaded with loots of plunder from the war, such as the fountain of Kronborg Castle. On their way southwards through the Sound De Ruyter intercepted the ships and arrested them, much to the annoyance of both the French and the English negotiators, but his action did provide the Dutch with leverage in the negotiations. The ships were not released until the peace negotiations had been finalised. The peace treaty was signed on June 7. It largely followed the Roskilde

Treaty of 1658 with the exception of the ceding of the island of Bornholm and the county of Trondheim in Norway which were returned to the Danish King. According to the treaty Denmark had to supply the ships needed to transport all Swedish troops out of the country so the following weeks were busy ones. De Ruyter assisted for about a month. On August 4 the last Swedish troops left the port of Elsinore, the embarkation point for most of them.

During his stay in Denmark De Ruyter had proved himself an extremely loyal, energetic and steadfast ally. Whether the obvious Danophilia he displayed, especially during the spring of 1660, had something to do with his acquaintance with Niels Juel cannot be said, but his services were richly rewarded by King Frederik III who on August 10 elevated him to knighthood[20], gave him an annuity of 800 *Rigsdalers* and presented him and his officers with medals and other favours. On August 13 De Ruyter left Copenhagen with his fleet heading for the Netherlands.

The island of Gorée off Cape Verde.

Water colour by Joannes Vingboons, 1665,
National Archive, The Hague

Aldus vcrthoont Hcm Het Ey

Ot Goeree geleegen an Cabo verde.

CHAPTER 8

Michiel de Ruyter's Expedition to West Africa and America, 1664-1665

Henk den Heijer

■ Introduction

For almost two months, Hieronymus van Beverningk had unsuccessfully been negotiating peace with the English in the castle of Breda when he wrote to Grand Pensionary Johan de Witt on 23 May 1667 that he was expecting little compliance from the other side unless the Dutch were to achieve a quick and resounding success in the war.[1] That did not fall on deaf ears. After consultation with the States General, the Grand Pensionary decided to execute a plan he had devised earlier to destroy the English fleet in its home port. He ordered Michiel de Ruyter to get the fleet in readiness for an expedition to England and stationed his brother Cornelis on board the *Zeven Provinciën* as a representative of the States General. What followed is history: the Dutch fleet destroyed a number of the enemy naval vessels laid up near Chatham and led the English flag ship *Royal Charles* in triumph to the Republic. England was forced to its knees with this heavy and especially humiliating blow and signed the peace treaty on 31 July 1667 in the Breda castle, thereby ending the Second Anglo-Dutch War.

The raid on Chatham is looked upon as the most glorious moment in Michiel de Ruyter's career, but that image needs some adjusting. The Admiral was not informed of the real purpose of the expedition by Cornelis de Witt until he had reached the Thames estuary. When, on 22 June, part of his fleet under the command of Willem Joseph van Ghent and in the presence of Cornelis de Witt wreaked havoc on the laid up English naval force, he had come down with an illness and was not present on the scene of action. De Ruyter did not arrive until the heaviest blows had been dealt. However, Gerard Brandt, the first biographer of Michiel de Ruyter, sang the admiral's praises for this daring action as if he were a new Hannibal. He thus created a myth that has lived on to the present day.[2]

This chapter is not so much about the end as about the beginning of the Second Anglo-Dutch War in which De Ruyter did play an important role. At the beginning of October 1664 the Admiral left the Mediterranean on the orders of Johan de Witt for a secret mission to West Africa. When he returned to the Republic with his fleet ten months later, the country had already been at war with England for some months. The actions of De Ruyter in West Africa, the Caribbean and near Newfoundland were to lead directly to the Second Anglo-Dutch War. This chapter examines why the States General dispatched Michiel de Ruyter to West Africa and America with a fleet, what actions the Admiral undertook there and what results he achieved.

■ Mounting tensions

Michiel de Ruyter's expedition to West Africa came at the tail end of a long process in which tensions between England and the Republic had steadily increased; tensions that would eventually lead to war. Over the past years, historians have come up with ideological and political explanations to account for De Ruyter's expedition and the outbreak of the Second Anglo-Dutch War, but the economic motive behind the expedition and the war is still given precedence.[3] As of the 1640s, the Republic had considerably consolidated its economic position in Europe and beyond at, among others, England's expense. England's economic position had seriously weakened due to the Civil War. Merchants in the Republic had profited from this and had taken over trade positions from the English. What was important for the Dutch was that they gained a firm foothold in the English colonies in the Caribbean and in North America, which would enable them to tap the production of sugar and tobacco. They supplied slaves and European goods in exchange for tropical produce. The English attempted to consolidate their economic position in relation to the Dutch during the First Anglo-Dutch War (1652-1654) but the main issue of that conflict had to do with European matters revolving around the renewal of the 1651 Navigation Act, breaking the Dutch hegemony in North Sea fishing and saluting the English flag at sea.[4]

The First Anglo-Dutch War had not solved the trade conflicts outside Europe. The two countries were in fierce competition with each other in Asia, West Africa and America. The Dutch were still in an advantageous position there thanks to their large trading companies. In 1602, the Dutch East India Company (Verenigde Oost-Indische Compagnie – VOC) had been established by order of the States General. This company, which held the Dutch monopoly on trade and shipping in Asia, pursued an aggressive policy, ousting its competitors from various lucrative markets. In Asia, the Dutch East India Company had pressed the Portuguese ever harder and had succeeded in obtaining trade monopolies in cinnamon, nutmeg, mace and cloves. The Dutch, moreover, refused to hand over the island of Run, one of the Banda Islands that the English had been laying claim to for years. As much had been agreed in the Treaty of Westminster of 1654, but the Dutch East India Company did not at all relish the idea of handing over one of its spice islands.[5]

Also in the Atlantic area, tension mounted between the two countries. Since the foundation of the Dutch West India Company (WIC) in 1621, the Dutch had set up a network of colonies and trading posts from which products were shipped to the Republic. Moreover, after the Peace of Westphalia in 1648 the Dutch had succeeded in considerably strengthening their trading position in the Caribbean. Curaçao quickly developed into a trading centre for the Spanish colonies on the mainland. Slaves and European goods were exchanged for cacao and other tropical agricultural produce. However, the Dutch merchants did not confine themselves to Curaçao. They also had commercial dealings with Barbados, St. Kitts and other English islands in the Caribbean.[6] The English Parliament had forbidden this trade, but the planters on the islands took little heed. As long as their own merchants could not sufficiently supply the colonies, they would avail themselves of the services offered by the Dutch. English colonists in North America did much the same: they used New Netherland as an illegal intermediate station for the import of European products and the export of American ones. Under the West India Company New Netherland had developed from a small trading post on the Hudson into a sizeable colony in the basin of this river. The Dutch possessions, wedged between English colonies, had been a thorn in the side of the English for years. West Africa may have been the last problem area where Dutch and English interests clashed, but it certainly was not the least. Since the 1650s the English had been trying to breathe new life into their trading and shipping with West Africa, but they felt thwarted by the West India Company that considered the coast its exclusive trading domain.

After his accession to the throne in 1660, Charles II seemed initially to strive for good relations with the Republic. After all, he had spent part of his exile in the Republic. Besides, if he were to strengthen his position after the Restoration, it was important that he brought back peace and stability to the country. Conflicts, let alone war with the Republic, did not appear to be in his interests. Even so, a lobby of

London merchants and nobles soon announced its wishes to promote England's overseas interests, which would inevitably entail conflict with its main economic rival: the Republic.[7] The lobby's first feat was to breathe new life into the Navigation Act, whose main purpose was to curb Dutch trading and shipping with England and the English colonies. James, duke of York and brother to the king, was the best-known member of this group. What is more, he had been among the founders and shareholders of the Company of Royal Adventurers trading into Africa (CRA). In December 1660 Charles II granted the CRA a royal charter giving the new company the exclusive rights to trade with West Africa. From then on, relations between England and the Republic rapidly deteriorated.

It was the CRA's intention to set up as quickly as possible a trading network in West Africa and to that end it sent a squadron under the command of Robert Holmes to Cape Verde. In March 1661 he dropped anchor off the island of Gorée, the WIC's most important trade centre in the Senegambia area. Holmes is supposed to have given the Dutch on the island to understand that on behalf of the CRA he claimed the exclusive trading rights to the entire West African coast, from Cape Verde to the Cape of Good Hope. The Dutch were to vacate their establishments in West Africa within a few months.[8] It is impossible to prove whether he actually said this, but the fact remains that shortly afterwards Holmes took possession of St Andrews Island in the mouth of the river Gambia. The island had already been claimed by the Dutch. Next came extending the trading network on the Gold Coast where the English already possessed some trading posts. Over the years 1662-1663 CRA agents opened factories in Takoradi, Cabo Corso and Komenda, places that the WIC felt it had exclusive trading rights to. By way of counteraction, the Company embargoed all trade at these factories and brought in several English ships.[9] At the same time, the political pressure increased on both sides in Europe. In London the Dutch ambassador Michiel van Gogh tried to convince the English that the CRA was violating the historic trading rights of the Dutch in Africa, while in The Hague the English envoy Sir George Downing attempted to get the States General to take measures against the acts of aggression on the part of the WIC.[10]

Relations between the Dutch and the English on the Gold Coast took a dramatic turn for the worse when the WIC captured the erstwhile Swedish fort at Cabo Corso in June 1663. The CRA, which also had a factory there, was about to make Cabo Corso its trading centre on the Gold Coast. News of the Dutch action was therefore not received well in London. In possession of Elmina and Cabo Corso, the WIC might well start laying down the law permanently on the Gold Coast, which had to be prevented. James, who besides being director of the CRA was also the head of the Royal Navy, ordered Robert Holmes to sail to West Africa with a fleet to put things right. On 1 December 1663 Holmes left for Cape Verde with two warships from the Royal Navy and eight vessels from the CRA. Upon his arrival he seized three Dutch vessels, sank two and took possession of the island of Gorée with the forts Nassau and Oranje on behalf of the CRA.[11] He left a small garrison behind on the island and subsequently left for the Gold Coast to safeguard the CRA's interests there the hard way. An attack on WIC fort Saint Anthony in Axim proved unsuccessful, but more to the east, fort Witsen was rather easily made to surrender after it was stormed and fired at from the ships. But the hardest task, seizing the Dutch possessions on the eastern part of the Gold Coast, was yet to come. As Holmes appeared with his vessels off Cabo Corso, director-general Johan Valckenburgh was just laying siege to the Danish fort Frede-

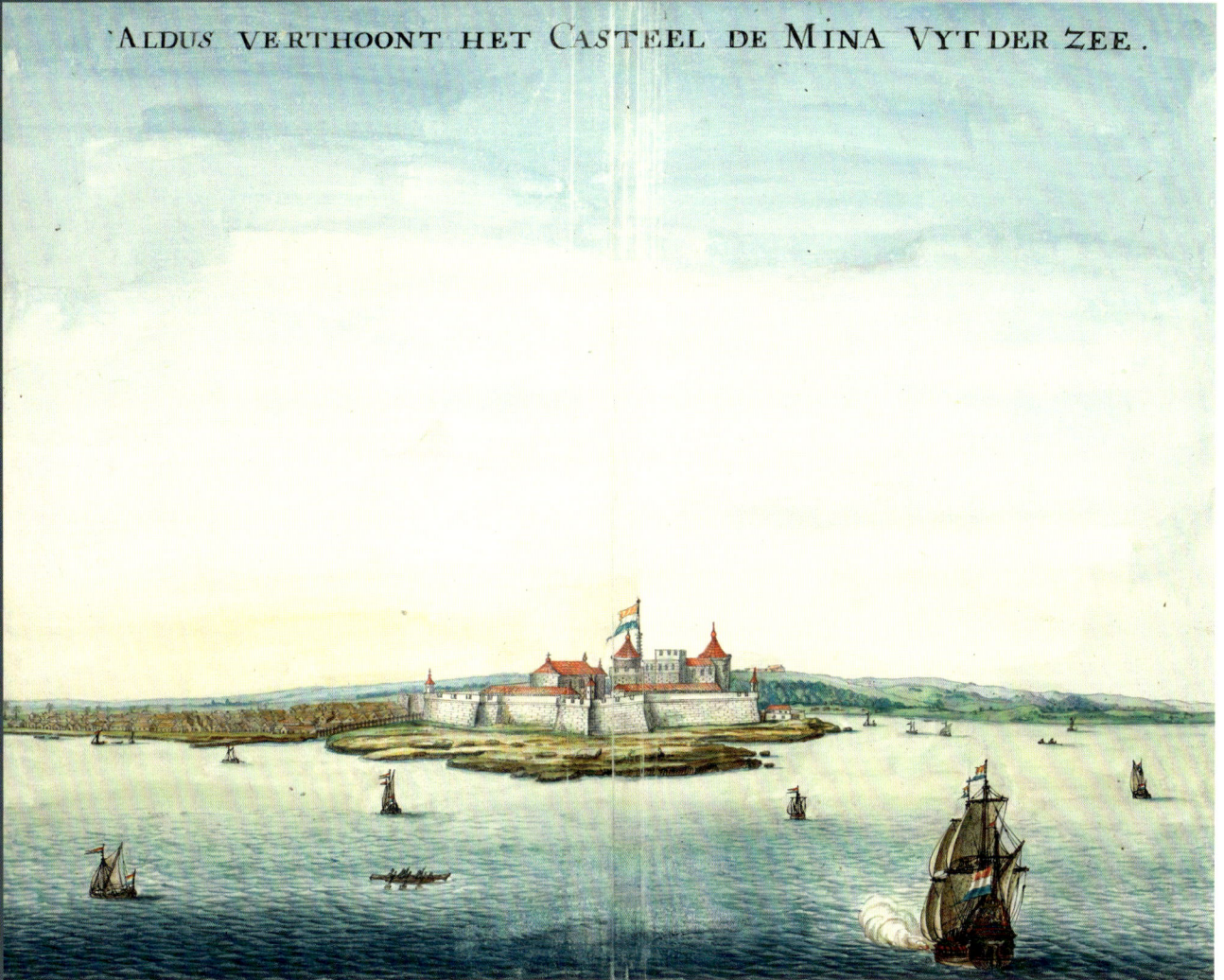

`ALDUS VERTHOONT HET CASTEEL DE MINA VYT DER ZEE.`

The Castle of Elmina seen from the sea.

Water colour by Joannes Vingboons, 1665,
National Archive, The Hague

ricksborg, which was also situated in this place.[12] Valckenburgh retreated with his
forces to Elmina, but he left a small garrison in the former Swedish fort with which
to ward off an English attack on Cabo Corso. But Holmes was not to be put off. He
launched an attack on the fort with a combined English, Danish and African force
and succeeded in forcing the Dutch occupying forces to surrender.[13] Thus, Cabo
Corso, henceforth called Cape Coast, fell into the hands of the English for good.
Holmes subsequently went on to seize the Dutch establishments at Adja and
Anomabu to the east of Cabo Corso, and then sailed home.

In The Hague the actions of the English were watched closely. Johan de Witt, the
Grand Pensionary of Holland and the leader of the Republicanist faction in the States
General, advocated maintaining the status quo. The Grand Pensionary intended to
achieve this by eliminating potential conflicts through clever diplomacy and
alliances. He realised all too well that the Republic was an economic giant, but could
only maintain that position in Europe with the military support of others. Only if the
worst came to the worst, and business interests threatened to be seriously harmed,
were Johan de Witt and his allies in the States General prepared to take military
action.[14] That moment was drawing near in the spring of 1664. Even before Holmes'
action in West Africa was known in the Republic, news arrived from London about

growing anti-Dutch sentiments in the English Parliament. In a Parliamentary report Dutch merchants were made out to be the main obstacles to the expansion of English shipping and trade. Parliament thus advised the king to take fitting measures in order to safeguard English commercial interests with an eye to the future.[15] At the same time it was rumoured in the Republic that the English were secretly getting a war fleet in readiness with which to intercept the returning VOC fleet.

Early in March 1664 a new step towards war was made when Charles II granted his brother James the patent to the trading and shipping with the colonies in North America. It was a public secret that the colonists little heeded the Navigation Act that had been renewed in 1660 and conducted illegal trade via New Netherland. Seizing the Dutch colony thus was top priority with the duke of York. He would then be able to control smuggling and, what was more, exercise power over an area ranging unbroken from Nova Scotia in the north to Carolina in the south. Two months after the patent had been granted, a squadron of three frigates with some three hundred soldiers on board left Portsmouth for New Netherland. The expedition was led by

Richard Nicolls. The governor of the colony, Petrus Stuyvesant, had already been informed of Nicolls' coming when the latter's ships appeared off New Amsterdam in August. With only a limited force at his disposal and with a population on the brink of panic on his hands, the governor could do little else but yield the colony. On 6 September he officially ceded New Netherland to the English, after Nicolls had promised him to guarantee free immigration from and trade with the Republic.[16]

■ Counteraction from the States General

While the call for war became louder in England, the States General took measures to protect the Dutch shipping and trade against possible acts of aggression from the English. The admiralties sent advice yachts to the English Channel in order to warn merchantmen sailing home about the English. In addition, a naval squadron under Cornelis Tromp was put to sea to accompany the returning VOC fleet safely home. The Republic, meanwhile, worked hard at expanding the war fleet and stocking up on gunpowder and shipping requirements.[17] Those activities did not escape the notice of the English. Charles II's government responded by increasing naval expenses, and had warships prepared and ordered English, Scottish and Irish sailors to stand by for duty in the war fleet.

Tensions also mounted in the diplomatic sphere. In The Hague, Ambassador Sir George Downing continued to bombard the Dutch with reproaches that they were forcefully thwarting English commercial interests in West Africa. Championing the cause of the CRA and acting on its behalf, he also put in a claim with the States General against the WIC.[18] While Downing was lodging his complaints, word arrived in the Republic that Robert Holmes had taken a number of company vessels and possessions in West Africa. On 21 July 1664 captain Andries Cornelissen Vertholen, who had only recently arrived from Elmina on the WIC ship *Eendracht*, gave an account of Holmes' actions to the States General.[19] A week later, the representatives for the States of Zeeland and Stad en Lande (Groningen) in the States General called for fitting measures against the English aggression in West Africa.[20] Meanwhile, the Dutch ambassador in London, Michiel van Gogh, had lodged a protest against Holmes' conduct. In front of Van Gogh Charles II denied most emphatically that he had commissioned Holmes to attack Dutch possessions, and promised to launch an investigation. Upon his return to England Holmes was indeed interrogated as to his conduct in Africa and he was even committed twice to the Tower, but these were mere diversions to give the Dutch the impression that their protests were taken serious by the English.[21]

The good intentions of Charles II and the English Parliament were given little credit in the Republic. Virtually everyone was convinced that the English wanted to strengthen their trading position in and outside Europe at the expense of the Republic and would not shun violence. No matter how, the States General wanted to safeguard the trading interests of the WIC in West Africa and asked the admiralties for advice. Of the five admiralties, only the admiralty of Friesland, a province with no interests in the WIC, abstained from advice and promises of support. The Admiralties of Amsterdam, Maze, Noorderkwartier and Zeeland, however, were willing to supply the States General with twelve warships to be sent on an expedition to West Africa if it could be financed.[22] The States General adopted the admiralties' advice and on 9 August decided to dispatch a fleet of twelve ships to Africa to retake the forts and factories captured by the English. An amount of 600,000 guilders was allotted for fitting out the fleet, which would be commanded by captain Jan van Kampen.[23] It was additionally decided to add a force of four hundred mariners to the fleet. On paper, this looked a solid plan, but Johan de Witt and his confidants very much doubted its feasibility. The English were, on the whole, well-informed of the decisions of the States General through spies and their ambassador Downing. It was therefore highly likely that they would intercept the ships in the English Channel with a war fleet. As a precaution, the fleet would be escorted until they were well past the English Channel by a few warships under Fleet Admiral Jacob van Wassenaar-Obdam, but even then it was by no means certain whether Van Kampen would be able to continue his voyage to Africa unharmed. It would, moreover, take weeks if not months before the ships were ready to depart.

Before the plan for an expedition to Africa was discussed in The Hague, the secretary of the Amsterdam admiralty, David de Wildt, had already presented Johan de Witt with a brilliant alternative. He suggested that the Grand Pensionary did not send Van Kampen to West Africa but De Ruyter, who was with a fleet in the Mediterranean. This plan should be given as little publicity as possible in order not to alarm the English untimely. De Witt adopted De Wildt's plan and steered it almost noiselessly through various political organs. First of all, he took some representatives of the States of Holland into his confidence. The Amsterdam deputies opposed the plan. Of old, they had had greater interests in the VOC than in the WIC and the Amsterdam deputies deemed the risk of a war with England too high. They further argued that it was De Ruyter's duty to protect the Dutch merchantmen in the Mediterranean. A temporary withdrawal of his fleet could put the ships there in grave danger. Even so, the Grand Pensionary persevered and put the proposal to the vote in the States of Holland. When the Amsterdam representatives understood they would be outvoted, they too endorsed the plan.[24] The next step was to inform a number of representatives of Gelderland, Groningen and Zeeland who De Witt knew were to be trusted. Finally, the proposal was put to the States General in full in a very cunning way. On 11 August the resolution to dispatch twelve vessels under Van Kampen to West Africa was read at high speed to the deputies at the Generality. Those present failed to notice that De Witt and De Wildt's new plan had been cleverly worked into the old proposal and voted to have it executed. Only those who had been taken into the Grand Pensionary's confidence knew the real purpose of the resolution.[25] Now that the decision had been taken, it was important to inform De Ruyter as secretly and quickly as possible of his new assignment. Three similar letters were couriered overland to Cadiz, Alicante and Malaga. Sooner or later De Ruyter was to drop anchor there in order to forage.[26]

■ Manoeuvring in the Mediterranean

In the spring of 1664 Michiel de Ruyter had been commissioned by the States General to take a fleet to the Mediterranean. It had every appearance of a rather routine job. From 1654 he had been sailing southwards almost annually to protect the Dutch vessels from Barbary corsairs. Besides convoying merchantmen and hunting for privateers, he would occasionally also enter into peace negotiations with Barbary states. In 1662, for instance, he had come to an agreement with the dey of Algiers. The latter guaranteed the Dutch free goods – free shipping in exchange for a steep ransom for all sailors on board Dutch vessels that had been brought in at Algiers.[27] In practice, however, ransom was rarely paid and the arrangement amounted to very little. In 1664 De Ruyter had to make another attempt at reaching a peace settlement with the dey. To that end the diplomat Johan Bertrand de Mortaigne had come aboard his ship. Should De Mortaigne be unsuccessful, then De Ruyter was authorized to launch an attack on Algiers and its privateers.[28]

On 13 April De Ruyter had gone aboard the *Spiegel*, the flagship of his fleet, which consisted of twelve vessels and a supply fluyt, at the roadstead of Texel. The Amsterdam Admiralty had supplied six warships while the Admiralties of Maze and Noorderkwartier had each fitted out three. The Maze vessels were commanded by Aart Jansz van Nes while the Noorderkwartier ships were under the command of Jan Cornelisz Meppel. Michiel de Ruyter, who commanded the Amsterdam squadron, was in supreme command of the entire fleet. The vessels, with altogether 516 guns and 2318 sailors on board, were of rather diverse quality. The flagship *Spiegel* was only a year old, but the *Prinses Louise* from the Maze Admiralty had seen service since 1646. Likewise, the *Rode Leeuw* and the *Caleb* from the Noorderkwartier Admiralty had been as good as written off as far as their life span went.

On 19 June De Ruyter dropped anchor at the roadstead of Algiers. A day later negotiations on the ransoming of Dutch sailors and the *'free shipping - free goods'* arrangement started. However, the negotiations were not very successful. The dey argued that his privateers had a right to bring in Dutch vessels as long as the Dutch did not pay the agreed ransom. Authorized by the States General to ransom the sailors, De Ruyter was willing to pay a maximum of 600 guilders per prisoner, but after only a few days the price per head had already risen to 720 guilders. On 4 July the admiral summoned a council of war where it was concluded that it was impossible to do business with the Algerians.[30] That very same day he left with his ships for Alicante to take in victuals and water. There, he received a letter from the Amster-

The fleet of Michiel De Ruyter in the Mediterranean, 1664

Admiralty	Captain	Name vessel	Cannon	Crew
Amsterdam	Michiel Adriaansz de Ruyter	Spiegel	68	315
Amsterdam	Gidion de Wildt	Provincie van Utrecht	58	265
Amsterdam	Willem van der Zaen	Geloof	50	24
Amsterdam	Isaack Sweers	Middelburg	36	165
Amsterdam	Hendrick Adriaensz.	Damiaten	32	135
Amsterdam	Jacob Cornelisz Swart	Edam	34	135
Amsterdam	Enno Doedesz Star	Groene Kameel	8	30
Maze	Aart Jansz van Nes	Prinses Louise	40	175
Maze	Leendert Haexwant	Rotterdam	34	123
Maze	Jan van Nes	Harderwyck	34	150
Noorderkwartier	Jan Cornelisz Meppel	Noorderkwartier	50	285
Noorderkwartier	Dirck Gerritsz Pomp	Rode Leeuw	36	150
Noorderkwartier	Govert 't Hoen	Caleb	36	150

Source: Brandt, *Het leven en bedryf*, 273-274.[29]

dam admiralty warning him for possible acts of aggression from the English. At precisely that moment, an English naval squadron of fourteen vessels under Captain John Lawson had dropped anchor at the roadstead of Cadiz. The English had spread rumours that war between their country and the Republic was imminent.[31] During the months of July and August De Ruyter's ships cruised the western basin of the Mediterranean Sea, escorting merchantmen through the Strait of Gibraltar. Meanwhile, the movements of the English fleet were closely watched. There were, however, no signs of a hostile atmosphere. On passing thirteen English vessels of war off Tangiers the English were, against custom, even the first to fire a salute.[32]

■ Secret commission from the States General

To all appearances relations between the Dutch and the English in the Mediterranean were fine, but in reality they were playing cat and mouse. De Ruyter made sure that his ships were continually in the neighbourhood of Dutch merchantmen thus keeping Lawson from launching a surprise attack. Tension between the two parties may have been great but when they met at sea or in port, salutes were fired on both sides and flag officers would pay each other the customary courtesy visits. It is in this atmosphere of mistrust that on 1 September De Ruyter arrived at Malaga for the umpteenth time. That very same day he received the express letter that the States General had sent him three weeks earlier. In it, De Ruyter read that he was to leave as quickly as possible for Cape Verde and from there, for the Gold Coast in order to recapture all the forts and factories seized by Holmes. All this had to be done in total secrecy. He was not to inform anyone, not even his flag officers, about the purpose of the expedition until they had passed the Strait of Gibraltar. Great amounts of victuals, firewood and water were stocked up as quickly as possible for the long voyage. The arrival of the courier and the sudden provisioning of the fleet had not escaped the attention of Lawson, who was in the neighbourhood with his ships. Intrigued, he inquired of Willem van der Zaen, who was paying him a courtesy visit on board his ship, what the Dutch plans were. The latter informed the English commander that the Dutch were intending to cruise around the Strait of Gibraltar and hunt down Barbary corsairs.[33] Shortly afterwards, both the Dutch and the English ships sailed for Cádiz. On 5 October De Ruyter sailed his ships out of the Bay of Cádiz in the direction of the Atlantic Ocean. Before he left, De Ruyter let Lawson, riding offshore at anchor, know that he was on his way to Salee, a corsairs' nest on the Atlantic coast of Morocco. That was a likely destination. On board the English fleet was also rear admiral Sir Thomas Allin, who was to take over command from John Lawson. When De Ruyter passed his ship, Allin noted in his log book that *"He came under our sterne and asked me how I did, and saluted me with 7 guns and drank to me. I drank to him and answered him 7; he thanked me 3, the which I answered; when De Ruyter was clear from the fleet he shot 7 guns to bid sir John farewell"*.[34]

This show of friendliness was no more than an act of two admirals who knew full well how their countries stood vis-à-vis each other. Had the English known the real reason for De Ruyter's departure, they would not have fired salutes but real cannonballs instead.

Two days after his departure from Cadiz and out of sight of the English fleet, De Ruyter convened the council of war on board the *Spiegel* in order to disclose the true purpose of the voyage. The flag officers were then told of the plan to sail to Cape Verde via the Canary Islands in order to recapture the island of Gorée from the English. Then the journey would continue to the Gold Coast. How well De Ruyter had managed to keep the mission a secret appeared from the reactions of all on board who were completely taken by surprise by the plan. But the crew did not complain; they were counting on handsome spoils that would be to their advantage as well.[35] Until that time, however, there were some problems to overcome. There were, for instance, no mates on board who had earlier sailed to West Africa. They had, moreover, no sea charts or atlases for the coastal area. Only one quartermaster on the *Rode Leeuw* had some knowledge of the forts on Gorée. It is with that scant knowledge that De Ruyter and his men had to make do.[36]

■ Recapturing Gorée

While the mates set course for Cape Verde, preparations were set in train on board the ships for an amphibious operation. De Ruyter assumed that upon spotting the superior strength of the Dutch the English on Gorée would quickly surrender, but in case they did not, he could always take a force into battle. In earlier operations he had gained experience with land attacks from sea. In November 1659, for example, during the Northern Wars, De Ruyter had led a successful landing operation on the Danish island of Fyn.[37] The war council decided that, if necessary, a large force would have to be brought ashore with sloops. They would be under the command of Johan Bertrand de Mortaigne, meanwhile promoted to the rank of colonel and earlier the diplomat who had unsuccessfully mediated the execution of the 1662 peace treaty in Algiers.[38] De Mortaigne had 350 sea soldiers at his disposal. If there were any English merchantmen in the roadstead of Gorée, those would have to be eliminated first. Only then could the landing operation and the assault on the forts on the island be launched. Soldiers who were the first to throw grenades into the forts, were promised extra remuneration. The spoils were to be divided among all those on board after the conquest.[39]

On 21 October the fleet rounded Cape Verde and a day later it reached the island of Gorée, which lay behind it. There, eight English merchantmen as well as a warship were riding at anchor. The Dutch fleet approached the English ships in fan-shaped formation, which made escape almost impossible. To their utter surprise, the English saw the superior numbers approach slowly and did not think to offer resistance. Affecting surprise, the English governor George Abercromby did, however, wonder what De Ruyter's act of aggression in times of peace was all about. He answered rather curtly that in the name of the States General he was claiming the island that Holmes had earlier and wrongfully so, taken possession of. The English warship was allowed to depart freely after her commander had declared he would not get involved in any battle. The masters of the merchantmen, for their part, were prepared to transfer the freight that belonged to the cRA to the Dutch on payment of the freightage. To this De Ruyter also agreed. Abercromby, who was now completely on his own, requested ten days to consider the matter but the council of war gave him no more than twenty-four hours. The governor then abandoned all attempts at resistance and ceded the island with the forts to the Dutch. After their surrender, the English and their ships were granted unopposed withdrawal; they were allowed to leave for other English settlements in West Africa. Only the yacht *Spion* was confiscated on behalf of the wic and renamed *Goeree.* Incidentally, two English merchantmen sailed of their own volition together with the Dutch to the Gold Coast. De Ruyter and his men had behaved extremely correctly during the action and the winding up of the capitulation. Even so, rumours were later spread in England that the Dutch were to have perpetrated acts of cruelty on Gorée. Those fabrications had been made up by the conquered in order to mask their surrender and defenceless retreat.

Towards the end of October the war council officially transferred the island to the wic. The fiscal Johannes Celarius was appointed as its temporary governor. Each ship was subsequently to supply ten sailors and soldiers for the Gorée garrison. In return they got a pay increase as well as the guarantee that they would be relieved by the fleet of Jan van Kampen.[40] However, those who stayed behind could not know that in the end, the States General cancelled Van Kampen's expedition. On 6 November De Ruyter left with a slightly depleted crew for the Gold Coast.

▪ Actions on the Gold Coast

Bad weather, crosscurrents and lulls caused the fleet to make rather slow progress. Victuals and water were rationed. Halfway down the voyage they put in at Sierra Leone to stock up on supplies and clean the ships. There, De Ruyter learnt that three Dutchmen were imprisoned in the local English factory and that a short while ago a Dutch ship had been captured. The council of war then decided to free the prisoners and to seize in reprisal all the commodities of the English. One of the Dutch prisoners turned out to have died meanwhile but the other two were liberated by a force led by Willem van der Zaen. Nearly 17,000 pounds of ivory, large amounts of metalwork, textiles and provisions were carried off.[41] After this necessary, yet financially attractive delay the voyage continued. In the end, two months after they had left Gorée, the fleet passed Cabo Tres Puntas, the most westerly point of the Gold Coast in the beginning of January 1665.

De Ruyter learnt from some Africans that there were fourteen Dutchmen in the nearby wic fort of Batenstein. That would be his first port of call on the Gold Coast. The head of the fort, officer Bartholomeus Rietbeeck, advised him to recapture fort Witsen near Takoradi, which had been seized by Holmes. The war council adopted the advice and that very same day the ships left for the fort, where they dropped anchor outside shooting range. Meanwhile, De Ruyter had informed director-general Johan Valckenburgh in Elmina of his arrival at the Gold Coast.

The following morning De Ruyter sent midshipman Reinout van Coevorden in a sloop to the coast in order to demand the fort's surrender. Though waving a white flag as he approached the beach, he was yet bombarded with muskets and cannonballs. Van Coevorden could not but go back to the fleet without having accomplished his mission. On board the *Spiegel* the war council next decided on a landing operation and on storming the fort. Over four hundred soldiers and sailors were distributed over twelve sloops. They were under the command of captains Jacob Cornelisz Swart, Jan du Bois and Jan van Nes, and count Johan van Hoorn who was in supreme command of the landing operation. The landing and storming took place under cover of the guns of the five smallest ships to come closest under the coast. On the beach and from behind dug-in canoes hundreds of African allies of the English put up a fierce resistance, but even so the landing forces succeeded in putting them to flight. They pursued the Africans all the way to their settlement, which was burnt down. Then, the troops concentrated on fort Witsen where the English had meanwhile hoisted the white flag. But they kept the gateway locked so scaling ladders and grenades were required after all to force surrender. Only thirteen Englishmen turned out to be present in the fort. There was not much loot to be had for the Dutchmen as the English had earlier shipped their commodities to Cormantijn as a precaution.

The day after the recapture, some thousand African auxiliaries arrived in two to three hundred canoes from Elmina. They were accompanied by two company servants who carried a letter from Johan Valckenburgh for De Ruyter. It said that he was to lay waste to fort Witsen as the costs for its upkeep were too high. While the Dutchmen blew up the fort, the Elminans pillaged the environment looking for African adversaries. Those they could get hold of were straightaway killed and decapitated. Now that they had dealt with the English in Takoradi, the Dutch could head for Elmina. There, De Ruyter and his men were welcomed by Johan Valckenburg. It took them days to unload the spoils that were stored in the castle.[42] While the ships were riding at anchor, an advice yacht from the Republic arrived on 10 January carrying letters for De Ruyter. From these, and from the oral information given by the master of the yacht Govert Hermansz, it became clear that the English had fitted out a fleet of thirty warships under Prince Rupert for an expedition to West Africa. The States General set against this the twelve warships of Jan van Kampen that were shortly to be added to De Ruyter's fleet. Meanwhile, De Ruyter was ordered to capture or sink all armed English ships he encountered, whether warships or merchantmen.[43] Thus, the tone for war was set. The letter was dated 21 October 1664, so it was very likely that Rupert and Van Kampen were already underway. De Ruyter took absolutely no risk and dispatched a yacht to scan the seas for approaching fleets. Further, preparations were made to have the fleet completely at the ready. The two English merchantmen that he had promised safe-conduct at Gorée, but that were still part of his fleet, were as yet declared to be prizes and fitted out as fire ships.

De Ruyter planned to first recapture Cabo Corso from the English but director-general Valckenburgh was of a different opinion. He requested that De Ruyter first dealt with the English headquarters at Cormantijn where local ruler Jan Kabesse had perpetrated acts of cruelty against the Dutch with the knowledge of the English governor Francis Selwyn.[44] At first, De Ruyter wanted to await the arrival of Rupert and Van Kampen but on 4 February the war council agreed all the same to attack Cormantijn. Again, an amphibian operation was decided on. Since it was expecting more resistance – after the assault on fort Witsen the English were ready for anything – the war council decided to deploy a landing force of some eight to nine hundred. Count Jan van Hoorn was again given supreme command of the force. To the force were also added twelve hundred armed Elminans in four to five hundred canoes. From the landward side the force would be backed by auxiliaries of Fante, who had been bribed by Valckenburgh. The plan was to capture the English lodges in Anomabu and Adja on the way to Cormantijn but that plan fell through because of the absence of Fante.[45] Later Adja was captured as yet.

The attack on Cormantijn was launched on 8 February. The landing forces had been provided with instructions, weapons and scaling ladders. The Elminans wore white linen neck cloths to distinguish them from the African allies of the English in the turmoil of the battle. Before the assault governor Selwyn received a written demand to surrender from De Ruyter but he did not react to this. Unknowingly, Selwyn thus sealed the fate of a great number of Africans and Europeans whose lives were violently lost. The landing operation was begun after a heavy firing on Cormantijn from the ships. As an extra incentive to the troops, De Ruyter had promised them unlimited plundering. He could not have foreseen that that promise would result in a veritable Armageddon. The Elminans stormed toward the African allies of the English and put them to a cruel death. They beheaded their opponents and then put their hands in the bloody larynxes while whooping with delight.[46] Shooting around, the Dutch landing forces ran with their scaling ladders towards the fort. The English inside the fort feared they would also be killed by the Elminans and opted for a quick surrender to the Dutch. Jan Kabesse and some African faithful followers were the only ones to put up resistance. Governor Selwyn could only just prevent him from blowing up the fort. Kabesse then cut the throats of his son and two slaves, and committed suicide. The Dutch made 58 Englishmen prisoners of war, bringing them quickly to a place of safety before the murderous Elminans could get at them. Then the fort was plundered by a frenzied crowd of soldiers and sailors. Great quantities of alcohol were consumed during this looting and acts of violence broke out whereby a number of men lost their lives.[47] The day after, De Ruyter and his officers were hard pressed to restore order and discipline among the soldiery. Upon his departure he left 52 crew members behind who were to protect the fort together with 10 WIC personnel and 10 Africans. The crew was to be relieved as soon as possible by company servants. Valckenburgh renamed the fort Amsterdam and appointed Samuel Smit as its commander.[48]

■ To the West Indies and Newfoundland

Having recaptured Cormantijn De Ruyter returned to Elmina where on the day of his arrival a ship from the Republic carrying letters from the States General put in as well. One of the letters said that the English had decided not to send Prince Rupert to West Africa with a fleet. They thus no longer posed an immediate threat and the States General had therefore decided not to send the relief fleet under Jan van Kampen to the Gold Coast, as had been planned. But in other areas danger had increased. Another letter stated that English privateers had seized various Dutch ships in European waters. Besides, an English naval squadron under the command of Richard Nicolls had seized the colony of New Netherland in September 1664. Officially, war had not yet broken out between the two countries but in practice that made little difference. The States General no longer harboured any illusions about keeping the peace and had it in mind to now repay the English in kind. Michiel de Ruyter was commissioned to cross the ocean with his fleet and then to cause as much damage as he could to the English colonies in the Caribbean and in North America. He was also to try and recapture New Netherland and seize all English merchantmen he encountered on his voyage.

It took the crew days to provision the ships and get them ready for sailing. It was decided to leave 24 volunteers behind as reinforcements to the garrisons on the Gold Coast. Towards the end of February the ships were ready to sail. On 27 February Director-General Johan Valckenburgh invited the officers of the fleet to a farewell dinner at the castle from which De Ruyter was absent due to illness. But the captive

Fort Cormantijn, later renamed
Fort Amsterdam.

Drawing by G. Heermans, 1706, Nederlands
Scheepvaartmuseum, Amsterdam

English governor Francis Selwyn did make an appearance at the table. That very same day the fleet consisting of twelve warships, a fluyt for the provisions and a fire ship departed from the roadstead of Elmina. Having spent eight weeks on the Gold Coast De Ruyter was happy to leave with the greater part of his crew. The Europeans feared the stretch of coastline because of the tropical diseases that claimed a great number of victims but the crew members had miraculously escaped that fate. The ships sailed in a south-easterly direction for two weeks before getting a favourable wind just south of the equator which enabled them to put about westwards to start the crossing to the Caribbean. During the crossing De Ruyter and his captains had to draw on all their seamanship to keep the ships, which were of diverse sailing capacities, together. Some days' sailing from Barbados the admiral convened his officers on board the *Spiegel* for a council of war. It was decided to seize all English ships they would come across in the Caribbean. Only the merchantmen that were riding at anchor before a French island were to be spared. France was an ally of the Republic that had to remain out of the conflict.[49]

On 30 April De Ruyter sailed his ships into the Bay of Barbados where over thirty ships were riding at anchor. The Dutch came straightaway under fire from the forts and the ships. During the attack De Ruyter took care of an English warship while his captains focused on the merchantmen and the forts. Resistance, however, was so fierce that after ninety minutes De Ruyter resolved to break off hostilities. His ships had been damaged considerably and all had casualties to tend to and deaths to mourn. It was decided to head for the nearby French island of Martinique. There the Dutch were given a warm welcome by the authorities and the local population. De Ruyter, however, wanted to lose as little time as possible. He had the dead buried with military honours, ordered the damage to ships and rigging to be repaired as quickly as possible and told his men to stock up water and victuals. Even before the entire fleet was ready to sail some ships were sent ahead to see if any English merchantmen could be captured in the neighbourhood. The squadron succeeded in overpowering nine ships off Montserrat but the freight they had on board was of little value. At Nevis they failed to capture a large frigate with valuable merchandise. However, a couple of days later Captain Isaac Sweers succeeded after all in seizing the ship loaded with ivory, indigo, sugar and tobacco. Some of the vessels that had been captured were sold on the French island of St. Christopher (St. Kitts) for about twelve thousand pounds of sugar each. The next stop was St. Eustatius where De Ruyter and his men were given an enthusiastic welcome by their fellow countrymen. Once more, various prize ships were sold in return for cotton, sugar and other produce. De Ruyter simply had too few men to man all those ships. On 17 May the voyage continued north with twenty ships. The original fleet of twelve warships, the supply fluyt and the fire ship, had now been enlarged with five prize ships laden with booty and the Rotterdam merchantman *Sint Petrus*.

The States General had asked De Ruyter to recapture the colony of New Netherland from the English, but then for unknown reasons abandoned their plan. The English had probably long since been informed of the arrival of the fleet and had put the colony in a state of defence. De Ruyter gave bringing the prize ships with their rich rewards safely home priority over an uncertain assault of New Netherland, especially after news had reached him of the official declaration of war between England and the Republic.[50] On 11 June the war council on board the *Spiegel* decided to call at Terraneuve (Newfoundland) in accordance with the States General's wishes. The captains were told to cause as much damage as they could to the English merchantmen and cod fishers active there. Then they were to take in water for the voyage home. Finally, they were to set course for the south-eastern tip of the Faroer Islands from where they would travel the last leg of the voyage together. In this time of war it was too risky to sail home separately. There was not much loot to be had at Terraneuve. Off St. John's various merchantmen were seized, besides fishing vessels. Six set of cannon were taken from the land and loaded into one of the prize ships as booty. On the other hand, though, De Ruyter also showed himself a generous and mild conqueror who had bread and goods distributed among the poor fishermen at St. John's. The English sailors of the captured prizes were given three ships and victuals with which they could return home. These acts of De Ruyter's belied the rumours that the Dutch behaved atrociously towards those they had conquered. The crew of a ship recently arrived from Barbados had spread rumours that the Dutch had cut off the ears, noses and private parts of English prisoners of war in Guinea.[51] On 20 June the signal for departure was given. A month later the fleet passed the

The fleet of Michiel de Ruyter arrives in the Wester Ems, July/August, 1665.

Drawing by Willem van de Velde the Elder, 1665, National Maritime Museum, Greenwich

Faroer Islands. For reasons of security it was then decided to sail above the Shetland Islands along to the Norwegian coast and from there as quickly as possible to the Republic.

■ Coming home and looking back

On 6 August the fleet arrived at Delfzijl where De Ruyter and his men were given a hero's welcome.[52] For the occasion the ships were decorated with English flags that had been captured. On his expedition, De Ruyter had not lost a single ship and only very few men. That amounted to a small miracle, given the length of the expedition and the dangerous tasks carried out on the way. Still, what had the expedition brought the Republic?

The action of De Ruyter had, in any case, led directly to the outbreak of the Second Anglo-Dutch War. As soon as news of the recapturing of Gorée reached the English, Sir Thomas Allin had launched an attack on the Dutch Smyrna fleet off Cadiz in December 1664. From that time on ships were seized by both sides until March 1665 saw the drafting of an official declaration of war.[53] From a political and military viewpoint the expedition can be said to have been a great success. Johan de Witt and his allies had grown convinced after the actions of Holmes and Nicolls that war with England was inevitable. With the expedition they clearly showed that the Republic was prepared to fight for its trading interests and overseas possessions.

De Ruyter had succeeded in recapturing the Dutch forts and factories in West Africa earlier taken by Holmes. Only the erstwhile Swedish fort at Cabo Corso remained in English hands. He had thus safeguarded the Dutch trade position in the area for the next decades. The actions in the Caribbean and in North America may have been less successful but they too caused considerable damage to English shipping.

From a financial point of view the expedition had been more than cost-effective. In West Africa a number of ships, large amounts of ivory and European commodities had been seized. At Barbados and other islands in the Caribbean sixteen merchantmen had been taken as prize while at Newfoundland another seven ships had been seized. Some of the captured ships that De Ruyter was not able to man were sold in the Caribbean for valuable tropical agricultural produce. The spoils that had been left behind in Elmina and the ships that were sold in the Caribbean yielded the State some 230,000 guilders. It is not known how much the remaining prizes and spoils fetched in the Republic, but the amount must have been considerable.[54]

Michiel de Ruyter, who had been promoted to Admiral of the Fleet during his absence, was appointed commander-in-chief of the fleet shortly upon his return.

That made De Ruyter, as Ronald Prud'homme van Reine argues in his biography, 'unquestionably the most distinguished Dutch naval officer'.[55] After that, he played a leading part in the battle with the English at sea. The peace treaty that was drawn up in Breda on 31 July 1667 stated that the company forts recaptured by De Ruyter in West Africa, including the erstwhile English headquarters at Cormantijn, were to remain in Dutch hands. The CRA, responsible for Holmes' expedition and therefore indirectly also for De Ruyter's, went bankrupt in 1672. Its successor, the Royal African Company, would in the decades to come be the WIC's great adversary in West Africa, but by that time Michiel de Ruyter had long since been added to the pantheon of fallen sea heroes.[56]

CHAPTER 9

De Ruyter versus Duquesne

A Battle to the Death

Michel Vergé-Franceschi

*The battle of Agosta (Etna),
April 22nd, 1676.*

*Painting by Abraham Storck, around 1680,
Nederlands Scheepvaartmuseum,
Amsterdam*

On 29 April, 1676, Michiel Adriaenszoon De Ruyter, sixty-nine years of age, succumbed to his wounds in the waters off Syracuse. Europe prepared to pay homage to this Spanish Grandee and posthumous duke of Ruyter, born in Vlissingen in the house of a brewery worker. King Louis XIV of France saw in him 'a man who did honour to humanity', and at sea many were the crew that made way for the vanquished fleet carrying his remains to home port in Holland. Everything had begun a year earlier.

It was during the first great war waged by Louis XIV (reigned 1643–1715) that De Ruyter found death in Sicilian waters. France, though Catholic, had long liked the Dutch, though Calvinist. In fact, the enmity between the most important of the seven provinces that would eventually form the United Provinces and France's principal adversary, the Habsburgs, was of long standing. That enmity was especially acrimonious with the Spanish Habsburg, Philip II of Spain (1555–1598). He was the son and heir of Charles V (1500–1558), the first Habsburg to ascend to the thrones of Castile and Aragon on the deaths of his grandfather, Ferdinand of Aragon (1516), and of his grandmother, Isabelle of Castile (1504). Early on Philip II ran into trouble with the Protestants of the North. A conflict between the Catholic king and the *Geuzen*, or Sea Beggars, could not help but last, and it did. For eighty years, from 1568 to 1648, the Hollanders, the Zeelanders, the Frisians and others waged their war of independence against kings Philip II, Philip III (1598–1621) and Philip IV (1621–1665). Finally, in 1648, with the Treaties of Westphalia, their independence was recognized and the seven provinces became the United Provinces, just as the thirteen American colonies would later become the United States of America after another war of independence (1778–1783), one which also pitted the fleets of England and France against each other. In the Hispano-Batavian conflict, the France of Cardinal Richelieu (1626–1642) was always on the Dutch side, the better to fight the King of Spain during the long Franco-Spanish conflict of 1635–1659. At the end of those wars Louis XIV was able to strip from his mother's brother, King Philip IV of Spain, several possessions: Roussillon, Perpignan, Céret and Salses ('the most beautiful fortress' then standing), Artois and Arras with its belfries. With this French help the Calvinist Dutch came to be powerful merchants with a near monopoly in the spice trade, having gradually wrested it away from the Portuguese heirs[1] of Vasco da Gama, who had opened the way for it in 1498 by landing at Kozhikode (Calicut). As a result, Jean-Baptiste Colbert (1619-1683)[2] found on coming to power in 1661 a situation very different from that which Cardinal Richelieu had faced. So radically had things changed in a little less than forty years that in 1664 and in 1667/1671, Colbert would wage two trade wars, called 'Tariff Wars', against the Sea Beggars' descendants. To keep the Dutch from flooding the French market with their goods, he persuaded Louis XIV to levy a considerable tax on Dutch imports such as herring from the North Sea, dried fish, spices from the Orient, manufactured goods, velvet from Utrecht, canvas from Haarlem, sheets from Leiden, Delftware, precious stones and diamonds cut in Amsterdam. At the same time, he created the *Compagnie du Nord* and the *Compagnie du Levant*, to export French goods such as wine, eau de vie, sheets, fabrics and other luxury articles. In the future, these items would travel under the French flag to the Low Countries, the Baltic and the Mediterranean.

The country of polders perceived a grave threat to its near monopoly of redistribution in European trade. Hindered in export as in import, the United Provinces decided to take action using its navy, which it owed partly to Maerten Harpertszoon

Tromp,[3] admiral of the fleet of Holland, and to the Dutch fluytes, those highly efficient cargo carriers which were pillars of large-scale international commerce. Faced with a populous France of some twenty million people, the Dutch of fewer than two million saw their future put in jeopardy through the maritime ambitions of the great Colbert. From 1669 onwards Pomponne, the French king's ambassador at The Hague, watched Dutch trade diminish, with fluytes often forced to remain at port for lack of freight. There was jealousy and jeering on both sides. Jean-Baptiste de Valbelle,[4] *chef d'escadre* under Louis XIV and commander and then bailiff of the Sovereign Order of Malta, referred to the Dutch as 'those cheese eaters'.[5] Their country he scorned as 'the land of burgomasters'. Passions rose. Both sides sought allies. France looked to unusual quarters: England! A man and minister of superior intelligence, Colbert was aware of France's naval inferiority relative to the Dutch, who had a strong naval tradition. In fact, the Dutch dominated production of all things of any value in the world of the 1670s. They built the best canals. Their gazettes were superior, so much so that in imitation Richelieu created the *Gazette de France*. The best fortresses before the advent of the great French engineer Sebastien le Prestre de Vauban were built '*à la hollandaise*'. The best ships too were of 'Dutch manufacture', and great French sailors like the Dieppois Abraham Duquesne (ca. 1604–1688)[6] were happy to work in the United Provinces with engineers and shipwrights from Holland. It was from there that Colbert drew many shipcarpenters and master carpenters. To fight these experts of the sea who had spawned the likes of Tromp and most recently De Ruyter, it is hardly surprising that France sought out English allies, for Albion had at its disposal the Royal Navy, sailing since the 1540s when the Tudor king Henry VIII launched it. Louis XIV and Colbert held the heirs of Drake, Raleigh, Hawkins and Frobisher in high esteem. The linchpin of this Anglo-French rapprochement was Henrietta of England (1644–1670), sister of Charles II of England, first cousin to Louis XIV and wife of the duc d'Orléans. Not long before her death, and the famous oration pronounced at her funeral by the renowned Bishop Bossuet ('*Madame se meurt, Madame est morte*'), she urged her brother, the king of England, to ally with her brother-in-law, the king of France. Charles II got lively encouragement from another quarter: his Breton mistress, Louise de Keroualle. Also, France was rich and England needed money. Indeed, in 1662 Charles II had been obliged to sell Dunkirk to his cousin, Louis XIV. On 1 June, 1670, the Treaty of Dover was signed. England and her fleet would remain allied to France until the Treaty of Westminster, signed in February, 1674, by Charles II and the United Provinces. Holland for her part also sought allies and found one in Spain, busily nourishing her rancour for France. The Spain of 1659, Catholic, lame, beaten at the battle of Rocroi in 1643 (the very day of Louis XIII's funeral, in the basilica of Saint-Denis), beaten at sea at Guetaria, at Cádiz, at Tarragona, at Cartagena, hoped to rebuild herself in 1672 through an alliance with her old Calvinist enemies.

Louis XIV and Charles II of England declared war on Holland in April, 1672. The pretext was that Dutch ships had insulted the Union Jack. The terrible threat of a double offensive, by land and by sea, descended on the Dutch as 120,000 men marched on Holland while the combined French and English fleets planned a landing in Zeeland. The armies followed their prestigious leaders, Condé and Turenne. The invaders envisioned a short war to end by Christmas, 1672. The prediction underestimated Dutch resistance. On 7 June, 1672, at Solebay (or Southwold Bay,[7] or Sousbay) off the coast of Suffolk, a single fearsome sailor held in check the combined

| DE RUYTER – DUTCH ADMIRAL

The battle of Schooneveld with por-traits of the commanding naval officers.

Print attributed to Romeyn de Hooghe, around 1673, Maritiem Museum Prins Hendrik, Rotterdam

fleets of vice-amiral d'Estrées[8] and Prince Rupert[9]: De Ruyter. The French officers still lacked experience, though they took the English Navy for their model, and De Ruyter had little trouble saving the United Provinces from a landing. Meanwhile, at enormous cost, the Dutch onshore held off the invading troops by opening the dykes of Muiden and flooding the flat land. Drama. Pain. So much pain, in fact, that the Dutch Republicans lost their grip on power, which they had held since 1650. The Grand Pensionary of Holland, Johan de Witt (1625–1672), was assassinated in The Hague in August along with his brother, Cornelis (1623–1672). Both were massacred by a mob of supporters of the Orangist party of William III who was made stadholder and took charge of the resistance to the French. Heir of the House of Nassau, he succeeded in dragging Spain, a country beaten in 1659 by Louis XIV and Mazarin, into the war against France. He also succeeded in the same way with the Habsburgs of Vienna. The war became a traditional match up: France against the House of Habsburg, as in the times of Francis I, of Richelieu and of Mazarin.

On 7 and 14 June, 1673, there was a new Anglo-French naval assault. The duke of York, now lord high admiral, and the comte Jean d'Estrées started the first battle of Schooneveld, fought one year to the day after the Battle of Solebay (7 June 1672/7 June 1673).[10] It was followed a week later by the second battle of Schooneveld, also called the battle of Walcheren.[11] De Ruyter resisted and kept them from landing new troops in Holland. On 21 August, 1673, at the battle of the Texel[12] the third attempt at an Anglo-French landing in Holland also ended in failure. The French army had to retreat from Holland and concentrate its efforts on Spain which entered the war against the *Roi Très Chrétien* on 15 October, 1673. Those efforts would focus notably on Franche-Comté.

Vice Admiral and marshall Jean II,
comte d'Estrées (1624-1707).

Painting by Jean-Pierre Franque, around
1825-50, from the RMN collection, photo-
grapher unknown, Musée de Versailles,
Versailles

Charles II received little support for the war from his people. Part of English opinion could not understand the alliance between a Stuart and Louis XIV, deemed at once too Papist and too absolute. Some wanted an alliance with the United Provinces, which, like England, was Protestant. Many reproached him for the sale, and thus the loss, of Dunkirk, which had profited France. Finally, there were ugly rumours floating around the duke of York's squadron. French officers, some said, had intervened little in the various battles of 1673 and had wilfully left their English ally to combat the Dutch adversary so that the fleets of De Ruyter and the duke of York would destroy each other and permit the French navy to become the world's greatest. Certain English officers spoke even of secret orders from Louis XIV to his naval officers instructing them in this Machiavellian design.[13] In these circumstances Charles II signed the second Treaty of Westminster with the United Provinces on 19 February, 1674, and proclaimed his neutrality. The brand-new French fleet, resurrected in 1661, found itself pitted against the two oldest navies in the world: Holland's, commanded by the illustrious De Ruyter, and Spain's, which in the previous century (1588) had launched reputedly 'invincible' armadas. To Spain's navy was added that of Naples, another part of the Habsburg king's realm.

The balance of strength between the two sides switched. Beginning in the summer of 1674, Cornelis Tromp roamed the French Atlantic coast. He did not hesitate to ransom Noirmoutier and a few islands. Then he threatened Rochefort, whose foundations Colbert was then trying to lay through his first cousin, Colbert du Terron.[14] Work on this new arsenal had only begun in 1665–1666. Meanwhile, on 20 July, 1674, as Tromp roamed, who was all the way off in Martinique trying to seize the island, French since 1635? None other than De Ruyter. Always De Ruyter.[15] Having stopped the king from landing French troops on Dutch soil, he now attacked Fort-Royal de la Martinique. Colbert, fortunately for him, had a cousin there too, a cousin of high quality: *capitaine de vaisseau* Renart d'Amblimont,[16] whose undistinguished birth stood in inverse relation to his talent. With a single frigate of thirty-six cannon, *Les Jeux* and four merchant vessels from Saint-Malo, Bordeaux, Toulon and La Ciotat, d'Amblimont resisted the Dutch and inflicted serious damage,[17] so serious that De Ruyter backed off and repaired to the United Provinces in failure.[18] D'Amblimont reaped his reward: a marquisate, newly established under the name of d'Amblimont, covering one-eighth of Champagne's wine country.

Curiously, with De Ruyter back in Europe the so-called war 'of Holland' now had as principal theatre of naval operations... the Mediterranean. Certainly, England's withdrawal gave the war a less maritime and more Continental dimension, for France had to battle the Habsburgs of Vienna and most of the German princes with the exception of Bavaria's ruler, who stayed neutral. At sea France had to battle the Spanish fleet as well as the Dutch. It is true that operations in the North were far from negligible. There France could count on the support of Sweden which suffered various setbacks in fighting with the Brandenburgers and Denmark. Still the Mediterranean was where most of the French, Dutch and Spanish naval forces were to be found. The revolt at Messina was to blame. With the Messinese in Sicily revolting against Philip IV of Spain, Louis XIV sent help. It arrived on 27 September, 1674, under Valbelle. This was a good way for Louis to reassert his presence in the western Mediterranean where the Spanish had already stripped his father of the Lerin Islands in 1635.[19] On 3 January, 1675, despite the Spanish blockade, Valbelle supplied Messina a second time. On 11 February, 1675, Vivonne[20] and Duquesne defeated the Spaniards in the first battle of Stromboli, near the Lipari Islands. On 26 June, witnessing the French navy's success in the Mediterranean, the United Provinces sent in De Ruyter to support the Spanish fleet for six months and to protect Dutch trade. Colbert was quite logically alarmed.

On 11 July, 1675, at five o'clock in the morning Colbert, who had been secretary of state in the navy since 1661, was worried. Nothing like the wee hours for confidences. Colbert wrote a note to his son Seignelay, who would succeed him on his death, in 1683. Colbert was perplexed:

"Mulling over the navy's affairs, I must admit, my son, that I have been reflecting on a painful subject. As you know, De Ruyter is headed for the Mediterranean. He will have under his command twenty-two Dutch and fourteen Spanish ships of the line, with nineteen galleys. If the duc de Vivonne is obliged to remain ashore to command the army, as it seems he will be, then the king's naval army, ships of the line and galleys will be commanded by sieur Duquesne, and it is this which pains me, for I can find nothing in Duquesne's heart or mind to compare with De Ruyter's. You must ensure that this observation is made before the king, without exaggeration. It will let His Majesty know that you are thinking only of what is good for him and for his glory, and that must also incite you to make these remarks at every occasion. I know

Pas-Caart van de MIDDELANDSCHE ZEE.

Vertoonende in twee deelen.

Nieulyck uytgegeven A.º 1654.

Namen van d'Eylanden Hoecken en Havens, gheleegen in dit weste= lijcke deel der Middelandsche Zee.

HISPANJA

Catalonia

Valentia

Algarve

Andaluzia

Granada

Murcia

Calis

Fezza

BARB

ITALIA

GRECIA

SICILIA

Morea

Candia

BARBARIA

t'Amsterdam.
By Frederick de Wildt inde Calverstraat
by den Dam inde dry Crabben.

Chart for navigation of the Mediterranean with lists of islands

Print by Frederick de Widt, around 1660, Amsterdam, Map Collection, University of Amsterdam

quite well that the king's thirty ships of the line are better equipped, better armed, better led than those of Holland, that the crews aboard the king's ships of the line are stronger and made up of better, braver men, that the Spanish ships of the line are poorly handled, poorly equipped and, in a word, that the king's thirty ships of the line, ten fire ships and twenty-four galleys ought naturally to vanquish everything that they might encounter in the Mediterranean. But, I admit, the heart and mind of the commanding officer trouble me."[21]

On 17 August Duquesne contributed to the capture of Agosta, raining heavy cannon fire on the forts of Vittoria and Piccolo and forcing their surrender.[22] On 2 September Tourville tried to assuage the fears that Colbert had inspired in Seignelay: "I believe", he wrote to his young friend, "that it would not ill affect the king's affairs if it were M. Duquesne who led us against our enemies. He seems to me as well intentioned as he is clever and able."[23] On 16 September Duquesne received orders to return to Toulon, winter there and, above all, prepare for future operations. On 17 October Louis xiv wrote to Vivonne: "As of now I am sending to Toulon my orders for the immediate and tireless refitting and careening of all my ships of the line... my intention being to put them to sea again precisely on 1 December, under the command of M. Duquesne, and have them join you."[24] In October Vivonne learned of De Ruyter's imminent arrival in the theatre of operations. On 8 November Colbert addressed his orders to Duquesne. On the 19th Duquesne informed his superior of "Reutre's [De Ruyter's] arrival... in Cádiz" at the beginning of November. On the 23rd Duquesne was ready to cast off but was painfully short of funds to complete his final preparations. "I am forced... to pawn... whatever china I have," he confessed to Colbert. For this "refined Norman",[25] known to be quite "stingy", this was a real sacrifice. Since his food stipend had not yet been paid, he did in fact need to advance money out of his own pocket to pay for his food and that of his entire staff. He resigned himself to it, in accordance with the custom of the times. He concluded, "I have forgotten to inform you that I have had two large bronze cannon of thirty-six calibre put in naval storage. They were in the two forts that I took with my division at Agosta. One is burst open, the other broken at the bore."

Just before casting off, Duquesne informed the court that he wanted to have his son Henri[26] aboard, to train him, and he recommended to Colbert the son of his brother Jacob[27], Abraham Duquesne-Guiton,[28] grandson of former La Rochelle mayor Jean Guiton. He wrote:

"He departed on the king's ships as lieutenant in 1670, going to Persia. He had several adventures, including a prison term of three years in Batavia. He returned to Europe on an English ship, for two hundred ecus. I can assure you that he was already a very good officer before that voyage. His father was killed in service, by cannon blast; may it please you to consider him a good subject, and have him paid as much of his salary as you see fit, to make up in some measure for the miseries of his last voyage. It would give me great joy if you could give him employment aboard my ship on the present occasion. He has come a long way in search of it, with a great desire to distinguish himself. I hope that you will send him back quickly and believe me your most humble and obedient servant."

On 16 December Duquesne's squadron left Toulon.

On 8 January, 1676, the first battle between De Ruyter's Dutch fleet and the

French one took place. The two squadrons confronted each other twenty-five leagues off Messina. The encounter bears the name of the second battle of Stromboli, or the battle of Alicudi. De Ruyter commanded eighteen ships of the line, four fire ships, six snows and two tenders, which prince William III, stadholder of Holland, had entrusted to him on 26 July, 1675. He had left Amsterdam on 29 July with six thousand men and thirteen hundred cannon.

Both the French and the Dutch claimed victory, but though the day was not yet won Duquesne did obtain a positive result. On 22 January he entered Messina and the populace hailed him as the victor. From Messina, Duquesne addressed his battle report to Colbert:

"The Dutch opened fire on us from a fair distance, although without our firing before they were within range as we approached Reutre... His continual artillery fire deprived us of our principal manoeuvres, killed and put out of commission our premiers officiers mariniers. *However, in the heavy fire between us and the enemy, at about two in the afternoon, with a cool wind blowing, one of our fire ships was dispatched. If not for the calm that reigned during its approach, the fire ship would have had its effect on the Dutch admiral, but that very calm gave him enough time to cut its masts with cannon fire. A similar accident through the calm occurred with one of the fire ships in the van, commanded by the marquis de Beauvoisis, who was killed. And again, towards the end of the battle, the fire ship under chevalier de La Galissonnière[29] sank after several cannonades. Reutre, his division and his vanguard retreated... The galleys advanced to withdraw the enemy ships most abused in the battle, which was over before the day was through, without all the gains that we might have hoped for... Nevertheless, having stolen the wind from Reutre, who had twenty-five warships, we attacked and made him fall back for as long as the wind permitted, compelling him to give us berth, and receiving no opposition from him as far as the lighthouse, ahead of the ten ships from Messina come to join us on the evening of the 10th, when a very dangerous gust rose up there and caused several collisions... The ships of my division that were nearest... followed me; and they show the signs of it on their masts, yards and sails, in their manoeuvres, and everywhere else. Sieurs de Langeron[30] and de Cou[31] and chevalier de Lhéry remained at their posts... Chevalier de Tourville is a good subject who merits a command... Sieur de Villeneuve-Ferrière[32] was injured in the thigh by cannon fire, which has put him out of commission. To sieur de Montreuil, a* capitaine *aboard my ship, whom I have found brave, ambitious for honour and possessed of very good sense in battle, I have given orders to command... until such time as sieur de Villeneuve is in a condition to act. Chevalier de Chaumont,* major de l'armée... *conducted himself with great presence of mind and strength wherever he found himself. It is he who at court could report to the king on the conduct of each man, if His Majesty so commands him, for he is always knowledgeable... You cannot, Monseigneur, decline to obtain leave from the King to make sieur Pallas[33] a capitaine; he has long deserved it, notably since he began serving with me as a* lieutenant. *You were previously informed; thus, Monseigneur, I hope that you will follow through on the promise that you have lately made to him, with my assurance that you gain a good subject in the navy. Sieur chevallier... lieutenant... has had his leg broken by cannon blast; he is a skilled and worthy naval man and deserves promotion. I will say nothing to you of my relations serving with me [his son Henri and his nephew Duquesne-Guiton]; I will let the public speak to you of them whenever you might be kind enough to inquire."*[34]

The *Gazette de France* honoured Duquesne. "On this occasion," it reads, "De Ruyter carried himself with all the experience and strength that one should expect from his great reputation... Sieur Duquesne, for his part, has made it clear that in ability and courage he is a worthy opponent to sieur De Ruyter." On 20 February Louis XIV addressed to Duquesne a personal letter of congratulations, and most of his battle companions praised him unconditionally. "Words can but inadequately convey the good conduct of sieur Duquesne, who has fulfilled his duties as a *général* [35] as ably as one can desire and to the approval of all the *capitaines*, unanimous in their accounts of his merit."[36] D'Alméras,[37] the royal navy's number-three *lieutenant général* after Duquesne and Martel, wrote to Colbert on 10 January, 1676, "M. Duquesne's combat happily succeeded."[38] On 24 January M. de Villedieu, for his part, wrote: "One can add nothing to what all those gentlemen say about M. Duquesne's bravery and good conduct."[39] Such was the praise for the French commander that anxiety ran high in the Dutch squadron. That anxiety was forgotten only momentarily when, on 24 March, the captains addressed their "birthday wishes" to De Ruyter who was turning sixty-nine. Even so, De Ruyter admitted, "The French have done marvels."

Duquesne nevertheless remained prudent, for De Ruyter's squadron was intact. In addition, his own military staff was uneven, and he did not shrink from criticizing it:

> *"The officers and capitaines who have served only in the Mediterranean are not apt to observe orders and signals for the running of a ship and for battle as fully as they ought to do, for they lack practice. Indeed, without the proper experience, they have trouble even agreeing to them. We recognize this as the advantage that the Dutch have over us, of sailing at almost all times, notably in the presence of their enemies, night and day, in battle; and thus do they avoid among themselves the collisions to which we aboard the king's ships are all too subject. Should His Majesty do me the honour of perpetuating my command in his armies, I shall be obliged to obtain strong protection from him, that I might force those officers and capitaines to observe naval exercise, and that, even when it befalls us to be at sea in winter and in our enemies' presence, it might be best that I indicate the proper ships and capitaines for such service."*

As he had figured, Duquesne found it necessary, on 22 April, 1676, to confront De Ruyter in what would be the old Dutchman's final battle. The two enemy squadrons having met just off Agosta, the encounter is remembered as the battle of Etna. Since 19 April De Ruyter's main objective had been to capture Agosta, which had fallen into French hands on 17 August, 1675. On 22 April the squadrons of Holland and France faced off on a sea "no more agitated than the canal of Versailles." Duquesne commanded the centre, d'Alméras, who had joined him after the second battle of Stromboli (Alicudi), commanded the van and Jean Gabaret[40] had command of the rear. Duquesne's fleet had the twenty ships of the line that fought at Alicudi, the ten from d'Alméras' division from Messina, eight or nine fire ships, two frigates and five tartanes. The Hispano-Batavian fleet had De Ruyter at the van, De Haen[41] at the rear and the Spanish admiral don Francisco Periere-Freire de La Cerda at the centre. The Dutch had seventeen ships of the line, six snows, four fire ships and two longboats. The Spanish had ten ships of the line, one fire ship, one tender and nine galleys. In all, the enemy had 1,450 cannon arrayed against the 1,772 aboard Duquesne's ships.

After a mere half-hour of combat De Ruyter fell victim to sustained fire from the *Lys*, commanded by d'Alméras. His left foot was torn off, his right leg broken, his

right ankle shattered. With these grave wounds, he fell from the poop deck, suffering a contusion to his head on impact. A half-hour later, on the French side, d'Alméras was killed in turn, as was *capitaine de vaisseau* Tambonneau.[42] Villette-Mursay's son,[43] only twelve years old, was slightly injured. The struggle continued for six hours, ending with a Dutch retreat to Syracuse that evening. Duquesne lost only five hundred men versus seven hundred on the Dutch side. The most illustrious of those, De Ruyter, was in agony aboard his ship. La Cerda asked to visit him. De Ruyter refused, replying that he had "seen enough poltroons to last a lifetime." Charles II of Spain would soon recall his admiral.

In France the navy was praised to the skies, even by officers of the army and princes of royal blood, Condé among them. Louis XIV commissioned a painting, *La Victoire d'Agosta*, to be executed by the Flemish painter Van Beecq.

On 22 May, 1676, Duquesne thanked Seignelay for his congratulations, given on the occasion of the first battle (Alicudi), and informed him of the second (Etna):

"Monseigneur, I have received with great joy the honour you have done me with your letter of 23 February, concerning our last battle with Reutre. I am in your debt, Monseigneur, for the esteem that you have seen fit to accord me even before I have had the honour of meeting you. I hope that you will have nothing to regret, Monseigneur, and that you will find satisfaction in conveying once again to the king the certain news of a second battle that we have given Reutre and the Spanish, as you will see in the journal my nephew [Duquesne-Guiton] will submit to you. I may also assure you that I am doing everything in my power to prepare our forces for departure... Since our return from Messina, when I learned of the honour done me by the king, your father and you yourself from your respective letters, sieur Valbelle has been unable to refrain from hatching his plots... [In the] cabal is, among others, sieur [Jean] Gabaret, who knows not whom to blame for his having received no letter of congratulations either from the king or from you... You are aware, Monseigneur, of sieur de Valbelle's most pernicious spirit... Pray, Monseigneur, take steps to assure peace within the corps, that we may all serve the king with joyful hearts... All will be well once the cabal has no leader."[44]

After these lines attacking Valbelle, a Provençal officer like another before him, Paul, whom Duquesne liked no better though both were devout Catholics and knights of Malta, Duquesne requested certain compensation for *capitaine de vaisseau* de Pallas, praising his "merit" and "ability", for "sieur Ris ... [an] *aide-major* who has lost his hand to a cannonball and was hit in the thigh by the same", and for a few others. He also thanked Seignelay for having obtained special grace from the king for his son Henri, a boy of fifteen. "I found out only today", he wrote, "that you had obtained honour for my son from the command of the *Parfait*; for this, Monseigneur, I am very much obliged to you."

Seignelay transmitted to Colbert all of Duquesne's remarks and notes. In the margins, Colbert wrote, "To my son. Observe what he says of Valbelle and of Gabaret. In the navy, nothing is more important than eliminating every sort of intrigue and cabal." After the battle of Etna, as after Alicudi, Duquesne had plenty of advice for Colbert:

"I hope that His Majesty will soon have the satisfaction of seeing his navy in high repute, if it please him to purge certain troublemakers and other mercenaries who sow division in her ranks; as for the rest, there are very fine men who begin to show promise and from whom we should expect much. There are some who are accustomed to debauchery when at harbour or port, and who are insufficiently exact in observing orders for running a ship and avoiding collisions, in the absence of extraordinary severity. I am obliged, with regret, to supply it lest I give them an excuse to disobey my orders on some important occasion. I have reason to be happy with the advice and conduct of MM. de Preuilly, de Valbelle and de Tourville and of the Marquis d'Amfreville, who deserves promotion. Chevalier de Lhéry has also distinguished himself on all occasions."

After the battle of Etna, Duquesne took charge as the unofficial commander of all naval personnel, able to bestow the graces of the king. Already supreme in matters of shipbuilding and port infrastructure, he now became omnipresent in all matters.

Truth be told, Colbert was delighted. He wrote:

"Monsieur, I cannot express how deeply I am touched by the glory that you have brought to the king's armies in the second battle that you have just fought, and also by the glory that you have won for yourself. I have no doubt that His Majesty will let you know of the satisfaction that He has received from your two fine acts in the campaign... Rest assured that your every counsel for the king's service will be followed; above all, set yourself to obtaining obedience and regularity throughout the king's navy, and ensure that there is neither cabal nor document that might harm you in the king's eyes."[45]

While De Ruyter's remains, saluted, they say, by cannon volleys from French ports, sailed for the United Provinces, Duquesne soared high in honour. Soon, in 1682, he would be created marquis du Quesne, and the king would give him the 300,000 *livres* needed to buy, near Étampes, the lands of Bouchet, of Val-Petit and of Bouchet-Val-grand, in the county of Montlhéry (1681). In effect, thus ended the careers of the two greatest Calvinist sailors of the seventeenth century. Legend has it that Duquesne requested, in vain, to be appointed the *vice-amirauté du Levant*, that is, commander of the Mediterranean fleet, saying to the king: "I am Protestant, but my service is catholic." The bon mot is no doubt apocryphal but Duquesne's services were indeed catholic from the siege of Rochelle in 1628, where he served against his coreligionists, to the death of the seventeenth century's greatest sailor, Michiel de Ruyter, whose name lived on by coincidence in the eighteenth century, in Toulon, borne by men of no relation to him.

CHAPTER 10

De Ruyter and his flag officers

Jaap R. Bruijn

De Ruyter worked with many flag officers. In his early years he had a few fellow flag officers. In 1652 when he was appointed vice-commodore of the Admiralty of Zeeland and was going to command a section of the fleet, none of the five admiralties, not in Zeeland nor in Holland nor in Friesland, had more than one flag officer in permanent service. Only in subsequent years did the number of flag officers increase, though slowly, and then it exploded in 1664-1665. The initiative for the sudden expansion of the officers' corps came from the admiralty Admiralty of Zeeland. The other four admiralties quickly followed Zeeland's example.

The growth in the number of flag officers ran parallel to an expansion of the fleet. A great building program in 1653 and a new one in 1664 resulted in a battle fleet of such a size that more flag officers than ever before were required. By then, the Dutch navy had become a full-grown modern navy, able to match any major opponent. In August 1665, after his return from the West, De Ruyter was appointed admiral of the fleet. He sat at the top of a hierarchy of fifteen rear admirals, vice admirals and lieutenant admirals. There were three of each per admiralty. He became the supreme commander of the fleet immediately after his return from the expedition to the Mediterranean, West-Africa, the Caribbean and New-Foundland. Though his return had been much desired, it was still rather unexpected. His squadron consisted of twelve men-of-war, equipped by the three admiralties in Holland. The ships were commanded by twelve officers of whom nine either were already flag officers or were soon appointed as such. These men had gotten to know their commander and themselves pretty well on a journey of about fifteen months. There had been some bitter disputes on the first part of the trip. It is likely, however, that De Ruyter learned to accept and perhaps to appreciate collaboration with colleagues who were not fully compatible while they learned to understand and accept his ideas about order and discipline and about tactics and strategy. The expedition probably had a great impact upon De Ruyter's leadership in later years.

In this chapter an outline of the old and new structure plus the composition of the flag officers' corps is sketched in a period when naval officers became professionals. De Ruyter's position amidst his fellow flag officers before he became admiral of the fleet is described and some of the characteristics of his principal colleagues are given. The situation later in his career was different. De Ruyter was soon by far the oldest officer in the fleet. Still he had close relations with some of these younger flag officers. During the Third Anglo Dutch War he had most of his closest and dearest colleagues around him in his own squadron but he must have felt almost alone on his last two expeditions in 1674 and 1675.

Vice Admiral Witte Cornelisz de With (1599-1658)

Painting by an unknown artist after a portrait by H.M. Sorgh dated 1654, 1677, Nederlands Scheepvaartmuseum, Amsterdam

■ Changes in the structure of the flag officers' corps

It was a long-standing tradition that noblemen commanded the fleet. They were thought to have had a military and fighting background. Two members of the Van Duivenvoorde-Van Wassenaer family held the position of lieutenant admiral from 1578 till 1623.[1] A bastard son of Prince Maurice had the rank from 1625 to 1627. It was only natural. Things changed in 1629 when 'commoner' Piet Heyn (1577-1629) was appointed lieutenant admiral. But he was soon killed in action and a new nobleman succeeded him. That was Philips van Dorp (1587-1652), who had long been a naval officer. As a commander, however, Van Dorp was a disaster and in 1637 he was forced to resign. The 'commoner' Maerten Harpertsz Tromp (1598-1653) was his successor, a most fortunate choice as it turned out.

The tradition of noble admirals was broken but another tradition remained entrenched: the admiral of the fleet had to be from Holland and he had to be appointed by the States of that province. It remained the prerogative of that province. The three Holland admiralties shared the cost of the office: Amsterdam paid the monthly wage of 300 guilders, Rotterdam the victualling allowances and the Noorderkwartier an extra bonus.[2] This prerogative stayed unassailable until 1690, when the lieutenant admiral of Zeeland, Cornelis Evertsen de Jongste (1642-1706) commanded the Dutch fleet in joint Anglo-Dutch operations against France. That only happened once.

The appointment of an admiralty's flag officer was a decision of the provincial States of Zeeland, Holland or Friesland. The admiralties nominated candidates in their respective provinces, from rear admiral to lieutenant admiral. The substantial seventeenth century increase in the number of subordinate flag officers took a long time to materialise. From 1637 the admiralty of Zeeland had a vice admiral and a commodore: Johan Evertsen (1600-1666) and Joost Banckert (1599-1647). At the outbreak of the First Anglo-Dutch War in 1652, Zeeland because of the death of Banckert had only a vice admiral. Temporary appointments, as had been the custom, followed. De Ruyter's position was also meant to be temporary. In 1653 Johan Evertsen's brother, Cornelis (1610-1666), became a permanent commodore.[3] The picture would not change until December 1664.

It was no different with the three Holland admiralties. At Rotterdam Witte de With (1599-1658) was vice admiral from 1637. He had several temporary rear admirals as his colleagues, men who had provisional appointments for one campaign or fighting season. Jan Verhaeff (1600-c. 1662) was made a permanent rear admiral in 1653, and at his death he was succeeded by Aert van Nes (1626-1693). De With's position was given to Egbert Kortenaer (c. 1605-1665) in 1659. The admiralty of the Noorderkwartier only appointed its first flag officer in 1652. That was rear admiral Pieter Florisz (c. 1609-1658) who in 1653 was promoted to vice admiral. At his death Jan Meppel (1609-1669) was named his successor. Florisz's position of rear admiral was filled up by Jacob de Boer (1600-1655), but then left vacant till 1659 when Volkert Schram (1622-1673) became the new rear admiral. In 1652 the greatest naval organization in the Dutch Republic, the admiralty at Amsterdam, did not have a single permanent flag officer. De Ruyter became its vice admiral in 1653, while Cornelis Tromp (1629-1691) was appointed rear admiral. The admiralty in Friesland had no flag officer until 1665!

Lieutenant Admiral Aert van Nes (1626-1693).

Painting by Bartholomeus van der Helst with a sea-scape by Ludolf Backhuysen, 1668, Rijksmuseum, Amsterdam

An adequate corps of flag officers was obviously not the concern of the naval administration, neither during the First Anglo-Dutch War nor in the following decade. When needed, temporary rear admirals and commodores were the solution. Some captains were simply upgraded. It was cheaper to pay the monthly captain's wage of 30 guilders than a rear admiral's 100 guilders. To clarify the structure, in 1654 there were three vice admirals (Johan Evertsen, De With and Florisz) and three rear admirals (Verhaeff, Cornelis Tromp and De Boer). Ten years later not much had changed. There were no more flag officers, only four new names: Kortenaer, Meppel, Van Nes and Schram. After Maerten Tromp was killed in 1653, Jacob van Wassenaer van Obdam (1610-1665) succeeded him as admiral of the fleet. He was a nobleman and his appointment was a product of the embarrassment that no active flag officer was thought qualified for the job. Authority, seniority and enough naval experience were required from a naval officer. No one fulfilled those three requirements so once again a high nobleman with military qualifications, as a half a century before, became admiral of the fleet.

The incomplete and unbalanced structure of the flag officers' corps was at odds with the professionalization of the navy itself. Huge building programs were under way from 1653 and were soon expanded even more. Naval administrators accepted the demise of the system of renting merchantmen to serve as temporary warships. In engagements with a strict line-of-battle, as more and more was the case with the English and the Dutch, armed merchantmen turned out to be of no value. In 1654, shortly before the peace of Westminster, the States General stipulated that the sixty newly built men-of-war be considered national property and not be sold by any of the five admiralties which had happened with some ships at the end of the Eighty Years' War in 1648. A huge naval dockyard and arsenal ('*'s Lands Zeemagazijn*') was built in Amsterdam in 1655-1656. Grand Pensionary Johan de Witt arranged adequate funding for this 'new' navy.

It looked as if the development of a proper corps of flag officers had been forgotten. The States of Zeeland broke the silence on this issue, that was in December 1664.[4] National interest was not the motivation for this step. The province had always been eager to provide the fleet with the supreme commander or at least with the second in command. After MaertenTromp's death in August 1653, vice admiral Johan Evertsen had not been accepted by Holland as the temporary supreme commander. On the eve of the Second Anglo-Dutch War Zeeland appointed Johan Evertsen to its own and long vacant lieutenant admiralship, taking for granted that its highest flag officer would now be the second man in the fleet. Six weeks passed before Holland reacted by upgrading its three vice admirals to the rank of lieutenant admiral in the three respective admiralties and immediately filled the top slots of vice and rear admirals. Holland now had ten flag officers. The States of Friesland then also decided to have its own brand-new flag officers and, in March 1665, created its own lieutenant, vice and rear admirals. All of a sudden Van Wassenaer van Obdam had fifteen flag officers. Zeeland's original plan to let Evertsen become second-in-command failed. That job went to Cornelis Tromp who took command of the fleet after Van Wassenaer van Obdam's death in the battle of Lowestoft in June 1665.

Though it looked ridiculous to more than double the size of the flag officers' corps in four months time and for Friesland that may have been the case, overall the increase was long overdue. Short-lived upgrading of captains was out of date in a professional and standing navy. The number of warships moreover was going to be doubled as a result of the large building program of 60 ships started in 1664. These new ships were all larger than the existing ones. Fighting was now done in the more formalized line of battle. The fleet was composed of three squadrons, each subdivided in three '*smaldelen*' (divisions). Each ship had its place in the line-of-battle. The nine different divisions each required one flag officer. The admiral included, ten flag officers had to be in place during a battle. Other, lower flag officers commanded convoy activities or operated against the Barbary corsairs in the Mediterranean.

De Ruyter was promoted to lieutenant admiral at Amsterdam in the big wave of promotions in 1664-1665. The admiralship of the fleet came seven months later in August 1665. Most of his new colleagues were known to him, but the composition of the flag officers' corps changed constantly. Flagships were deployed in the frontline in battle and their commanders often placed themselves prominently on board, though that was forbidden. Several of them were killed in the sharp and bloody engagements of the Second and Third Anglo Dutch Wars. The deaths meant there were numerous shifts in the corps and De Ruyter soon found himself the senior in age and experience.

What types these colleagues were and with whom De Ruyter had special relations, is sketched in the next two paragraphs.

■ Flag officers in the period 1652-1664

De Ruyter had been in naval service once before. That was in 1641-1642 as the third in command of an auxiliary fleet sent to Portugal. In 1652 almost all his colleagues were new to him. He only knew Pieter Florisz and, of course, his fellow townsman from Flushing, Johan Evertsen. De Ruyter must have been familiar with several other naval captains in Flushing. We know, however, little about the social relations between individual flag officers and captains on board and ashore. The council-of-war was the place where they invariably and consistently met each other. De Ruyter was lucky in that he entered service in time to see how Tromp handled his fleet as its supreme commander. That great admiral had to fight a war with inadequate means and was faced with the ingratitude of the political leaders in 1652 and 1653. It would not be much different for De Ruyter at the end of his own career.

Witte de With, the vice admiral of Rotterdam and Tromp's perennial rival, was in 1653 the most obvious successor as admiral of the fleet. That did not happen. De With's career in the navy had begun in 1622, when he became a captain of the Rotterdam admiralty. De With certainly was a flag officer of great fame. In his earlier years he had served in Asia and South America, and had assisted Piet Heyn in capturing a rich Spanish treasure fleet in 1628. During the thirties and forties he fought against Dunkirk and Ostend privateers, and in 1644 and 1645 he commanded huge convoys through the Sound when diplomatic relations with Denmark were very strained. He clashed, however, with admiral Tromp, whom he thought to be no more than his equal rather than his superior. De With was a very courageous man, a champion of boarding tactics in battle, but lacked sufficient social graces in circumstances when these were required. He was a hot-tempered man. De Ruyter himself described an example. In 1656 Dutch diplomats visited the Dutch fleet at the roadstead of Gdańsk. When they were on board De With's ship, the vice admiral got irritated for some reason and began to curse his guests. He called them corrupt and abusers of the wives of captains at sea.[5] Such incidents disqualified him for the highest position in the fleet. Another thing was his behaviour in 1650. Three years before, De With had been sent on an impossible mission to Brazil in order to save the last remnants of the Dutch presence there. His ships did not receive any further support, not even much needed extra victuals. In 1650 he decided to return home without having orders to do so. On his return he was arrested, but after a long trial he was rehabilitated.[6] De With was definitively not the man to succeed Tromp and to command a fleet that would have to adjust to the line-of-battle tactics demonstrated in 1653 by the anticipated English opponent. In November 1658 De With was killed in the battle of the Sound.

As said Van Wassenaer van Obdam, a high-ranked nobleman and lieutenant general of cavalry, succeeded Tromp. He was an influential member of the States of Holland and of the States General as well. He had never been to sea before. He always suffered from gout and on board he was surrounded by at least four servants and two special cooks. His first years in command were reasonable and Kortenaer served as his flag captain. In later years, however, Van Wassenaer van Obdam became something of a lame duck. The boards of admiralty at Amsterdam and Hoorn/Enkhuizen accused him of weak leadership in the battle of the Sound of 1658 and afterwards. The question was not resolved and both admiralties refused to admit him in their meetings during the following four years.

On board the esteem Van Wassenaer van Obdam enjoyed for his noble birth and status as a distinguished army general was great. Both qualifications inspired respect among naval captains and flag officers who were simple commoners and were always rated lower than army officers. No critical remarks from De Ruyter are known. He served under Van Wassenaer van Obdam's command in 1656, 1657, 1658 and briefly in 1659. During the summer of 1656 he wrote on Sundays almost weekly in his ship's log: 'I have attended a good sermon (*'schone predycasye'*) on board the Admiral's ship'. This may be an indication of good personal relations between the two men.[7]

Pieter Florisz had not been a candidate for Tromp's position. He was in age a peer of De Ruyter and had been born at Monnickendam. In May 1652 he had become rear admiral of the Noorderkwartier Admiralty, after having been its captain from 1644. His appointment as vice admiral came on the same day as De Ruyter's, November 11, 1653. Not much is known about their personal relations. They had met twice before, in 1640 and 1641. Florisz had been a master of a West-Indiaman, and in 1641 captain in the fleet sent to Portugal, serving in De Ruyter's division. The admiralty of Zeeland had then insisted on the position of rear admiral for De Ruyter at the expense of a senior colleague of Florisz in the Noorderkwartier.

Florisz was one of the many naval officers who participated in nearly all major and minor campaigns of their days. As with the others, for him being a naval officer became an occupation. He was present in the Baltic with Witte De With in 1644, in all engagements of the First Anglo-Dutch War and under Van Wassenaer van Obdam in the Baltic in 1656, off Portugal in 1657 and off Denmark in 1658. He was killed in the battle of the Sound, together with De With. Like De Ruyter he was twice a widower. In 1654 he married again. This time the bride was the daughter of a Hoorn burgomaster. His promotion to vice admiral had not been automatic. Initially only Monnickendam supported him, the other cities of the Noorderkwartier nominating other candidates. Hoorn's argument had been the rank of rear admiral was high enough for him![8]

Johan Evertsen was not a candidate in 1653 either, as mentioned before. He was an old hand in De Ruyter's eyes. Born in 1600 and serving the navy since time immemorial, he was above all a seasoned vice admiral. At the age of 19 Evertsen had become a naval captain. His family had strong traditional links with the navy. Johan himself held the position of vice admiral for almost 30 years, that was from 1637. It was only in December 1664 that he became lieutenant admiral, the event that triggered the wave of promotions.[9] He was probably the most experienced flag officer. His seaman's career had been a fighting life. He commanded a squadron in the battle

Pieter Floris.

of the Downs in 1639 and after that he had his first quarrel with De With. He had been through all kinds of weather at sea. He fought on board armed merchantmen, but also on full blown ships-of-the-line like the *Walcheren*. He had reported to meetings of the States General and had been consulted by that body. Nevertheless, in his own mind he suffered undeserved humiliation because he was never accepted as second in command. In 1659 he demonstrated how painful it was for him to serve under De Ruyter, his former subordinate, younger in age and seniority. When visiting De Ruyter's flagship, Evertsen showed very little respect for his commander. De Ruyter wisely decided to tolerate this behaviour for a while. Tactful contact by De Ruyter improved relations between the two men. Evertsen's wounded pride is understandable, but he proved a difficult colleague for his fellow officers. He never resigned, thereby blocking further promotion for his much younger brother, Cornelis Evertsen (1610-1666). Cornelis was not a man of the past and enjoyed a more compliant character than his brother. He befriended De Ruyter early on. At anchor in the Sound in June 1656, De Ruyter was very happy to hear from his family at home that Cornelis had returned safely from Cadiz in Spain. 'God be thanked', he jotted down.[10] The two Evertsen brothers were killed in 1666.

The careers of De Ruyter's colleagues were extremely varied. In the first decade of the 'new' navy as yet there was no clear career pattern as yet. One could first have been a master in the merchant marine, but could have started as an ordinary naval seaman too. A good social background and a parental network did help a man to become a lieutenant and a captain. But there were opportunities for old tars as well. Kortenaer is a representative of this category. He came from Groningen and was a gunner and mate on board ships of the Rotterdam admiralty. In 1652 he was mate and in 1653 captain on Maerten Tromp's flagship. Then until 1659 he was Van Wassenaer van Obdam's flag captain. This landlubber admiral repeatedly asked for Kortenaer's assistance and advice. Kortenaer's eye and right hand had been mutilated in battle. In 1659 he was appointed vice admiral as the successor of De With. An interesting, but untrue, anecdote is told about him. In the spring of 1659 the Danish king bestowed the Order of the White Elephant on him. Kortenaer carefully inspected the elephant hanging on his breast. When asked why he was looking so carefully at the beast, he answered 'who is going to feed this animal?' An annual allowance was the result. Kortenaer, however, did not receive this high distinction. He just got a gold medal, hanging on a cord.[11]

'*Se non è vero, è ben trovato*'. Kortenaer's answer, however, would not have been impossible or unlikely. Till then he had only been a, though highly appreciated, flag captain. This was a position in which one earned a monthly wage of 100 guilders and no more. A flag captain felt left behind compared to other captains, let alone the flag officers. For those two categories the monthly wage was only secondary. The financial rewards gained by the ships' provisioning system were much and much higher. The victualling of a man-of-war was a captain's or a flag officer's concern. He received a daily allowance fixed at about 7 '*stuivers*' per seaman and soldier and 9 '*stuivers*' per officer, 20 '*stuivers*' equalling one guilder. It was the so-called '*kostpenningen*', provisioning pennies. Food rations were prescribed. The purchase and transportation of the victuals and drinks were even the highest ranking officer's responsibility. For transportation he received another allowance. There was an officially accepted margin of profit from each daily allowance, varying between one third and one fifth.[12]

Large ships with more people to feed and longer expeditions offered higher earnings. Kortenaer up to 1659 had missed out on those benefits. His junior colleague Isaac Sweers (1622-1673), for instance, had earned about 12,000 guilders from provisioning in 1655-1658, while he only had his flag captain's salary.[13] A captain's monthly wage was no more than 30 guilders. In May 1659, Kortenaer was promoted to vice admiral. His financial situation improved rapidly and considerably. A year later he could afford to buy a new house at Rotterdam. Not long after he had been promoted to lieutenant admiral, Kortenaer was killed in the battle of Lowestoft in June 1665. He was only a couple of years older than De Ruyter but unfortunately nothing is known about the relations between the two men.

■ From 1665 with a team of flag officers

In 1665 De Ruyter had become admiral of the fleet. Much had changed since he entered naval service in 1652. He had matured at the same time as the navy. Year after year he had participated in all kinds of naval activities. He must have met almost all the captains and flag officers in person, and must have acquired extensive experience in commanding ships, squadrons and fleets. The long expedition to the Mediterranean, West-Africa and the West in 1664-1665 may be said to have been crucial in this respect. Nine out of twelve of his officers were or later became flag officers, though three of them soon retired or were killed in battle. His 'men' profited from the recent expansion of the flag officers' corps too.[14]

The numbers of flag officers after 1664 and the frequent changes in the composition of the corps prohibit an examination of the individual characteristics of the men involved. They were also a less interesting group. The flag officers in the previous period, small in number, showed a great variety in background, professionally and socially. After 1664 that was much less the case. Though the naval ranks were still open to outsiders, few joined to become captains. David Vlugh (1623-1673) from Enkhuizen was one of the few who did. For many years he was a master of an armed merchantman until in 1665 he became a captain of the Noorderkwartier Admiralty. A rear admiralship followed quickly in 1666. In previous years he had cooperated several times with naval expeditions, carrying materiel for the warships. Vlugh showed great courage. He died during the first battle at Schoneveld in June 1673, the same day as his father-in-law, vice admiral Schram.[15]

In and after the second Anglo-Dutch War a large proportion of flag officers and captains were professional naval seamen, connected for a number of successive years with the navy. They participated almost full-time in naval expeditions, having no opportunity to become involved in any other occupation, neither at sea nor on shore. Sweers is a good example. He spent his youth in Spain and Brazil, that is before he entered naval service in 1649. In the period 1655-1668 he was continually at sea: almost ten out of every twelve months on average, earning a great deal of money. It was not much different for most of his colleagues.

To be a flag officer was a full-time job in most of the years in the period 1650-1680. There were few years of general peace. The three wars against England attract most attention, but disputes with Portugal and Baltic affairs absorbed major naval efforts as well. And in 1672 came war with France. Fighting the different Barbary States had become almost routine. As a consequence, there were plenty of opportunities for flag officers and captains to meet each other. De Ruyter, in particular, introduced frequent councils-of-war to consult his comrades and to give them instructions. But other commanders as well invited their colleagues to their flagships to discuss the conditions of ships and crews or to read and interpret the instructions of the States General and the admiralties.

A flood of instructions and regulations had been issued by the States General in 1664-1666. These covered a whole range of subjects. The Articles of War for the maintenance of order on board were revised in 1664 and supplemented a year later. General signal books were made available, also to merchantmen travelling in convoy. The relations between naval and army officers were described. A list of bounties was put up as well as a list of financial compensations in case of mutilations while in naval service. The required material supplies on board were also listed. In May 1666,

Rear Admiral David Vlugh

Print by F.H. Weissenbruch,, around 1850,
Marinemuseum, Den Helder

De Ruyter himself provided his flag officers and captains with fighting instructions. The interpretation and application of all this paperwork were already good reasons for councils-of-war![16] The years 1668-1670 were rather peaceful. In 1671, however, the hard core of the fleet was concentrated in the southern part of the North Sea. There was no war as yet. De Ruyter used this golden opportunity for all kinds of exercises and manoeuvres. He also discussed ideas about the formation of the line-of-battle and what to do in case of a disruption in the opposite line. A break-through, as soon applied in the first battle of Schoneveld, may have been analysed, and perhaps the concentration of forces in the battle of the Texel too.

Flag officers and captains got to know each other pretty well. Not everyone was even-tempered. Disputes and major rows could not be avoided and broke out at times among commanders. The ships' logbooks and the reports to the authorities mentioned some but undoubtedly not all of them. A few we know about. After the battle of Solebay in 1672, rear admiral Jan de Haen (1630-1676) accused Schram and Vlugh of serious neglect of duty, whereupon the prosecutor of the fleet demanded a death sentence. A unanimous council-of-war, however, decided on cashiering for the two men. According to De Ruyter, the accusation was caused by personal prejudice ('houde vrocken'). A similar case occurred shortly after the second battle of Schooneveld on June 14, 1673. Lieutenant admiral Cornelis Tromp and again De Haen blamed vice admiral Sweers of neglect of duty during the battle. Vice admiral Jan de Liefde was also accused. Inspection of Sweers' heavily damaged ship proved the contrary. Old resentments could explain these false accusations, noted De Ruyter in his logbook. The confrontation between Tromp and Sweers became such a blinding row that both men would have begun to fight, if others had not come between them.[17]

De Ruyter could be rude and grudging towards his flag officers. On the long expedition of 1664-1665 vice admiral Meppel was his main victim. He did not strictly obey De Ruyter's regulations as to shore leave, the supply of water, and each one's place in the sailing order. Meppel was fined. The vice-admiral, however, accused his superior of his own inconsistency in the application of the regulations. That was much to De Ruyter's annoyance. Later, nevertheless, De Ruyter hung Meppel's portrait on the wall in his house.[18]

A fleet was always divided and subdivided in squadrons and divisions. Each had its own organizational structure. The admiralties of Amsterdam, Rotterdam and Zeeland had most of their ships in their own squadrons. The two other admiralties had their contingents allocated to one or more of these squadrons. De Ruyter was always put in command of the Rotterdam squadron with its own flag officers. It was this admiralty's prerogative and the flag ship was by tradition from Rotterdam. In 1671-1673 Aert van Nes, Jan de Liefde (1619-1673) and Jan van Nes (1631-1680) were De Ruyter's standing mates. Certain captains also regularly belonged to his squadron. His son Engel (1649-1683) and his stepson Jan van Gelder (1647-1673), both from Amsterdam, were among them. There are no indications of much rivalry and tension in De Ruyter's contingent as there was in the Amsterdam squadron. Most flag officers involved in the quarrels of 1672 and 1673 belonged to that admiralty.

In the absence of an admiral general the Grand Pensionary, Johan de Witt, assured himself of a powerful position in the complex labyrinth that was Dutch naval administration. He controlled several lines of communication and instigated important decisions in various matters. Promotion to captain and flag officer required quality, but good relations with the relevant rulers too. Quite a few burgomasters put in a good word for their sons or other relatives, when soliciting Johan De Witt's support for their respective candidates. The Grand Pensionary could be strict and he tried to avoid nominations of poorly qualified officers. A characteristic example of his judgment is the case of Jacob van Meeuwen (1619-1678) of Dordrecht. In 1667 Van Meeuwen's promotion to rear admiral was expected. Even though Johan's brother recommended their cousin, De Witt refused support. According to him, Van Meeuwen lacked judgment. 'Excessive drinking has spoilt his brains or perhaps a former illness has done him harm', he said.[19]

A career in the navy increasingly attracted the younger sons of the ruling class. The navy had developed into a great and rather well organized institution, offering regular active service and good financial rewards for its captains and flag officers. Regents' families could expect their sons to be good candidates for these positions, certainly when the boys had started as midshipmen on board the ships of well-known captains. Apart from a few who held honorary positions, all of the flag officers could show a more or less impressive record of commands. Some officers built up such reputations that distinguished families vied with each other to send their sons to serve under these officers as midshipmen. Particularly in the 1660's and early 1670's, youngsters from foreign navies found their way into the service of Dutch captains and flag officers. From France came, for instance, Jean Bart and the Count De Guiche, while future Danish admirals Cort Adeler and Niels Juel and the nobleman Rosencrans received their tactical instruction in the Dutch navy. A position on board De Ruyter's ship was highly sought after. The instructions and discussions must have been held in the Dutch language which in the maritime affairs of those days was often the *lingua franca*.

The list of names of captains and flag officers in De Ruyter's fleet and later includes many families who belonged to the ruling class or to the nobility. Just a random selection: from Amsterdam Gideon de Wildt (1620-1665), from Brielle Philips van Almonde (1644-1711), Van Meeuwen from Dordrecht, from Middelburg Salomon le Sage, from Schiedam Eland du Bois (1642-1676), and from Vlaardingen Gerard Callenburg (1642-1722). Noblemen were, for example, Willem Joseph, baron van Ghent (1626-1672) and Hans Willem Aylva (1635-1691). Traditional naval families continued to send their boys to sea. An exceptional case is the Evertsen family of Flushing. The two brothers Johan and Cornelis were the third generation of naval officers in the family. Three of their sons kept this tradition alive and played important roles in Zeeland and in the national navy too. The best known examples are Cornelis Tromp and Engel de Ruyter. There is no doubt that their fathers' reputations and influence affected their very quick advancements.

Cornelis Tromp was a lieutenant at the age of 16, captain at 20 and rear admiral at 24 in 1653. He certainly had a high opinion of himself since after his father's death he offered to succeed him as admiral of the fleet! Engel de Ruyter was 15 years old when he joined his father on the expedition of 1664-1665.[20] His step brother Jan van Gelder and his brother-in-law Johan de Witte were on board as well. In 1668 and only 19, Engel commanded a ship-of-the-line! Promotion to rear admiral followed in 1673. The marked rise in social status of naval officers is well illustrated by both Cornelis Tromp and Engel de Ruyter. The frequent commands provided them with wages, bounties and in particular with the provisioning pennies and prestige. The two men are perhaps extreme examples, but several of their colleagues rose in similar ways. In 1674 three flag officers and two captains were put in the highest category by municipal assessors in Rotterdam when the town imposed a sort of income tax.[21]

In 1667 Tromp married a very rich widow, Margaretha van Raephorst, who was living along the most prestigious of Amsterdam canals: the Herengracht and soon after that the Keizersgracht. But more important, she owned an attractive summer residence at 's Graveland, south-east of Amsterdam. After it had been demolished by the French army in the war of 1672, it was rebuilt in the shape of a ship; from the eighteenth century on it was called '*Trompenburg*'. Engel de Ruyter, a bachelor, opted for a summer residence too. In 1680 he bought a manor, to be called '*Ruytervelt*', at Breukelen along the river Vecht. Wealthy people from Amsterdam had a strong preference for property in this area. Rear admiral Geleyn Evertsen (1655-1721), son of Cornelis, was a rich man in the province of Zeeland. In 1690 he had a manor built near Middelburg. He named it '*Zeerust*', refuge from the sea.[22]

■ Befriended colleagues

We know little about colleagues whom De Ruyter truly befriended. One has to take into consideration that he was first of all a family man. His colleagues were birds of different feathers. It is likely that De Ruyter felt himself closer to colleagues with a long seafaring background than those with military or upper class roots, although his contacts with the Grand Pensionary were very amicable.

His contemporaries were familiar with his tremendous row with Cornelis Tromp after the Two Days' battle in August 1666, and Tromp's dismissal. This affair was no secret to the man in the street nor was the difficult reconciliation of both men thanks to Prince William III's pressure in April 1673. The new start began poorly with Tromp's accusations levelled against Sweers, but there are no further reports about personal antagonism or problems. Cornelis Evertsen's early death in 1666, already mentioned, was sincerely deplored by the admiral and his family.

Fellow flag officers Adriaen Banckert (c. 1620-1684), Aert van Nes and Jan de Liefde must have had much in common with De Ruyter. They were all at sea from their youth onwards and often they had participated in the same expeditions, endured the same hazards and enjoyed the same victories. In their later years, they had their sons as captains in their squadrons or they had brothers around them. Banckert was also from Flushing. In 1631 he joined his father Joost as a midshipman and from then on he only served the admiralty of Zeeland. That was his permanent employer. He became a vice admiral in 1665 and a lieutenant admiral in 1666. No details are known about his personal relations with De Ruyter. It is said that both men regularly discussed tactical manoeuvres of the fleet. Banckert's son Adriaen was captain in the fleet of 1673.

Banckert was always in command of a squadron. Aert Van Nes and De Liefde, however, belonged to De Ruyter's squadron of mainly Rotterdam ships. Both men were from Rotterdam. A couple of times Van Nes took command when De Ruyter was sick or absent. He had no son as a captain in the fleet, for he married late: in 1665. He was a captain in 1652 and his promotions to the three ranks of flag officer occurred in 1662, 1665 and 1666. Van Nes was a prominent man in the city of Rotterdam, living in an exclusive area. His younger brother Jan van Nes regularly joined him in the same expeditions. Jan was always one step behind his older brother Aert: captain in 1659, rear admiral in 1666 and vice admiral in 1673. It was like Cornelis Evertsen in Zeeland. The two brothers were both present on the extended voyage of 1664-1665.

Jan de Liefde was probably De Ruyter's dearest colleague and friend after Cornelis Evertsen died. Their wives were friends as well. In 1668 De Ruyter and Anna van Gelder were present at the baptismal ceremony of De Liefde's daughter. De Ruyter was one of the witnesses and Anna was the godmother. De Liefde's son Pieter was second flag captain on the 'Zeven Provinciën' in 1672 and 1673. De Liefde himself became rear admiral in 1665 and vice admiral the next year. He and Van Nes had family connections through their wives whose mothers were cousins. De Liefde's second wife was a daughter of the secretary of the Rotterdam admiralty, the most important man in the local naval administration. De Liefde's wife and Anna van Gelder joined their husbands in April 1673, when they sailed together in the admiralty's yacht from Rotterdam to Hellevoetsluis to say farewell. Jan de Liefde would not return, for he was killed in the battle of Texel on August 21. De Ruyter's beloved

stepson Van Gelder was killed there too. Engel de Ruyter wrote in his logbook on August 22: *'in the afternoon I sailed with Father to brother Van Gelder and to vice admiral De Liefde to see, for the last time, their dead bodies'.* After that De Ruyter immediately arranged the provisional promotion of Jan de Liefde's elder brother, Cornelis (1617-1673), to rear admiral. Cornelis enjoyed this position only a few weeks, for he died on September 25.[23] The battle of the Texel was an important victory, but the Dutch admiral of the fleet suffered great personal losses.

It got worse for the old admiral. He had proved his historic value for the Dutch Republic by safeguarding the country from an invasion from the sea. The destruction of an independent state had been averted. De Ruyter was no longer needed. Cornelis Tromp was the rising star in the navy, being William III's great favourite. The old admiral was sidetracked. In 1674 he was given command of a second rate expedition to the West Indies. None of his former flag officers accompanied him. He had to be content with his son Engel, now a rear admiral, his son-in-law Johan de Witte and Banckert's son. His vice admiral was Cornelis Evertsen, the son of Johan. Tromp, however, was heading a great attack on the French Atlantic coast. Van Nes and Banckert were his top admirals. After this expedition both men retired from naval service and stayed at home.

De Ruyter had outlived his usefulness. In 1675 he was 68! He had survived almost all of his former colleagues. Nevertheless, he did not stop and he accepted the same kind of haughty treatment by the authorities as Tromp had endured in the First Anglo-Dutch War. In August 1675 he set off to the Mediterranean, not accompanied by any of his relatives or old colleagues and friends. His vice admiral was De Haen, a formidable and quarrelsome person. His third in command was a man who had only been a seaman since 1672.[24] The contrast with earlier days could not have been greater.

CHAPTER 11

De Ruyter in Paint

Ronald Prud'homme van Reine

According to a persistent myth, Michiel de Ruyter was a man of such modesty that he set no great store by having himself immortalized in painting. All portraits made during his life are said to have come about in spite of himself rather than thanks to him. This is certainly true of the etched and engraved portraits of him. In De Ruyter's lifetime, some forty or so (depending on how one counts) prints were published, especially by Amsterdam printers.[1] They were sold in bookshops to admirers and everyone else who took an interest. In the seventeenth century, prints were a popular wall decoration, not least because they were relatively cheap. And indeed, very many portraits of De Ruyter have been preserved as prints, suggesting that the number of copies must have been very high.

The painted portraits of De Ruyter present a different case, however. As a rule, these were commissioned by De Ruyter himself and only rarely so for the art market. Relatively few private individuals will have owned a painted portrait of the admiral.[2] Presumably not many paintings of De Ruyter were made in the seventeenth century with them in mind. It is not without good reason that early in 1668, the Italian prince Cosimo de Medici, who had met De Ruyter, searched in vain for portraits that bore a good likeness to De Ruyter.[3]

The Rotterdam painter Abraham Westervelt (ca. 1620-1692) painted a series of portraits of naval heroes on a small panel that sold at about ten guilders each.[4] These can still be found in, for instance, inventories of flag officers. Several have been preserved to this day, but remarkably none depicting De Ruyter, which seems to indicate that Westervelt did not stock particularly many. Of Maerten Tromp, in contrast, several portraits have come down.

■ Portraits for the market

The most important seventeenth-century copies of the portrait of De Ruyter were done after the example of the 1667 'state portrait' by Amsterdam artist Ferdinand Bol (1616-1680), one of Rembrandt's pupils. In 1663 Bol had already produced two history paintings for the council boards of the Amsterdam Admiralty. In this portrait De Ruyter is depicted in a classical pose. It shows him as proud a man as he had ever been. He is dressed in a long black-brown officer's coat with a steel hauberk while on his breast he is wearing the chain and medallion of the Order of Saint Michael. From his side hangs the richly-wrought sword that the Amsterdam Admiralty had presented him with towards the end of 1666. In his right hand, resting on a globe that emphasizes both his world-wide working area and his fame, he holds his comman-

Michiel de Ruyter

Painting by Ferdinand Bol with a seascape by Willem van de Velde the Younger, 1667, Mauritshuis, The Hague

der's baton. The globe sits on a table, together with a compass and a navigational chart. In a number of portraits the coast of Flanders can be distinguished on the chart, a reference to the Four Days' Battle, which had taken place there. De Ruyter is standing before a long heavy curtain that highlights his authority and a balustrade behind which a seascape is visible. It prominently features the *Zeven Provinciën*, painted, it is assumed, by Willem van de Velde the Younger. We look at the Fleet Admiral in the lofty pose he has adopted from a low angle. This angle in particular makes the whole especially impressive and it is for this reason that this picture has become the standard portrait of the naval hero. But surely, this 'state portrait' does not tell us much about De Ruyter's real appearance in those times. As much is obvious from the long, smooth fingers of his right hand clasping the commander's baton: these are not the fingers of a rough sea dog.

The contemporary copies of this portrait, presumably usually produced in Bol's studio, are simplified versions with fewer extra figures. The table with the globe, for instance, as well as other objects are missing from these portraits; the subject has undone the top buttons of his coat and holds the baton in a different way. These fairly large pictures, usually set in beautifully carved frames with armorial trophies, must first and foremost have been intended for public buildings. There are also different versions of the portrait, painted by Bol himself, that show De Ruyter with his head slightly tilted to the left. It was such a version of the portrait, doubly dated 1668/1669, that the admiral presented to the king of Denmark, who in 1660 had raised him to the peerage and had bestowed an annuity on him. Finally there are some versions of the portrait by Bol which hardly bear any likeness, for instance one recently discovered dated 1674, which shows De Ruyter for the first and last time in a very fashionable but therefore uncharacteristic allonge-wig. These portraits must have been produced for a relatively low price, probably outside Bol's studio.[5]

■ Official portraits

At the request of the States General De Ruyter made each of the five admiralties a present of a copy of his portrait by Bol in the course of 1667.[6] These paintings are replicas, and show differences as to details. By way of thanks for his gift, De Ruyter received in his turn a present from all five boards. Owing to the fact that the resolutions (decrees) of three of those admiralties have been preserved, three gifts from De Ruyter and the return presents have been recovered.

The Amsterdam Admiralty accepted De Ruyter's painting on 15 June 1667. Well over four months later, on 19 October, when the Second Anglo-Dutch War had come to an end with the Breda Peace Treaty, the admiralty decided to present De Ruyter with a gift in return for his present. They subsequently settled, probably after consultation with De Ruyter, on a handsome sword with a hilt especially wrought for the occasion. The Rotterdam Admiralty received De Ruyter's portrait as early as 10 May: they were after all his employers. It was immediately decided to hang the work of art. It was not until 1 March 1668 that a gilt water pitcher was commissioned by way of thanks to De Ruyter, at the value of 1200 guilders. In Zeeland some dissension arose over the question whether the portrait of a Fleet Admiral of Holland should be accepted just like that. It was queried whether this would not constitute a sign of contempt towards their own flag officers. However, the consideration that De Ruyter

had offered them the painting to show his appreciation for his training and functions within the Zeeland Admiralty removed all objections. A resolution adopted on 6 June 1667 shows the members of the Zeeland Admiralty as delighted with De Ruyter's generous donation. In gratitude, they decided to send the Fleet Admiral the complete *Atlas Maior* by Joannes Blaeu, including all appendices. These were extremely valuable folios containing hand-coloured topographic maps. On 3 December 1667, the chamber suited the action to the word.[7]

Of the five copies, four are still extant. They are in the Rijksmuseum in Amsterdam, the Mauritshuis in The Hague, the Westfries Museum in Hoorn and the National Maritime Museum in Greenwich. A fire in the building of the Frisian admiralty in Harlingen may have destroyed the fifth copy in 1771. The existence of a sixth copy has been argued on the grounds that the Admiralty of the Noorderkwartier held alternating meetings in Hoorn and Enkhuizen. However, there is no evidence for this and also, it does not seem likely that this minor admiralty was the only chamber to receive a second copy of De Ruyter's portrait by Bol. One of the locations possibly made do with a copy of the portrait on a smaller panel or with a print. Only the portrait in Hoorn is, incidentally, absolutely certain to have come from the admiralty building in that town.[8]

Once donated, the portrait of supreme commander De Ruyter hung in the council chambers of all the admiralties in the Republic. He had been placed on a pedestal, and enjoyed general recognition as the fleet's chief commander.

Another special commission concerned the portrait that De Ruyter had painted of himself in 1669 by the Amsterdam artist Karel Dujardin (1622-1678).[9] This painting too was probably intended for the King of Denmark, who was to receive several portraits of De Ruyter. Never has De Ruyter been depicted in a more warlike stance than by Dujardin here. He is standing in a full suit of armour, in front of a great red blood flag with his family coat of arms; in the background his warship is visible. The admiral of the fleet is shown as determined, clasping his commander's baton with his right hand. He is presented from a low perspective, which renders his appearance especially distinguished. In this portrait De Ruyter may look like a giant; in reality, however, he was a man of average length.

■ Hendrick Berckman and Middelburg painting

Five portraits of De Ruyter painted by the Middelburg artist Hendrick Berckman (1629-1679) have survived to the present day. Three of these have come down together with the pendant portraits of his third wife Anna van Gelder. Commissioned by De Ruyter, these paintings were painted from life and must have hung in his house.[10] They date, in chronological order, from 1655, 1660, 1664, 1668 and 1675. It is not impossible that there were more portraits of De Ruyter by Berckman, that those were lost or that their subject has not been recognized yet. It was, for instance, common practice to have wedding portraits painted in the year of one's wedding. Such wedding portraits exist of some of De Ruyter's colleagues, including Cornelis Tromp, Isaac Sweers and Jan van Brakel. We may therefore assume that similar portraits of De Ruyter and Anna van Gelder were indeed painted shortly after their wedding early in 1652.

At the time of his first marriage in 1631 and his second, five years later, the master mariner and first mate of a whaling ship cannot have had enough money for a por-

Dit beelt dat wyst u aen, een RUYTER na het leven,
Die met syn houte paert soo Ridderlyck hem droeg:
Men sag hem in het slaen, noyt voor syn viant beven,
Hy toond en hem het swaert, en quam hem voor den boeg:
Dien RUYTER wil ick hier, voor eenen Ridder achten,
Dewys allien de daet, doch maeckt een Edelman,
Hoe dat ick hem vir cier, noch speelen myn ghedachten,
Hoe dat hem onsen Stael, syn trou beloonen can.   Cudemans.

Cornelis Banheyningh exc.   Anno 1654.

trait painter of repute. Yet it should by no means be ruled out that he even then commissioned portraits painted or drawn on small panels. The oldest engraved portrait known to exist of De Ruyter dates from 1654 and was executed by Hendrick Udemans from Middelburg.[11] Depicted as a coarse and simple man, he looks very different from the flag officer he was to become. Thus, we are unlikely to find an unidentified portrait of De Ruyter from the period before the First Anglo-Dutch War. Comparisons will always be made to a representation of De Ruyter from later years, but he presumably looked very different before 1652.

As a counter argument against the idea that a painted picture of De Ruyter was already in existence in 1652, it could be reasoned that as vice-commander of the Zeeland Admiralty he received an as yet relatively modest income. On those grounds, then, it could be argued that his first portrait in oil did not come about until the year 1655, when he moved to Amsterdam upon being offered a good position with a regular income as vice-admiral of the Amsterdam Admiralty. Yet then, it is remarkable that he returned to a Middelburg artist to have his portrait painted while Amsterdam abounded with so many good painters. And that makes it likely that indeed, De Ruyter had sat earlier before a Zeeland artist.

Middelburg is located on Walcheren, the main island in the province of Zeeland, one of the wealthiest of the Republic's provinces. Trade and shipping thrived, and this was also beneficial to Middelburg painting in the first half of the seventeenth century. Also prompted by collectors of herbs and flowers, Middelburg was the centre of floral painting in the first decades of that century.[12] Ambrosius Bosschaert and his pupils painted a great many compositions with flower arrangements. In 1613 he left for Bergen op Zoom, but his work in Middelburg was continued by Christoffel van den Berghe and Jacob van Geel. The latter was mainly engaged in painting landscapes. Between 1614 and 1625, Adriaen Pietersz. van de Venne was also working in Middelburg, producing large historical representations and portraits. Other portrait painters working in Middelburg in this period were Salomon Mesdach and Cornelis Eversdijck. In the second quarter of the seventeenth century, painting there was slightly in decline, but around 1650 it showed some signs of revival. This is especially due to the arrival of some new artists such as Daniël de Blieck, a painter of church interiors, Johannes Goedaert, a floral painter, Laurens Craen and Adriaen Coorte, both still-life painters, and Cornelis Jonson van Ceulen, Willem Eversdijck and Hendrick Berckman, all portraitists.

Born in Klundert in 1629, Berckman presumably studied under Haarlem-based Philips Wouwerman and later worked with Thomas Willeboirts Bosschaert and Jacob Jordaens in Antwerp.[13] He is thought to have painted cavalry engagements and figure paintings, but these no longer exist. His group portraits of the Flushing and Middelburg militia were likewise lost. Among Berckman's commissioners was Prince Hendrick van Nassau, governor of Hulst. Portraits of him by Berckman were also made into prints. Between 1652 and 1654 Berckman lived in Leiden. In 1655 he joined the guild in Middelburg, where he would live ever since.

■ The 1655 portrait

Berckman turned out sound, slightly old-fashioned looking portraits, and this may well have attracted De Ruyter to him. What is more, he must have been cheaper than

Michiel de Ruyter

*Painting by H. Berckman, 1655, Zeeland
Maritime Museum, Flushing*

Michiel de Ruyter

*Painting by Karel van Mander, 1656-1658.
Skokloster Castle, Sweden.
Photograph by Jens Mohr*

many a colleague of his in Amsterdam, which surely also counted with the thrifty De Ruyter. The milieu of the Zeeland admirals proved a good catchment area from which Berckman drew his clientele. Colleagues of De Ruyter whose portraits he also painted from 1655 included Johan Evertsen (circa 1655) and Adriaen Banckert (circa 1655, 1672 and 1673). De Ruyter thus appears to have carefully weighed his options before he approached Berckman in 1655 in order to have his portrait painted.

In all likelihood, Berckman also painted Anna van Gelder's portrait in 1655 as a pendant, as he would in the years to come. It is not hard to explain why this is no longer known today. In former centuries such portraits would often become separated as the portrait of the naval hero was deemed the more important while the portrait of the wife who had not played a major role in the national history was no longer set great store by. Once the paintings are separated, the portrait of the wife is with the passage of time no longer recognized and is hung or stored as the representation of some unknown lady. It does occasionally happen that, centuries later, such a pendant portrait turns up again, but of course it may also be lost in the meantime.

Vice Amiral
de Reuter.

Michiel de Ruyter

Painting by H. Berckman, 1660, Zeeland
Maritime Museum, Flushing

Anna van Gelder

Painting by H. Berckman, 1660, Zeeland
Maritime Museum, Flushing

Michiel de Ruyter

Painting by H. Berckman, 1664, National
Maritime Museum, Greenwich

Anna van Gelder

Painting by H. Berckman, 1664, National
Maritime Museum, Greenwich

After the fashion of his times Berckman painted De Ruyter in 1655 against a neutral background.[14] Across his black-brown officer's coat the admiral is wearing a broad baldric embroidered with gold thread, whose colour makes it an eye-catching item. From a triple gold chain around his neck hangs the gold medallion that De Ruyter received from the States General by way of thanks for the valour he had shown in the Battle of Portland between 28 February and 2 March 1653. De Ruyter must have sat for this portrait in the first half of 1655, shortly before or at the very time of his moving to Amsterdam. In July 1655 he left on an expedition to the Mediterranean, from which he would not return until the beginning of May 1656, when he arrived before Texel.

Over the next few years, De Ruyter and Anna van Gelder were to become regular clients of Berckman, so they must, apparently, have been very satisfied with his work. They were clearly prepared to make the very long journey in order to visit his studio. They needed to take a canal barge across the canals of Holland to subsequently reach the islands of Zeeland by regular barge. Doubtless such appointments would usually be combined with family visits and cannot have been thought inordinately tiresome. De Ruyter still had many relatives and acquaintances living on Walcheren.[15] Moreover, in 1663 his one but eldest daughter Alida had come to live in Flushing after her marriage to Johan Schorer, a member of the town council. After his death in 1664, she was married again three years later, this time to the Flushing minister, Thomas Potts. The couple continued to live in Flushing.

During an expedition to Denmark in 1656, the most important Dutch naval officers, including De Ruyter, were painted at the request of the Danish king by the Dutch-born painter Karel van Mander, then living in Denmark. In a short period of time he managed to capture the naval officers very much as they were in real life. The paintings are nowadays kept in the Swedish castle of Skokloster, not far from Stockholm.[16]

■ The 1660 and 1664 portraits

The year 1660 provided De Ruyter with another good reason to have his portrait painted. In 1659, the Danish king had presented him with a gold chain of honour together with ditto pendant in gratitude for his deeds during the war with Sweden; he had raised him to the Danish peerage (heritable in the male and female line) and had promised him an annuity of eight hundred rix-dollars for the rest of his life. And he had been given a family coat of arms.

The manner in which De Ruyter had himself painted by Berckman for the second time shows that he had become a different, more distinguished man than he used to be in his Zeelandic days.[17] For the first time we see him depicted in an aristocratic pose, as far as his hips. In his left hand he is clasping the gold chain of honour and pendant with the portrait of the king of Denmark. In his right hand he holds a cane with a white handle while a sword with a gold hilt hangs from his left side. Behind a curtain, to the right in the background, some ships riding at sea can be distinguished, done to emphasize the function of the subject. The painter thus followed the practice that many portraitists adopted as customary around this time. To cap it all, his brand-new coat of arms is depicted at the top left, which given his relatively humble origins, cannot but have instilled a sense of pride in him. Anna van Gelder is pictured in a pendant, holding a red velvet psalter in her left hand as a sign of her piety. She is wearing rings on both hands; on her right hand, on her thumb.

De Ruyter had returned from Denmark in the beginning of September 1660, therefore the paintings were finished in the last months of that year. Between July 1661 and April 1663 De Ruyter was on an expedition to the Mediterranean that would prove most profitable. A great amount of loot was taken from the Barbary corsairs from North Africa. Peace treaties were entered into with the Algerians and Tunisians. For the time being, the only corsairs that could cause trouble were those from Tripoli. However, they never made an appearance in the winter months, so De Ruyter could take no more action against them during the last months of the expedition. When De Ruyter and his colleagues returned before Texel in April 1663, they were given a joyful welcome. In pamphlets and odes the vice-admiral was acclaimed as the conqueror of Barbary privateering.

Exceptionally, it took almost a year this time before De Ruyter went back to sea. The good earnings of the latest expedition and the extra leisure time must have persuaded him in the first months of 1664 to commission Hendrick Berckman to paint his portrait for the third time. A pendant portrait of Anna van Gelder was likewise composed again.

Dress, pose and background are on the whole very similar to those in the picture of De Ruyter made four years earlier.[18] The family coat of arms has again been given a prominent place at the top left. This time, however, for the sake of variety, his left hand rests on a cane with an ivory handle. A similar cane from the property of De Ruyter's descendants is kept in the Rijksmuseum.[19] An important difference between this portrait and the previous one concerns the stern expression De Ruyter is now wearing. His hair is now at shoulder length. This suddenly makes him look much more like De Ruyter as we all know him from the portraits by Bol and Dujardin.

Anna van Gelder is holding a fan in her hand while behind a balustrade we can make out a garden, a well-known device in contemporary portraits of women. As in all subsequent portraits of her, she wears a black dress, with a broad white collar and white cuffs and, on her head, a little black cap. At the top right, a striking feature is her family crest, occurring here for the first and the last time in any portrait of her. It clearly marks the independence of the woman who was De Ruyter's help and stay. After all, she was the one who made sure his ship was victualled and arranged his financial affairs while he was at sea.

These paintings are executed in a grander fashion than were those before them. They are done on a larger panel, and now both have scenes in the background. The background scene in De Ruyter's portrait depicting ships has clearly been done with much more care than had been devoted to that in the 1660 portrait.

■ The family portrait by Jurriaen Jacobson and the 1668 portraits by Berckman

The next three years saw De Ruyter's long but successful expedition to Africa and America, the battles in the Second Anglo-Dutch War and the raid on the Medway. These events made a national hero of De Ruyter. As we saw, his portrait was hung in the council chambers of the admiralties. Jan Lievens painted portraits of the heroes who had featured in the Four Days' Battle, i.e. De Ruyter and Cornelis Tromp.[20] Unfortunately, we now only know these from prints. A print depicting De Ruyter and Tromp returning triumphantly in a chariot was hung in all Dutch town halls.[21] Also, in honour of these two admirals as well as of Zeeland Fleet Admiral Cornelis Evertsen the Elder, who had been killed in action, raised-relief portrait medals were struck after a design by Wouter Muller. Their triumphant victories over the English during the raid on the Medway led a number of De Ruyter's colleagues, including the Rotterdam Admiral of the Fleet Aert van Nes and Vice-Admiral Jan de Liefde, to commission portraits of themselves that paraded their successes. Amsterdam-based Bartholomeus van der Helst, a highly popular artist with the upper ten, was to execute these.[22]

In August 1665, De Ruyter had been appointed Admiral of the Fleet for Holland and West-Friesland and had thus become supreme commander of the war fleet. That also meant a substantial increase in income. And naturally, he would after the Second Anglo-Dutch War commission another portrait of himself holding his commander's baton. Yet during the war, De Ruyter must have conceived of the idea to have a large family portrait painted. He could now easily afford such a large canvas. It would seem that De Ruyter was inspired by the desire to have a representation of his children as they were growing up. Between 1652 and 1667 he had spent approximately 130 out of 204 months at sea. He had thus barely seen his children grow up. That loss could not be undone. However, a family portrait could provide some small compensation.

He did not approach Hendrick Berckman for this painting, although the latter had painted militia pieces and would certainly have been capable of executing a family portrait. But this time, De Ruyter opted to stay close to home. Amsterdam artist Jurriaen Jacobson (ca. 1625-1685) succeeded in landing the commission.[23] Jacobson had been born in Hamburg and is known to have studied under Frans Snijders in Antwerp. He lived in Amsterdam from about 1662 until 1668. In that year he left for Leeuwarden, where he would spend the rest of his life. Apart from portraits, Jacobson also painted historical pieces, hunting scenes and still lifes. The painting of De Ruyter's family is the only large family portrait Jacobson is known to have done.

It was far from unusual for the upper classes in the seventeenth-century Republic to have family portraits made.[24] On the other hand, not every affluent family would actually do so. Similar family portraits of naval officers are extremely scarce, although we should of course allow for the possibility that many were never recognized as such or were lost. Only fairly recently was a portrait of the Tromp family discovered, painted by Jacob Delff the Younger around 1647, and presumably commissioned by Fleet Admiral Maerten Harpertsz Tromp.[25] A similar family portrait of the Evertsen family is recorded as having existed as well.[26] A painting thought to depict the Banckert family was recently put in another family's name.[27]

A panel this size entailed vast expenses and true to himself, De Ruyter cut down on the costs. He did so, first of all, by choosing Jurriaen Jacobson, who may have been a very skilful artist but who did certainly not belong to the leading portrait painters. De Ruyter would not approach Ferdinand Bol, Bartholomeus van der Helst or Isaac Luttichuys for private commissions, as his colleagues did. Secondly, De Ruyter did not have Jacobson paint the family portrait true to life, which meant a considerable lowering of the costs. The De Ruyters now would not have to pose for hours.

As his example Jacobson used existing paintings of the several family members from the preceding decade.[28] De Ruyter's son Engel was presumably copied after a childhood portrait from 1658, when he was nine years old. De Ruyter's oldest daughter Cornelia and her husband Johan de Witte were copied after wedding portraits done by Hendrick Berckman in 1659. De Ruyter's stepson Jan van Gelder, depicted with a bunch of grapes, as well as his younger daughters Alida, Margaretha and Anna, seen

Michiel de Ruyter and his family. The Admiral and his wife, Anna van Gelder, are flanked by his stepson, Jan van Gelder (to the right of the couple), and their children, Cornelia (right) with her husband Jan de Witte, Alida (middle) and Engel (left with a falcon). In the foreground two little daughters, Margaretha (left) and Anna (right) play with De Ruyter's grandson, Cornelis de Witte.

Painting by Jurriaen Jacobson, 1667, Rijksmuseum, Amsterdam

Signature and date on the family portrait.

playing with his oldest grandson Cornelis de Witte, were surely likewise done after existing portraits (possibly not all of which were painted but could have been drawn).

The rather illegible date that Jacobson added to his signature has caused a great deal of confusion as to when the painting was actually painted. When, at the beginning of the twentieth century, the painting arrived in the Rijksmuseum from the estate of De Ruyter's descendants, this date was read as 1662. To this day, art historians stubbornly insist on the correctness of this reading because this year also tallies with the ages of the people depicted.[29] However, they do then not take into account that all the subjects were painted after the example of other portraits and that, therefore, the family portrait may well have been finished in a different year than the age of some suggests.

The catalogue of paintings of the Rijksmuseum for 1934 contains a picture (a so-called cliché) of the date of the painting that just as convincingly allows the year to be read as 1667.[30] For a variety of reasons, this date is much more likely than 1662. In 1662, De Ruyter was in the Mediterranean, fighting privateers. As stated earlier, he had left on this expedition in May 1661, not to return until April 1663. Now it is not inconceivable that De Ruyter had commissioned the family portrait in the beginning of 1661. Yet it would have come at a strange moment during his career: he was still only a vice-admiral and had portraits made of himself and his wife as recently as 1660. It is thus much more probable that he commissioned this large canvas after his promotion to Fleet Admiral and supreme commander.

Moreover, there are a number of indications in the painting that rule out the date 1662. For instance, De Ruyter did not receive the pendant belonging with the Order of Saint Michael that is clearly visible around his neck until 1666, when the French king Louis xiv conferred this honour on the Fleet Admiral as a reward for his bravery during the Four Days' Battle. Likewise, it was in 1666 that De Ruyter received from the Amsterdam Admiralty the sword of honour that hangs from his side. Advocates of the 1662 dating have always disposed of these details arguing they could have been added on to the painting at a later date.[31] However, that cannot possibly be true for the commander's baton that De Ruyter is holding firmly in his outstretched left hand. It is the first time that De Ruyter is carrying this baton because he was only appointed supreme commander of the fleet in 1665. And this is also why in Berckman's 1664 portrait of him his hand is resting on a cane.

Anyone comparing the representations of De Ruyter and Anna van Gelder in the family portrait with the 1664 and 1668 portraits of the two spouses by Berckman will draw the conclusion that Jacobson borrowed rather a lot from these. Particularly the 1668 portraits seem to have served as his examples. De Ruyter is depicted in a partly unbuttoned black-brown officer's coat, with the pendant of the Order of Saint Michael and his commander's baton. In the family portrait, De Ruyter has remarkably been given a square, wide plain linen collar that in 1667 would have been rather old-fashioned but that he also wore in the portrait of 1664. In the 1668 portrait by Berckman he is wearing the much more modern jabot. In her 1668 portrait, Anna van Gelder is shown holding a fan, just as she was in 1664. Her face in 1668 is more like that in the family portrait than that in the 1664 portrait. The same goes for De Ruyter's face.

Medaillion of the Order of Saint Michael, signifying the knighting of Michiel de Ruyter by the King of France.

Enamel, 1666, Nederlands Scheepvaart-museum, Amsterdam

In any case, it is clear that the 1660 portraits by Berckman are much further removed from the family portrait than are the 1664 and 1668 pictures when it comes to likeness, dress and attributes. Now, how to explain that in 1667 Jacobson based himself on portraits dating from 1668? It is not too hard to explain. In 1667 Berckman may well have had a painted or drawn modello of these portraits ready. De Ruyter may have given those to Jacobson.

Then the question remains why Jacobson put De Ruyter's oldest grandson Cornelis de Witte (born in 1660) in a central position rather than his second grandson Michiel de Witte (born in 1662) and his first granddaughter Cornelia Schorer (born in

Michiel de Ruyter

Painting by H. Berckman, 1668,
ex-Kralinger Museum, Rotterdam
Photograph by Ton Sipman

Anna van Gelder

Painting by H. Berckman, 1668,
ex-Kralinger Museum, Rotterdam
Photograph by Ton Sipman

1663). That, I think, can be accounted for by the decision to place the first male heir from the next generation in this painting centre stage, in the middle of the representation. It is not without reason that De Ruyter proudly points his baton at him. Representing the other grandchildren would have resulted in a very crowded composition and would probably have looked rather arbitrary to De Ruyter in 1667. His younger daughters, his stepson Jan van Gelder, not omitting his son Engel were yet to marry. De Ruyter must have expected to have many more grandchildren, not least a real family heir. And indeed, over the next years, fourteen more grandchildren would be born, though Engel would never marry and thus never present De Ruyter with a grandson. The pater familias himself was to witness the birth of seven of those grandchildren.

De Ruyter's youngest daughter Anna, who not yet thirteen had died of the plague in August 1666, has also been immortalized in the family portrait. Before her stands a basket with a garland, which may well be taken as a funeral wreath.[32] Fond as they were of their children, De Ruyter and his wife must have insisted on her being included in the picture. It is, moreover, not inconceivable that by August 1666, Jacobson had already made his first sketches for the composition of the painting.

As was usual, the artist will have painted the background of the painting in close consultation with his commissioner. Contrary to expectation perhaps, this background does not depict a sea with ships but an Italian garden with cypresses and an obelisk in ruins. The sculpture of a putto blowing a whelk shell and De Ruyter's baton are the only references to his life as a naval officer. De Ruyter had the family portrait hung in a central place in the reception room of his house.[33] There, it hung among portraits of the Princes of Orange and representations of mythological figures. There was not a single sea piece. Perhaps he chose not to be reminded for once of the sea in this room but preferred to create a warmer atmosphere instead. Everything directly connected with his professional life was stored in his office, in the cellar and in the attics. During his many voyages in the Mediterranean, De Ruyter must often have enjoyed such landscapes as shown in the background of this painting.

The new portrait of De Ruyter that Berckman finished in 1668 depicts him as a relatively simple man, with a baton in his hand and a view towards the sea, with his ship, the *Zeven Provinciën*. The family crest has been included again at the top right corner. A representative of the States General and the burgomaster of Dordrecht, Cornelis de Witt as well as several naval officers who had played an important part in the raid on the Medway commissioned renowned artists in 1667 and 1668 to paint portraits of them that glorified their deeds. Cornelis de Witt carried it rather far: he asked portraitist Jan de Baen from The Hague to make a large panel for the council chamber of the Dordrecht town hall depicting him triumphant with a cornucopia overflowing at his feet and angels soaring above his head, blowing trumpets.[34] In this sense, the 'state portraits' of De Ruyter by Bol and Dujardin were also quite something. But De Ruyter would not commission something so ostentatious for himself. His 1668 portrait by Berckman lacks all reference to the raid on the Medway.[35] The pendant portrait of Anna van Gelder has also been kept fairly simple. As usual, she is wearing some jewellery, including ear drops, a brooch, strings of pearls around her arms and a ring. Her right hand holding a fan rests on a chair while behind her a landscape can be seen to the left of a column, a symbol of steadfastness.

■ Portraits of the children

In the preceding decade, De Ruyter's children and their partners also had separate portraits made of themselves. We have already mentioned the 1659 wedding portrait of Cornelia de Ruyter and Johan de Witte by Hendrick Berckman.[36] They had similarly shown a preference for the artist from Middelburg, which is remarkable as the couple settled in Rotterdam. In 1661, six years before his marriage to Alida de Ruyter, Thomas Potts also had himself portrayed by Berckman. Of Engel and Margaretha de Ruyter, childhood portraits from the mid-sixties have survived. Until recently, they were among the property of the heirs of the Elias family, together with the 1668 portraits of De Ruyter and Anna van Gelder. This branch of the family is descended from Margaretha Somer, a daughter of Margaretha de Ruyter and the Amsterdam Reverend Bernardus Somer, who were married in 1673. Attempts at attributing the unsigned portraits of Engel and Margaretha de Ruyter from the mid-sixties are much disputed. Given their style, they cannot have been done by Berckman. The names that come up most frequently are those of Jurriaen Jacobson, Herbert Tuer from Nijmegen and Cornelis Jonson van Ceulen the Younger from Utrecht, the son of the portraitist who some decades earlier worked in Middelburg.[37]

Engel posed himself in quasi-Roman dress, which calls to mind the portraits that Cornelis Tromp had Jan Mijtens paint of himself in 1661 and 1668. He stands before a column, his right hand resting on a plumed helmet, his left hand akimbo. To the left in the background, we can make out the sea. Wearing a fine dress and holding a string of pearls in her hands, Margaretha stands near a large fountain. A landscape with trees is visible in the background.

In 1668, Engel de Ruyter and Jan van Gelder had their portraits painted by Jan

Andries Lievens, the son of Jan Lievens.[38] They are depicted in extremely handsome attire and each has a dog at heel. That year, they had both been appointed captain with the Amsterdam Admiralty. Moreover, Engel had been especially invited to the English court to be knighted by King Charles II. For fellow captains with less distinguished fathers, commissioning a well-known artist to execute such a painting was well-nigh impossible: a captain's income would never suffice for that purpose. As the portraits were done as pendants and on large panels, they were most likely meant to hang side by side in the house of their parents.

What is more, the next year Engel had a large 'official portrait' made of himself by Ferdinand Bol, who two years earlier had painted the picture of his father for the admiralties.[39] It is most improbable that this portrait of Engel was meant for the Amsterdam Admiralty; after all, he was still merely a captain. Even so, the painting is set in a valuable carved frame emblazoned with armorial trophies, just as his father's portraits of 1667 were. It may have been intended for Engel's own house, located next to his parents' at the Binnenkant on the newly created island called the Waalseiland (nowadays Prins Hendrikkade) in Amsterdam. Engel moved into that house around 1669. The inventory drawn up after his death lists only one portrait of him, which could be this painting by Bol.[40]

■ The 1675 portrait

As we know, De Ruyter sat for Karel Dujardin in 1669. Since then, many years would elapse before De Ruyter had his portrait painted again, for the last time, by Berckman. The reason is obvious. By 1669 De Ruyter will, for the time being at least, have had enough of sitting for his picture. In 1672, the *rampjaar* (disaster year), the Republic's economy collapsed after the attacks by France, England and the city-states of Münster and Cologne. As a result, the art market likewise slumped as well-to-do patrons stayed away. Famous artists like Willem van de Velde the Elder and his son Willem van de Velde the Younger left for England in search of a livelihood. De Ruyter would certainly have had the means to commission new portraits of himself and his wife but he put this off, possibly because he was kept busy at the fleet. All the same, several prints appeared in 1673 with the portrait of De Ruyter, who had reaped great fame that year in the Battle of Schooneveld and the Battle of Texel.[41]

Even so, we do have a last portrait of De Ruyter by Berckman, dated 1675. De Ruyter must have sat for it because in this painting his face looks considerably older than in previous representations and for the first time, he is depicted with grey hair. The sitting could only have taken place in the months prior to his last expedition to

the Mediterranean, for which he left Rotterdam towards the end of July to go to his ship the *Eendracht* that was lying ready off Hellevoetsluis.

De Ruyter had by then become a mere shadow of the sturdy, imposing seafarer of bygone days. He suffered constantly from sudden, severe attacks of an illness that was called 'gravel' in his times and was caused by a stone in his kidney or bladder. It had given De Ruyter a corpulent body. Perhaps Berckman took this into consideration and for this reason painted the body of the admiral concealed in a suit of armour, with to the right, a sea battle in the background.[42] Or, another possible reason could of course lie in De Ruyter's not having sufficient time to pose for a very long time and being no longer capable of this at his age. Berckman painted him in the same suit of armour and in the same position he had in 1673 captured his colleague Adriaen Banckert in. All he needed to do was add De Ruyter's face and his medallion of the Order of Saint Michael to the portrait he had made of Banckert. We do not know of a pendant portrait of Anna van Gelder but the portraits may with time have become separated.

Thus, De Ruyter had himself painted five times by Berckman. All in all, together with his official portraits by Bol and Dujardin, the family portrait by Jacobson, the 1656 painting from Denmark by Van Mander and the no longer extant portrait by Jan Lievens of 1666 we arrive at some ten different contemporary portraits in oil. For the making of copies, one of the versions of the portrait by Bol appears to have been favoured at the time for a model. Of the other portraits, only a very limited number of copies have survived.

With ten different portraits, De Ruyter is well up on the list of most frequently immortalized naval heroes.[43] In fact, he is only surpassed by Cornelis Tromp, whom I have not without reason once called the 'national record-holder portraits' of the seventeenth century. To this day, we have some fourteen different portraits of Tromp, the vast majority of which were commissioned by him and painted by prominent Amsterdam portraitists. That number may actually grow in the future. Only a couple of years ago, a large, hitherto unknown painted portrait of Cornelis Tromp turned up at an auction in New York, painted by Jan Mijtens in 1661.[44]

When De Ruyter follows so closely on the vain Tromp, coming second in numbers of portraits in oil, then that does mean something. Vanity does not necessarily come into it. De Ruyter lived a long life and therefore had more time in which to have himself immortalized than had many of his colleagues. Moreover, he was the supreme commander of the fleet for over ten years, serving in two major naval wars with important sea battles. Yet the proposition that he rather not had his portrait painted out of modesty is no longer tenable.

■ A posthumous portrait

The 1675 painting ends the set of portraits that Berckman painted of De Ruyter over the years. There is, however, an interesting coda to this history. It was very common practice for the relatives of a naval hero to have a large posthumous portrait painted of him after his death. Often the descendants will have financed this with the sum of money they received as a tribute from the States General upon the hero's demise. This is what presumably happened in the Van Galen and Stellingwerf families, who had posthumous portraits painted by Bartholomeus and Lodewijk van der Helst, respectively.[45]

Michiel de Ruyter

Painting by H. Berckman, 1675,
Instituut Collectie Nederland,
Amsterdam/ Rijswijk
Photography by Ton Sipman

It is not known whether the De Ruyter family received a similar financial gift. It would appear that they did not, given that payment of the costs for the admiral's funeral, which the relatives and the admiralty had advanced, was a long time coming. Be that as it may, the family doubtless received back payments from the admiralty over time. Besides, De Ruyter left approximately 350,000 guilders, so his next of kin were hardly poverty-stricken. Engel de Ruyter, for instance, commissioned Emanuel de Witte in 1683 to paint a canvas representing the choir of the New Church [Nieuwe Kerk] in Amsterdam and in the centre showing the impressive marble tomb of the naval hero admired with interest by countless visitors.[46]

Some years previously, the family must have commissioned two more large portraits of Michiel de Ruyter and Anna van Gelder. They approached Ferdinand Bol for the posthumous painting of De Ruyter. It was only natural that De Ruyter, fallen in action, would one more time be depicted as a proud hero and therefore Bol was asked to do a painting in the style of the 1667 'state portrait'. This also suggests why the family did not ask Berckman to paint this picture: after all, his portraits of De Ruyter were much less warlike. Karel Dujardin was no option as he had meanwhile gone to live in Italy, where he died in 1678.

Bol depicted De Ruyter in this new portrait in much the same posture as he had

Anna van Gelder

Painting by H. Berckman, about 1678,
Zeeland Maritime Museum, Flushing

adopted in the portrait that the admiral had sent to the king of Denmark in 1669.[47] De Ruyter is shown in full armour as he was in Dujardin's 1669 painting and in Berckman's picture of 1675. The increasingly heroic nature of the portraiture of naval heroes from the seventies onwards made representations of admirals in full armour extremely popular.[48] Apparently, there was a desire to ever strongly emphasize the myth of power and invincibility. In practice, of course, suits of armour were never worn on board as they would have been extremely impractical.

There are some striking differences with the 'state portrait' of 1667. For the first time, De Ruyter is seen wearing an orange sash on his left arm, which seems to express devotion to the House of Orange. For the first time too, a little Moor can be seen at De Ruyter's side, a figure that though it was very usual to include in portraits of rulers yet was conspicuously absent from all the pictures that were made during De Ruyter's life.[49] De Ruyter, for one, had apparently set no great store by this addition. Such little black boys suited families who lived in great style in their splendid town houses located within the ring of canals in the centre of Amsterdam, and who had a retinue of servants. Not so De Ruyter, who had little domestic help and lived in a plain sailors' district on the IJ.[50] There is reason to suspect that the orange sash and the little Moor were added at the instigation of Engel de Ruyter. He led a more luxurious lifestyle than his father, and could boast a summer house in Breukelen.[51] Further, Engel had not been close friends with Johan de Witt like his father and will have applauded a clear reference to the House of Orange. In the background of this new portrait by Bol, an encounter at sea can be seen, which could represent the raid on the Medway. In the 1667 portrait, only the *Zeven Provinciën* could be seen; an episode from the Anglo-Dutch Wars was probably deemed less felicitous as this painting was meant for the council chambers of the admiralties.

For the pendant to the posthumous painting of her husband by Bol Anna van Gelder once more turned to trusted Hendrick Berckman. It must have been one of his last commissions: he died in 1679. Berckman painted Anna, who had visibly aged, in familiar attire, with the customary items of jewellery and sitting on a chair. Behind the curtain, a landscape can be seen in the background. The chair is easily explained. Towards the late seventies, Anna van Gelder could no longer walk properly. In 1677 she had had a bad fall while hanging out the laundry on the clothes lines in the attic at home.[52] The paintings were set in very beautiful, carved frames with martial trophies, which conveys a sense of their belonging inseparably together. They probably hung in Engel de Ruyter's home until his death in 1683 and then in Anna van Gelder's, until she passed away in 1687. The frames fit in remarkably well with the frame of Engel's 1669 portrait by Bol as well as with that of a smaller-sized version of the 1667 portrait of De Ruyter by Bol, which has survived in its original frame to this day and was part of the family estate.[53]

In 1687 Gerard Brandt's big biography of De Ruyter appeared, dedicated to Anna van Gelder. At the beginning of his book the writer had included a print after the posthumous portrait by Bol.[54] This representation would gain great notoriety because of this print as well as on the basis of some later copies in oil.[55] Since it was soon forgotten that the portrait had been painted posthumously, it would ironically give rise to mistaken conclusions about the person of De Ruyter. The orange sash was often adduced as proof that De Ruyter was, after all, and contrary to what was generally assumed, an ardent advocate of the House of Orange. The little black boy was to provide many a twentieth-century detractor who wished to accuse De Ruyter of slave trade and imperialism with ammunition. Painted true to life so many times and still judged on a posthumous portrait. Sic transit gloria mundi.

Select bibliography

- Abun-Nasr, Jamil M., *A History of the Maghrib in the Islamic Period* (Cambridge 1991).
- Akveld, L.M., a.o. (eds.), *In het kielzog. Maritiem-historische studies aangeboden aan Jaap R. Bruijn bij zijn vertrek als hoogleraar Zeegeschiedenis aan de Universiteit Leiden* (Amsterdam 2003).
- Anderson, R. C. (ed.), *The Journal of Edward Montagu, First Earl of Sandwich, Admiral and General at Sea, 1639-1665* (London 1929).
- Anderson, R.C. (ed.), *The Journals of Sir Thomas Allin* (Navy Records Society 1939).
- Anderson, R. C. (ed.), *Journals and Narratives of the Third Dutch War* (London 1946).
- An-Naciri, Aḥmad ibn Khalid, *Kitab el-Istiqca li Akhbar doual el-Maghrib el-Aqca* (Casablanca 1997).
- Anonymous, *Newes from Mamora, or a Summary Relation Sent to the King of Spaine...*, trans. W. Squire (1614).
- Anonymous, *The Life of Michael Adrian de Ruyter, Admiral of Holland* (1677).
- Asaert, G., a.o. (eds.), *Maritieme Geschiedenis der Nederlanden*, 4 volumes, (Bussum 1976-1978).
- Asch, R. G., Durchhardt, H. (eds.), *Der Absolutismus - ein Mythos? Strukturwandel monarchischer Herrschaft* (Cologne 1996).
- Askgaard, Finn, *Kampen om Østersøen* (Copenhagen 1974).

- Bardet, J.-P., Dupâquier, J. (eds), *Histoire des populations de l'Europe: I. Des origines aux prémices de la révolution démographique* (Paris 1997).
- Barfod, Jørgen H., *Niels Juel liv og gerning* (Århus 1977).
- Beik, W. H., *Absolutism and society in seventeenth-century France* (Cambridge 1985).
- Bjerg, Hans Christian, Frantzen, Ole L., *Danmark i Krig* (Copenhagen 2005).
- Blankert, A., *Ferdinand Bol (1616-1680): Een leerling van Rembrandt* (The Hague 1976).
- Blok, P.J., *Michiel Adriaanszoon de Ruyter* ('s-Gravenhage 1928).
- Blok, P., *The Life of Admiral De Ruyter*, trans.

G.J. Renier (London 1933).
- Boon, P., *Bouwers van de zee: zeevarenden van het Westfriese platteland, c. 1680-1720* (The Hague 1996).
- Boxer, C.R., *The Dutch seaborne empire 1600-1800* (London 1965).
- Brady, T.A., Oberman, H., Tracy, J.D. (eds.), *Handbook of European history, 1400-1600*, vol. 1 (Leiden 1994).
- Brandt, G., *Het leven en bedryf van den heere Michiel de Ruiter, hertog, ridder ende L.Admiraal Generaal van Hollandt en Westvrieslandt* (Amsterdam 1687).
- Brandt, G., *Het leven en bedrijf van den here Michiel de Ruiter* (Amsterdam 1701 edition).
- Brand, H. (ed.), *Trade, Diplomacy and Cultural Exchange: Continuity and Change in the North Sea Area and the Baltic, c.1350-1750* (Hilversum 2005).
- Braudel, Fernand, *The Mediterranean and the Mediterranean World in the Age of Philip II*, trans. Silan Reynolds, 2 vols. (London 1975).
- Brewer, J., *The sinews of power: War, money and the English state, 1688-1783* (London 1989).
- Broos, B., Van Suchtelen, A., *Portraits in the Mauritshuis 1430-1790* (Zwolle-The Hague 2004).
- Bruijn, J.R. (ed.), *De oorlogvoering ter zee in 1673 in journalen en andere stukken* (Groningen 1966).
- Bruijn, J.R., Klein, P.W. (eds.), *Honderd jaar Engelandvaart. Stoomvaartmaatschappij Zeeland, Koninklijke Nederlandsche Postvaart NV 1875-1975* (Bussum 1975).
- Bruijn, J.R., Gaastra, F.S., Schöffer, I., *Dutch-Asiatic Shipping in the 17th and 18th Centuries* (The Hague 1979).
- Bruijn, J.R., *The Dutch navy of the seventeenth and eighteenth centuries* (Columbia (S.C.) 1993); 2nd edition St. John's NF 2011.
- Bruijn, J.R., *Varend Verleden. De Nederlandse oorlogsvloot in de 17de en 18de eeuw* (Amsterdam 1998).
- Buisman, J., *Duizend jaar weer, wind en water in de Lage Landen*, 5 volumes (Franeker 2000-2006).

- Capp, Bernard, *Cromwell's Navy: The Fleet and the English Revolution, 1648-1660* (Oxford 1989).
- Castries, Comte Henri de, (ed), *Les sources inédites de l'histoire du Maroc, Première série, Dynastie Saadienne*, Tomes 1-6, Archives et bibliothèques des Pays-Bas (Paris 1906-1923).
- *Catalogus der schilderijen, pastels, miniaturen, aquarellen, tentoongesteld in het Rijksmuseum te Amsterdam* (Amsterdam 1934).
- Cau, C.S. e.a. (ed.), *Groot Placaet-Boeck, vervattende de placaten, ordonnantien ende edicten van de Hoog Mogende Heeren Staaten Generael der Vereenighde Nederlanden (…)*, vol. 4 (The Hague 1705).
- Cavelli-Björkmann, G. (ed.), *Face to face. Portraits from five centuries* (Stockholm 2001).
- Chappell, E. (ed.), *The Tangier Papers of Samuel Pepys* (Navy Records Society 1935).
- Claydon, Tony, *Europe and the Making of England, 1660-1760* (Cambridge 2007).
- Clark, George, *The Seventeenth Century* (Oxford 1967).
- Clissold, Stephen, *The Barbary Slaves* (London 1977).
- Coindreau, Roger, *Les corsaires de Salé* (Casablanca 1993).
- Colenbrander, H.T., *Bescheiden uit vreemde archieven omtrent de groote Nederlandsche zeeoorlogen 1652-1676*, 2 volumes (The Hague 1919).
- Corbett, Julian S. (ed.), *Fighting Instructions, 1530-1816* (2nd edition London 1971).

- Daaku, K.Y., *Trade and Politics on the Gold Coast 1600-1720. A Study of the African Reaction to European Trade* (Oxford 1970).
- Dan, Pierre, *Histoire de Barbarie et de ses corsaires* (Paris 1637).
- Dantzig, A. van, *Forts and Castles of Ghana* (Accra 1980).
- Dapper, Olfert, *Déscription de l'Afrique* (Amsterdam 1686).
- Davids, K., Lucassen, J. (eds), *A miracle mirrored: The Dutch Republic in European perspec-*

tive (Cambridge 1995).

- Davids, K., a.o. (ed.), *De Republiek tussen zee en vasteland* (Apeldoorn 1995).
- Davies, J.D., *Gentlemen and Tarpaulins: The Officers and Men of the Restoration Navy* (Oxford 1991)
- Davies, J.D., *The Battle of the Texel, 11 August 1673: The Climactic Sea Battle of the Anglo-Dutch Wars* (Woodbridge, forthcoming).
- Davies, K.G., *The North Atlantic World in the Seventeenth Century* (Minneapolis) 1974.
- Davies, Robert C., *Christian Slaves, Muslim Masters: White Slavery in the Mediterranean, the Barbary Coast and Italy, 1500-1800* (New York 2003).
- De Bruin, G., *Geheimhouding en verraad. De geheimhouding van staatszaken ten tijde van de Republiek (1600-1750)* (The Hague 1991).
- De Jong, M., *'Staat van Oorlog': Wapenbedrijf en militaire hervorming in de Republiek der Verenigde Nederlanden, 1585-1621* (Hilversum 2005).
- De Jongh, E., *Portretten van echt en trouw. Huwelijk en gezin in de Nederlandse kunst van de zeventiende eeuw* (Zwolle-Haarlem 1986).
- De Vries, J., Van der Woude, A., *The first modern economy. Success, failure, and perseverance of the Dutch economy, 1500-1815* (Cambridge 1997).
- Den Heijer, H., *De geschiedenis van de WIC* (Zutphen 1994).
- Den Heijer, H., *Goud, ivoor en slaven. Scheepvaart en handel van de Tweede Westindische Compagnie op Afrika, 1674-1740* (Zutphen 1997).
- Dessert, D., *Argent, pouvoir, et société au Grand Siècle* (Paris 1984).
- Dessert, Daniel, *La Royale: Vaisseaux et marines du Roi-Soleil* (Paris 1996).
- Downing, B. M., *The Military Revolution and political change: Origins of democracy and autocracy in early modern Europe* (Princeton 1992).
- Durot, E., *Henri Duquesne (1662–1722), Huguenot réfugié en Suisse* (Chambery 1997–1998)

- Eekhout, L., *Het admiralenboek. De vlagofficieren van de Nederlandse marine 1382-1991* (Amsterdam 1992).
- Ekberg, Carl J., *The Failure of Louis XIV's Dutch War* (Chapel Hill 1979).
- Ekin, Des, *The Stolen Village: Baltimore and the Barbary Pirates* (Dublin 2006).
- Elias, J.E., *Het voorspel van den Eersten Engelschen oorlog*, 2 volumes (The Hague 1920).
- Elias, J. E., *De vlootbouw in Nederland in de eerste helft der 17de eeuw, 1596-1655* (Amsterdam 1933).
- Eloufrani, Mohamed Esseghir, *Nuzhat al-ḥadi bi-akbar muluk al-qarn al-ḥadi* (Rabat 1988).
- Engels, Marie-Christine, *Merchants, Interlopers, Seamen and Corsairs: The Flemish Community in Livorno and Genoa 1615-1635* (Hilversum 1997).
- Enthoven, V., *Zeeland en de opkomst van de Republiek: Handel en strijd in de Scheldedelta, c. 1550-1621* (Leiden 1996).
- Enthoven, V., Acda, G., Bon, A. (eds.), *Een saluut van 26 schoten. Liber Amicorum aangeboden aan Ger Teitler bij zijn afscheid als hoogleraar aan het Koninklijk Instituut voor de Marine* (Amsterdam 2005).

- Fahlborg, Birger, *Sveriges yttre politik 1664-1668* (Stockholm 1949).
- Fahlborg, Birger, *Sveriges yttre politik 1668-1672* (Stockholm 1961).
- Feld, M.D., *The structure of violence: Armed forces as social systems* (London 1977).
- Fisher, Sir Godfrey, *Barbary Legend: War, Trade, and Piracy in North Africa, 1415-1830* (Oxford 1957).
- Fox, Frank L., *A Distant Storm: The Four Days' Battle of 1666 The Greatest Sea Fight of the Age of Sail* (Rotherfield 1996).
- Fruin, R., Japikse, N. (ed.), *Brieven aan Johan de Witt 1648-1672, tweede deel, 1660-1672* (Amsterdam 1922).
- Fulton, Thomas Wemyss, *The Sovereignty of the Sea: An Historical Account of the Claims of England to the Dominion of the British Seas, and of the Evolution of the Territorial Waters: with special reference to the Rights of Fishing and the Naval Salute* (2nd edition; New York 1976).

- Gaastra, F.S., *De geschiedenis van de VOC* (Zutphen 1991).
- Gaastra, F.S., *The Dutch East India Company. Expansion and Decline* (Zutphen 2003).
- Glete, Jan, ed., *Naval History, 1500-1680* (Aldershot 2005).
- Glete, Jan, *Navies and Nations: Warships, Navies and State Building in Europe and America, 1500-1860* (Stockholm 1993).
- Glete, Jan, *War and the State in Early Modern Europe: Spain, the Dutch Republic and Sweden as fiscal-military States, 1500-1660* (London 2002).
- Gorski, P. S., *The Disciplinary Revolution: Calvinism and the rise of the state in Early Modern Europe* (Chicago 2003).
- Grapperhaus, F. H. M.. *Convoyen en licenten* (Zutphen 1986).
- Grove, G.L., *Journalen van de Admiralen Van Wassenaer-Obdam (1658/59) en De Ruyter (1658/59)* (Amsterdam 1907).

- Haak, B., *Hollandse schilders in de Gouden Eeuw* (Amsterdam 1984).
- Hacquebord, L., Vroom, W. (eds.), *Walvisvaart in de Gouden Eeuw. Opgravingen op Spitsbergen* (Amsterdam 1988).
- Hajji, Mohamed, *Al-Zawiyah al-Dilaiyah wa-dawruha al-dini wa-al-ilmi wa-siyasi* (Rabat 1988).
- Haley, K.H.D., *The British and the Dutch: Political and Cultural Relations through the Ages* (1988).
- Harrison, John, *The Tragical Life and Death of Muley Abdala Melek the Late King of Barbary* (Delph 1633).
- 't Hart, M. C., *The making of a bourgeois state: War, politics and finance during the Dutch revolt* (Manchester 1993).
- Hattendorf, John B. (ed.), *Oxford Encyclopedia of Maritime History* (New York 2007).
- Hattendorf, John B., Unger, R.W. (eds.), *War at Sea in The Middle Ages and the Renaissance* (Woodbridge 2003).
- Hatton, Ragnhild, *Europe in the Age of Louis XIV* (2nd edition; London 1979).
- Hebb, David Delison, *Piracy and the English Government* (Aldershot 1994).

- Heers, Jacques, *The Barbary Corsairs: Warfare in the Mediterranean, 1480-1580*, trans. Jonathan North (London 2003).
- Hernán, Enrique García, Maffi, Davide (eds), *Guerra y Sociedad en la Monarquía Hispánica: Política, estrategia y cultura en la Europa moderna (1500-1700)*, vol. 1 (Madrid 2006).
- *Het staatsche leger*, 8 vols. in 10 parts (Breda and The Hague 1911-64).
- Hoogewerff, G.J. (ed.), *De twee reizen van Cosimo de Medici prins van Toscane door de Nederlanden (1667-1669). Journalen en documenten* (Amsterdam 1919).
- Hopkins, J. F. P. (trans. and ed.), *Letters from Barbary 1576-1774: Arabic Documents in the Public Record Office* (Oxford 1982).

- Israel, J.I., *Dutch primacy in world trade 1585-1740* (Oxford 1989).

- Jacobs, J.A., *Een zegenrijk gewest. Nieuw-Nederland in de zeventiende eeuw* (Amsterdam 1999).
- Jal, Augustin, *Abraham Duquesne* (Paris 1873).
- James, A., *Navy and Government in Early Modern France, 1572-1661* (Woodbridge 2004).
- Japikse, N., *De verwikkelingen tusschen de Republiek en Engeland van 1660-1665* (Leiden 1900).
- Joffé, George (ed.), *North Africa: Nation, State, and Region* (London and New York 1993).
- Jones, J. R., *The Anglo-Dutch Wars of the Seventeenth Century* (London 1996).
- Jong, M. de, '*Staat van Oorlog': Wapenbedrijf en militaire hervorming in de Republiek der Verenigde Nederlanden, 1585-1621* (Hilversum 2005).
- Jonker, J., Sluyterman, K., *Thuis op de wereldmarkt. Nederlandse handelshuizen door de eeuwen heen* (The Hague 2000).
- Junge, Hans-Christoph, *Flottenpolitik und Revolution* (Stuttgart 1980).
- Julien, Charles André, *Histoire de l'Afrique du Nord: Tunisie, Algérie, Maroc* (Paris 1956).
- Justesen, O., *Danish Sources for the History of Ghana 1657-1754*, vol. 1 (Copenhagen 2005).

- Kilian, J.M., *The paintings of Karel du Jardin. Catalogue raisonné* (Amsterdam-Philadelphia 2005).
- Kitson, Frank, *Prince Rupert: Admiral and General-at-Sea* (London 1998).
- Klooster, W., *Illicit Riches. Dutch Trade in the Caribbean, 1648-1795* (Leiden 1998).
- Klopp, O., *Admiral de Ruyter* (Hannover 1858).
- Knight, R.J.B., *The Pursuit of Victory: The Life and Achievement of Horatio Nelson* (2005).
- Korteweg, J., *Kaperbloed en koopmansgeest. 'Legale' zeeroof door de eeuwen heen* (Amsterdam 2006).

- Lachmann, R. M., *Capitalists in spite of themselves: Elite conflict and economic transitions in early modern Europe* (Oxford 2000).
- Lane-Poole, Stanley, *The Barbary Corsairs* (London 1984).
- Laroui, Abdallah, *L'histoire du Maghreb: un essai de synthèse* (Casablanca 2001).
- Latham, R., Matthews, W. (eds), *The Diary of Samuel Pepys*, 11 vols. (1970-83).
- Lavery, Brian, *The Ship of the Line. Vol. 1: The Development of the battlefleet, 1650-1850* (Annapolis 1983).
- Lemmers, A., *Van werf tot facilitair complex. 350 jaar marinegeschiedenis op Kattenburg* (The Hague 2005).
- Lesger, C., *Handel in Amsterdam ten tijde van de Opstand. Kooplieden, commerciële expansie en verandering in de ruimtelijke economie van de Nederlanden ca. 1550 -ca. 1630* (Hilversum 2001).
- Lind, H.D., *Kong Frederik den tredies Sømagt* (Odense 1896).
- Lloyd, Christopher, *English Corsairs on the Barbary Coast* (London 1981).
- Lowenheim, Oded, *Predators and Parasites: Persistent Agents of International Harm and Great Power Authority* (Ann Arbor 2007).
- Lynn, J. A., *Giant of the Grand Siècle: The French army, 1610-1715* (Cambridge 1997).
- Lynn, J. A., 'Revisiting the great fact of war and Bourbon absolutism: The growth of the French army during the Grand Siécle', in: Enrique García Hernán & Davide Maffi (eds),

Guerra y Sociedad en la Monarquía Hispánica: Política, estrategia y cultura en la Europa moderna (1500-1700) (Madrid 2006).

- Maarleveld, T.J., *Archaeological heritage management in Dutch waters: exploratory studies* (Leiden 1998).
- Middelkoop, N. (ed.), *Kopstukken. Amsterdammers geportretteerd 1600-1800* (Bussum-Amsterdam 2002).
- Milo, T.H., *Wassenaer en de zeemacht. Jacob van Wassenaer van Obdam en zijn tijd* (Wassenaar 1965).
- Milton, G., *Nathaniel's Nutmeg* (New York 1999).
- Moes, E.W., *Iconographia Batava. Beredeneerde lijst van geschilderde en gebeeldhouwde portretten van Noord-Nederlanders in vorige eeuwen*, 2 vols. (Amsterdam 1897-1905).
- Muller, F., *Beschrijvende catalogus van 7000 portretten van Nederlanders* (Amsterdam 1853).

- Nørregard, G., *Danish Settlements in West Africa 1658-1850* (Boston 1966).
- North, D. C., *Structure and change in economic history* (New York 1981).
- North, D. C., *Understanding the process of economic change* (Princeton 2005).

- Ollard, R., *Man of War. Sir Robert Holmes and the Restoration Navy* (London 1969).
- Ormrod, D, *The rise of commercial empires: England and the Netherlands in the Age of Mercantilism, 1650-1770* (Cambridge 2003).
- Oudendijk, J., *Johan de Witt en de zeemacht* (Amsterdam 1944).

- Panhuysen, L., *De ware vrijheid. De levens van Johan en Cornelis de Witt* (Amsterdam 2005).
- Parker, D., *Class and state in Ancien Regime France: The road to modernity?* (London 1996).
- Parker, G., *The Army of Flanders and the Spanish Road, 1567-1659* (Cambridge 1972).
- Parker, Kenneth, "Reading 'Barbary' in Early Modern England, 1550-1685", in: *The Seventeenth Century* 19.1 (2004), 88.
- Parrott, D., *Richelieu's army: War, government*

and society in France, 1624-1642 (Cambridge 2001).

- Pascon, Paul, *La maison d'Iligh et l'histoire sociale du Tazerwalt* (Rabat 1984).

- Pechot, L., *Histoire de L 'Afrique du Nord Avant 1830* (Alger 1914).

- Pincus, S.C.A., *Protestantism and patriotism. Ideologies and the making of English foreign policy, 1650-1668* (Cambridge 1996).

- Playfair, R. L., *The Scourge of Christendom: Annals of British Relations with Algiers prior to the French Conquest* (London 1884).

- Powell, J. R. (ed.), *The Letters of Robert Blake Together with Supplementary Documents* (London 1937).

- Powell, J.R., Timings, E.K. (eds.), *The Rupert and Monck Letterbook* (London and Colchester 1969).

- Prak, Maarten Roy, *The Dutch Republic in the Seventeenth Century*, trans. Diane Webb (Cambridge 2005).

- Price, J. L., *Holland and the Dutch Republic in the seventeenth century: The politics of particularism* (Oxford 1994).

- Probst, Niels M., *Christian 4.s flåde* (Copenhagen 1996).

- Probst, Niels M., *Niels Juel, vor største flådefører* (Copenhagen 2005).

- Prud'homme van Reine, R.B., e.a., *Ter navolging. Maritieme kunst en curiosa uit de Kweekschool voor de Zeevaart* (Amsterdam-Zutphen 1992).

- Prud'homme van Reine, R.B., *Biografie van Michiel Adriaenszoon de Ruyter* (Amsterdam and Antwerp 1996); 6th edition, 2007

- Prud'homme van Reine, R.B., *Schittering en schandaal: Biografie van Maerten en Cornelis Tromp* (Amsterdam and Antwerp 2001).

- Rahn, Werner (ed.), *Deutsche Marinen im Wandel: Von Symbol nationaler Einheit zum Instument internationaler Sicherheit* (München 2005).

- Redlich, F., *The German military enterpriser and his work force: A study in European economic and social history*, 2 vols. (Wiesbaden 1964-65).

- Reinders, H.R., *Modderwerk. Het uitdiepen van de haven van Amsterdam in de tweede helft van de zeventiende eeuw* (Rapport Rijksdienst IJsselmeerpolders 1978-19Abw).

- *Remonstrantie Aen de Hoog Mogende Heeren de Staten Generael der Vereenighde Nederlanden; overgegeven den III Juny 1664. By de Heeren de Bewinthebberen van de Geoctroyeerde West-Indische Compagnie der Vereenighde Nederlanden* (Amsterdam 1664).

- *Resolutie vande Edele Groot Mogende heeren Staten van Hollandt ende West-Vrieslandt; Item een Missive van hare Hoog Mogende de heeren Staten Generael der Vereenighde Nederlanden; Mitsgaders een Missive vanden Directeur Generael Johan van Valckenburgh (...)* (The Hague 1665).

- Roding, J., Heerma van Voss, L. (eds.), *The North Sea and Culture (1550-1800)* (Hilversum 1996)

- Rogers, C. J., *The Military Revolution Debate: Readings on the military transformation of Early Modern Europe* (Boulder 1995).

- Rogers, P. G., *A History of Anglo-Moroccan Relations to 1900* (London 1970).

- Rogers, P.G., *The Dutch in the Medway* (London 1970).

- Rodger, N.A.M., *The Command of the Ocean: A Naval History of Britain, 1649-1815* (London 2004).

- Rommelse, G., *The Second Anglo-Dutch War (1665-1667)* (Hilversum 2006).

- Roos, D., *Twee eeuwen varen en vechten. Het admiralengeslacht Evertsen* (Flushing 2003).

- Rowen, Herbert H., *John de Witt, Grand Pensionary of Holland, 1625-1672* (Princeton 1978).

- Rowlands, G., *The dynastic state and the army under Louis XIV: Royal service and private interest, 1661-1701* (Cambridge 2002).

- Sainsbury, W.N. (ed.), *Calendar of State Papers, Colonial Series, America and West Indies 1661-1668* (London 1880).

- Scheurleer, D.F., *Michiel Adriaensz de Ruyter, Leven en daden naar berichten en afbeeldingen van tijdgenoten* (The Hague 1907).

- Schutte, O., *Repertorium der Nederlandse vertegenwoordigers residerende in het buitenland 1584-1810* (The Hague 1976).

- Sebag, Paul, *Tunis au XVIIe siècle: une cité barbaresque au temps de la course* (Paris 1989).

- Shaw, W.A., *The Knights of England* (Oxford 1906).

- Sigmond, P., Kloek, W., *Sea Battles and naval heroes in the 17th-century Dutch Republic* (Amsterdam 2007)

- Smuts, M. (ed) *The Stuart Court and Europe: Essays in Politics and Political Culture* (Cambridge 1996).

- Sonnino, Paul, *Louis XIV and the Origins of the Dutch War* (Cambridge 1988).

- Storrs, C., *The resilience of the Spanish Monarchy, 1665-1700* (Oxford 2006).

- Susi, Mohamed al-Mukhtar, *Iligh qadiman wa-ḥadithan* (Rabat 1966).

- Temple, Sir William, *Observations upon the United Provinces of the Netherlands* (Cambridge 1932).

- Terpstra, H., *Jacob van Neck. Amsterdams admiraal en regent* (Amsterdam 1950).

- Thieme, U., Becker, F., *Allgemeines Lexikon der bildenden Künstler*, 37 vols. (Leipzig 1907-1950).

- Thompson, E.M. (ed.), *Letters of Humphrey Prideaux to John Ellis* (Camden Society 1875).

- Thompson, I. A. A., *War and government in Habsburg Spain, 1560-1620* (London 1976).

- Tilly, C., (ed.), *The formation of national states in Western Europe* (Princeton 1975).

- Tilly, C., *Coercion, capital, and European states, AD 990-1990* (Oxford 1990).

- Tønnesen, A., *'Al het Hollandse volk dat hier nu woont'. Nederlanders in Helsingør, circa 1550-1600* (Hilversum 2003).

- Tunstall, Brian, *Naval Warfare in the Age of Sail: The Evolution of Fighting Tactics, 1650-1815* (Annapolis 1990).

- Van Deursen, A. Th., Bruijn, J.R., Korteweg, J.E., *De Admiraal: De Wereld van Michiel Adriaenszoon de Ruyter* (Franeker 2007).

- Van den Broek, L., Jacobs, M., *Christenslaven. De slavernij-ervaringen van Cornelis Stout in Algiers (1678-1680) en Maria ter Meetelen in Marokko (1731-1743)* (Zutphen 2006).

- Van Doorn, J. A. A., *Een sociologische benadering van het organisatieverschijnsel in het bijzonder gebaseerd op een analyse van het militaire systeem* (Leiden 1956).

- Van Foreest, H.A., Weber, R.E.J., *De Vierdaagse zeeslag 11-14 Juni 1666* (Amsterdam 1984).
- Van Hoboken, J.R., *Witte de With in Brazilië 1648-1649* (Amsterdam 1955).
- Van Krieken, G., *Kapers en kooplieden. De betrekkingen tussen Algiers en Nederland 1604-1830* (Amsterdam 1999).
- Van Krieken, G., *Corsaires & marchands: les relations entre Alger et les Pays-Bas, 1640-1830* (Bouchène 2002).
- Van Lottum, J., *Across the North sea. The impact of the Dutch Republic on international labour migration, c. 1550-1850* (Amsterdam 2007).
- Van Nimwegen, O., *'Deser landen crijchsvolck'. Het Staatse leger en de militaire revoluties 1588-1688* (Amsterdam 2006).
- Van Someren, J.F., *Beschrijvende catalogus van gegraveerde portretten van Nederlanders*, 3 vols. (Amsterdam 1888-1891).
- Van Thiel, P.J.J., De Bruyn Cops, C.J., *Prijst de lijst. De Hollandse schilderijlijst in de zeventiende eeuw* (Amsterdam-The Hague 1984).
- Van Vliet, A.P. *Vissers en kapers. De zeevisserij vanuit het Maasmondgebied en de Duinkerker kapers (ca. 1580-1648)* (The Hague 1994).
- Van Vliet, A.P., *Vissers in oorlogstijd. De Zeeuwse zeevisserij in de jaren 1568-1648* (Middelburg 2003).
- Van Vliet, A.P., *'Een vriendelijcke groetenisse'. Brieven van het thuisfront aan de vloot van De Ruyter (1664-1665)* (Franeker 2007).
- Vermeesch, G., *Oorlog, steden en staatsvorming: De grenssteden Gorinchem en Doesburg tijdens de geboorte-eeuw van de Republiek, 1570-1680* (Amsterdam 2006).
- Vergé-Franceschi, M., *Campagnes de mer sous Louis XIV* (Paris 1991).
- Vergé-Franceschi, M., *Abraham Duquesne: Huguenot et marin du Roi Soleil* (Paris 1992).
- Vergé-Franceschi, M., *Chronique maritime de la France d'Ancien Régime (1492–1792)* (Paris 1998).
- Vergé-Franceschi, M., *Henri le Navigateur* (Paris 1994)
- Vergé-Franceschi, M., *Colbert ou la politique du bon sens* ((2nd edition, Paris 2005).
- Verhoog, P. (ed.), *De reis van Michiel Adriaens-zoon de Ruyter in 1664-1665* (The Hague 1961).
- Villiers, P., *Les corsairs du littoral: Dunkerque, Calais, Boulogne de Philippe II à Louis XIV (1568-1713)* (Villeneuve d'Ascq 2000).
- Von Wurzbach, A., *Niederländisches Künstler-Lexikon*, 3 vols. (Wenen-Leipzig 1906-1911).
- Vreugdenhil, A., *Lists of Men-of-War. 1650-1700: Part IV, Ships of the United Netherlands, 1648-1702* (London 1938).
- Vries, J. de & Woude, A. van der, *The first modern economy: Success, failure, and perseverance of the Dutch economy, 1500-1815*, Cambridge, 1997.
- Vries, R. J. de, 'Population', in: T. A. Brady, H. Oberman, & J. D. Tracy (eds), *Handbook of European history, 1400-1600*, (Leiden 1994).

- *Waerachtigh Verhael vande Grouwelicke en Barbarische Moorderye, begaen door de Engelschen in Guinea aen Onse Nederlandsche Natie* (Middelburgh 1665).
- Wallerstein, I., *The modern world-system,* vol. 1 (New York 1974).
- Warnsinck-Delprat, C.E. (ed.), *Reijse gedaen bij Adriaen Schagen aen de croonen van Sweden ende Polen inden jaere 1656* (The Hague 1968).
- Warnsinck, J. C. M., *Admiraal de Ruyter. De Zeeslag op Schooneveld, juni 1673* (The Hague 1930).
- Weber, R.E.J., *De seinboeken voor Nederlandse oorlogsvloten en konvooien tot 1690* (Amsterdam 1982).
- Wegener Sleeswijk, A., *De Gouden Eeuw van het fluitschip* (Franeker 2003).
- Wheeler, James Scott, *The Making of a World Power: War and the Military Revolution in Seventeenth Century England* (Phoenix Mill 1999).
- Wiersum, E., *Egbert Meussen Cortenaer* (Assen 1939).
- Wilson, P. H., *German armies: War and German politics, 1648-1806* (London 1988).
- Wilson, Peter Lamborn, *Pirate Utopias: Moorish Corsairs & European Renegadoes* (New York 2003).

- Zeller, Gaston, *Histoire des Relations Internationales, publiée sous la direction de Pierre Renouvin. Tome 3: Les Temps Modernes. Deuxième partie. De Louis XIV à 1789* (Paris 1955).
- Zook, G.F., *The Company of Royal Adventurers Trading into Africa* (Lancaster 1919).
- Zwitzer, H. L., *'De militie van den Staat': Het leger van de Republiek der Verenigde Nederlanden* (Amsterdam 1991).

References

1 The Maritime World of the Dutch Republic

[1] S. Hart, 'Rederij', in: G. Asaert a.o. (eds.), *Maritieme Geschiedenis der Nederlanden,* vol. 2, Bussum 1977, 106-125, i.l. 108-111.

[2] A.P. van Vliet, *'Een vriendelijcke groetenisse'. Brieven van het thuisfront aan de vloot van De Ruyter (1664-1665),* Franeker 2007, 285-287; letter by Jean de Witte to Cornelia de Ruyter, 3.11.1683 in the collection of the Stichting De Ruyter, section 13, box 11, no. 91.

[3] J. de Vries and A. van der Woude, *The first modern economy. Success, failure, and perseverance of the Dutch economy, 1500-1815,* Cambridge 1997, 344-347.

[4] H.R. Reinders, *Modderwerk. Het uitdiepen van de haven van Amsterdam in de tweede helft van de zeventiende eeuw,* Rapport Rijksdienst IJsselmeerpolders 1978-19Abw.

[5] De Vries and Van der Woude, *The first modern economy,* 34-36 and 179-187.

[6] J. Buisman, *Duizend jaar weer, wind en water in de Lage Landen,* vol. 4 (1575-1675), Franeker 2000, 10, 445, 448 and 685; ibidem, vol. 5 (1675-1750), Franeker 2006, 860-863.

[7] H. Terpstra, *Jacob van Neck. Amsterdams admiraal en regent,* Amsterdam 1950; J.R. Bruijn, *The Dutch navy of the seventeenth and eighteenth centuries,* Columbia (S.C.) 1993, 35-38.

[8] C.R. Boxer, *The Dutch seaborne empire 1600-1800,* London 1965, 32-34.

[9] A. Lemmers, *Van werf tot facilitair complex. 350 jaar marinegeschiedenis op Kattenburg,* The Hague 2005, 30.

[10] A. Wegener Sleeswijk, *De Gouden Eeuw van het fluitschip,* Franeker 2003, 28 and fig. 5; The Hague, National Archive, Admiraliteits Archieven 3256 (ms. 1694).

[11] T.J. Maarleveld, *Archaeological heritage management in Dutch waters: exploratory studies,* Leiden 1998, 81-103.

[12] De Vries and Van der Woude, *The first modern economy,* 295-303; J.R. Bruijn, *'Scheepswerven in de 17de eeuw',* in: Werfkroniek. Bouwverslag van de Zeven Provinciën en andere verhalen over ambachtelijke scheepsbouw op de Batavia-werf, Lelystad 1989, 6-16.

[13] J.I. Israel, *Dutch primacy in world trade 1585-1740,* Oxford 1989, 73-79; J. Jonker and K. Sluyterman, *Thuis op de wereldmarkt. Nederlandse handelshuizen door de eeuwen heen,* The Hague 2000, 35-39.

[14] Bruijn, *'Postvervoer en reizigersverkeer tussen de lage landen en Engeland* (ca. 1650-ca. 1870)', in: P.W. Klein and J.R. Bruijn (eds.), *Honderd jaar Engelandvaart. Stoomvaartmaatschappij Zeeland, Koninklijke Nederlandsche Postvaart NV 1875-1975,* Bussum 1975, 19-52, i.l. 23-33; Amsterdam, Municipal Archive, Not. Records. 674, 176 (1.5.1637).

[15] C. Lesger, *Handel in Amsterdam ten tijde van de Opstand. Kooplieden, commerciële expansie en verandering in de ruimtelijke economie van de Nederlanden ca. 1550 -ca. 1630,* Hilversum 2001, chapters 5 and 6.

[16] J.E. Elias, *Het voorspel van den Eersten Engelschen oorlog,* The Hague 1920, 61; J.V. Th. Knoppers, "De vaart in Europa", in: G. Asaert a.o. (eds.), *Maritieme Geschiedenis der Nederlanden,* vol. 3, Bussum 1977, 226-261, i.l. 226; J. van Lottum, *Across the North sea. The impact of the Dutch Republic on international labour migration, c. 1550-1850,* Amsterdam 2007, 207; Hoorn, Westfries Archief, Oud Archief Enkhuizen, 424, no. 1587.

[17] Wegener Sleeswijk, *De Gouden Eeuw,* chapters 3 and 6.

[18] Van Lottum, *Across the North Sea,* 206-207.

[19] O. Schutte (eds.), *Repertorium der Nederlandse vertegenwoordigers, residerende in het buitenland 1584-1810,* The Hague 1976, 259 and 265-269; Lesger, Handel in Amsterdam, 233-234; A. Tønnesen, *'Al het Hollandse volk dat hier nu woont'. Nederlanders in Helsingør, circa 1550-1600,* Hilversum 2003.

[20] For a short introduction see: Bruijn, *'De walvisvaart: de ontplooiing van een nieuwe bedrijfstak',* in: L. Hacquebord and W. Vroom (eds.), *Walvisvaart in de Gouden Eeuw. Opgravingen op Spitsbergen,* Amsterdam 1988, 16-24 and the other articles in this publication.

[21] A.P. van Vliet, *Vissers en kapers. De zeevisserij vanuit het Maasmondgebied en de Duinkerker kapers (ca. 1580-1648),* The Hague 1994, 204 and 319; idem, *Vissers in oorlogstijd. De Zeeuwse zeevisserij in de jaren 1568-1648,* Middelburg 2003, 103 and 109.

[22] A recent and good survey of the history of Dutch privateering is: J. Korteweg, *Kaperbloed en koopmansgeest. 'Legale' zeeroof door de eeuwen heen.,* Amsterdam 2006.

[23] J.R. Bruijn, F.S. Gaastra and I. Schöffer, *Dutch-Asiatic Shipping in the 17th and 18th Centuries,* vol. III (The Hague 1979), nos. 5515-5517.

[24] Ibidem, vol. I (The Hague 1987), chapter 9. A general survey offers Gaastra, *The Dutch East India Company. Expansion and Decline,* Zutphen 2003.

[25] H.J. den Heijer, *De geschiedenis van de WIC,* Zutphen 1994, 31; idem, *Goud, ivoor en slaven. Scheepvaart en handel van de Tweede Westindische Compagnie 1674-1740,* Zutphen 1997, 122-123.

[26] J. Lucassen, *'Zeevarenden',* in: G. Asaert a.o. (eds.), *Maritieme geschiedenis der Nederlanden,* vol. 2, 126-158, i.l. 132; Bruijn, *'Zeevarenden',* in: ibidem, vol. 3, 146-190, i.l. 147; Van Lottum, Across the North Sea, 206-207.

[27] O. van Nimwegen, *'Deser landen crijchsvolck'. Het Staatse leger en de militaire revoluties 1588-1688,* Amsterdam 2006, 54 and 421.

[28] P. Boon, *Bouwers van de zee: zeevarenden van het Westfriese platteland, c. 1680-1720,* The Hague 1996, 129-130.

[29] J. van Lottum and S. Sogner, *'Het verhaal van Magnus en Barbara: migratiegeschiedenis in het klein',* in: Holland, 39 (2007), 65-79; Van Vliet, in: Holland, 39 (2007), 65-79; Van Vliet, 'Een vriendelijke groetenisse' 201.

[30] A. Little, *'British seamen in the United Provinces during the seventeenth century Anglo-Dutch Wars: the Dutch navy – a preliminary sur-*

vey', in: H. Brand (ed.), *Trade, diplomacy and cultural exchange. Continuity and change in the North Sea and the Baltic c. 1350-1750*, Hilversum 2005, 75-92, i.l. 87-91; P. Villiers, *Les corsairs du littoral: Dunkerque, Calais, Boulogne de Philippe* II à *Louis XIV (1568-1713)*, Villeneuve d'Ascq 2000, 190; J.R. Bruijn, *Varend Verleden. De Nederlandse oorlogsvloot in de 17de en 18de eeuw*, Amsterdam 1998, chapter 10.

2   Michiel Adriaenszoon de Ruyter and his Biographer Gerard Brandt

[1] Biographies based on original research: G. Brandt, *Het leven en bedrijf van den heere Michiel de Ruiter*. Amsterdam 1687; P.J. Blok, *Michiel Adriaanszoon de Ruyter*. The Hague 1928; R. Prud'homme van Reine, *Rechterhand van Nederland. Biografie van Michiel Adriaenszoon de Ruyter*. Amsterdam-Antwerp 1996.

[2] National Archives The Hague, The Netherlands. De Ruyter Collection (Acquired 1896), 233 (notes about his family made by De Ruyter, continued by his daughter Cornelia); P.K. Dommisse, *Michiel Adriaansz. De Ruyter en zijn naaste familie. Eensluidend afschrift der te Vlissingen aanwezige genealogische bronnen en brieven, met eenige aanteekeningen.* Vlissingen 1907; *Het nageslacht van Michiel Adriaensz. De Ruyter. Samengesteld door het Centraal Bureau voor Genealogie te 's-Gravenhage*. The Hague 1957.

[3] L. van den Bosch, *Leeven en daden der doorlugtighste zeehelden en ontdeckers van landen dezer eeuwen*. Amsterdam 1677.

[4] B. Piélat, *La vie et les actions mémorables de l'admiral De Ruyter, Duc, Chevalier et Lt. Amiral Général des Provinces Unies*. Amsterdam 1677 [actually 1681 or later].

[5] *The life of Michael Adrian de Ruyter, Admiral of Holland*. London 1677.

[6] K. Porteman and M.B. Smits-Veldt, *Een nieuw vaderland voor de muzen. Geschiedenis van de Nederlandse literatuur 1560-1700* (Amsterdam 2008), 766-772. For the collaboration between Gerard Brandt and Joannes Vollenhove, see: G.R.W. Dibbets, *Joannes Vollenhove (1631-1708) dominee-dichter. Een biografie* (Hilversum 2007), 74-81 and 305-331.

[7] University Library Amsterdam, Manuscripts, O 16 g, d.11-3-1677.

[8] Ibidem, O 15 s, d. 13-1-1676.

[9] Ibidem, O 16 f, d. 17-2-1677.

[10] Ibidem, O 16 t, undated (1677).

[11] Ibidem, O17 b and c, d. 3-1 and 8-2-1681.

[12] Ibidem, O 17 e and g, d.18-7-1681 and 19-2-1682.

[13] J. de Haes, *Het leven van Geeraert Brandt* (The Hague 1740), 52.

[14] University Library Amsterdam, Manuscripts, O 17 t, d. 7-12-1684.

[15] Ibidem, O 17 u, d. 9-2-1685.

[16] Ibidem, O 17 s, d. 28-11-1684.

[17] Ibidem, O 17 u, d. 9-2-1685.

[18] Brandt, *Leven en bedrijf*, 58 (Fourth edition Amsterdam-Rotterdam-The Hague 1746 was consulted).

[19] Ibidem, Foreword.

[20] Prud'homme van Reine, *Rechterhand*, 14, 15.

[21] Brandt, *Leven en bedrijf*, 986.

[22] Prud'homme van Reine, *Rechterhand*, 27.

[23] Brandt, *Leven en bedrijf*, 4.

[24] Ibidem, 5.

[25] Ibidem, 6.

[26] Ibidem, 15-19; National Archives The Hague, De Ruyter Collection (Acquired 1896), 190; Prud'homme van Reine, *Rechterhand*, 54, 55.

[27] Public Record Office, State Papers Foreign 84, 185, fo. 184, received 19/29-11-1669; R. Prud'homme van Reine, *Schittering en schandaal. Biografie van Maerten en Cornelis Tromp* (Amsterdam-Antwerp 2001), 294, 295.

[28] Brandt, *Leven en bedrijf*, 762.

[29] Ibidem, 740-746; Prud'homme van Reine, *Rechterhand*, 249-253; Prud'homme van Reine, *Schittering*, 295, 296.

[30] Prud'homme van Reine, *Rechterhand*, 189.

[31] Ibidem, 293.

[32] Brandt, *Leven en bedrijf*, 988.

[33] Ibidem, 'Opdragt'.

[34] Ibidem, 2.

[35] H. Duits, ''De groote waterheldt': een eerste verkenning van Geeraardt Brandts biografie Het leven en bedryf van den heere Michiel de Ruiter (1687)'. In: *Tydskrif vir Nederlands en Afrikaans* 9 (2002), 47-65, especially 52-56.

[36] Brandt, *Leven en bedrijf*, 1-37.

[37] Ibidem, 985-991.

[38] H. Duits, ''Een cieraadt zyner eeuwe'. Over Geeraardt Brandts karakterschets van zijn held in Het leven en bedryf van den heere Michiel de Ruyter (1687)'. In: M van Vaeck et al. (Eds.) *De steen van Alciato. Literatuur en visuele cultuur in de Nederlanden. Opstellen voor prof. dr. Karel Porteman bij zijn emeritaat* (Leuven 2003), 229-248, especially 240-247.

[39] C. Lawrence, 'Hendrick de Keyser's Heemskerck monument: the origins of the cult and iconography of Dutch naval heroes'. In: *Simiolus. Netherlands quarterly for the history of art* 21 (1992), 265-295. See also: R. Prud'homme van Reine, Zeehelden, Amsterdam-Antwerp 2005.

3 Merchants, Diplomats, and Corsairs

[1] Some of the texts which represent this tendency include R. L Playfair's *The Scourge of Christendom* (1884), Stanley Lane-Poole's *The Barbary Corsairs* (1890), Stephen Clissold, *The Barbary Slaves* (1977), and Robert C. Davies, *Christian Slaves, Muslim Masters* (2003).

[2] Sir Godfrey Fisher, *Barbary Legend: War, Trade, and Piracy in North Africa, 1415-1830* (Oxford: Clarendon Press, 1957) 6-7.

[3] Kenneth Parker, 'Reading 'Barbary' in Early Modern England, 1550-1685,' *The Seventeenth Century* 19.1 (2004): 88.

[4] Parker, 'Reading 'Barbary', 89-93.

[5] P. L. Wilson, *Pirate Utopias: Moorish Corsairs & European Renegadoes* (Brooklyn, NY: Autonomedia, 2003).

[6] Wilson, *Pirate Utopias*, 14-15.

[7] Wilson, *Pirate Utopias*, 29,

[8] Notable examples of this new, critical scholarship include A. Hess, *The Forgotten Frontier* (1978), D. D Hebb, *Piracy and the English Government* (1994), N. Matar, *Turks, Moors and Englishmen* (1999), G. van Krieken, *Corsaires & marchands* (2007).

[9] Fernand Braudel, *The Mediterranean and the Mediterranean World in the Age of Philip* II, vol. I (London: Fontana/Collins, 1975) 629-631.

[10] Braudel, *The Mediterranean and the Mediterranean World*, 635.

[11] Maarten Roy Prak, *The Dutch Republic in the Seventeenth Century*, (Cambridge: Cambridge University Press, 2005) 23-24.

[12] Van Krieken, *Corsaires & marchands: les relations entre Alger et les Pays-Bas, 1640-1830.* (Bouchène, 2002) 17.

[13] Van Krieken, *Corsaires & marchands*, 19-20.

[14] Van , *Corsaires & marchands*, 21.

[15] Van Krieken, *Corsaires & marchands*, 24.

[16] Van Krieken, *Corsaires & marchands*, 26.

[17] David Delison Hebb, *Piracy and the English Government* (Aldershot, Hants, England: Scolar Press, 1994) 83.

[18] Hebb, *Piracy and the English Government*, 88-90.

[19] Mansell's punitive expedition against Algiers was renewed in May 1621 with a blockade of the port. However, the failure to come to any acceptable arrangement over the liberation of English slaves demonstrated the limitations of the military approach.

[20] Hebb, *Piracy and the English Government*, 84.

[21] Van Krieken, *Corsaires & marchands*, 29.

[22] Van Krieken, *Corsaires & marchands*, 31-32.

[23] Gérard Van Krieken, 'Trois Représentants Hollandais a Tunis (1616-1628),' *IBLA: Revue de L'Institut Des Belles Lettres Arabes* 137 (1976): 50-51.

[24] Krieken, *Corsaires & marchands*, 38. Murad Rais was a native of Haarlem who became a notorious renegade corsair in Algiers. After Algiers he spent a few years in Salé where he was elected Admiral of the Fleet. Towards the end of 1620s he moved back to Algiers where he continued to carry out raids on European ships. His most spectacular feat was the raid against the Irish village of Baltimore in June 1631 which was the object of a recent account, Des Ekin, *The Stolen Village: Baltimore and the Barbary Pirates* (Dublin: O'Brien, 2006).

[25] Krieken, 'Trois Représentants Hollandais a Tunis', 53.

[26] Van Krieken, *Corsaires & marchands*, 44.

[27] Marie-Christine Engels, *Merchants, Interlopers, Seamen and Corsairs: The 'Flemish' Community in Livorno and Genoa 1615-1635* (Hilversum: Verloren, 1997), 73.

[28] 'Ratification par Moulay Zidan du traité du 24 décembre 1610,' *Les sources inédites de l'histoire du Maroc.* Comte Henri de Castries, Première Série, Dynastie Saadienne. Tome I, Archives et bibliothèques des Pays-Bas (Paris: Ernest Leroux, 1906) 613-621.

[29] 'Lettre de Moulay Zidan aux États-Généraux 10 août 1611,' *Les sources inédites*, tome I, 670.

[30] 'Lettre des États-Généraux à Moulay Zidan 27 décembre 1610,' *Les sources inédites*, tome I, 589.

[31] 'Lettre de Moulay Zidan aux États-Généraux 10 août 1611', *Les sources inédites*, tome I, 669.

[32] 'Lettre de Moulay Zidan aux États-Généraux 28 septembre, 1611,' *Les sources inédites*, tome I, 673.

[33] Anonymous. *Newes from Mamora, or, a Summary Relation Sent to the King of Spaine of the Good … God to Giue in Taking, and Suprising, of Mamora, a Port in Barbary*. Trans. W Squire, 1614.

[34] See M. E. Eloufrani, *Nuzhat al-hadi bi-akbar muluk al-qarn al-hadi*, ed O. Houdas (Rabat: Maktabat al-Talib, 1988); A. K. An-Naciri, *Kitab el-Istiqca li Akhbar doual el-Maghrib el-Aqca*, vol. 6 (Casablanca: Dar el Kitab, 1997).

[35] In 1612 when Zidan was engaged in fighting the insurrection of the *marabout* Abou Mahali, he was allowed to purchase ammunition in the United Provinces to the value of 15.155 florins, 'Résolution des États-Généraux, 20 septembre, 1612,' *Les sources inédites de l'histoire du Maroc.* Comte Henri de Castries, Première série, Dynastie Saadienne. Tome II, Archives et bibliothèques des Pays-Bas (Paris : Ernest Leroux, 1907) 155-156.

[36] In August 1616, Zidan sent a letter of thanks to the States General for allowing him to hire a Dutch ship to transport his envoys to Europe, 'Lettre de Moulay Zidan aux États-Généraux, 4 novembre, 1616,' *Les sources inédites*, tome II, 714-717.

[37] In 1612 during the insurrection of *marabout* Abou Mahali, when Zidan was compelled to flee Marrakech, he commanded a French captain to carry his treasured goods including some 3000 books to the port of Santa Cruz. The French vessel was intercepted by a Spanish warship and the books were seized and sent to Madrid. In an attempt to recover the lost books, Zidan sent envoys to France and requested the help of Dutch authorities to intervene on his behalf at the courts of France and Spain. Much to his frustration, these coordinated efforts met with failure. 'Lettre de Moulay Zidan aux États-Généraux, 27 juin, 1612,' *Les sources inédites*, tome II, 106-108

[38] Between 1609 and 1649 at least four members of the Pallache family conducted missions for the King of Morocco at The Hague; see Herman Obdeijn, 'Les relations entre le Maroc et les Pays-Bas: un aperçu historique,' *Le Maroc et la Hollande: études sur l'histoire, la migration, la linguistique et la sémiologie de la culture* (Rabat: Faculté des lettres et des sciences humaines, 1988) 61-71.

[39] 'Journal d'Albert Ruyl 20 novembre 1623-20 juillet 1624,' *Les sources inédites de l'histoire du*

Maroc. Comte Henri de Castries, Première série, Dynastie Saadienne. Tome III, archives et bibliothèques des Pays-Bas (Paris: Ernest Leroux, 1912) 506-535.

[40] There are several references to these incidents in Dutch archives. In May 1614, the States General wrote to Zidan to request the release of six Dutch captives held in Morocco, *Les sources inédites,* tome II, 300. On 14 December 1622, Albert Ruyl noted in his journal that two months earlier a Dutch ship coming from Muscovy bound for Leghorn had been captured by a corsair from Salé. The value of ship and cargo was estimated at 160 000 Florins; see *Les sources inédites,* tome III, 269-270.

[41] Eloufrani, *Nuzhat al-hadi,* 254.

[42] An-Naciri, *Kitab el-Istiqca,* vol. 6, 78-81.

[43] Adrien Matham, *Voyage d'Adrien Matham au Maroc 1640-1641* (La Haye: M. Nijhoff, 1866).

[44] 'Journal d'Adriaen Matham 1 septembre 1640 - 12 novembre 1641,' *Les sources inédites de l'histoire du Maroc.* Comte Henri de Castries, Première série, Dynastie Saadienne. Tome IV, archives et bibliothèques des Pays-Bas (Paris: Ernest Leroux, 1913) 596-599.

[45] Blok, *The Life of Admiral De Ruyter,* Trans. G J Renier (London: Ernest Benn, 1933)17-20.

[46] 'Journal de 'La Salamandre' 21 janvier-3 août 1644,' *Les sources inédites de l'histoire du Maroc.* Comte Henri de Castries, Première série, Dynastie Saadienne. Tome V, archives et bibliothèques des Pays-Bas (Paris: Ernest Leroux, 1920) 576-577.

[47] 'Journal de 'La Salamandre' 21 janvier-3 août 1644,' *Les sources inédites* tome V, 581.

[48] It is reported in the biography of De Ruyter by Gerard Brandt that Sidi Ali ben Moussa coveted a piece of cloth and sought to purchase it at a price lower than De Ruyter could afford. Despite his earnest threats, the marabout could not prevail on De Ruyter to sell the item at the desired price. In the midst of haggling De Ruyter offered the piece as a present saying that he preferred to dispose of it in such an amicable manner rather than cause a devaluation of his other merchandise. The *marabout,* who was not mollified by this act of generosity and perceived the proud and resolute character of De Ruyter, walked out much angered. Later when his temper cooled

down, he returned to ask De Ruyter to agree to his offer. Seeing the firm attitude of his guest, he turned to his followers and in lavish words praised the conduct and courage of De Ruyter, laying his palm on the bare chest of his guest and placing the other's hand against his, thus indicating the everlasting bond of friendship and mutual affection that united them. See Geeraert Brandt, *La vie de Michel de Ruiter, lieutenant-amiral-general de Hollande et de West-Frise: Ou est comprise l'histoire maritime des provinces unies, depuis l'an 1652, jusques a 1676* (Amsterdam: P. & J. Blaeu, 1698), pp12-13. See also Blok, *The Life of Admiral De Ruyter,* 27-28.

[49] 'Journal de 'La Salamandre' 3 décembre 1645 - 17 août 1646,' *Les sources inédites* tome V, 614-615.

[50] 1646 - 15 septembre 1647,' *Les sources inédites* tome V, 627.

[51] In 1640, Sidi Ali ben Moussa lost Draa to the rising Sharif Sidi Mohamed from Sijilmasa; see Eloufrani, *Nuzhat al-hadi,* 301-302.

[52] Mohamed al-Mukhtar Susi, *Iligh qadiman wa-hadithan,* ed. Mohamed ibn Abdallah Rudani (Rabat: Al-Matbaah Al-Malakiyah, 1966) 20-23.

[53] Jerome Bookin-Weiner, 'Corsairing in the Economy and Politics of North Africa,' *North Africa: Nation, State, and Region,* ed. George Joffé (London and New York: Routledge, 1993) 20.

[54] 'Lettre de Sidi Abdallah aux États-Généraux 3 octobre, 1651,' *Les sources inédites,* 297.

[55] Eventually, the new taxes were suspended but were enacted much later in the new treaty.

[56] 'Lettre de David de Vries aux États-Généraux 4 juin 1652,' *Les sources inédites* tome V, 330.

[57] 'Lettre des États-Généraux aux Salétins, 19 juin 1654,' *Les sources inédites* tome V, 389.

[58] 'Lettre de David de Vries aux États-Généraux 20 juillet 1654,' *Les sources inédites* tome V, 396.

[59] 'Pièces relatives à la capture de la barque de Brahim Er-Rais,' *Les sources inédites* tome V, 455.

[60] 'Lettre de M. de Ruyter à l'Amirauté d'Amsterdam, 6 octobre, 1654,' *Les sources inédites* tome V, 449.

[61] 'Lettre de M. de Ruyter à Sidi Abdallah, 11 octobre, 1654,' *Les sources inédites* tome V, 477.

[62] 'Lettre de Sidi Abdallah à M. de Ruyter, 8 octobre, 1655,' *Les sources inédites* tome V, 491-492.

[63] 'Lettre de David de Vries aux États-Généraux,

20 novembre, 1654,' *Les sources inédites* tome V, 536-537.

[64] 'Instructions pour David de Vries, 21 juin 1655,' *Les sources inédites de l'histoire du Maroc.* Comte Henri de Castries, Première série, Dynastie Saadienne. Tome VI, archives et bibliothèques des Pays-Bas (Paris: Ernest Leroux, 1923) 24-30.

[65] 'Lettre de Sidi Abdallah à M. de Ruyter, 8 octobre, 1655,' *Les sources inédites* tome VI, 80.

[66] 'Lettre de l'Amirauté d'Amsterdam aux États-Généraux, 27 decembre, 1655,' *Les sources inédites* tome VI, 226-227.

[67] 'Instructions pour David de Vries, 23 mai, 1656,' *Les sources inédites* tome VI, 271-276.

[68] 'David de Vries à l'Amirauté d'Amsterdam 25 août 1656,' *Les sources inédites* tome VI, 292.

[69] 'Instructions pour David de Vries, 1 décembre, 1656,' *Les sources inédites* tome VI, 309-311.

[70] 'Lettre de David de Vries aux États-Généraux, 25 mars, 1657,' *Les sources inédites* tome VI, 337-339.

[71] 'Traité entre les Pays-Bas et Salé, 22 mars, 1657,' *Les sources inédites* tome VI, 323-329.

[72] 'Lettre de M. de Ruyter à Sidi Abdallah, 20 avril, 1657,' *Les sources inédites* tome VI, 348-49.

[73] Blok, *The Life of Admiral De Ruyter,* 125.

[74] The total number of Dutch slaves held in Algiers was estimated at 400 according to Dutch consul, Andries van der Burgh in 1662; see Krieken, *Corsaires & marchands,* 60.

[75] Van Krieken, *Corsaires & marchands,* 53.

[76] 'Lettre de M. de Ruyter aux États-Généraux, 21 novembre, 1655,' *Les sources inédites* tome VI, 208.

[77] 'Journal de M. de Ruyter, Juillet 1655-2 mai 1656,' *Les sources inédites* tome VI, 230-234.

[78] 'Lettre de L'Amirauté d'Amsterdam aux États-Généraux, 27 décembre, 1655,' *Les sources inédites* tome VI, 226.

[79] Blok, *The Life of Admiral De Ruyter,* 151.

[80] Van Krieken, *Corsaires & marchands,* 55.

[81] Van Krieken, *Corsaires & marchands,* 56.

[82] Van Krieken, *Corsaires & marchands,* 57-58.

[83] Van Krieken, *Corsaires & marchands,* 60-61.

[84] Van Krieken, *Corsaires & marchands,* 62.

[85] Blok, *The Life of Admiral De Ruyter,* 168.

[86] Van Krieken, *Corsaires & marchands,* 64-65.

[87] Van Krieken, *Corsaires & marchands,* 62, 65.

[88] Blok, *The Life of Admiral De Ruyter,* 175-176.

[1] J. de Vries and A. van der Woude, *The first modern economy: Success, failure, and perseverance of the Dutch economy, 1500-1815*, Cambridge 1997; D. Ormrod, *The rise of commercial empires: England and the Netherlands in the Age of Mercantilism, 1650-1770*, Cambridge 2003.

[2] C. Tilly, *Coercion, capital, and European states, AD 990-1990*, Oxford 1990, 11, 53, 60, 62, 76, 94 and 150; B.M. Downing, *The Military Revolution and political change: Origins of democracy and autocracy in early modern Europe*, Princeton 1992, 212-238; R.M. Lachmann, *Capitalists in spite of themselves: Elite conflict and economic transitions in early modern Europe*, Oxford 2000, 147-170 and 269-270.

[3] C.J. Rogers, *The military revolution debate: Readings on the military transformation of Early Modern Europe*, Boulder 1995; J. Glete, *War and the state in early modern Europe: Spain, the Dutch Republic and Sweden as fiscal-military states, 1500-1660*, London 2002, 45-47.

[4] I. Wallerstein, *The modern world-system*, vol. 1, New York 1974, 199-221; J.I. Israel, *Dutch primacy in world trade, 1585-1740*, Oxford 1989, 410-415.

[5] M.C. 't Hart, *The making of a bourgeois state: War, politics and finance during the Dutch revolt*, Manchester 1993; J.L. Price, *Holland and the Dutch Republic in the seventeenth century: The politics of particularism*, Oxford 1994; K. Davids and J. Lucassen,(eds), *A miracle mirrored: The Dutch Republic in European perspective*, Cambridge 1995, esp. 438-460; V. Enthoven, *Zeeland en de opkomst van de Republiek: Handel en strijd in de Scheldedelta, c. 1550-1621*, Leiden 1996; Glete, *War*, 140-173; P.S. Gorski, *The disciplinary revolution: Calvinism and the rise of the state in Early Modern Europe*, Chicago 2003, 39-78; M. de Jong, '*Staat van Oorlog': Wapenbedrijf en militaire hervorming in de Republiek der Verenigde Nederlanden, 1585-1621*, Hilversum 2005; G. Vermeesch, *Oorlog, steden en staatsvorming: De grenssteden Gorinchem en Doesburg tijdens de geboorte-eeuw van de Republiek, 1570-1680*, Amsterdam 2006.

[6] J. Glete, *Navies and nations: Warships, navies*

and state building in Europe and America, 1500-1860, 2 vols, Stockholm 1993; Glete, *War*, 155-157 and 162-165.

[7] C. Tilly (ed.), *The formation of national states in Western Europe*, Princeton 1975; Downing, *The military*.

[8] R.G. Asch and H. Durchhardt (eds), *Der Absolutismus - ein Mythos? Strukturwandel monarchischer Herrschaft*, Cologne 1996 ; I.A.A. Thompson, *War and government in Habsburg Spain, 1560-1629*, London 1976; D. Dessert, *Argent, pouvoir, et société au Grand Siècle*, Paris 1984 ; W.H. Beik, *Absolutism and society in seventeenth-century France*, Cambridge 1985; D. Parker, *Class and state in Ancien Regime France: The road to modernity?* London 1996; D. Dessert, *La Royale: Vaisseaux et marins du Roi-Soleil*, Paris 1996 ; J.A. Lynn, *Giant of the Grand Siècle: The French army, 1610-1715*, Cambridge 1997; D. Parrott, *Richelieu's army: War, government and society in France, 1624-1642*, Cambridge 2001; G. Rowlands, *The dynastic state and the army under Louis XIV: Royal service and private interest, 1661-1701*, Cambridge 2002; A. James, *Navy and government in early modern France, 1572-1661*, Woodbridge 2004.

[9] J. Brewer, *The sinews of power: War, money and the English state, 1688-1783*, London 1989; J.S. Wheeler, *The making of a world power: War and the military revolution in seventeenth century England*, Phoenix Mill 1999.

[10] J.A.A. van Doorn, *Sociologie van de organisatie: Beschouwingen over organiseren in het bijzonder op een onderzoek van het militaire systeem*, Leiden 1956. M.D. Feld, 'Middle-class society and the rise of military professionalism', in: M. D. Feld, *The structure of violence: Armed forces as social systems*, London 1977, 169-203.

[11] D.C. North, *Structure and change in economic history*, New York 1981; North, *Understanding the process of economic change*, Princeton 2005.

[12] For theoretical concepts, Glete, *War*, 1-9 and 42-66.

[13] J.-P. Bardet, and J. Dupâquier (eds), *Histoire des populations de l'Europe: I. Des origines aux prémices de la révolution démographique*, Paris

1997 ; R.J. Vries, 'Population', in: T. A. Brady, H. Oberman, and J. D. Tracy (eds), *Handbook of European history, 1400-1600*, vol. 1, Leiden 1994, 1-50; De Vries and Van der Woude, *The first*, 46-57; Glete, *War*, 72-73, 143-144 and 178-181.

[14] Glete, *War*, 10-41.

[15] G. Parker, *The Army of Flanders and the Spanish Road, 1567-1659*, Cambridge 1972; P.H. Wilson, *German armies: War and German politics, 1648-1806*, London 1988, 34-35, 45-54, 90-93 and 105; Glete, *War*, 83-96; C. Storrs, *The resilience of the Spanish Monarchy, 1665-1700*, Oxford 2006, 17-62; A.P. van Vliet, *Vissers en kapers: De zeevisserij vanuit het Maasmondgebied en de Duinkerker kapers (ca. 1580-1648)*, The Hague 1994.

[16] J.A. Lynn, 'Revisiting the great fact of war and Bourbon absolutism: The growth of the French army during the Grand Siécle', in: Enrique García Hernán and Davide Maffi (eds.), *Guerra y Sociedad en la Monarquía Hispánica: Política, estrategia y cultura en la Europa moderna (1500-1700)*, vol. 1, Madrid 2006, 49-74.

[17] Glete, *War*, 34-35 and 202-210.

[18] *Het Staatsche Leger*, 8 vols in 10 parts, Breda and The Hague, 1911-64, vol. 2, 344-371, vol. 3, 290-295, vol. 4, 355-359; H.L. Zwitzer, '*De militie van den Staat': Het leger van de Republiek der Verenigde Nederlanden*, Amsterdam, 1991, 175-177; Wilson, *German armies*, 44-57 and 87-129.

[19] F. Redlich, *The German military enterpriser and his work force: A study in European economic and social history*, 2 vols, Wiesbaden 1964-65; Zwitzer, '*De militie*'; Glete, *War*, 155-162; O. Van Nimwegen, '*Deser landen crijchsvolck': Het Staatse leger en de militaire revoluties, 1588-1688*, Amsterdam 2006.

[20] Glete, *Navies*, esp. 146-152, 195, 211 and appendices 1 and 2; Storrs, *Resilience*, 63-105.

[21] Glete, *Navies*

[22] Glete, *Navies*, esp. 152-158 and appendix 2. I am grateful to Mr R. H. C. van Maanen who has sent me his unpublished lists of Dutch warships.

[23] F.H.M. Grapperhaus, *Convoyen en licenten*, Zutphen 1986.

[24] For a general history of the Dutch navy, J.R. Bruijn, *The Dutch navy of the seventeenth and*

eighteenth centuries, Columbia 1993; enlarged and revised edition as *Varend verleden: De nederlandse oorlogsvloot in de zeventiende en achttiende eeuw*, Amsterdam 1998.

[25] Glete, *Navies*, 411-413.

[26] Glete, *War*, 134.

[27] Lists of Dutch warships and their armament in 1628, 1631 and 1654, Admiraliteitscolleges, XXXVII, 79, Nationaal Archief, The Hague; similar, but slightly different lists for 1628, 1629, 1631, 1633 and 1654, Staten Generaal 1550-1796, nos 8049, 8050, 8051, 8053, 8059, Nationaal Archief, The Hague. Photocopies of the latter have been sent to me by Mr James C. Bender. He has also suggested that the dimensions of warships of the Maas Admiralty built until 1652 in the lists of 1654 are measured in Maas feet of 309 mm, not Amsterdam feet of 283 mm. My own calculations of armament/size relations confirm this. This means that the well-known fleet flagships *Aemilia* (1634) and *Brederode* (1646) (explicitly listed as measured in Maas feet) were larger than assumed in the literature.

[28] J.E. Elias, *De vlootbouw in Nederland in de eerste helft der 17de eeuw, 1596-1655*, Amsterdam 1933; A. Vreugdenhil, *Lists of Men-of-War. 1650-1700: Part IV, Ships of the United Netherlands, 1648-1702*, London 1938. Glete, *Navies*, 152-158, 161-167 and 178-187.

[29] Vreugdenhil, *Lists*; Glete, *Navies*, 187-206.

5   Navies, Strategy, and Tactics in the Age of De Ruyter

[1] I am grateful to Jaap Bruijn and Jan Glete for their constructive critiques on an earlier draft of this chapter.

[2] N.A.M. Rodger, 'The Development of Broadside Gunnery, 1450-1650', in: *Mariner's Mirror*, 82 (1996), 301-324; reprinted in: Jan Glete, ed., *Naval History, 1500-1680*. The International Library of Essays on Military History. Aldershot: Ashgate, 2005. 239-262.

[3] Jan Glete, 'Naval Power and Control of the Seas in the Baltic in the 16th Century' in: John B. Hattendorf and Richard Unger, *War at Sea in The Middle Ages and the Renaissance*. Woodbridge: Boydell Press, 2003, 217-232. For a summary of the contrasting slower naval development on the southern Baltic shore, see John B. Hattendorf, 'Deutschland und die See: Historische Würzeln deutscher Seestreitkräfte bis 1815', in: Werner Rahn, hrsg., *Deutsche Marinen im Wandel: Von Symbol nationaler Einheit zum Instrument internationaler Sicherheit.* (München: R. Oldenbourg Verlag, 2005), 17-40.

[4] For a succinct overview, see 'Chronology of War and Peace, Civil and International' in: Ragnhild Hatton, *Europe in the Age of Louis XIV.* (London: Thames and Hudson, 1969 and 1979, 227-228.

[5] For a summary of recent interpretations, see David Davies, 'Wars, Maritime: Dutch Wars' in: John B. Hattendorf, ed., *Oxford Encyclopedia of Maritime History.* New York and Oxford: Oxford University Press, 2007, 4:325-329. See also, Simon Groenveld, 'The English Civil War as a Cause of the First Anglo Dutch War, 1640-1652', in: *The Historical Journal*, 30, 3 (1987), 541-566; Hans-Christoph Junge, *Flottenpolitik und Revolution.* Veröffentlichungen des Deutschen Historischen Instituts London, band 6. (Stuttgart: Klett-Cotta, 1980); Bernard Capp, *Cromwell's Navy: The Fleet and the English Revolution, 1648-1660.* Oxford: Clarendon Press, 1989.

[6] Tony Claydon, *Europe and the Making of England, 1660-1760.* Cambridge: Cambridge University Press, 2007, 133-40, 152.

[7] Glete, *War and the State in Early Modern Europe: Spain, the Dutch Republic and Sweden as Fiscal-Military States, 1500-1660.* London and New York: Routledge, 2002. 162-171.

[8] The statistics in Glete, *Navies and Nations: Warships, Navies and State Building in Europe and America, 1500-1860.* Stockholm: Almqvist & Wiksell International, 1993, 1:179, 186 have been modified by personal communication with Jan Glete reflecting his latest research and: Martin Bellamy, *Christian IV and his navy: A political and administrative history of the Danish navy 1596-1648*, Brill, Leiden, 2006, pp. 261-279. No reliable statistics are available for Spain.

[9] This figure for Dutch warships is actually for 1642.

[10] *Ibid.*, 204

[11] Glete, *Navies and Nations,* 1:156, 130. In comparing the numbers of Dutch and English warships, the number of Dutch ships can be misleading as they were generally smaller than the English ships, as the displacement figures in the table above suggests.

[12] Rodger, *The Command of the Ocean: A Naval History of Britain, 1649-1815.* London: Allen Lane, 2004, 2.

[13] Brian Lavery, *The Ship of the Line.* Vol. 1: *The Development of the battlefleet, 1650-1850.* Annapolis: Naval Institute Press, 1983. 1, 18-23. Little recent comparative study has been done of Dutch frigate designs from the 1640s and their relationship to developments in English ship design.

[14] *Ibid.,* 22-23.

[15] James S. Wheeler, 'Prelude to Power: The Crisis of 1649 and the Foundation of English Naval Power', in: *Mariner's Mirror*, 81, 2 (May 1995), pp. 148-155; reprinted in: Glete, *Naval History,* 229-236.

[16] Wheeler, 'English Financial Operations during the First Dutch War, 1652-1654', in: *The Journal of European Economic History*, 23, 2 (Fall 1994), 329-343. See also James Scott Wheeler, *The Making of a World Power: War and the Military Revolution in Seventeenth Century England.* Stroud: Sutton Publishing, 1999, 43-48.

[17] Wheeler, *Making of a World Power,* 46.

[18] Bruijn, *The Dutch Navy of the Seventeenth and Eighteenth Centuries.* Columbia: University of South Carolina Press, 1993, 70-71, and Bruijn, *Varend Verleden: De Nederlandse Oorlogsvloot in de 17de en 18de Eeuw.* Amsterdam: Uitgeverij Balans, 1999, 92-93. See also, 'Resolution of Admiral Tromp…' in: Julian S. Corbett, ed., *Fighting Instructions, 1530-1816.* Publications of the Navy Records Society, vol. 29. London: Navy Records Society, 1905; reprinted London: Conway Press, 1971; Annapolis: Naval Institute

Press, 1971, 91.

[19] See Thomas Wemyss, Fulton, *The Sovereignty of the Sea: An Historical Account of the Claims of England to the Dominion of the British Seas, and of the Evolution of the Territorial Waters: with special reference to the Rights of Fishing and the Naval Salute*. London: William Blackwood and Sons, 1911; reprinted in facsimile, Milwood, NY: Kraus Reprint, 1976.

[20] Brian Tunstall, *Naval Warfare in the Age of Sail: The Evolution of Fighting Tactics, 1650-1815*. Edited by Dr. Nicholas Tracy. (Annapolis: Naval Institute Press, 1990), 18.

[21] Corbett, *Fighting Instructions*, 99-103; J.R. Powell, ed., *The Letters of Robert Blake Together with Supplementary Documents*. Publications of the Navy Records Society, vol. 76. London: Navy Records Society, 1937, 467-471.

[22] Powell, *Blake Letters*, 471-476.

[23] Bruijn, *Dutch Navy*, 73-74; *Varend Verleden*, 95-97.

[24] Glete, *Navies and Nations*, 1:192, 195 as modified by personal communication with Jan Glete; Bellamy, *Christian IV and his navy*, 261-279.

[25] *Ibid.*, 204.

[26] See Alan James, *Navy and Government in Early Modern France, 1572-1661*. Royal Historical Society Studies in History New Series. Woodbridge: The Boydell Press, 2004.

[27] See Daniel Dessert, *La Royale: Vaisseaux et marines du Roi-Soleil*. Paris: Fayard, 1996.

[28] Lavery, *Ship of the Line*, 30-32, 59-60.

[29] Herbert H. Rowen, *John de Witt, Grand Pensionary of Holland, 1625-1672*. Princeton: Princeton University Press, 1978, 78-83; Bruijn, *Dutch Navy*, 75-82; *Varend Verleden*, 103-107.

[30] Tunstall, *Naval Warfare*, 22-24; Corbett, *Fighting Instructions*, 122-130.

[31] Bruijn, *Dutch Navies*, 77; *Varend Verleden*, 100-101.

[32] R.C. Anderson, ed., *The Journal of Edward Montagu, First Earl of Sandwich, Admiral and General at Sea, 1639-1665*. Publications of the Navy Records Society, vol. 44. London: Navy Records Society, 1929, 224: 3 June 1665.

[33] *Ibid*, 269-270: 29 August 1665.

[34] R.E.J. Weber, 'The Introduction of the Single Line Ahead as a Battle Formation by the Dutch,

1665-1666', in: *Mariner's Mirror*, 73 (1987), 5-19; reprinted in: Glete, *Naval History*, 313-327.

[35] *Ibid.*, 320-21.

[36] Gaston Zeller, *Histoire des Relations Internationales*, publiée sous le direction de Pierre Renouvin. Tome 3: *Les Temps Modernes. Duexième partie. De Louis XIV à 1789*. (Paris: Librairie Hachette, 1955), 25.

[37] See H.A. van Foreest en R.E.J. Weber met medewerking van J.F. van Dulm en J.A. van der Kooij, *De Vierdaagse Zeeslag 11-14 Juni 1666*. Verhandelingen der Koninklijke Nederlandse Akademie van Wetenschappen, Afd. Letterkunde, Nieuwe Reeks, Deel 126. Werken Uitgegeven door de Commissie voor Zeegeschiedenis, XVI. Amsterdam: B.V. Noord-Hollandsche Uitgevers Maatschappij, 1984; and Frank L. Fox, *A Distant Storm: The Four Days' Battle of 1666 The Greatest Sea Fight of the Age of Sail*. Rotherfield: Press of Sail Publications, 1996..

[38] Rodger, *Command of the Ocean*, p. 75.

[39] Corbett, *Fighting Instructions*, 129-130.

[40] *Ibid*.

[41] Corbett, *Fighting Instructions*, 148-149, misdated as 1672, but 18 July 1666 as documented in: Tunstall, *Naval Warfare*, 27-30.

[42] Weber, 'The Single Line Ahead', 325.

[43] These changes are reflected in De Ruyter's instructions of 6 August 1667 in: R.E.J. Weber, *De seinboeken voor Nederlandse oorlogsvloten en konvooien tot 1690*. Verhandelingen der Koninklijke Nederlandse Akademie van Wetenschappen, Afd. Letterkunde, Nieuwe Reeks, Deel 112. Werken Uitgegeven door de Commissie voor Zeegeschiedenis, XV. Amsterdam: B.V. Noord-Hollandsche Uitgevers Maatschappij, 1984, Doc. 21; 102-114.

[44] P. G. Rogers, *The Dutch in the Medway*. London: Oxford University Press, 1970.

[45] Lavery, *Ship of the Line*, 1:32-36.

[46] Paul Sonnino, Paul, *Louis XIV and the Origins of the Dutch War*. Cambridge: Cambridge University Press, 1988, 176.

[47] For this agreement, see Birger Fahlborg, *Sveriges yttre politik 1664-1668*. Kungl. Vitterhets-, historie- och antikvitetsakademiens handlingar. Stockholm: Wahlström & Widstrand (1 kommission), 1949, and *Sveriges yttre politik 1668-1672*.

Stockholm: Almqvist & Wiksell, 1961.

[48] J. R. Jones, *The Anglo-Dutch Wars of the Seventeenth Century*. London; Longman, 1996, 179-188.

[49] Sonnino, *Louis XIV*, 191.

[50] Bruijn, *Dutch Navy*, 88; *Varend Verleden*, 115.

[51] Tunstall, *Naval Warfare*, 32; Corbett, *Fighting Instructions*, 133-163.

[52] Anderson, ed., *Journals and Narratives of the Third Dutch War*. Publications of the Navy Records Society, vol. 86. London: Navy Records Society, 1946, 13-22, 95-101, 156-57, 164-184; Michel Vergé-Franceschi, *Abraham Duquesne: Huguenot et marin du Roi Soleil*. Paris : Éditions France-Empire, 1992, 254-260; J.D. Davies, *Gentlemen and Tarpaulins: The Officers and Men of the Restoration Navy*. Oxford: Clarendon Press, 1991, 171.

[53] Rodger, *Command*, 83; Bruijn, *Dutch Navy*, 89; *Varend Verleden*, 117.

[54] Frank Kitson, *Prince Rupert: Admiral and General-at-Sea*. London: Constable, 1998, 246-289.

[55] J.C.M. Warnsinck, *Admiraal de Ruyter. De Zeeslag op Schooneveld, juni 1673*. 's-Gravenhage: Martinus Nijhoff, 1930, 44-59; Tunstall, Naval Warfare, 35; J.R. Bruijn, ed., *De Oorlogvoering ter Zee in 1673 in Journalen en Andere Stukken*. Werken uitgegeven door het Historisch Genootschap. Derde serie, no. 84. Groningen: J.B. Wolters, 1966, 55-56, 114-15; Anderson, *Third Dutch War Journals*, 32-36, 300-02, 319-20, 334, 377, 386,387.

[56] Jones, *Dutch Wars*, 206; Tunstall, *Naval Warfare*, 36; Bruijn, *Oorlogvoering*, 60, 118-20; Anderson, *Third Dutch War Journals*, 37-40, 303, 322, 336, 378, 379, 389.

[57] Bruijn, *Oorlogvoering*, 89-90, 152-54, 184-85, 205-09; Anderson, *Third Dutch War Journals*, 46-53, 311, 355-62, 381, 386, 390-4.

[58] Carl J. Ekberg, *The Failure of Louis XIV's Dutch War*. Chapel Hill: University of North Carolina Press, 1979, 161-170.

1 I am grateful to Frank Fox and Peter Le Fevre for their comments on an earlier version of this essay.

2 *The Life of Michael Adrian de Ruyter, Admiral of Holland* (1677), 56-7.

3 *The Tangier Papers of Samuel Pepys*, ed. E. Chappell (Navy Records Society, vol. 73, 1935), 314.

4 *Barlow's Journal*, 1. 275; *Calendar of the Manuscripts of the Marquess of Ormonde, KP, Preserved at Kilkenny Castle* (Historical Manuscripts Commission), New Series, VII (1911), 509.

5 C.R. Boxer, 'Admiral De Ruyter through English Eyes', *History Today*, 26 (1976), 232.

6 Boxer, 'De Ruyter', 233.

7 *The Life*, 13-14.

8 Bodleian Library, Oxford: Carte MS 35, fo. 506. The episode referred to here probably took place in 1643 rather than 1644: R. Prud'homme van Reine, *Rechterhand van Nederland. Biografie van Michiel Adriaenszoon de Ruyter* (Amsterdam 1996), 43-7 and 194.

9 Boxer, 'M.A. De Ruyter, 1607-76', *The Mariner's Mirror*, 44 (1958), 5; A. Little, 'British Seamen in the United Provinces During the Seventeenth Century Anglo-Dutch Wars: The Dutch Navy – A Preliminary Survey', *Trade, Diplomacy and Cultural Exchange: Continuity and Change in the North Sea Area and the Baltic, c.1350-1750*, ed. H. Brand (Hilversum, 2005), 88.

10 *The Life*, 48-9.

11 *The Diary of Samuel Pepys*, ed. R. Latham and W. Matthews (11 vols., 1970-83), vi. 186.

12 *The Rupert and Monck Letterbook*, ed. J.R. Powell and E.K. Timings (Navy Records Society, vol. 112, 1969), 239.

13 *Rupert and Monck Letterbook*, 277.

14 *The Journals of Sir Thomas Allin*, ed. R.C. Anderson (Navy Records Society, vol. 79, 1939), 1. 154-5. Cf. *The Manuscripts of J.M. Heathcote, Esq., Conington Castle* (Historical Manuscripts Commission, 50, 1899), 155.

15 *Pepys's Diary*, vi. 42, 43, 46. Cf. S.C. Pincus, *Protestantism and Patriotism: Ideologies and the Making of English Foreign Policy, 1650-68* (Cambridge, 1996), 290-1.

16 H.T. Colenbrander, *Bescheiden uit vreemde archieven omtrent de groote Nederlandsche zeeoorlogen 1652-1676*, (The Hague, 1919). 1. 269.

17 *Pepys's Diary*, viii. 309.

18 *Pepys's Diary*, vii. 228.

19 *Pepys's Diary*, vii. 231, 234.

20 Cf. ibid., 291.

21 Carte MS 222, fo. 108.

22 *The Life*, 45.

23 R. Ollard, *Man of War: Sir Robert Holmes and the Restoration Navy* (1969), 137-8 and *passim*.

24 Although there seems to have been no reference to the fact in contemporary English sources, De Ruyter in fact was already a knight, having received the honour from King Frederick III of Denmark in 1659.

25 *The Life*, 8-10, 95.

26 *The Life*, 113-14.

27 Sir William Temple, *Observations Upon the United Provinces of the Netherlands*, ed. G.N. Clark (Cambridge, 1932), 71.

28 The National Archives, Kew, SP 84/188/77 (cited by Boxer, 240).

29 For the numbers of Britons serving in the Dutch fleet, see Little, 'British Seamen', 76-92.

30 Cited by A. Patterson, '"Crouching at Home, and Cruel when Abroad": Restoration Constructions of National and International Character', *The Stuart Court and Europe: Essays in Politics and Political Culture*, ed. M. Smuts (Cambridge, 1996), 223 and pp. 210-27 passim. Cf. K.H.D. Haley, *The British and the Dutch: Political and Cultural Relations through the Ages* (1988), 107-9.

31 R. Loeber, 'English and Irish Sources for the History of Dutch Economic Activity in Ireland, 1600-89', *Irish Economic and Social History*, 8 (1981), 71.

32 D.D. Aldridge, 'The Lauderdales and the Dutch', *The North Sea and Culture (1550-1800)*, ed. J. Roding and L. Heerma van Voss (Hilversum 1996), 296.

33 *Calendar of State Papers, Domestic Series, 1667*, 341, 354, 372, 382, 385, 393-4.

34 *London Gazette*, no. 181, 5-8 August 1667, cited by Boxer, 'De Ruyter', 239. A similar version of the story is given in *The Life*, 60-3.

35 *The Manuscripts of His Grace the duke of Portland, Preserved at Welbeck Abbey* (Historical Manuscripts Commission), III (1894), 323.

36 Cited by Boxer, 'M.A. De Ruyter, 1607-76', *The Mariner's Mirror*, 54 (1958), 13.

37 Bodleian Library, Oxford, Rawlinson MS A185, fos. 221-2.

38 J.D. Davies, *Gentlemen and Tarpaulins: The Officers and Men of the Restoration Navy* (Oxford, 1991), 16-66; N.A.M. Rodger, *The Command of the Ocean: A Naval History of Britain, 1649-1815* (2006), 112-24.

39 J. Binns, 'Sir John Lawson: Scarborough's admiral of the red', *Northern History*, 32 (1996), 90–110.

40 *The Life*, 28.

41 Davies, 'Harman, Sir John (d. 1673), naval officer', *The Oxford Dictionary of National Biography* (2004).

42 Davies, *Gentlemen and Tarpaulins*, 150-1, 162-3.

43 *The Life*, 32.

44 S. Pincus, *Protestantism and Patriotism: Ideologies and the Making of English Foreign Policy, 1650-1668* (Cambridge, 1996); 339; 345; G. Rommelse, *The Second Anglo-Dutch War (1665-1667) - International Raison d'Etat, Mercantilism and Maritime Strife* (Hilversum, 2006), 132, 150.

45 *The Life*, 6.

46 The English possession of the cautionary towns was referred to in the virulently hostile pamphlet of 1664, *The Dutch Drawn to the Life* (pp. 16-17).

47 Davies, *The Battle of the Texel, 11 August 1673: The Climactic Sea Battle of the Anglo-Dutch Wars* (Woodbridge, forthcoming).

48 Boxer, 'M H Tromp, 1598-1653', *The Mariner's Mirror*, 40 (1954), 44-5.

49 *Calendar of State Papers, Domestic, 1673-5*, 601.

50 Boxer, 'De Ruyter', 240.

51 Prud'homme van Reine, *Schittering en schandaal: Biografie van Maerten en Cornelis Tromp* (Amsterdam, 2001), 353-7.

52 Carte MS 243, fos. 172v, 211v.

53 *Letters of Humphrey Prideaux to John Ellis*, ed. E.M. Thompson (Camden Society, new series XV, 1875), 32, 35.

54 British Library, M636/28, Sir Ralph Verney to Edmund Verney, 8 January 1675.

55 *Calendar of State Papers, Venetian, 1673-5*, 345, 356, 360-1; GEC[okayne], *The Complete Baronetage*, IV. 70. The special remainder seems to have been academic, for no other Tromp claimed the baronetcy after the admiral's death in 1691.

56 W.A. Shaw, *The Knights of England* (Oxford, 1906), II. 250; Carte MS 243, fos. 211-12; *Calendar of State Papers, Domestic, 1673-5*, 601.

57 *Calendar of State Papers, Domestic, 1676-7*, 131; Boxer, 'De Ruyter', 240.

58 I am grateful to Dr Peter Le Fevre for this point.

59 *The Life*, 115.

60 *Calendar of State Papers, Domestic, 1676-7*, 452; *The Manuscripts of S.H. Le Fleming, Esq., of Rydal Hall* (Historical Manuscripts Commission, 1890), 130.

61 R.J.B. Knight, *The Pursuit of Victory: The Life and Achievement of Horatio Nelson* (2005), 529-30.

7   Danish Perspectives on De Ruyter's Role in the Nordic Conflicts

1 Where not specifically noted, this chapter is based on Niels M. Probst, *Christian 4.s flåde*, Copenhagen 1996 and Probst, *Niels Juel, vor største flådefører*, Copenhagen 2005. See also Jørgen H. Barfod, *Niels Juel, liv og gerning*, Århus 1977.

2 Finn Askgaard, Finn, *Kampen om Østersøen,*, Copenhagen 1974, p. 48: "de förnämsta sjöhanar här mitt i Kungen av Danmarks land och på dess strömmar".

3 G.L. Grove, *Journalen van de Admiralen Van Wassenaer-Obdam (1658/59) en De Ruyter (1658/59)*, Amsterdam 1907.

4 H.D. Lind, *Kong Frederik den tredjes Sømagt*, Odense 1896, p. 99.

5 Askgaard, p. 196-7.

6 Askgaard, p. 249f.

7 Askgaard, p. 359.

8 P.J. Blok, *The Life of Admiral De Ruyter* (translated by G.T. Renier), London 1933, p. 128f. Further O. Klopp, *Admiral de Ruyter*, Hannover 1858; Ronald Prud'homme van Reine, *Rechterhand van Nederland. Biografie van Michiel Adriaenszoon de Ruyter*, Amsterdam/Antwerpen 1998; D.F. Scheurleer, *Michiel Adriaensz de Ruyter, Leven en daden naar berichten en afbeeldingen van tijdgenoten*, The Hague 1907. See also the chapter by J.R. Bruijn in this volumebook.

9 Askgaard, p.357-364.

10 Lind p.200. The promise was not redeemed until 1732 when the debt was once and for all settled with the payment of 24.000 *Rigsdalers*.

11 Askgaard, p. 416f.

12 Grove 1907, *Journalen*.

13 H.C. Bjerg and O. L. Frantzen, *Danmark i Krig,*, Copenhagen 2005, p. 139

14 Bjerg and Frantzen, pp. 134-137.

15 Askgaard, pp 421-422.

16 Bjerg and Frantzen, pp.138-140.

17 Blok, p. 142.

18 Grove, *Journalen.* 1907

19 Askgaard, p. 443.

20 Grove, Michiel de Ruyters Optagelse i den danske Adel og hans forhold til Kongerne Frederik III og Christian V', in: *Personalehistorisk Tidsskrift Femte række, II Bind 1905*, gives a full transcription of the Royal patent of nobility, de Ruyters letter of gratitude to the King and various other correspondence regarding his nobility.

8   Michiel de Ruyter's Expedition to West Africa and America, 1664-1665

1 R. Fruin and N. Japikse (eds.), *Brieven aan Johan de Witt 1648-1672, tweede deel, 1660-1672*, Amsterdam 1922, 354-355.

2 R.B. Prud'homme van Reine, *Rechterhand van Nederland. Biografie van Michiel Adriaenszoon de Ruyter*, Amsterdam 2002, 13.

3 G. Rommelse, *The Second Anglo-Dutch War (1665-1667)*, Hilversum 2006, 195-201. For the ideological explanation, see S.C.A. Pincus, *Protestantism and patriotism. Ideologies and the making of English foreign policy, 1650-1668*, Cambridge 1996.

4 K.G. Davies, *The North Atlantic World in the Seventeenth Century*, Minneapolis 1974, 306.

5 F.S. Gaastra, *De geschiedenis van de VOC*, Zutphen 1991, 45; G. Milton, *Nathaniel's Nutmeg*, New York 1999, 355-356; Rommelse, *The Second Anglo-Dutch War*, 87-88.

6 W. Klooster, *Illicit Riches. Dutch Trade in the Caribbean, 1648-1795*, Leiden 1998, 42; Davies, *The North Atlantic World*, 291.

7 N.A.M. Rodger, *The Command of the Ocean. A Naval History of Britain 1649-1815*, London 2004, 65.

8 R. Ollard, *Man of War. Sir Robert Holmes and the Restoration Navy*, London 1969, 66-71; G.F. Zook, *The Company of Royal Adventurers Trading into Africa*, Lancaster 1919, 30.

9 F. Binder and N. Schneeloch, 'Dirck Dircksz. Wilre en Willem Godschalk van Focquenbroch geschilderd door Pieter de Wit te Elmina in 1669' in: *Bulletin van het Rijksmuseum*, 1979, number 1, 16; *Resolutie vande Edele Groot Mogende heeren Staten van Hollandt ende West-Vrieslandt; Item een Missive van hare Hoog Mogende heeren Staten Generael der Vereenighde Nederlanden; Mitsgaders een Missive vanden Directeur Generael Johan van Valckenburgh (…)*, 's Gravenhage 1665, Brief van Johan Valckenburgh; W.N. Sainsbury (ed.), *Calendar of State Papers, Colonial Series, America and West Indies 1661-1668*, London 1880, 135.

10 Rommelse, *The Second Anglo-Dutch War*, 94-95.

11 Ollard, *Man of War*, 88-93.

12 For the problems with the Danes on the Gold Coast, see the *Remonstrantie Aen de Hoog Mogende Heeren de Staten Generael der Vereen-*

ighde Nederlanden; overgegeven den III *Juny 1664. By de Heeren de Bewint-hebberen van de Geoctroyeerde West-Indische Compagnie der Vereenighde Nederlanden*, Amsterdam 1664.

13 O. Justesen, *Danish Sources for the History of Ghana 1657-1754*, volume 1, Copenhagen 2005, 16-17; G. Nørregard, *Danish Settlements in West Africa 1658-1850*, Boston 1966, 26; Zook, *The Company*, 44-47. The Dutch surrendered on 3 May 1664.

14 L. Panhuysen, *De ware vrijheid. De levens van Johan en Cornelis de Witt*, Antwerp and Amsterdam 2005, 302; W. Troost, 'Een maritieme of continentale diplomatie? De buitenlandse politiek van Johan de Witt tot Willem V' in: K. Davids et.al. (ed.), *De Republiek tussen zee en vasteland*, Apeldoorn 1995, 274-275.

15 N. Japikse, *De verwikkelingen tusschen de Republiek en Engeland van 1660-1665*, Leiden 1900, 313-314.

16 J.A. Jacobs, *Een zegenrijk gewest. Nieuw-Nederland in de zeventiende eeuw*, Amsterdam 1999, 164-165.

17 J.K. Oudendijk, *Johan de Witt en de zeemacht*, Amsterdam 1944, 88-91; Rommelse, *The Second Anglo-Dutch War*, 104-105; A.P. van Vliet, '*Een vriendelijcke groetenisse'. Brieven van het thuisfront aan de vloot van De Ruyter (1664-1665)*, Franeker 2007, 24.

18 Japikse, *De verwikkelingen*, 326-328, 380-384.

19 Ibidem, 348.

20 Ibidem, 354; *Waerachtigh Verhael van de Grouwelicke en Barbarische Moorderye, begaen door de Engelschen in Guinea aen Onse Nederlandsche Natie*, Middelburgh 1665.

21 Ollard, *Man of War*, 129-130; Rommelse, *The Second Anglo-Dutch War*, 105-106; Sainsbury, *Calendar of State Papers*, 285.

22 Van Vliet, '*Een vriendelijcke groetenisse*', 26. At the founding of the WIC Friesland had not succeeded in obtaining a share in the Company and was not keen to defend its interest. See H. den Heijer, *Goud, ivoor en slaven. Scheepvaart en handel van de Tweede Westindische Compagnie op Afrika, 1674-1740*, Zutphen 1997, 41-42.

23 P. Verhoog and L. Koelmans, *De reis van Michiel Adriaanszoon de Ruyter in 1664-1665*, The Hague 1961, 17; Van Vliet, '*Een vriendelijcke groetenisse*', 26.

24 G. de Bruin, *Geheimhouding en verraad. De geheimhouding van staatszaken ten tijde van de Republiek (1600-1750)*, The Hague 1991, 311.

25 G. Brandt, *Het leven en bedryf van den heere Michiel de Ruiter, hertog, ridder ende L.Admiraal Generaal van Hollandt en Westvrieslandt*, Amsterdam 1687, 294.

26 Ibidem, 294-296; Japikse, *De verwikkelingen*, 354-356; De Bruin, *Geheimhouding*, 310-314.

27 C.S. Cau et.al. (eds.), *Groot Placaet-Boeck, vervattende de placaten, ordonnantien ende edicten van de Hoog Mogende Heeren Staaten Generael der Vereenighde Nederlanden (…)*, part 4, 's Gravenhage [the Hague] 1705, 292-294; L. van den Broek and M. Jacobs, *Christenslaven. De slavernij-ervaringen van Cornelis Stout in Algiers (1678-1680) en Maria ter Meetelen in Marokko (1731-1743)*, Zutphen 2006, 27.

28 The detailed instructions for De Ruyter are to be found in Brandt, *Het leven en bedryf*, 270-273.

29 According to Verhoog and Koelmans (*De reis*, 23) the fleet had been fitted out with 516 set of cannon and a crew of 2272.

30 Van den Broek and Jacobs, *Christenslaven*, 29; G. van Krieken, *Kapers en kooplieden. De betrekkingen tussen Algiers en Nederland 1604-1830*, Amsterdam 1999, 43-46.

31 Brandt, *Het leven en bedryf*, 285-286.

32 Verhoog and Koelmans, *De reis*, 63. Between 1662 and 1684 Tangier was in English hands and was the home base of the English fleet in the Mediterranean.

33 Prud'homme van Reine, *Rechterhand van Nederland*, 132.

34 Quoted from Verhoog and Koelmans, *De reis*, 69-70.

35 P.J. Blok, *Michiel Adriaanszoon de Ruyter*, 's-Gravenhage [The Hague] 1930, 215.

36 Brandt, *Het leven en bedryf*, 305.

37 Prud'homme van Reine, *Rechterhand van Nederland*, 109-111.

38 Brandt, *Het leven en bedryf*, 306; O. Schutte, *Repertorium der Nederlandse vertegenwoordigers residerende in het buitenland 1584-1810*, 's-Gravenhage [The Hague] 1976, 178 (no 124).

39 Blok, *Michiel Adriaanszoon de Ruyter*, 216; Brandt, *Het leven en bedryf*, 306-307.

40 Van Vliet, '*Een vriendelijcke groetenisse*', 40.

41 Brandt, *Het leven en bedryf*, 319-323.

42 Ibidem, 325-329; Verhoog and Koelmans, *De reis*, 244-245.

43 Brandt, *Het leven en bedryf*, 330-332.

44 Ibidem, 335-341.

45 Fante was one of the many Akan-speaking peoples on the Gold Coast. K.Y. Daaku, *Trade and Politics on the Gold Coast 1600-1720. A Study of the African Reaction to European Trade*, Oxford 1970, 4, 16-17.

46 Verhoog and Koelmans, *De reis*, 83.

47 Brandt, *Het leven en bedryf*, 353.

48 Ibidem, 354-355; A. van Dantzig, *Forts and Castles of Ghana*, Accra 1980, 35; Verhoog and Koelmans, *De reis*, 85.

49 Brandt, *Het leven en bedryf*, 362-363.

50 Prud'homme van Reine, *Rechterhand van Nederland*, 147. According to Brandt (*Het leven en bedryf*, 366) De Ruyter had been informed on 7 May 1665 by the crew of a Dutch fluyt coming from La Rochelle about the official outbreak of the Second Anglo-Dutch War.

51 Brandt, *Het leven en bedryf*, 372-373.

52 Verhoog and Koelmans, *De reis*, 102-103.

53 Rommelse, *The Second Anglo-Dutch War*, 113 and 120-121.

54 Blok, *Michiel Adriaanszoon de Ruyter*, 233-234.

55 Prud'homme van Reine, *Rechterhand van Nederland*, 153.

56 H. den Heijer, *De geschiedenis van de WIC*, Zutphen 1994, 80.

9 De Ruyter versus Duquesne

1 Michel Vergé-Franceschi, *Henri le Navigateur*, Éditions du Félin, 1994, reissued in 1998, translated into Portuguese in 2000 by the Institut Piaget, Lisbon.

2 Vergé-Franceschi, *Colbert ou la politique du bon sens*, Éditions Payot, 2004; reissued by Livre de Poche–Payot, 2005.

3 Maerten Harpertszoon Tromp (b. 1598, Brielle, Holland–d. 1653, killed at sea off Terheijde, Holland). Dutch admiral. He battled the Spanish fleet from 1624 to 1648, then the English squadrons from 1651 to 1653, finding death against the latter. Son of a frigate captain, he is remembered by posterity for reputedly having had a broom tied to his mainmast, symbolically sweeping the English from the seas, as he chased the English admiral Robert Blake all the way to the mouth of the Thames, in December,1652, after fighting him in the second battle of Goodwin Sands. Maerten Harpertszoon was the father of Cornelis Tromp (b. 1629, Rotterdam–d. 1691, Amsterdam), also a Dutch admiral.

4 Jean-Baptiste de Valbelle was commander and then bailiff of the Sovereign Order of Malta (b. ca. 1627, Marseille–d. 1681, La Reynarde, near Marseille). *Chef d'escadre* of Provence (1673). He was an invaluable auxiliary to Vivonne and to Duquesne in the Sicilian fighting against De Ruyter. Indeed, the marquis de Villette-Mursay wrote in his memoirs: "In the war at Messina … Valbelle was M. de Vivonne's precursor…. He brought first aid to the Messinese." See Vergé-Franceschi's critical edition of the memoirs of de Villette-Mursay: *Campagnes de mer sous Louis XIV*, Éditions Tallandier, 1991.

5 Letter from Valbelle, 8 June 1673, written after the first battle of Schooneveld. Cited without archival reference in Augustin Jal, *Abraham Duquesne*, 1873.

6 Vergé-Franceschi, *Abraham Duquesne*, Éditions France-Empire, 1992.

7 As Villette-Mursay spells it.

8 Jean II d'Estrées, comte d'Estrées (b. 1624, Solothurn, Switzerland–d. 1707, Paris). *Vice-amiral du Ponant* (the Atlantic fleet) at the creation of the *vice-amirauté* in 1669 and future *maréchal de France*, d'Estrées owed his *vice-amirauté* to his cousin Beaufort's mysterious disappearance at Candie, in 1669. The late duc de Beaufort was the son of César, duc de Vendôme, himself the bastard son of Henry IV and his favourite Gabrielle d'Estrées, Jean's aunt. Beaufort had been France's *Grand-maître de la navigation et commerce* since 1665, after succeeding his own father. D'Estrées thus had a legitimate claim to the post but Colbert had it eliminated by Louis XIV in 1669. It thus became necessary to give the *vice-amirauté* to d'Estrées as compensation for his lost inheritance even though he was no sailor. A land officer until 1667, he gained admission to the navy only in 1668. At the time of his nomination as *vice-amiral du Ponant*, he had commanded only a single squadron, destined for the Antilles (1668). At the beginning of the war with the Dutch, having scarcely got his sea legs in a second campaign (1670) against the Barbary pirates (Tunis, Salé, Algiers), he was commander-in-chief throughout the beginning of operations and in combat at Solebay, Schooneveld, and Texel (1672–1673). In 1674 he cruised along the French coast to defend it against the Dutch menace. His very mixed success in 1672–1673 moved Louis XIV to revoke his command in favour of Vivonne, brother of Mme de Montespan.

9 James Stuart, duke of York (b. 1633, London–d. 1701, Saint-Germain-en-Laye, France). Before ascending to the thrones of England as James II and of Scotland as James VII after the death of his brother, Charles II, in 1685, James Stuart was lord high admiral of the English fleet. Unlike the comte d'Estrées, he was a real sailor. In 1664, for example, he took the famous colony of New Amsterdam from the Dutch, giving it his own name: New York. He also wrote the celebrated *Fighting Instructions* for the Royal Navy in 1665. These quickly became the model for Colbert's navy, from 1669 on. At the outbreak of war with Holland, the duke of York was in command of the English squadron, combined with the French squadron, under the command of comte Jean d'Estrées. At Solebay (7 June 1672) he was aboard the *Royal Prince*, which came under heavy attack from De Ruyter. No longer able to manoeuvre, he boarded the *St Michel* under Sir Robert Holmes. When that ship was in turn heavily damaged, he boarded the *London*, commanded by Edward Spragge. Twice during the battle the duke of York was hit "in the stomach" by a violent shower of splinters, but the buffalo corset that he always wore under his jerkin cushioned both blows. With the outcome of the battle still very uncertain, the duke of York abandoned active command of the squadron to his first cousin, Prince Rupert. He was the chief of the admiralty when the death of Charles II made him king of England, Scotland, and Ireland.

10 The English and French squadrons had joined on 26 May in the harbour at Saint Helens, near Portsmouth, as they had in 1672, on the eve of the battle of Solebay. The English fleet was made up of about fifty ships of the line (forty-nine, fifty, or fifty-four, depending on the source), twenty-four fire ships and eight frigates. It was under the command of Prince Rupert, duke of Cumberland and first cousin to both Charles II and the duke of York, who had relinquished command of the squadron on 20 June, 1672, thirteen days after Solebay, in apparent admission of his failings in the Anglo-French defeat. The French fleet was made up of twenty-seven ships of the line, three frigates, ten fire ships and nine *barca-longas*. It was under the command of d'Estrées, as in 1672. On 3 June the combined squadrons discovered De Ruyter west of the port of Ostend. De Ruyter had under his command fifty or fifty-two ships of the line, twenty-four to thirty fire ships, twelve to fourteen frigates and fourteen or fifteen yachts. The battle took place on 7 June, 1673. The English vanguard, under Prince Rupert, engaged the Dutch vanguard, under Cornelis Tromp. The French centre, under d'Estrées, attacked the Dutch centre, under De Ruyter. The English rear guard, under Spragge, went after the Dutch rear guard. The Dutch suffered considerably. Their losses, it appears, outnumbered the combined losses of the English and the French, who each counted

three hundred wounded or killed. The French lost eight fire ships, six captains killed and three wounded.

[11] On 14 June, 1673, the leaders of the various squadrons remain unchanged; De Ruyter (Dutch), d'Estrées (French), Rupert (English). As the comte d'Estrées put it, the affair was nothing but "a big skirmish". The long cannonade nevertheless went on until ten at night and raised the total number of French losses from the battles of 7 and 14 June, 1673, to 212 killed and 224 wounded. On 18 June peace talks began at Cologne with Sweden as mediator. Holland agreed to cede to France only three cities, including Maastricht, and consented to salute England's war flag. Thanks to De Ruyter's resistance, the United Provinces could show intransigence. Peace talks were broken off. On 3 August the United Provinces received the support of Spain, the Habsburgs of Vienna, and the duc de Lorraine. On 21 August a new naval battle was fought at Texel.

[12] The battle of Texel was fought after the two battles of Schooneveld, which d'Estrées described as "vain illusions serving no purpose". The forces present at Texel were the same as those at the two previous battles, but slightly augmented on both sides. The French squadron, reinforced by the marquis de Martel's division, now had thirty ships of the line, nine fire ships, four frigates, nine *barca-longas* and three fluyts. The English squadron had sixty ships of the line, twenty-five fire ships, and forty transports. De Ruyter commanded seventy-five ships of the line and frigates, twenty-five fire ships, and eighteen yachts, all crewed by 20,376 men. D'Estrées led the vanguard in a tenacious fight against its Dutch counterpart under Banckert, commander of the Zeeland squadron. Prince Rupert and the centre fought De Ruyter and the Dutch centre. At the rear Tromp engaged Spragge, who drowned during the fighting. The particularly indecisive battle occasioned some violent polemics between Prince Rupert and comte d'Estrées, the former accusing the latter of having left him to face De Ruyter alone for too long.

[13] Just after the battle of Walcheren, or second battle of Schooneveld, the *lieutenant général des armées navales*, the marquis de Martel, wrote of his commanding officer: "Monsieur d'Estrées has dishonoured the nation. Everything turns on him, for the captains would have done their duty had he led them to it. In none of our combats has M. d'Estrées ever carried out any vigorous action. Last year [after the battle of Solebay], what he did to Duquesne [disgraced by the king in 1673] cries out to God for vengeance. In truth, one may say that he is a sad case, much disparaged among the English." From London, Croissy, the ambassador of the king of France and Colbert's brother, wrote to his nephew Seignelay: "That lampoon does more harm to the king's interests than any of the daily Spanish and Dutch attempts to ruin the French alliance." Martel was immediately imprisoned. Augustin Jal, *Abraham Duquesne*, 1873: cited without archival reference, but Jal was the curator of the Archives de la Marine in Paris and his work is of exceptional quality.

[14] Charles Colbert du Terron (b. ca. 1619, Reims, France–1684, Paris), naval quartermaster.

[15] De Ruyter already knew Martinique, having been there in 1665. In June–July, 1674, with twenty ships of the line and about thirty lighter ships, 4,336 sailors, 3,886 soldiers, and 1,142 guns, he went there to begin the conquest of the French Antilles. With a French population of five thousand, the island was then the strongest of the French colonies in the Antilles, next to Saint-Domingue. Its population was greater than those of Guadeloupe, Marie-Galante, Saint-Martin, Saint-Barthélemy, Saint-Croix, and Grenada combined.

[16] Thomas-Claude Renart de Fuchsamberg, marquis d'Amblimont (b. 1642, Mouzon-sur-Meuse, France–d. 1700, Fort-Royal de la Martinique).

[17] According to the *Mercure hollandais*, the Dutch had 35 officers dead or wounded, 159 men dead, and 380 wounded! The figures were exaggerated in France, where there was talk of four hundred Dutch killed and eight hundred wounded.

[18] So decisive was the victory over De Ruyter that to commemorate it Louis XIV, as was his wont, had a medal struck. It showed victory hovering over a wrecked ship of the line and a Dutchman in chains in the presence of a Carib. The *Gazette de France* published shining praise of d'Amblimont.

[19] Vergé-Franceschi, *Chronique maritime de la France d'Ancien Régime (1492–1792)*, Éditions Sedes, 1998.

[20] Louis-Victor, vicomte de Rochechouart, comte and then duc de Mortemart and Vivonne (b. 1636, Paris–d. 1688, Chaillot, France), *général des galères* and *maréchal de France*. Elder brother of Mme de Montespan. It was at Rosas that he received the Messinese emissaries who came to ask for Louis's help against the Catholic king. Vivonne became *vice-roi* of Sicily on 1 January, 1675. He suffered a light contusion at the first battle of Stromboli on 11 February, 1675. On 25 July, 1675, Louis XIV named him *commandant général des forces navales de Méditerranée*, and Vivonne acted literally as *vice-amiral du Levant*, that is, of the Mediterranean fleet, the post having been vacant from its creation in 1669 until 1689. That was because Duquesne refused to abjure his Protestant faith to obtain it. With Duquesne's death in 1688 the king gave it to Tourville (1689). On 2 August, 1675, Vivonne, aged thirty-nine years, received the baton of a *maréchal de France*, to his own astonishment.

[21] Letter from Colbert to Seignelay, 11 July 1675, cited in Michel Vergé-Franceschi, *Abraham Duquesne, marin huguenot du Roi-Soleil*, Paris, France-Empire, 1992, note 466.

[22] During the operations Vivonne had twenty-nine ships of the line and twenty-four galleys under his command.

[23] Letter from Tourville to Seignelay, 2 September 1675, in Vergé-Franceschi, *Abraham Duquesne*, note 467.

[24] Letter from the king to Vivonne, 17 October, 1675. *Ibid.*, note 468.

[25] The expression is Colbert's.

[26] Eric Durot, *Henri Duquesne (1662–1722), Huguenot réfugié en Suisse*, Mémoire de Maîtrise under the direction of Michel Vergé-Franceschi, Université de Savoie, Chambéry, 1997–1998.

[27] Jacob Duquesne, married to Suzanne Guiton in 1646. Michel Vergé-Franceschi, doctoral thesis *d'état-ès-lettres*, *Les Officiers généraux de la marine royale*, Université de Paris X–Nanterre,

1987, 7 vol., 3,547 pp., Librairie de l'Inde, Paris, 1990.

[28] *Lieutenant général des armées navales* (b. ca. 1650, Nantes–d. 1724, Bellebat, near Rochefort). In 1721, in The Hague, he published *Le Voyage fait aux Indes Orientales par une escadre de six vaisseaux commandée par M. Duquesne par ordre de la Compagnie des Indes Orientales.*

[29] Roland Barrin, chevalier then marquis de la Galissonnière (b. 1646, Nantes, France–d. 1737, Poitiers, France), future *chef d'escadre*. *Enseigne de vaisseau* in 1669, *lieutenant de vaisseau* in 1671. He had command of a mere fire ship in 1676, a post generally assigned to officers without "birth", which was not his case. Villette-Mursay wrote in his memoirs that at the battle of Melazzo (1676) he showed "signs of valour and good conduct". *Mémoires du marquis de Villette-Mursay*, critical edition, ed. Michel Vergé-Franceschi, Éditions Tallandier, Paris, 1992, biographical note on la Galissonnière.

[30] Joseph Andrault, marquis then comte de Langeron (b. 1649 Saint-Pierre de Langeron, Nivernais, France–d. 1711, Sceaux, France), future *lieutenant général des armées navales*. After the victory over the Hispano-Batavians at Palermo and De Ruyter's death, he was sent to the court. There he confirmed the king's victory (2 June, 1676).

[31] Pierre de Cou (b. ca. 1630, Arvert, France– 1676, killed at the battle of Etna).

[32] François de Villeneuve de Ferrière (b. 1643, La Rochelle, France–d. 1676, Messina). Killed at the second battle of Stromboli (Alicudi).

[33] M. de Pallas (b. ca. 1630, Apt, France–d. 1702, Havana). In 1675 Vivonne said that he was "a very good subject".

[34] Duquesne's report, January 1676, in Vergé-Franceschi, *Abraham Duquesne*, note 470.

[35] In the seventeenth century the term *général de mer* is as common as *amiral*.

[36] Anonymous account, 25 January, 1676, in Vergé-Franceschi, *Abraham Duquesne*.

[37] Guillaume, marquis d'Alméras (b. ca. 1620, Montpellier, France–d. 1676, battle of Etna), *lieutenant général des armées navales.*

[38] Letter from the marquis d'Alméras to Colbert, 10 January, 1676, in Vergé-Franceschi, *Abraham Duquesne*, p. 472.

[39] *Ibid.*

[40] Jean Gabaret (b. 1631, Île de Ré, France–d. 1697, Rochefort, France), *lieutenant général des armées navales.*

[41] Jan Den Haen (b. ca. 1620–d. 1676, Palermo, Italy). At the battle of Palermo he took a cannonball to the head while standing on part of the netting (the *saint-aubinet*) of the admiral's ship. The man who became his *contre-amiral*, Pieter van Middellandt, drowned in the same battle.

[42] The chevalier de Tambonneau (b. ca. 1640, Paris–d. 1676, battle of Etna).

[43] Philippe Le Vallois, marquis de Villette-Mursay (1632–1707), first cousin to Mme de Maintenon and *Lieutenant général des armées navales*, was a converted Huguenot.

[44] Letter from Duquesne to Seignelay, 22 May, 1676, in Vergé-Franceschi, *Abraham Duquesne*, note 473. The former cabal, with respect to the present one, is that of the "*fouquettistes*" in the king's navy. They were clients of *surintendant* Nicolas Fouquet who was arrested by order of the king in Nantes in 1661 and died in Pignerol in 1680.

[45] Letter from Colbert to Duquesne, 30 May, 1676. Vergé-Franceschi, *Abraham Duquesne*, note 474.

10 De Ruyter and his Flag Officers

[1] For data on flag officers see L. Eekhout, *Het admiralenboek. De vlagofficieren van de Nederlandse marine 1382-1991*, Amsterdam 1992. Be aware that not all information is correct. For the composition of the fleets I have consulted G. Brandt, *Het leven en bedrijf van den heere Michiel de Ruiter*, Amsterdam 1701 edition.

[2] T.H. Milo, *Wassenaer en de zeemacht. Jacob van Wassenaer van Obdam en zijn tijd*, Wassenaar 1965, 27.

[3] D. Roos, *Twee eeuwen varen en vechten. Het admiralengeslacht Evertsen*, Flushing 2003, 213 and 475.

[4] J.R. Bruijn, *The Dutch navy of the seventeenth and eighteenth centuries*, Columbia S.C. 1993, 111-114.

[5] R.B. Prud'homme van Reine, *Rechterhand van Nederland. Biografie van Michiel Adriaenszoon de Ruyter*, Amsterdam 1996, 95-96.

[6] W.J. van Hoboken, *Witte de With in Brazilië 1648-1649*, Amsterdam 1955.

[7] Milo, *Wassenaer*, 23-31; C.E. Warnsinck-Delprat (ed.), *Reijse gedaen bij Adriaen Schagen aen de croonen van Sweden ende Polen inden jaere 1656* (Werken Linschoten Vereeniging LXIX), The Hague 1968, from p.146 passim.

[8] J. Brozius, 'Het leven en bedrijf van Pieter Florisz', in: *Levend Verleden*, special issue of the Heldersche Historische Vereniging 2007, 11-25; Prud'homme van Reine, *Rechterhand*, 68.

[9] Roos, *Twee eeuwen varen*, 130, 217-219 and 227-228.

[10] Prud'homme van Reine, *Rechterhand*, 106, 109, 211; Warnsinck-Delprat (ed.), *Reijse*, 143 and 148.

[11] E. Wiersum, *Egbert Meussen Cortenaer*, Assen 1939, 30; J.C.M. Warnsinck, 'Cortenaer', in: *De Gids*, 104 (1940), 229-256.

[12] Bruijn, *The Dutch navy*, 49-50 and 116-118.

[13] Municipal Archive Amsterdam, Particuliere Archieven 21; J.R. Bruijn, 'Isaäc Sweers, 1622-1673. Beroepsofficier in een nog niet bestaand korps', in: V. Enthoven, G. Acda and A. Bon (eds.), *Een saluut van 26 schoten. Liber Amicorum aangeboden aan Ger Teitler bij zijn afscheid als hoogleraar aan het Koninklijk Instituut voor de Marine*, Amsterdam 2005, 131-138.

[14] They were: Aert and Jan van Nes, Gideon de Wildt, Willem van der Zaan, Isaäc Sweers, Enno Doede Star, Leender Haexwant, Jan Meppel, Govert 't Hoen. See: P. Verhoog (ed.), *De reis van Michiel Adriaanszoon de Ruyter in 1664-1665*, Werken Linschoten Vereeniging LXII, The Hague 1961 and A. P. van Vliet, 'Een vriendelijcke groetenisse'. Brieven van het thuisfront aan de

vloot van De Ruyter (1664-1665), Franeker 2007.

[15] W.C. Thijssen, 'David Vlugh. «Enkhuiser heldt»', in: Levend Verleden, 44-63.

[16] For the text of these instructions and regulations, see: H.A. van Foreest and R.E.J. Weber, De Vierdaagse zeeslag 11-14 Juni 1666, Amsterdam 1984, 115-158 and R.E.J. Weber, De seinboeken voor Nederlandse oorlogsvloten en konvooien tot 1690, Amsterdam 1982, 73-114.

[17] Brandt, Het leven, 739 and 756; J.R. Bruijn (ed.), De oorlogvoering ter zee in 1673 in journalen en andere stukken, Groningen 1966, 62, 122-123, 125-126; Thijssen, 'David Vlugh', 57.

[18] Verhoog (ed.), De reis, 33-35 and 273; Prud'homme van Reine, Rechterhand, 201.

[19] Bruijn, The Dutch navy, 115.

[20] Prud'homme van Reine, Rechterhand, 205-209.

[21] Bruijn, The Dutch navy, 118.

[22] Prud'homme van Reine, Schittering en schandaal. Biografie van Maerten en Cornelis Tromp,

Amsterdam 2001, 270-274 and 390-397; L.M. Akveld and J.R. Bruijn, 'Een ooggetuige over Chatham', in Spiegel Historiael 2 (1967), 322-329; Roos, Twee eeuwen varen, 403-405.

[23] N. Scheltema, 'De geslachten van Van Nes geseyt Boer Jaep en De Liefde (Groenrijs)', in: Rotterdamsche Historiebladen, afd. III, Rotterdam 1880, 415-495; Bruijn, De oorlogvoering, 185-186; Prud'homme van Reine, Rechterhand, 211, 212.

24 Prud'homme van Reine, Rechterhand, 300.

11 De Ruyter in Paint

[1] F. Muller, Beschrijvende catalogus van 7000 portretten van Nederlanders (Amsterdam 1853), 220-222, nos. 4622-4649; J.F. van Someren, Beschrijvende catalogus van gegraveerde portretten van Nederlanders. 3 volumes (Amsterdam 1888-1891), III, 540, 541, nos. 4702-4716; *R.B. Prud'homme van Reine, Zeehelden, (Amsterdam-Antwerp 2005), 153.

[2] F.A. Geurdes, 'Helden aan de wand: de zeventiende-eeuwse particuliere verzamelaars van admiraalsportretten'. Student Thesis University of Utrecht 2007. The version used is available on the website of the University Library Utrecht, www.igitur.nl. The author searched a random number of inventories of collectors of paintings for portraits of De Ruyter and Maerten and Cornelis Tromp. In fourteen inventories he discovered portraits of the two Tromps while in only four he came across a portrait of De Ruyter. Three out of four portraits found of De Ruyter were accompanied by a portrait of Cornelis Tromp.

[3] G.J. Hoogewerff (ed.), De twee reizen van Cosimo de Medici prins van Toscane door de Nederlanden (1667-1669). Journalen en documenten (Amsterdam 1919), 74-76.

[4] Prud'homme van Reine, 'De zeventiende-eeuwse zeeheldenportrettenreeks van Abraham Westervelt'. In: Bulletin van het Rijksmuseum 43 (1995), 96-112.

[5] Prud'homme van Reine, Rechterhand van Nederland. Biografie van Michiel Adriaenszoon de Ruyter (Amsterdam-Antwerp 1996), 215, 216. For the portrait in a private collection in Rotterdam:

Geschiedkundige tentoonstelling van het Nederlandsche zeewezen te 's-Gravenhage (The Hague 1900),148, nr. 1295 (toegeschreven aan Ferdinand Bol); E.W. Moes, Iconographia Batava. Beredeneerde lijst van geschilderde en gebeeldhouwde portretten van Noord-Nederlanders in vorige eeuwen (2 delen; Amsterdam 1897-1905), II, 304, nr. 29 (ascribed to Jurriaen Ovens, 1623-1678).

[6] R. van Luttervelt, 'Het officiële portret van De Ruyter door Bol'. In: Bulletin van het Rijksmuseum 1 (1953), 33-34; A. Blankert, Ferdinand Bol (1616-1680): Een leerling van Rembrandt (The Hague 1976), 63, 64, 124-128, nos. 76-87ff; P.J.J. van Thiel and C.J. de Bruyn Cops, Prijst de lijst. De Hollandse schilderijlijst in de zeventiende eeuw (Amsterdam-The Hague 1984), 219, 220, no. 54; B. Broos and A. van Suchtelen, Portraits in the Mauritshuis 1430-1790 (Zwolle-The Hague 2004), 42-46, no. 5.

[7] Prud'homme van Reine, Opkomst en ondergang van Nederlands gouden vloot, chapter 7 (Amsterdam-Antwerp 2009), 218-256.

[8] In contrast to Broos and Van Suchtelen, Portraits, 45. They argue that the copy in the Mauritshuis in The Hague must definitely have come from the Amsterdam Admiralty on the grounds that it ended up in the museum in 1894 via the Navy models' room [de Marinemodellenkamer] of the Royal Navy and that all pieces in that collection belonged to the Amsterdam Admiralty. However, they pass over the fact that the Nationale Konstgallerij, the Rijksmuseum's predecessor, received into its collection the portrait by Bol from the Amsterdam Admiralty in

1799, a second from the Rotterdam Admiralty in 1800 and a third from the Zeeland Admiralty in 1808. In all likelihood, the Rijksmuseum is now in possession of the portrait from the Zeeland Admiralty, but in the absence of any further details as to what happened with the other portraits this is uncertain. If this supposition proves correct, then the Rotterdam copy should now be in Greenwich. See: E.W. Moes and E. van Biema, De Nationale Konstgallerij en het Koninklijk Museum. Bijdrage tot de geschiedenis van het Rijksmuseum (Amsterdam 1909), 187, 188.

[9] J.M. Kilian, The paintings of Karel du Jardin. Catalogue raisonné (Amsterdam-Philadelphia 2005), 47, 48, 206, 207, no. 112. The author assumes that Dujardin still had the portrait of De Ruyter in his possession at the time of his death since such a painting is listed in the inventory of his estate. However, this must concern a modello for the portrait, because it is hardly conceivable that the painter did not sell the portrait himself. Elbert Bol, Ferdinand's son, also had a portrait of De Ruyter at the time of his death in 1709.

[10] P.J. Blok, 'Inventaris van De Ruyter's inboedel, opgemaakt 22-24 maart 1677'. In: Bijdragen en Mededelingen van het Historisch Genootschap 49 (1928), 187-213. This inventory mentions only two portraits of De Ruyter as such, but the older portraits must by then have been divided among the children and thus were not included in the inventory.

[11] Prud'homme van Reine, Rechterhand, 87.

[12] B. Haak, Hollandse schilders in de Gouden

Eeuw (Amsterdam 1984), 203-208, 342-344, 424.

[13] A. von Wurzbach, *Niederländisches Künstler-Lexikon.* 3 volumes (Vienna-Leipzig 1906-1911), I, 86, 87; U. Thieme and F. Becker, *Allgemeines Lexikon der bildenden Künstler.* 37 volumes (Leipzig 1907-1950), II, 377.

[14] Prud'homme van Reine, *Rechterhand*, 90.

[15] For this, see the correspondence of seventeenth-century relatives kept by the Foundation for the Promotion of the Memory of Michiel de Ruyter [Stichting Bevordering Nagedachtenis Michiel de Ruyter] in The Hague. Inventory on website www.deruyter.org.

[16] C.E. Warnsinck-Delprat (ed.), *Reyse gedaen bij Adriaen Schagen aen de croonen van Sweden ende Polen in den jaere 1656* (The Hague 1968), 41, 116; Prud'homme van Reine, *Rechterhand*, 96.

[17] Prud'homme van Reine, *Rechterhand*, 114.

[18] Prud'homme van Reine, *Rechterhand*, 121, 122.

[19] R. van Luttervelt, 'Herinneringen aan Michiel Adriaenszoon de Ruyter in het Rijksmuseum'. In: *Bulletin van het Rijksmuseum* 5 (1957), 27-71, especially 35. This is of course no conclusive proof that these concern one and the same walking cane as these were fairly common. Cf. P. Sigmond and W. Kloek, *Zeeslagen en zeehelden in de Gouden Eeuw* (Amsterdam 2007), 158.

[20] Van Someren, III, *Beschrijvende catalogus*, 541, no. 4709.

[21] Prud'homme van Reine, *Schittering en schandaal. Biografie van Maerten en Cornelis Tromp* (Amsterdam-Antwerp 2001), 258.

[22] Prud'homme van Reine, 'Paerlen op de kroon der Gallerij. De schilderijen van de zeventiende-eeuwse zeeofficierenfamilie Van Nes in het Rijksmuseum'. In: *Bulletin van het Rijksmuseum* 43 (1995), 96-112; R. Ekkart, 'Amsterdamse portretschilders in de zeventiende en achttiende eeuw'. In: N. Middelkoop (ed.), *Kopstukken. Amsterdammers geportretteerd 1600-1800* (Bussum-Amsterdam 2002), 28-45.

[23] Von Wurzbach, *Niederländisches Künstler-Lexikon*, I, 744; Thieme and Becker, *Allgemeines Lexikon*, XVII, 258, 259.

[24] E. de Jongh, *Portretten van echt en trouw. Huwelijk en gezin in de Nederlandse kunst van de zeventiende eeuw* (Zwolle-Haarlem 1986), 14-64; R.E.O. Ekkart, 'Seventeenth-century Northern-Netherlandish Group Portraiture'. In: G. Cavelli-Björkmann (ed.), *Face to face. Portraits from five centuries* (Stockholm 2001), 47-57.

[25] Prud'homme van Reine, *Schittering*, 121, 122.

[26] D. Roos, *Twee eeuwen varen en vechten 1550-1750. Het admiralengeslacht Evertsen* (Flushing 2003), 403.

[27] I. Verslype and G. Wuestman, 'Een groepsportret met een bewogen geschiedenis. Moderne onderzoekstechnieken leiden tot nieuwe toeschrijving'. In: *Bulletin van het Rijksmuseum* 54 (2006), 400-411. The painting turns out to have been painted by Willem Duyster and an unknown artist. The subjects have not been identified but given the composition of the group they are definitely not the Banckert family.

[28] Prud'homme van Reine, *Rechterhand*, 201. The childhood portrait of Engel de Ruyter is mentioned in E.W. Moes, *Iconographia Batava. Beredeneerde lijst van geschilderde en gebeeldhouwde portretten van Noord-Nederlanders in vorige eeuwen.* 2 volumes (Amsterdam 1897-1905), II, 302, no. 6658, 1.

[29] Most recently, W. Kloek in: Sigmond and Kloek, *Zeeslagen*, 162, 163.

[30] *Catalogus der schilderijen, pastels, miniaturen, aquarellen, tentoongesteld in het Rijksmuseum te Amsterdam.* Amsterdam 1934.

[31] Van Luttervelt, 'Herinneringen De Ruyter', 59. Because of the commander's baton in De Ruyter's hand Van Luttervelt mistakenly gave the dates for the portraits of De Ruyter by Dujardin of 1669 and by Berckman of 1668 as 1660 and 1661, respectively. This also lent plausibility to his dating the family portrait at 1662. It is, incidentally, most unfortunate that when some decades ago the painting by Jacobson was restored no report was drawn up mentioning the presence of additional touches.

[32] Prud'homme van Reine, *Rechterhand*, 202.

[33] Blok, 'Inventaris', 195.

[34] R. van Luttervelt, 'Herinneringen aan Johan en Cornelis de Witt in het Rijksmuseum'. In: *Bulletin van het Rijksmuseum* 8 (1960), 27-63, especially 49-53; Van Thiel and De Bruyn Cops, *Prijst de lijst*, 221, 222, no. 55.

[35] Prud'homme van Reine, *Rechterhand*, 197.

[35a] Recently the 1668 portraits were auctioned: Sale Christie's Amsterdam: *20 Rooms. The private collection of the late Mrs. Elias-Vaes. 27-29 April 2010*, pp. 73-75, cat.no. 163.

[36] These portraits were auctioned in Amsterdam in 1911 and sold to Germany. They have not been seen since. See Van Luttervelt, 'Herinneringen De Ruyter', 59.

[37] Information from the Iconographical Bureau [Iconografisch Bureau] in The Hague. Recently these portraits of Engel and Margaretha de Ruyter were auctioned: Sale Christie's Amsterdam: *20 Rooms (see note 35)*, pp. 76-79, cat.nos. 164, 165. The portrait of Engel de Ruyter is here ascribed to the circle of Jan de Baen and the portrait of Margaretha de Ruyter to the circle of Jan Mijtens.

[38] Van Luttervelt, 'Herinneringen De Ruyter', 67-70.

[39] Prud'homme van Reine, *Rechterhand*, 209.

[40] J.F.L. de Balbian Verster, 'Engel de Ruyter'. In: *Jaarverslag Vereeniging Nederlandsch Historisch Scheepvaart Museum 9* (1925), 59-83, especially 80, 81.

[41] Prud'homme van Reine, *Rechterhand*, 280.

[42] Prud'homme van Reine, *Rechterhand*, 295.

[43] The number of ten mentioned here is based on the portraits in oil discussed in this article. Other portraits by different painters mentioned in the literature I would consider as constituting another version, a copy, as being non-contemporary or as not representing De Ruyter. See the list of forty portraits in: E.W. Moes, *Iconographia Batava*, II, 302-304, no. 6661. Moes counted all portraits by Bol one by one and also included in his list a sculptured portrait. He further mentioned a number of anonymous portraits, which were mistakenly identified as representing De Ruyter. This also goes for the portraits he mentioned by G. Flinck, J. Backer and J. Ovens. He wrongly attributed the family portrait by J. Jacobson to J.B. Weenix.

[44] Information from the Iconographical Bureau [Iconografisch Bureau] in The Hague, auctioned at Sotheby's New York, 28-1-2005.

[45] Prud'homme van Reine, *Zeehelden*, 74, 87.

[46] Van Luttervelt, 'Herinneringen De Ruyter', 66; Sigmond and Kloek, *Zeeslagen*, 168, 169.

47 Blankert, *Ferdinand Bol*, 127, no. 86; Van Thiel and De Bruyn Cops, *Prijst de lijst*, 220.

48 Prud'homme van Reine, 'Op zijn paasbest. De Nederlandse zeeofficier uit de zeventiende eeuw geportretteerd'. In: L.M. Akveld et al. (eds), *In het kielzog. Maritiem-historische studies aangeboden aan Jaap R. Bruijn bij zijn vertrek als hoogleraar Zeegeschiedenis aan de Universiteit Leiden* (Amsterdam 2003), 395-408, especially 408.

49 E. Boer, 'Een moortje als versiering. De zwarte page in de Nederlandse schilderkunst'. In: *Spiegel Historiael 38* (2003), 296-301.

50 Prud'homme van Reine, *Rechterhand*, 200.

51 Prud'homme van Reine, *Rechterhand*, 345, 346.

52 Prud'homme van Reine, *Rechterhand*, 334.

53 This portrait of De Ruyter by Bol, executed on a smaller panel than were the portraits destined for the admiralties, nowadays hangs in the Zeeuws Museum in Middelburg. In the Nederlands Scheepvaartmuseum in Amsterdam, a similar version of the portrait of De Ruyter can be seen in its original carved frame. This latter is from the collection of the Vaderlandsch Fonds van de Kweekschool voor de Zeevaart [National Fund of the Seafarer's Training College]. It was donated in 1788 by Pieter van Winter. His daughter Lucretia Johanna van Winter donated De Ruyter's original Order of Saint Michael to the Kweekschool [Training College] in 1814; this is now also kept in the Scheepvaartmuseum in Amsterdam. Gerard Brandt was her great-great-great-grandfather. Both items thus may have come down from De Ruyter's biographer. For this, see: R.B. Prud'homme van Reine et al, *Ter navolging. Maritieme kunst en curiosa uit de Kweekschool voor de Zeevaart* (Amsterdam-Zutphen 1992), 19, 20, 31, 84, 85, 142, 143, 187.

54 G. Brandt, *Het leven en bedrijf van den Heere Michiel de Ruyter* (Amsterdam 1746, fourth edition), before the frontispiece.

55 The reprint of Brandt, *Het leven en bedrijf* in five volumes (Amsterdam 1794-1796), I, has before the title page a new print after the painting, done by Reinier Vinkeles, with the note that it at that time hung in the home of the widowed Mrs Elias. Equally well-known is the print after the painting by Jacob Houbraken in Jan Wagenaar's *Vaderlandse historie*, made in the middle of the eighteenth century. According to the legend, the painting then hung in the house of Margaretha le Leu de Wilhem (1708-1778), granddaughter to Margaretha de Ruyter. Her daughter Machtelina Henriette (1730) married Gerbrand Elias (1728-1769) and therefore was the widowed Mrs Elias mentioned in 1794. The family portrait by Jurriaen Jacobson also hung in the same family's house, before it was bought by the Amsterdam Rijksmuseum in 1912. A good nineteenth-century copy after the posthumous portrait by Bol can be seen in the Marinemuseum in Den Helder.

Index of ship names

Index of geographical names

Index of persons

Contributors

Karim Bejjit (1970) earned his MA in Postcolonial Studies from the University of Kent, UK (1996) and a Doctorat d'Etat (PhD) in English from Mohamed I University Oujda, Morocco (2000). He is currently Associate Professor of English at Hassan II University, Casablanca, where since 2000 he has taught seminars and lectures on English and American fiction, postcolonial theory, and European writings on North Africa. In 2007 he was a visiting scholar at NIAS (Netherlands Institute for Advanced Study) working on a book entitled *At the Gate of Barbary: English Colonial Texts on Tangier (1661-1684)*. His most recent publication is 'Tangier That Was: The Confessions of Samuel Pepys' in *Writing Tangier*, eds. Ralph M. Coury and Kevin Lacey (2009)

Jaap R. Bruijn (1938) in 2003 became emeritus professor of maritime history at Leiden University. He has published numerous books and articles on a variety of topics including the early modern Dutch Navy, shipping and commanders of the Dutch East India Company, privateering, 20th century Dutch whaling, trade unions in the Navy and a few shorter biographies of 18th and 19th century Dutch naval officers and of a fisher/merchant. With some of these studies he has enjoyed the cooperation with colleagues and former students. He also served as editor-in-chief of the four volume *Maritieme Geschiedenis der Nederlanden* (1976-78).

David Davies (1957) has published extensively on both naval and non-naval history. His first book was *Gentlemen and Tarpaulins: The Officers and Men of the Restoration Navy* (1991) and his second, *Pepys's Navy: Ships, Men and Warfare 1649-89* (2008), won the Samuel Pepys Prize for 2009. He is the Chairman of the Naval Dockyards Society, a Vice-President of the Navy Records Society, a member of the Council of the Society for Nautical Research and a Fellow of the Royal Historical Society. He was formerly Deputy Headmaster (Academic) of Bedford Modern School, and is now a full-time writer. He is also the author of the naval historical fiction series *The Journals of Matthew Quinton*, set in the Restoration period and beginning with *Gentleman Captain* (2009) and T*he Mountain of Gold* (2010). Website: *www.jddavies.com.*

Jan Glete (1947-2009) wrote about the Swedish company Boliden and Kreuger group in his 1975 doctoral dissertation. His interests migrated from 19th and 20th century Swedish industrial and economic history to European military and naval history and the formation of early modern fiscal-military states. His work on state formation has proven exceptionally influential. From 1999 he was a professor of history at Stockholm University. Among his works in English are the books *Navies and Nations: Warships and Navies and state building in Europe and America 1500-1860* (1993), *Warfare at sea 1500-1860: maritime conflicts and the transformation of Europe* (2000), *War and the state in Early Modern Europe: Spain, the Dutch Republic and Sweden as fiscal-military states 1500-1660* (2002), *Naval history 1500-1680* (2005) and his last book *Swedish Naval Administration 1521–1721: Resource Flows and Organisational Capabilities* (2010).

John B. Hattendorf (1941) has been the Ernest J. King Professor of Maritime History at the U.S. Naval War College at Newport, Rhode Island, since 1984, where he is also chairman, Maritime History Department, and museum director. A former naval officer, he holds his academic degrees in history from Kenyon College (A.B., 1964), Brown University (A.M., 1971), and the University of Oxford (D.Phil., 1979). He is the author, editor, co-author, or co-editor of more than 30 books, including serving as editor-in-chief of the *Oxford Encyclopedia of Maritime History* (2007). He has been awarded an honorary doctorate, the Caird Medal of the National Maritime Museum Greenwich, the U.S. Navy's Superior Civilian Service Medal, the Samuel Eliot Morison Award, and the Alfred Thayer Mahan Award for Literary Achievement. His most recent publication is *Talking About Naval History: A Collection of Essays* (2011).

Henk den Heijer (1950) earned his Ph.D at the University of Leiden, specializing in maritime history and the history of European expansion. He is professor of maritime history at the University of Leiden and the author of several articles and books on Atlantic history including *De geschiedenis van de WIC* (1994) and *De geoctrooieerde compagnie. De VOC en WIC als voorlopers van de naamloze vennootschap* (2005).

Rolof van Hövell tot Westerflier (1940) earned a LLM degree and a MA degree from the University of Leiden. He also he received a degree in comparative law (MCL) from Columbia University. He has spent the last forty years practicing law in The Netherlands Antilles, Rotterdam and Jakarta. Driven by his life-long passion for history, he founded Karwansaray Publishers in 2007, a company dedicated to promoting and sharing a multi-faceted view of history that crosses cultural and political boundaries. Some of his other productions include the successful *Ancient Warfare* and *Medieval Warfare* magazines. This book is the first in the Protagonists of History in International Perspective series. Future releases include *Marlborough: Soldier and Diplomat* (due out in March 2012) and an upcoming work on the Duke of Alba (due out in December 2012).

Niels M. Probst (1940), after training as a carpenter and studying house design as well as serving in the Danish air force as a fighter pilot, in 1971 joined Maersk Air. He eventually captained four- and twin-engined Boeing airliners and retired in 1990. Since the early 1980s he has published numerous articles on sixteenth and seventeenth century Danish warships, mainly in the quarterly journal Marinehistorisk Tidsskrift, which he has edited since 1998. Early in the 1990s he became a 'museum advisor' at the Royal Danish Naval Museum, serving during a short term as its director. After his main work, *Christian 4.s flåde* (*The Navy of Christian IV*) (1996), followed several smaller works on naval aviation and artillery. In 2005 he produced a special exhibition on Niels Juel at the Naval Museum and in that connection published a book about the Admiral. A model builder, he has supplied reconstruction draughts for ten display models in scales of 1:30 or 1:36 of ships dating from 1514 to 1670.

Ronald Prud'homme van Reine (1960) is an historian. His doctoral dissertation (1990) was a biography, *Jan Hendrik van Kinsbergen (1735-1819): Admiraal en filantroop.* He subsequently went on to publish, among other works, more biographies of naval heroes and general works on naval history: *Rechterhand van Nederland. Biografie van Michiel Adriaenszoon de Ruyter* (1996); *Schittering en schandaal. Biografie van Maerten en Cornelis Tromp* (2001); *Admiraal Zilvervloot. Biografie van Piet Hein* (2003); *Zeehelden* (2005); *Opkomst en ondergang van Nederlands gouden vloot. Door de ogen van de zeeschilders Willem van de Velde de Oude en de Jonge* (2009).

Michel Vergé-Franceschi (1951) is professor of modern history at the University of Tours (François Rabelais). He is the former director of the Laboratoire d'Histoire et d'Archéologie Maritime at the C.N.R.S./Paris IV-Sorbonne/ Musée National de la Marine and a specialist in the maritime history of France from the sixteenth to the eighteenth century. His *Abraham Duquesne* (1992) was awarded three literary prizes (Prix ACORAM, 1993; Prix Neptunia, 1993; Prix Meurand, 1993). Member of the Academie Française and of the Academie des Sciences Morales et Politiques, he was editor-in-chief of the Dictionnaire d'histoire maritime (2002) and is the author of *Histoire de la marine française au XVIIIᵉ siècle* (1998) and of *Chronique d'histoire maritime de la France, 1492–1792* (2000).